NF

31/10/97

95p

The people
of Roman Britain

Size, 5 feet 4 inches by 2 feet 2 inches.

The people
of Roman Britain

Anthony Birley

B T Batsford Ltd London

For Susanna, Ursula, and Hamish

Frontispiece A tombstone set up at Greatchesters on Hadrian's Wall to 'the spirits of the departed (and) his daughter Pervica' by an unknown soldier, presumably of Celtic origin in view of the girl's name (RIB 1747, where the first line is read as DIS M.: the SALVTE shown in this nineteenth-century rendering is a mistaken reading)

ISBN 0 7134 5935 2

Printed and bound in Great Britain by
Adlard & Son Ltd, The Garden City Press,
Letchworth, Herts

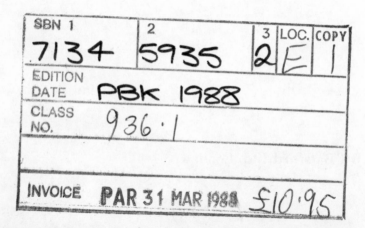

Contents

List of illustrations

Preface

It is exactly fifteen years since I completed *Life in Roman Britain*, a long span in human life, and it is rather a surprise to me that the book is still in print. Much has changed in the intervening period, with the spectacular increase in archaeological excavation and in publications on this subject. Of particular importance have been the creation of a journal of Romano-British studies (*Britannia*) and the appearance of Volume I of *The Roman Inscriptions of Britain*. Without RIB the present work could hardly have been undertaken. My first task, when I began work on the book three years ago, was to make an index of the names in RIB – which at present still lacks one – and of subsequently published inscriptions. I have tried to be as complete as possible, but I fear that some of the very numerous graffiti and other inscriptions in the *instrumentum domesticum* category (publication of which in RIB II is awaited impatiently) may have eluded me. The result is a book stuffed with personal names, Roman and Celtic in the main, with a copious sprinkling of Greek, German and other varieties. The title, *The People of Roman Britain*, will not, I hope, mislead. My intention is to describe the people who lived in Britain, either as permanent residents of the island or on Roman government service, whose names are known. They are dealt with by category, and the military naturally occupy a dominant position because of the nature of the evidence. Chapter II, which covers the emperors' dealings with Britain, provides a narrative framework, supplemented by the discussion of the governors and other high officials in Chapter III, while the last chapter looks ahead to the post-Roman period. Some of the characters will be familiar to many readers, although I have attempted to put figures such as Aulus Plautius or Sextus Julius Severus into perspective by discussing their family background. Some of the minor people have considerable interest. I at any rate derive some pleasure and instruction from the fact that the first named British sailor was a Devon man who served in the German fleet (*classis Germanica*: Chapter IX); or that the first known British 'civil servant' was a slave with a Greek name meaning 'blameless' (Anencletus: Chapter XV). The names alone can be informative, as I have tried to show with the British potters; and throughout the book I have aimed constantly to keep before the reader the fact that Britain was part of a great empire and was affected by its history. I ought to explain the system adopted for giving references. In view of the large numbers of names mentioned in each chapter, I thought it best to avoid cluttering up the text with note-numbers. Instead, all the individuals named in each chapter are listed in alphabetical order at the end of the book, chapter by chapter, with the evidence for each one; these lists are preceded by a brief bibliography. Inevitably, I have not been able to provide annotation for every statement, e.g. by listing all the auxiliary regiments known to have served in Britain to back up the remarks on p. 94 about the nature of the island's garrison. But I have tried to give chapter and verse for every one of the people of Roman Britain whom I have named.

It remains for me to thank all those who have made my task easier. First and foremost, I must mention my father, Eric Birley, whose published studies alone have been a great stimulus; how much I have benefited from discussion with him and from the opportunity to consult his unpublished work and files on the Roman army, only his former pupils will appreciate. I must also thank my Manchester colleagues, A. K. Bowman (now at Oxford), R. P. C. Hanson, G. D. B. Jones, and J. P. Wild, for giving me the benefit of their opinions on various matters; I must also thank Dr Bowman for making available a key name from the Vindolanda writing tablets in advance of full publication, and Professor Jones, for two names from unpublished inscriptions, and for help with illustrations. Mrs K. F. Hartley kindly gave advice, and new information, about mortaria-makers. My brother, Robin Birley, whose work at Vindolanda has aroused so much new public interest in Roman Britain over the past decade, has given friendly encouragement and practical assistance, particularly with illustrations. My friend and former pupil, P. A. Holder, has given valuable assistance on the *auxilia*. Last but by no means least I must mention Dr Graham Webster, who first encouraged me to write this book and who has been generous with his advice throughout. To all these and a host of others whose published work I have learned from, particularly those who have sent me offprints, I offer my thanks. Needless to say, I cannot evade responsibility for errors of fact or interpretation.

When I was writing *Life in Roman Britain*, I was a postgraduate student and research fellow. The present work has been written under very different conditions. As a full-time university teacher, with no sabbatical leave, I have taken much longer to complete it than I had hoped, and I must thank my publishers, particularly Mr Peter Kemmis Betty, for their understanding. To my wife and children, who have patiently endured, and tried to alleviate, the difficulties I have encountered on the way, I dedicate the book as a token of appreciation.

A.R.B.
Manchester, January 1979

A new edition has given the opportunity to correct misprints and to make a few minor improvements (notably on the status of King Cogidubnus, pp. 20, 24, 66, and on the remarkable centurion Maximius Gaetulicus, p. 78). Since 1979 a fascinating array of new people has been revealed by further ink writing-tablets from Vindolanda and by lead curse-tablets from Bath and Uley. It was tempting to try to make use of some of these; but the work is still in progress, and prudence dictates patiences, until full publication. Meanwhile, I can draw attention to three works not available to me when I prepared this book: P. A. Holder, *The Roman Army in Britain* (Batsford, 1980); A. K. Bowman and J. D. Thomas, *Vindolanda: The Latin Writing Tablets* (Britannia monograph no. 4); R. Goodburn and H. Waugh, *Epigraphic Indexes* to R.I.B. (Alan Stton, 1983). They all illuminate the people of Roman Britain. I would also like to single out the concise remarks by J. C. Mann, 'Epigraphic consciousness', JRS 1985, 204-6.

A.R.B.
Manchester, June 1987

Chapter I

Introduction

'What was once a whole world, you made into a single city' (*urbem fecisti quod prius orbis erat*). Thus the Gallic poet Rutilius Namatianus addressed Roma in the early fifth century. But as he cautiously made his way home in the autumn of the year 417, he surely knew that the barbarians were now in the Latin West to stay. His friend and fellow-Gaul Victorinus, with whom he stayed in Italy on his journey, had had to leave his native Toulouse – a band of invaders had captured it not long before. Victorinus had been governor (*vicarius*) of Britain, and Rutilius took the opportunity of paying his friend a pretty compliment in his poem: 'Ocean and Thule know his virtues, as do the fields ploughed by the wild Briton.' There Victorinus would always be remembered: although Britain was on the outer edge of the world, as governor he had behaved as if he were at its very centre. After all, Rutilius adds, it is more creditable to have striven to please such people, people whom it would not have been so discreditable to have displeased. Rutilius must have known, when he wrote, that Britain had been for eight years beyond the authority of the western emperor. That was not because of the barbarians alone, or because in AD 406–407 Britain's garrison had made its own emperors. The last of these usurpers, Constantine III, had been suppressed in 411. Britain was now outside the empire, permanently as it transpired, because its inhabitants had thrown out the Roman officials – presumably those of the usurper – in AD 409. Roman rule effectively ended in that year. What followed was 'sub-Roman', the age of Arthur, and the arrival of the peoples who became the English.

Rome took Britain from prehistory into history. The first named inhabitants of this island emerge in the pages of Julius Caesar. In the century that followed his invasions a score of dynasts in southern Britain put their names on coins. A few, such as Cunobelinus, 'Cymbeline', are mentioned by Roman writers as well; the others, ranging from Addedomaros to Volisios, are known from their coins alone. During the first few decades after the conquest by Claudius a further handful of leading Britons leave their imprint: in particular, Caratacus, the heroic king who kept British resistance alive for eight years, and the two contrasting queens, Boudica the inspiring figurehead of the great rebellion in AD 60, and the arrogant and hot-blooded Cartimandua, who betrayed Caratacus to Rome. Thereafter, apart from Calgacus, who vainly opposed the Roman advance into the Scottish Highlands in the 80s, the scions of the native Celtic aristocracy are submerged until the late fourth century, when figures like Cunedda appear.

Soon most of the Britons were to acquiesce in Roman domination. The client-king Tiberius Claudius Cogidubnus is an early portent, accepting Roman citizenship and privileges from the conquerors. Humbler Britons conscripted into the army were also to acquire Roman status, men like the Coritanian M. Ulpius Novantico, or his fellow-soldier M. Ulpius Longinus, who had already disguised his British origin by taking a Latin name even before becoming a citizen. But the fascination of studying the people of Roman Britain lies not merely in observing the transformation of Celts into Romans. The empire to which Britain was added was vast and heterogeneous. It stretched from the North Sea to Mesopotamia, from Transylvania to the Sahara. Even in the first century AD 'Roman' was no longer synonymous with 'Italian'. To be sure, most of the early governors and a high proportion of the first legionary garrison came from Italy. But before long Romans of other origins appear – men like the procurator Julius Classicianus, from the Celtic aristocracy of northern Gaul, and the governor Julius Agricola, from the colonial élite of Provence. In the second and third centuries the 'colonials' dominate the lists of Roman officials – the governors Lollius Urbicus, Antistius Adventus, and Alfenus Senecio, were all members of families domiciled in Numidia (Algeria), and Spain, Dalmatia, and the Greek-speaking provinces also contributed men, as indeed Italy herself still did.

The army that garrisoned Britain was not composed solely of legionaries, the élite citizen troops. An equal part was played by the regiments of cavalry and infantry conscripted from non-citizen peoples in the provinces, the *auxilia*. Those that served in Britain were drawn predominantly from the western provinces, but a few more exotic units are found, such as the Hamian archers from Syria. Many of these soldiers must have settled in Britain when their long years of service ended. This is specifically attested for the colony of veteran legionaries founded at Colchester, and may be inferred not only for the other first-century foundations, Lincoln and Gloucester, but for a host of individual veterans, auxiliaries as well as legionaries. No doubt, after a century or so the province provided a high proportion of recruits for its own garrison, and the distinctions between Romans and native Britons began gradually to disappear.

The limited quantity of evidence may not permit as systematic a study of the various strata in the population as might be wished. But what there is can none the less be exploited with profit. Analysis of the centurions who were in charge of the gangs of legionaries that built Hadrian's Wall allows us to observe, amongst dozens of men with colourless names – Julii or Valerii and the like – a few that stand out, the Greek Statilius Solon, or the curiously named Lousius Suavis, surely a Celt who had adapted his name to Roman forms. Occasional flashes of light are cast by individuals whose story can be pieced together, such as another centurion, Marcus Cocceius Firmus. One or two tombstones offer tantalizing glimpses into the society of Roman Britain – the elderly priest of Sulis, Calpurnius Receptus, buried at Bath by his widow, once his slave-girl, whose name is the Greek word meaning 'delicious'. A tombstone found at Cologne reveals the name of the first British sailor, a Devon man (Dumnonian) named Aemilius – who served in the German fleet. An altar dredged out of the North Sea off the Dutch coast and an inscription found at York tell us something about a merchant from Rouen who traded with Britain, Viducius Placidus. Taken as a whole, this kind of evidence at least gives us the flavour of Britain under Roman rule.

A variety of information has survived for the 366 years during which most of Britain was first a province, then several provinces, finally a diocese, of the empire. For the historical framework we depend on Roman writers, of whom two above all, Tacitus for the first century and Ammianus for the fourth, serve us remarkably well. Considering how remote Britain always seemed, from the vantage-point of the Mediterranean world, one can only be grateful for the amount of information we have; Tacitus' biography of Agricola really is a unique record for any province. The archaeology of Roman Britain has been intensively studied for the best part of a century, and informed interest goes back to Elizabeth I's antiquary William Camden. But for detailed knowledge of the population we are dependent on epigraphy, and here the picture is gloomier. In comparison with other outlying provinces, the volume of surviving inscriptions from Britain is meagre in the extreme. Those on stone (with a few on other materials) have indeed been admirably published, by Mr R. P. Wright, building on the devoted labours of R. G. Collingwood and other scholars; and it is greatly to be hoped that the *instrumentum domesticum*, the graffiti on pots, the writing-tablets, and the like, will also soon be available. But the fact remains that the total is very small. To some extent this is caused by the misfortune of geology: in much of the lowland zone, in particular, good stone is not readily available, and such inscriptions as there were still surviving in the fourth and early fifth centuries may well have been exploited in large quantities to provide stone and lime to build defences against the barbarians, or indeed by the barbarians themselves. The fifth-century inhabitants of Britain will have had scant respect for memorials of pagan Romans and Britons elegantly carved on Purbeck marble. It may also have been the case that the Celtic inhabitants of these islands never fully acquired the 'epigraphic habit' which the peoples of the Mediterranean and its hinterland took for granted in the few centuries immediately before and after the birth of Christ. The Celts were not by nature particularly retiring or unostentatious people, but they may, in Britain at least, have preferred other forms of display, rather than putting up inscriptions. Questions of literacy, and wealth, are doubtless also relevant. Britain was not an exceptionally impoverished country when the Romans arrived, and the presence of the garrison clearly brought a good deal of money here. But paying a skilled man to carve an inscription on a suitable piece of stone or bronze will have involved a considerable outlay; and the canny Britons may well have reflected that if their neighbours, or passers-by, could not read the result in many cases, because they were illiterate, inscriptions were an unnecessary luxury.

However this may be, some comment is called for on the distribution and nature of the epigraphic record in Britain. There are 2,314 inscriptions edited in *The Roman Inscriptions of Britain*, Volume I. Just under 100 are milestones, from various parts of the country. Of the remainder, the vast majority come from the military districts of the island, nearly 800 from Hadrian's Wall and its forts alone, and a further 600 or so from the outposts to the north and the forts of its southern hinterland, as far as Stainmore. If one adds the inscriptions from the legionary fortresses of York, Chester, and Caerleon, the stones from the Antonine Wall and other Scottish sites, and from the auxiliary forts south of the Hadrian's Wall zone, the number of 'civilian district' inscriptions remaining is scanty. One must take account, also, of the essentially military nature of the early epigraphy at cities such as Colchester, Cirencester, and Lincoln, where the tombstones of first-century legionaries and auxiliaries, and a few from later periods, make up a sizeable proportion of the yield. It is, fortunately, the case that plenty of the inscriptions from military areas relate to civilians or to soldiers' activities that are not strictly military.

Enough has been said to indicate why it is not possible in the case of Britain even to attempt a study of the social structure and population of the province on the lines of that done elsewhere in the empire, for example Pannonia, or Dalmatia. It must be acknowledged, in any case, that the work done on those areas is itself subject to criticism on methodological grounds. Not the least of the problems facing the historian is the lack of evidence for the size of the population. If one cannot make any valid assertions about that, it seems fruitless to extrapolate from the epigraphic record: the ratio between the known members of the population and the whole is unknown. Studying the people of Britain in the Roman period may thus appear to be a case of making bricks without straw. There is no point in denying this criticism as far as the civilian element in the population is concerned. So few inhabitants of the towns, so few of the landowners and peasantry, are known to us by name, that any generalizations about them will rightly be viewed with deep suspicion. Discussion of these categories of the inhabitants, who must, after all, have constituted the great majority of the population of Britain, must therefore be limited mainly to bare statements of the known names. Other categories offer some scope. During the first and second centuries AD the makers of mortaria (mixing bowls), for example, stamped their pots with their name or 'trademark'. Although the evidence is not yet available in conveniently accessible form, well over 200 names may be assembled, and these have something to tell us. Furthermore, as already indicated, the members of the garrison are relatively well recorded, and the evidence from Britain may be supplemented by scores of inscriptions from other parts of the empire. As far as the men who governed Britain, and officered the army, are concerned, we are exceptionally well provided with information. Although the majority of those concerned were only in Britain for a few years, they formed part of its history, and an analysis of their background and careers has a value in the wider context, the story of imperial Rome.

Many of the individuals discussed in this book are at first sight mere names and nothing more. But the elaborate Roman naming system makes it possible to learn a good deal about a person's origin and background from his names alone. In its most fully developed form the nomenclature of a male Roman citizen contained six elements. First came the *praenomen* or forename, such as Aulus, Gaius or Lucius, generally abbreviated to the first letter only, or to two or three letters in the cases of Sex(tus) and Ti(berius). Then came the *nomen gentilicium* – which will often be referred to in these pages as *nomen* or *gentilicium*, for short; this was the 'clan' or family name, and hence was the equivalent of the modern European surname. Most *nomina* terminated in -ius, such as Julius or Valerius, although there were a few rarer forms, ending in -anus or -enus, for example. The third element was the patronymic or filiation, the father's *praenomen* in the genitive case and *filius*, son: *M.f.*, *Marci filius*, 'son of Marcus'. This was followed by the tribe or 'voting-district', of which there were 35. This too was generally abbreviated, *Cl.* or *Cla.* for *Claudia*, *Fab.* for *Fabia*, and so on. After the tribe came the third personal name, the *cognomen*, originally a private, unofficial name, or nickname. In the final place came the man's place of origin, *origo*, or domicile, *domus*, such as Forum Julii (Fréjus in Provence). The full style of Julius Agricola would thus have been Cn(aeus) Julius L(uci) f(ilius) Ani(ensis) Agricola Foro Julii – but, not surprisingly, members of the ruling élite of the empire such as Agricola were not expected to set out the full rigmarole. Men of humbler status, such as common soldiers in the legions, for whom possession of Roman citizenship was one of their few assets, regularly did so.

For several centuries in early Roman history the first four of these elements had sufficed for registration or other official purposes, and in everyday usage the first two alone, *praenomen* and *nomen*, were enough. But *cognomina* were becoming increasingly common during the first century BC. There were barely a dozen common *praenomina*, and with the great spread of Roman citizenship there must have been literally hundreds of men called Marcus Valerius or Publius Cornelius in many communities. The use of a *cognomen* to distinguish Marcus Valerius Longus from other Marci Valerii was a practical necessity. In the meantime certain old-established noble families had used *cognomina* for centuries to distinguish themselves from humbler bearers of their *nomen*: only the patrician Julii used the *cognomen* Caesar. In the mid-first century BC some men, like Caesar, were generally referred to either by *praenomen* and *cognomen*, Gaius Caesar, or *nomen* and *cognomen*, Julius Caesar, but never by *praenomen* and *nomen*, Gaius Julius. But a number of Caesar's contemporaries, such as Antony, Marcus Antonius, were still content to do without *cognomina*.

The use of the *cognomen* had still not become universal by the time of the conquest of Britain. Thus the first governor, Aulus Plautius, had no other name, nor did Quintus Veranius, governor in the late 50s AD. But the last prominent Roman to be known by two names only was Aulus Vitellius, one of the ephemeral emperors of the year 69, and he must have been regarded as distinctly old-fashioned in this respect. From the reign of Claudius onwards the use of three names, the *tria nomina*, *praenomen*, *nomen* or *gentilicium*, and *cognomen*, was regarded as the norm for a Roman male, 'to possess the three names' meant 'to be a Roman citizen'. With the end of the free Republic the main electoral function of the 35 tribes naturally lost its importance. But for formal purposes the tribe continued to be listed, while it became increasingly necessary for the *origo* to be given, as more Romans were now domiciled elsewhere than at Rome itself.

The early tombstones of legionaries in Britain illustrate these developments. Some are traditional, giving the first four elements only, as with C. Valerius C.f. Maec., a soldier of the IXth legion buried at Lincoln – Gaius Valerius, son of Gaius, in the Maecian tribe. Another man from the IXth at Lincoln also lacks a *cognomen*, Gaius Saufeius, son of Gaius, in the Fabian tribe, but in his case the place of origin, Heraclea in Macedonia, is added: C. Saufeius C.f. Fab. Her. Men from II Adiutrix and XX Valeria Victrix buried at Chester a few years later have all six elements: C. Julius C. (f.) Cl. Quartus Cel., and C. Juventius C. (f.) Cla. Capito Apro – Gaius Julius, son of Gaius, Claudian tribe, Quartus, from Celeia, and Gaius Juventius, son of Gaius, Claudian tribe, Capito, from Aprus.

Roman girls for centuries had to be content with a single name, the *gentilicium*, with filiation: Julia C.f., Julia, daughter of Gaius, or Antonia M.f., Antonia, daughter of Marcus. On their marriage they took their husband's name, in the genitive, Julia Pompeii, Julia, wife of Pompeius. In some families of the aristocracy daughters were given *cognomina*: for example, we find Caecilia Metella. But during the first century AD it seems gradually to have become normal for women to have *cognomina*.

The widespread granting of the Roman franchise, *civitas*, from Caesar onwards, ensured a continual growth in the number of persons with the imperial *gentilicia*, Julius, Claudius, Flavius, Ulpius, Aelius, and Aurelius, to take only those which appear in the greatest numbers. It was natural – and it may have been encouraged officially – that new citizens should take the family name of the emperor who had, directly or indirectly, bestowed the privilege of Roman status on them. Thus the British king Cogidubnus, allowed a portion of southern Britain as a client-state under Roman protection, advertises his debt to Claudius (or to Nero) by bearing the names Ti(berius) Claudius. The British lady, Claudia

Rufina, whose charm and polite manners the poet Martial applauds in an elegant epigram, was doubtless the daughter or granddaughter of another beneficiary from the period immediately after the conquest. She also has a *cognomen*, and a standard Roman one at that, although 'raised among the sky-blue Britons', as Martial somewhat tactlessly put it. When *cognomina* became universal for male citizens, the women began to adopt them as well.

The first Roman citizen in a native family would be obliged, unless he altered his personal name, to keep it as his *cognomen*, as King Cogidubnus did. We see a typical example of the type in the British soldier in an auxiliary regiment serving in the Danubian area, M. Ulpius Novantico, from Ratae (Leicester). He has the *praenomen* and *nomen gentilicium* of the emperor Trajan and his original Celtic name as *cognomen*. But another man in the same unit, the *cohors I Brittonum*, from the Belgae of southern Britain, was already equipped with a Roman name, and became M. Ulpius Longinus on receiving *civitas* – his father, named as Saccius on his diploma, had been sufficiently influenced by the arrival of Roman rule to choose Longinus for his son in preference to a Celtic name like his own. Alternatively, Longinus may have been a second name given to the man when he joined the army. Cases of this kind may be noted with the Thracian cavalrymen buried in Britain, Longinus Sdapeze and Rufus Sita. But before long, it is clear that Roman names tended to predominate among large elements of the indigenous population in new provinces, and Britain is unlikely to have been an exception. There are certainly cases of Britons other than soldiers, not Roman citizens, but with Latin names: Grata, daughter of Dagobitus, buried at London, or Lucullus, son of Ammin(i)us, who made a dedication at Chichester.

On the other hand, there is evidence, particularly in the names on potters' stamps, of the continuance of Celtic names on into the late second century, and beyond. There is even a potter with a Latin name, Albinus, whose son, also a potter, had the Celtic name Matugenus. A further feature of the nomenclature of the Roman empire, particularly prevalent in the Celtic areas, was the practice of 'fabricating' *gentilicia*. In other words, recipients of Roman citizenship, instead of taking a new *nomen gentilicium*, converted their existing personal name, or that of their father. If, as was often the case, the new citizen or his father already had a Latin name, such as Secundus or Simplex, he would then be known as, for example, M. Secundius Secundus, or M. Simplicius Simplex. But if he had a Celtic name, and wished to keep it, he might call himself C. Indutius Felix. Examples of both these types are found in Britain, and although it is often presumed that their bearers are probably immigrants from Gaul, or – even more likely – from the Rhineland, it must be pointed out that we have specimens of the practice with persons who are surely British. One may cite the Tammonii of Silchester, the first of whom, T. Tammon(ius) Vitalis, was son of Saen(i)us Tammon(i)us. It should be mentioned, further, that Celtic families who behaved in this way were also capable of changing the '*gentilicium*' from generation to generation. We can observe this with C. Aeresius Saenus, veteran of the VIth at York, who called his son Saenius Agustinus, even though he was of course a citizen himself – as may indeed have been the case with the father of Tammonius Vitalis.

During the early empire, new citizens had a third choice. Instead of taking the name of the emperor, or adapting their own to conform with Latin practice, they might assume the *gentilicium* of the influential person, such as the governor of the province, who had gained the privilege for them. Such cases may be observed in other parts of the empire, for example in Lycia, where the first governor, Q. Veranius (later in Britain), perpetuated his memory by arranging such grants, as a number of Lycians with names like Q. Veranius Philagrus, or Q. Veranius Eudemus, demonstrate. There is not much sign of this having happened in Britain. Some of the relatively numerous Julii may, of course, have taken that name out of respect for or gratitude to the governors Julius Frontinus or Julius Agricola, but this cannot be proved. A few other cases are a little more probable, a Neratius or a Lollius, but still doubtful – for one thing this practice died out in the early second century at latest. Only where the official concerned had a very rare *gentilicium* is the connection fairly certain. An example from Britain is Javolenus: there are two possible bearers of this name, although the text is rather illegible in both cases. But if they were called this, their ancestors presumably gained citizenship through the patronage of the Flavian law officer *(juridicus)* Javolenus Priscus.

Another path to citizenship was through enslavement to a citizen. On being freed, by 'manumission' the ex-slave acquired his or her master's status and took the same *gentilicium*. Most slaves tended to be given Greek names, and it is thus difficult to tell whether a citizen with a Greek *cognomen* is really a Greek, from the eastern half of the empire, if no more details are given. The whole question of determining origins is indeed fraught with uncertainty. Fortunately, in the early period it was common practice to state a person's origin, as was seen with the legionary C. Saufeius. When this is not supplied, various other clues may be used.

One of these is the tribe. Analysis of the allocation of the communities of the empire into the 31 possible *tribus rusticae,* made by the Austrian scholar J. W. Kubitschek in 1889, is still the basis for examining the subject, although caution is required, and there are many gaps in our knowledge. But even so, one may be fairly confident that a certain number of tribes were never used outside Italy, and some were confined to a few towns within the peninsula. A few others are found only in Italy and a small handful of provincial cities, an example being the Aniensis, which is found at Agricola's home, Forum Julii, at Saragossa, and at Alexandria Troas, as well as at a handful of Italian towns. By contrast, there were certain tribes selected by particular emperors for the provincial communities to which they made bloc grants of *civitas*. Thus the Quirina, which Claudius, Nero and the Flavians used, is found very widely in north Africa, which benefited from grants made by those emperors.

Study of Latin personal names rests largely on two fundamental studies, by W. Schulze on the *gentilicia*, published in 1904, and on the *cognomina* by I. Kajanto, published in 1965. Regional studies help to complete these works, but for non-Latin names one must turn, for Britain, above all to Alfred Holder's three-volume *Alt-celtischer Sprachschatz* (1894–1916). An eminent Celtic philologist long ago warned that 'as usual with such encyclopaedic works, the result has been to endow it in the eyes of non-specialists with an authority sometimes greater than it deserves'. There is certainly a temptation, when a name seems non-Latin, to regard it as Celtic, a temptation to which Holder himself was evidently prone on occasion. It is particularly difficult to distinguish between Celtic and German names, not least because many Germans, or persons who described themselves as such, had Celtic names anyway.

A further aspect which requires mention is the apparent popularity of particular *cognomina*, or types of *cognomina*, in certain regions of the empire. It has long been recognized, for example, that names formed from past participles are particularly favoured in Roman Africa. Rogatus (meaning 'asked') is a good example: of the 714 epigraphic examples counted by Kajanto 650 are found in Africa. Similarly, Saturninus, although very common everywhere, was particularly favoured by the Africans, presumably influenced by the cult of the Punic deity equated with Saturn. In Celtic areas of the empire too, favourite Latin names may be observed, sometimes because they happened to resemble existing Celtic ones, or perhaps, in some cases, were translations of common native names. Names beginning Sen- (Senilis, Seneca, etc.) or Bell- (Bellus, Bellicus, Bellator), are examples. The evidence from Britain itself seems too small in quantity to satisfy a statistician, but it may none the less be observed that Vitalis, itself very common throughout the empire (1,028 examples, according to Kajanto, making it the eighteenth most popular in his total of 130,000), is found rather more frequently here than one would expect. Five of the British potters have this name, and there are 20 other examples, to which one may add two British soldiers serving overseas and the son of another (M. Ulpius Longinus, mentioned earlier). It comes equal fourth in popularity with Rufus in the province, after Maximus, Victor, and Secundus.

Other attempts at statistics may be meaningless also, but for what they are worth one may present some approximate figures for the bearers of various *gentilicia*, excluding those cases which are certainly or probably of immigrants, and restricting it to presumed natives of Britain:

Julii	63
Claudii	15
Flavii	33
Cocceii	2
Ulpii	9
Aelii	22
T. Aurelii	6
other Aurelii	77

The heavy concentration of Aurelii, reflecting Caracalla's grant of citizenship to all free *peregrini*, 'peregrines' or alien inhabitants of the empire in 212, is no surprise. The emperor himself was officially named M. Aurelius Antoninus, hence the new citizens in large numbers of cases assumed the *gentilicium* Aurelius. As for the large number of Julii, this may be attributable in large measure to an influx of Gauls, in the first decades after the conquest in particular, and to the settlement of veteran legionaries of that name. But of course, this is really little better than guesswork.

There are some 135 inscriptions from Britain in which a place of origin (*origo*) is specifically mentioned, in a few cases the person in question being simply from another part of Britain. Virtually every region of the empire is represented. Slightly more come from Germany than anywhere else, although Italians come very close behind. These Germans are in the main from the later period, while the Italians are from the first century of Roman rule. After a relatively short period, certainly by the year 200 or so, it became the exception to state an origin. This may have been partly because the soldiers, who have provided the bulk of the evidence, were by then mostly recruited in Britain. The Germans, on the other hand, were in a sense a self-consciously new element when they began to arrive in greater numbers in the third century. Men like Hnaudifridus and his soldiers at Housesteads on the Wall presumably saw some point in mentioning where their home was. Much of the rest of the garrison would not need to specify, for they would have been born locally.

By the third century, with all free subjects of Rome now citizens, and only new arrivals such as these German mercenaries having a different status, the old forms of Roman nomenclature must have seemed increasingly irrelevant. The *praenomen* begins to disappear well before this, all over the empire, and ceases to be used much in the third century. In the last century of Roman rule, particularly with the gradual adoption of Christianity, new styles of nomenclature begin to appear. Various examples will be seen in this work, particularly in the last chapter.

There is still room for further analysis of the inscriptions of Roman Britain. One might, for example, compile statistics of the women who are attested – less than 200. Something could be said about the information in the tombstones, of which there are about 465. About 25 have the formula *h(ic) s(itus) e(st)*, 'here he lies'. Just over 30 have the later wording, *Dis Manibus*, conventionally rendered 'to the divine shades', while more than 200 have *D.M.* or *D.M. s(acrum)* ('sacred'). Only four have *memoriae*, 'in memory of', while the remainder are too fragmentary to classify, or have no formula. It may be noted, further, that the ages of death, where given, range from infants under the age of two, to a veteran legionary at Caerleon who was allegedly 100; and that the commonest age of death was apparently 30, 35, or 40. But these figures have no real validity as evidence for life expectancy. They merely illustrate the tendency to round off ages to the nearest five years – and perhaps the greater likelihood of a person who died at this time of life being commemorated.

In spite of the extreme paucity of the evidence, judicious use of inscriptions from other parts of the empire helps to give us a fuller picture of the people who lived in Britain during the Roman period. Much of the book, admittedly, is devoted to people whose presence here was merely an episode in their lives. But they too form part of the history of this country. Since Roman society was categorized above all by rank, it is desirable here briefly to sketch the different *ordines*, into which the population of the empire, including Britain, was divided. At the apex stood the emperor, at first, until the 160s, alone, with the names Caesar and Augustus taken from the founders of the principate. By the time that Britain became part of the empire, there was no longer any doubt that the empire was a monarchy, and that monarchy an hereditary one. But the problem of the succession was never resolved. Some emperors had no sons, others had heirs who were unworthy. One expedient, first practised in the 160s, was for the emperor to take a colleague. In the third and fourth centuries this became standard practice for long periods. But there was always the danger that an ambitious general might attempt a *coup*. Britain was a breeding-ground for such usurpations, most of them unsuccessful – the exception was Constantine the Great, proclaimed emperor by dissident troops at York in 306.

Throughout the first two centuries of Roman rule in Britain, the generals, both the governors and the legionary commanders, were drawn from the highest order in the empire below the emperor himself, the senate. Its members were traditionally large landowners, at first almost all Italians. But during the first century AD the colonial élites of southern Gaul, southern Spain, and north Africa, and then rich men from the Greek-speaking provinces, entered the senate in increasing numbers; and the emperors themselves, from Trajan (AD 98–117) onwards were mainly of colonial or provincial origin. Other parts of the empire, the north-western provinces, including Britain and the Rhineland, and the Danubian and Balkan lands, lagged behind in this respect. The reasons were diverse: to some extent, the Celtic system of land-tenure may have been as much an obstacle as lack of 'culture', making it difficult for the Celtic chieftains who became Roman in name and outlook to accumulate the landed wealth that was required. At any rate, no certain British senators can be detected, for even King Cogidubnus turns out not to have been a *legatus Augusti*.

The next order of society, the *equites*, or 'knights', were for the most part men of similar stamp to the senators, on a smaller scale, a 'squirearchy' or local magnates. They furnished the bulk of the regimental commanders for the army, and could achieve positions of eminence as imperial procurators. Often the sons of such men entered the senate, and, particularly at times of crisis, they might be enrolled as members themselves. Not all the *equites* were of this type – some were ambitious men of relatively humble origin who obtained commissions and equestrian status at the same time, with the aid of a powerful patron.

Below the *equites* there was in theory an undifferentiated mass of Roman citizens. But within the citizen body some had particular privileges. The legionaries and veterans, above all the centurions, mostly men who had risen from the ranks, were in a superior position to most of their fellow-citizens. For one thing, they enjoyed regular wages, which was beyond the reach of most free men. Besides this, they had tax exemption and other privileges. Centurions could rise to equestrian rank in some cases, but all could count on being among the better-off members of society when they chose to retire. Ex-legionaries, too, are found among the local ruling élite in the urban communities of the empire, particularly in the *coloniae*. These élites are detectable as the 'curial class', that is, as the members of the councils, who sat in the *curia*, 'council-chamber', of their home-town as decurions. As the economic position of the empire began to worsen, the role of the decurions became less enviable, for they were squeezed by taxation – above all by the obligation to collect revenues for the government – more than most other groups. None the less, their enhanced status was recognized by the courts, and in Roman law the 'better-off', or 'more honourable', *honestiores*, were treated more favourably in some respects than the 'humbler', *humiliores*.

The rest of the inhabitants of the empire fell into this category. After the Edict of Caracalla, distinctions between citizen and non-citizen were swept aside. Up till then, non-Romans had had the opportunity of enhancing their status by entering the army. The 'auxiliary' regiments, *auxilia*, cavalry *alae* and infantry *cohorts*, were manned by provincials, who, from Claudius' time onwards obtained Roman citizenship after 25 years' service. In some parts of the empire, indeed, when there was a shortage of citizen recruits, non-Romans who fulfilled the requirements were given citizenship and enrolled in the legions.

Once all free inhabitants had become citizens, the division between legions and *auxilia* must have seemed somewhat irrelevant. But in any case, by the mid-third century the crisis that had gripped the empire had made drastic changes in the military system necessary. The emperor Gallienus (AD 260–268) broke with the tradition of using senatorial generals, and drastically reorganized the army, beginning a process which was taken further by his successors, culminating with the reforms of Diocletian and Constantine.

But for most of the population, these changes may well have seemed largely irrelevant to their daily lives. The empire's inhabitants were overwhelmingly peasants, living at or close to the subsistence level. As far as Britain is concerned, there is little information about their status – whether they were tenants or freeholders, or to what extent slave-labour was used on large estates. Certainly, the existence, particularly in the fourth century, of large villas, points to a considerable tenantry, no doubt tied to the land. But our sources are almost silent about the labour-force. Inscriptions from the countryside are very scarce, and the names provided by graffiti at rural sites generally give little clue to their owners' position in society.

There were, to be sure, other groups, representatives of which are considered in some of the chapters in this book – merchants, craftsmen, and slaves. Merchants and craftsmen generally had a low status in the Mediterranean world. It is difficult to tell to what extent this was so in Britain. There is some evidence for freedmen and slaves being involved in both groups. Slavery was certainly practised in Roman Britain, but there is no guarantee that it was on a large scale or that it had a major role in the economy of the country. It may well be that it was confined to the household, with slaves being used as domestic servants and by craftsmen in small workshops, and that there were no big estates on which the labour force was principally servile.

During the last decades of Roman rule there are hints that Britain was prospering and that individual Britons were coming to the fore. The emergence of Pelagius as a major figure in the Church during the late fourth and early fifth centuries is one sign of this. Another is the British origin of the usurpers Gratian and Constantine III, and of the latter's general Gerontius. Had Britain not been cut off from the empire in 409, many others might have been ready to participate in the affairs of Rome.

Chapter II
Britain and the Caesars

Britain first enters the light of history with the invasions of Julius Caesar. In the *Gallic War* he mentions only a few of the officers who accompanied him on his two expeditions. Apart from the tribune C. Volusenus, who reconnoitred the coast before the first invasion, of 55 BC, these were Q. Atrius, who guarded the fleet after the second invasion, Q. Laberius Durus, a military tribune who died in battle, and, the highest ranking officer, C. Trebonius, Caesar's *legatus*, 'lieutenant' or legionary commander. More Celts than Romans are named, in fact. Most prominent was Commius, chief of the Gallic Atrebates, who had influence in Britain and was sent there on an advance mission by Caesar. He also mentions six British chiefs, the most prominent of them Cassivellaunus of the Catuvellauni, along with Mandubracius of Essex, Cingetorix, Carvilius, Taximagulus, and Segovax, all of Kent, and a 'noble' general captured by the Romans, Lugotorix. These men almost all have compound names of the sort favoured by the Celtic aristocracy. Elements in their nomenclature recur among the population of Britain throughout the Roman period and beyond, particularly the termination – *orix*.

The presence in Britain of some of Caesar's other *legati* must be assumed – he needed commanders of senatorial rank for his legions. His *quaestor*, junior magistrate assigned to the proconsul of Gaul, M. Licinius Crassus, son of the great Crassus, was probably there, and the *legatus* Q. Tullius Cicero certainly was. Although Caesar does not mention him, we learn of his presence from letters exchanged by Quintus Cicero with his brother, the great orator, during the second expedition. In his *Commentaries,* of course, Caesar wanted to enhance his own reputation, and it did no harm to sprinkle his pages with the names of barbarian chiefs whom he defeated or brought over to Rome's side. But there was no need for him to detail the activities of too many subordinates: he wanted his readers to concentrate on his own achievements. Trebonius perhaps received a mention because Caesar was under an obligation to him – Trebonius, as tribune of the plebs in 55 BC, had passed a law extending Caesar's proconsulship for a second lengthy term; but he was later to turn against Caesar and to play a prominent part in his murder.

Britain was not left entirely alone between Caesar's second invasion in 54 BC and Claudius' expedition of AD 43. Caesar's claim to have received the islanders' submission was doubtless never abandoned by his successors. Augustus occasionally showed signs of sending in troops to reassert it; but he preferred to exercise influence through diplomatic pressure. Caesar's agent Commius had gone over to the anti-Roman side in 52 BC and fled to Britain in 51 or 50 when resistance ended in Gaul, having apparently expressed the wish never to meet a Roman again. In Britain he established a kingdom south of the middle Thames, where he struck coins. Three successors, Tincommius, Eppillus, and Verica span the period between the invasions, all implausibly described on their coinage as 'son of Commius'. Tincommius, in spite of Commius' feelings, was to take refuge in Rome during the last years of Augustus, who records the fact in his *Res Gestae*. The other two were to use the Latin word *rex*, 'king', on their coins, surely indicating that they were recognized by Rome, and regarded as clients of the emperor. Elsewhere in southern Britain coinage attests further British rulers. Tasciovanus of the Catuvellauni minted coins at Verulamium, and, for a short time only, at Camulodunum, capital of the Trinovantes. This suggests that he infringed Caesar's prohibition on Catuvellaunian expansion eastwards, but was obliged to withdraw after pressure from Augustus. A ruler called Addedomarus minted at Camulodunum for a time, to be replaced by Dubnovellaunus, earlier apparently ruling in Kent. But Dubnovellaunus was to take refuge in Rome, for he is mentioned as seeking Augustus' protection in the *Res Gestae*. It seems clear that he was driven out by the most famous of the pre-Roman rulers, Cunobelinus – Shakespeare's 'radiant Cymbeline', son of Tasciovanus. At about the time that Cunobelin moved in to control the south-east, Rome had incurred the great disaster in Germany, in AD 9. It may well be that he took advantage of this to break the treaty imposed by Caesar.

During the reign of Tiberius Cunobelinus' power in southern Britain grew and was consolidated. Soon after the old emperor's death in 37, one of Cunobelinus' sons, Adminius, fled to Caligula. This was a perfect pretext for Roman intervention, and Caligula prepared an invasion force in 40, only to abandon the attempt. His murder early in 41 might have ended Roman interest in Britain, but Cunobelinus himself died at about this time. His sons Togodumnus and Caratacus began expending their kingdom further. They seem to have gained control of part, at least, of the Dobunni, whose territory extended from the Mendips to the Cotswolds and beyond. Coins from this area reveal the names of rulers in the generation before the conquest, in abbreviated form, as Anted., Eisu., Catti., and Comux., followed by Corio. and Boduoc. There had already been Catuvellaunian encroachment into Verica's kingdom, the northern part of which seems to have been controlled by a brother of Cunobelin, Epaticcus, in the mid-20s. Now, soon after the accession of Claudius, Verica was expelled, and fled to the Romans. Claudius thus had a perfect pretext to invade. An invasion force of four legions was assembled, and, after some delay, led triumphantly into south-east Britain by Aulus Plautius. The emperor followed when victory was in sight, and received the surrender of 11 British kings in person.

As with Caesar's two invasions, that of AD 43 was undertaken, to a large extent at least, for political reasons. Claudius had come to the throne in surprising circumstances after the murder of Caligula in January 41, and was despised by the upper classes. There had been an attempted military coup in 42. The British expedition was admirably designed to give the new regime some much needed prestige. Claudius himself was desperately anxious to live up to the military reputations of his ancestors and of Caesar, whose name he had assumed, so it is not surprising that he participated personally. But he had to make very careful arrangements to ensure that his absence from Rome did not create the opportunity for another armed rebellion. His suite therefore included as *comites*, aides-de-camp, a number of men too dangerous to leave behind, D. Valerius Asiaticus, M. Vinicius, and Cn. Sentius Saturninus, all of whom had played a prominent part in the events of January 41. Other *comites* were Ser. Sulpicius Galba, who was to be emperor in 68–69, and members of Claudius' family – his son-in-law, who had inherited through his mother the prestigious names Cn. Pompeius Magnus; Magnus' father M. Licinius Crassus Frugi; and the youth to whom Claudius' infant younger daughter Octavia was betrothed, L. Junius Silanus, a descendant of Augustus. The antiquarian emperor, consciously treading in Caesar's footsteps, was thus able to imitate the great man by having a M. Crassus on his staff, and to go one better by taking a 'Pompey the Great'. There were, in addition, members of the palace household, C. Stertinius Xenophon, the court physician, Ti. Claudius Balbillus, son of Tiberius' astrologer Thrasyllus, the eunuch Posides, and probably the freedman chief secretary, Narcissus, whose presence with the army before embarkation is well attested. A detachment of the praetorian guard escorted the emperor on his brief foray, commanded by one of the prefects, Rufrius Pollio. A. Plautius, who led the invasion force and remained as first governor, is discussed in detail in the next chapter, but here it may be mentioned that a young kinsman of his, Ti. Plautius Silvanus Aelianus, was attached to Claudius' staff; and that two of his legionary commanders were T. Flavius Sabinus and the latter's younger brother, T. Flavius Vespasianus, the future emperor Vespasian. Vespasian's military reputation, to which he owed the command against the Jewish rebels and thus the throne, was based on his exploits in Britain. His elder son Titus had been a military tribune in the province, too, some 15 years later. It was thus no coincidence that renewed attention was paid to Britain by the Flavian dynasty. The first governor appointed by Vespasian was a kinsman, Q. Petillius Cerialis, probably his son-in-law, who had already been in Britain at the time of Boudica's revolt.

The imposition of Roman rule in 43 apparently involved the surrender of 11 British kings to Claudius. Togodumnus died in battle in the first season, and Caratacus continued the fight, from Wales, until his capture in 51. But some of the 11 who submitted were clearly confirmed as client-rulers, their frontiers regulated by Rome and their position protected and controlled by the legions. Verica may have recovered his kingdom, although this is not recorded, but in any case a new man was found to rule a portion of southern England in Rome's interest, either supplanting Verica or replacing him. Tacitus drily records, in the *Agricola*, that 'certain states (*civitates*) were assigned to Cogidumnus as king . . . for it is an ancient and long accepted custom of the Roman people to use, among other instruments of servitude, even kings'. He also noted that the man remained very loyal to Rome for a long time, 'as I recall', which suggests that Cogidumnus kept his throne until the 70s. A massive inscription at Chichester shows that this must have been his capital and that he had been enfranchised by the emperor, who family name he took; and that he spelt his name with a *b* instead of *m*: [Ti.] Claud(ius) [Co]gidubnus. He also paraded with the grandiose title *rex magnus Brit(anniae)* – meaning merely that he ruled over more than one British state; and is the likeliest candidate to have occupied the sumptuous palace discovered at Fishbourne, close to Chichester.

Less is known about the other native rulers. Two later clients of Rome are known, Cartimandua of the Brigantes and Prasutagus of the Iceni, but it is not clear whether they were already installed in 43. Some of Prasutagus' predecessors struck coins, which have been found widely in East Anglia, where the Iceni had their home. The earliest coins give the name or names CANS DVRO, interpretation of which is uncertain. Other coins give the names Saenu., Aesu., and Anted. The first of these is echoed after the conquest by the 'fabricated' *gentilicium* S(a)enius, while Aesu-, which must be derived from the Celtic god Esus, is found on a dedication at Roman Colchester by a freedman of Aesubilinus. Anted., probably Antedios, is thought to have been king of the Iceni at the time of the conquest; his name is the same as one found on the coins of the Dobunni, mentioned earlier. He may perhaps have remained in power until the Iceni rebelled in the year 47. Thereafter personal names disappear from the coinage, except for a group with the legend SVBIDASTO-ESICO, which remains obscure. Otherwise, the word ECEN or ECE appears, presumably the tribal name (*Eceni*). Prasutagus may have been installed by Rome after 47, with diminished powers. On his death in 60, Rome decided on annexation, and, as is too well known to require detailed treatment, his widow Boudica led the last major revolt in the province. Her name, it may be added, evidently means 'Victory', revealing her to have been a first-century British 'Queen Victoria'.

Further north, the Coritani of the East Midlands, whose chief town was to be Leicester (Ratae) under Roman rule, are not known to have offered resistance to Rome, nor can it be told whether they were allowed, initially, to retain their own ruler. Coins now shown to have been produced by the Coritani give a number of names of presumed kings, including Volisios, Dumnocoverus, Dumnove – llaunos, and Cartivel (launos?). At all events, by the 60s, Coritanian territory was firmly under direct Roman rule, and Rome's forces confronted the Brigantes of the Pennines. Our knowledge of the Brigantian royal house derives entirely from Tacitus, unless one is prepared to make use of the Welsh Triads. The Roman historian refers to them both in his *Histories,* under the year 69, and in his *Annals,* composed later but dealing with the reigns of Claudius and Nero. Quite exceptionally among Celtic peoples, the Brigantes had a queen regnant – Boudica, it must be stressed, had not been a monarch in her own right: she had been the consort of Prasutagus. The Brigantian ruler, Cartimandua, is described vividly in the pages of Tacitus, from which it is quite clear that she was 'a quisling queen': 'powerful from her nobility, she had increased her power when, by the capture through trickery of king Caratacus she appeared to have provided material for the triumph of Claudius Caesar'. Thus, Tacitus reveals, she had treacherously handed over the British resistance leader when he fled to the Brigantes for refuge after his defeat in 51. 'Wealth, and the extravagance that goes with success' followed. She repudiated her husband Venutius 'and gave his armour-bearer Vellocatus her hand in marriage. At once her house was convulsed by the scandal. The husband had the state (*civitas*) on his side, the adulterer had the lust and savagery of the queen'. In the *Annals,* Tacitus recounts how Venutius attempted to depose his former wife, who was kept in power by the support of Roman troops, early in the reign of Nero. But in 69, the year of the four emperors, when the British garrison was depleted, Venutius struck again, expelled Cartimandua and seized the kingdom. Within two years or so he had been overthrown: the great earthworks at Stanwix in the North Riding of Yorkshire probably represents the place where he mustered his hosts for his last stand. Neither he nor Cartimandua and her second husband are heard of again, although the queen is perhaps to be identified with the woman called Aregwedd Foeddawg, who by 'craft and deceit and treachery' placed Caradawc (Caratacus) in Roman hands, in the early Welsh poem. Cartimandua's name, it may be added, is thought to mean 'sleek filly', which seems curiously appropriate. Rather less fittingly, perhaps, Vellocatus means 'fighter of the good fight' – the meaning of Venutius is obscure.

Why the Brigantes should have had a female ruler is not clear. It may be that a substantial element in the population of the Pennines was pre-Celtic, and that the ruling Celtic aristocracy had found it politic to follow their customs. On the other hand, Rome may have imposed Cartimandua, if she were the only child of the previous ruler, to suit their own purposes. After this time, only two more British leaders are named. One of them, Arviragus, is known only from a passing mention in the poet Juvenal, and may even have been invented. The other is the Caledonian chief Calgacus, portrayed by Tacitus in the *Agricola*: he was the man against whom Agricola won his last, great battle, at the 'Graupian Mountain' somewhere in north-eastern Scotland. But Tacitus does not record his fate. What happened to the families of other British princes is unknown. Some, no doubt, gave their children Roman names and acquired Roman citizenship, thereby merging indistinguishably into the imperial background. One may wonder, for example, who were the parents or grandparents of Claudia Rufina, the elegant British lady married to a friend of the poet Martial, and living in Rome in the late first century. But speculation is fruitless. Only in the late fourth and early fifth centuries do British chiefs or princes re-emerge, men like Cunedda and Vortigern, who are treated in the last chapter of this book.

There was no occasion for an imperial visit to Britain by any of the three Flavian emperors or by Trajan. It was almost 80 years after the Claudian expedition before Hadrian came, in the year 122, bringing with him his friend Platorius Nepos as governor and an extra legion, VI Victrix. The biographer in the *Augustan History*, our only direct evidence, appears to dispose of Hadrian's stay in a single sentence: '. . . he made for Britain, where he set right many things and – the first to do so – drew a wall along a length of eighty miles to separate barbarians and Romans'. This sentence constitutes the only ancient literary source for the Wall having been built by Hadrian. But after this remark, and before resuming his account of Hadrian's travels with the words 'after settling matters in Britain he crossed to Gaul', the biographer inserts an anecdote. Septicius Clarus, prefect of the guard, and Suetonius Tranquillus, 'director of imperial correspondence' (or *ab epistulis*), were dismissed by Hadrian, for the rather obscure reason that 'they had at that time behaved in the company of his wife Sabina, in their association with her, in a more informal fashion than respect for the court household demanded'. The biographer adds that Hadrian would have divorced his wife as well, for being moody and difficult – 'if he had been a private citizen, as he himself used to say'. Quite what is behind this is impossible to say for certain. It might mean that either or both these men had been having an affair with Sabina, although it sounds as if she had complained to Hadrian that they had not shown her sufficient respect. At all events, there is no reason why the episode should not have occurred in Britain, as the context suggests, since prefect and chief secretary would normally be expected to accompany the emperor, while Sabina was certainly with him on some of his other travels, strained though their relationship was. The biographer uses the story to launch into an account of Hadrian's practice of using *frumentarii*, 'commissary agents', or secret police, to pry into the private life of his household and friends. The picture thus evoked is of the emperor striding bareheaded up and down the Whinsill as he planned the erection of his Wall, or showing off his knowledge of engineering by designing the bridge which bore his name, *pons Aelius*, at Newcastle, and breaking off to read the report of a *frumentarius* about the activities of his wife. Certainly, a contemporary poet, Florus, produced some doggerel about the emperor's plod among the Britons:

I don't want to be emperor, please,
To tramp round Britain, weak at the knees,
Or in the Scythian winter to freeze.

Hadrian's reply was in a similar vein:

And I don't want to be Florus, please,
To tramp round the pubs, into bars to squeeze,
To lurk about eating pies and peas,
And get myself infested with fleas.

Later in the second century Britain attracted attention on three further occasions. The first two involved wars against the northern barbarians, although neither Antoninus Pius in the early 140s nor his grandson Commodus in the early 180s, found it necessary or desirable to take personal charge. But both made considerable propaganda out of the campaigns, and Commodus revived for himself the title Britannicus that had been borne by Claudius' son. In the mid-180s came the first of numerous attempts by the army in Britain to make their own emperor, their choices being a legionary legate named Priscus and the governor Pertinax. Both refused, but the latter did achieve the purple for a few months in 193. His murder led to civil war, and this time the army of Britain got rather further. The governor D. Clodius Albinus was appointed Caesar by Severus in 193 and at the end of 195 was proclaimed Augustus by his troops. He led most of the army to Gaul in a bid to gain the empire, but was defeated by Severus at the battle of Lyons in February 197.

It was over 10 years after that before Severus came to Britain, but he may have had an interest in it for some time. His brother Geta had served as military tribune of the Legion II Augusta here in the 160s, and Severus must have been affected by the publicity given to the province in the 180s. He appointed his wife's nephew, Sex. Varius Marcellus, as procurator soon after defeating Albinus, so that he would have been well able to receive confidential reports on the situation from a person of trust. But his motives for launching the great expedition of 208 are difficult to gauge. He was a restless character, but he was well past his sixtieth birthday and, as a native of north Africa, suffering from gout or arthritis, was not ideally qualified for campaigning in northern Britain. There was certainly trouble in the north, but it is doubtful whether an imperial expedition was really necessary, as Herodian, the mediocre historian of the mid-third century claims. There may be some truth in the view of Cassius Dio, a contemporary of Severus, who knew him well, that the emperor was disgusted by the misconduct and bitter rivalry of his sons Caracalla and Geta, now aged 22 and 20, and hoped that they, and the army too, would benefit from a campaign. Dio adds that Severus, an expert in astrology, knew that he would not return. It was his last chance to make his mark and to give his sons some training in generalship.

He doubtless took a large staff of advisers with him, but few names are preserved. One of the praetorian prefects was there, the great jurist Papinian, a relative of the empress, Julia Domna, who was also in the party, as was another of her kinsmen, C. Julius Avitus Alexianus. Both these men were no doubt Syrians, as was Julia herself. The only other person known to have been in the imperial retinue was the freedman Castor. On the coins of 208 Severus is portrayed riding off to war, but Herodian records that he was carried in a litter, and Dio adds that he was transported through most of the enemy territory in this way. No doubt he ,wintered at York, but his campaign headquarters were probably at a new base on the south shore of the Tay, further north than the Romans had been since Julius Agricola's campaigns in the 80s.

During the first part of the *expeditio*, Severus' younger son Geta remained behind in the province, while Caracalla and his father were with the army in the north. It is just possible that Geta was the 'most impious Caesar' responsible for sentencing to death the martyr St Alban. But too little is known of Geta's activities, and the accounts of Alban's martyrdom are too unreliable, to make this certain. At all events, before the end of 209 Severus raised Geta to the rank of Augustus, and there were now for the first time three emperors reigning jointly, and all three were in Britain. At the end of 209 they all took the title Britannicus, even though the campaigns, in which the army had penetrated far to the north, had had only mixed success, and the Caledonians and Maeatae, the principal tribes, had remained very elusive, fighting a guerrilla war.

The *Augustan History* has a curious anecdote which, if authentic, probably belongs to the end of the campaigning season of 209. 'After giving a Moor his discharge, on the Wall (*apud vallum*), when he returned to the nearest *mansio*. . . and wondering what sort of man should meet him, he was encountered by a certain 'Ethiopian' (black man) from the military *numerus* (unit), with a wide reputation as a buffoon and a noted joker, carrying a cypress-garland.' Severus, enraged by the bad omen, ordered the man to be removed. Further bad omens followed, including one involving the emperor being taken to the wrong temple, that of Bellona. The story may be pure invention, but it does so happen that later in the third century a *numerus Maurorum*, a unit of Moors, was stationed at Burgh-by-Sands at the western end of Hadrian's Wall; and a shrine of Bellona is attested at Old Carlisle, 10 miles away.

The normally sober Cassius Dio supplies two further stories, one a little frivolous, the other more serious. After the conclusion of a treaty with the enemy, Julia Domna joked with the wife of a Caledonian named Argentocoxus about her people's sexual practices: the women apparently had 'free intercourse with men'. This may reflect Roman misunderstanding of the practices of a matriarchal society, but the woman replied – wittily, in Dio's opinion – 'We fulfil nature's demands much better than you Roman women: we openly associate with the best men, you commit adultery with the worst in secret.' This could be taken as a veiled allusion to the allegedly promiscuous private life of the empress.

His second story is much more remarkable. Caracalla, who was still behaving 'intemperately' and making no secret of his intention to kill his brother Geta if he got the chance, actually made an attempt on Severus' life, while they were riding out to discuss terms with the Caledonians. In full view of the Roman and the Caledonian armies, Caracalla 'reined in his horse and drew his sword as if to strike his father in the back' – Severus was mounted, in spite of the weakness in his legs. Only the outcry from their entourage caused him to desist. Severus said nothing at the time, and concluded the business with the enemy, but on returning to headquarters scornfully rebuked his son, in the presence of the prefect Papinian. Putting a sword within easy reach, he ended by telling Caracalla that if he really wanted to kill him he should do it now. If he shrank from doing it with his own hands, he should order Papinian to do it, since he, Caracalla, was also emperor, 'and Papinian will surely do anything that you command'. It may well have been as a result of this affair that Severus finally raised Geta to equal rank with himself and Caracalla.

During the years that he was in Britain Severus had to continue ruling the empire at long range. The clearest trace of this is preserved in the *Code of Justinian*, which includes 15 rescripts from him on different points of law. One of them, dated 5 May 210, was written 'at York (*Eboraci*)'. This probably represents only a small fraction of the business that he had to attend to. Not only the Roman equivalent of ministerial 'red boxes' would follow him to Britain, but petitioners of all kinds. An inscription from Ephesus records the travels of a local dignitary who had persistently pursued Severus as far as the extreme west of the empire.

On 4 February 211 Severus died at York. His body was cremated there and the ashes were placed in an urn of 'purple stone', as Dio describes it – perhaps it was Derbyshire Blue John. Caracalla and Geta at once made preparations to return to Rome and to fight it out between themselves. Caracalla failed to get the troops in Britain to murder Geta: the men remained loyal to him, in part because of his close resemblance to his father. Peace was made with the northern tribes and the garrisons were withdrawn from the newly annexed territory in Scotland. This seemingly marked the end of Roman attempts to conquer the whole island. Within less than a year Caracalla succeeded in murdering his brother: in Britain, no less than in the rest of the empire, the names of Geta were systematically erased from inscriptions on public buildings. In Britain it seems that the army may have been slow to carry out these instructions or in some other way showed its hostility. At all events, in 213 the governor Julius Marcus seems to have insisted that every unit demonstrate loyalty to Caracalla: at least half a dozen inscriptions, some datable to this year, include the same formula, *pro pietate ac devotione communi*, 'in token of their common duty and devotion' to the emperor. Meanwhile, by his famous Edict, probably proclaimed in 212, shortly after Geta's murder, Caracalla had conferred Roman citizenship on all free inhabitants of the Roman empire. The newly enfranchised all took Caracalla's *gentilicium*, Aurelius, which, already widespread after grants by the Antonine emperors, now at a stroke became the commonest in the empire.

Caracalla seems not to have been impressed by Julius Marcus' attempt to whip up loyalty, for the governor's own name was deleted on most of his inscriptions, which must indicate that he had been convicted of a serious offence. It seems probable that it was now that Britain was divided into two separate provinces. The northern frontier region was assigned to the commander of the VIth legion, who was upgraded to become governor of Britannia Inferior, while the other two legions came under the more senior, consular governor of Britannia Superior. This was designed to prevent too much power being concentrated in the hands of one man, as had happened with Clodius Albinus.

Britain was apparently tranquil for many decades after this, and the convulsions which weakened the empire almost to the point of collapse later in the third century had little direct impact here. A distant echo of a coup in the year 238 may be detected. A man who had once governed Britannia Inferior – in 216 – was proclaimed emperor in Africa. He lasted for only three weeks, and although by the end of that year his grandson, of the same names, became emperor, as

Gordian III, old Gordian's names had already been deleted from three inscriptions in the north of England. Two decades later events elsewhere affected Britain more directly, with the creation of the breakaway 'Gallic Empire' by Postumus in 260. Up till 273, when it was subjugated by Aurelian, Britain belonged to this *imperium Galliarum*, and a number of inscriptions attest the loyalty of the British army and civil population to the regime of Postumus and his successors Victorinus and Tetricus. But there is no evidence that these emperors ever crossed the Channel.

Three or four years after the restoration of central imperial control one of the British governors attempted a coup, but he was suppressed by a special emissary of the emperor Probus, with no disturbances. It was a very different matter in the year 286, when one of the most remarkable episodes in the history of Britain began: the establishment of the 'island empire', *insulae imperium*, by the naval commander Carausius. This man had been appointed to suppress piracy in the Channel. According to the sources, which are of course uniformly hostile, he had begun to keep recaptured booty for himself, and even to connive with the barbarian raiders to share the profits. When about to face retribution, he fled to Britain and rapidly gained control of the island, while also retaining a substantial belt of the Gallic coast, including the port of Boulogne.

. It has been argued that it was Carausius' usurpation of the title Augustus in 286 that obliged Diocletian to promote his deputy Maximian to this rank, thus making him co-emperor. Carausius issued coins depicting all three as fellow-rulers with the legend CARAUSIUS ET FRATRES SUI, 'Carausius and his brothers', when Maximian, after two or three years, abandoned attempts to overthrow him. But he was never given more than *de facto* recognition, and it was the embarrassment which his continued independence represented that caused Diocletian and Maximian to appoint deputies with title Caesar. The western Caesar, Constantius, was at once given the task of destroying the rebel 'empire'. In his first year, 293, he captured Boulogne, and it was probably this blow to Carausius' prestige that caused his removal and replacement by his finance minister Allectus. But it was not until 296 that Constantius was able to mount a successful invasion. His praetorian prefect Asclepiodotus met Allectus in battle somewhere in southern England and decisively defeated him. Constantius made a triumphant entry into London, a scene depicted on a famous medallion found at Arras. Britain's return to central rule was described as 'the restoration of the eternal light' of Roman civilization.

Carausius was a native of Belgium of humble extraction, who had served as a helmsman in the fleet in his youth, and was undoubtedly a talented commander. This much information the chroniclers of the fourth and fifth centuries supply. The contemporary orators add only vilification, and in any case concentrate on Allectus, the man in charge when the 'British empire' was brought to an end. The coinage struck by these two men provides some corrective – for one thing, they make it clear that the two usurpers made no appeal to British nationalism. They did their best to show themselves to be thoroughly Roman, and indeed one of Carausius' issues has a legend with a Virgilian allusion, as if to demonstrate that he was not the barbarous pirate of official propaganda. To be sure, his portraits hardly depict a cultured person. On the contrary, he looks a rather terrifying hirsute figure, with a large coarse face, and bull neck. But it would be fair to comment that 'his brothers', as he called them, were men of similar stamp.

After the reintegration of Britain into the empire, the western Caesar Constantius probably spent a good deal of time in the island, although no details are recorded. But he certainly came soon after his promotion to Augustus in 305, when Diocletian and Maximian abdicated, and was at York, after campaigning against the Picts, when he died in 306. The army of Britain then made its most important single contribution to world history, for the troops at York refused to accept the anti-dynastic arrangements of Diocletian, under which Constantius' son Constantine was excluded from the succession. They proclaimed Constantine emperor there on 25 July 306. Although it was five years before he gained control of Rome and the whole west and another 12 after that before he became sole master of the Roman empire, it was never forgotten whence he had set out on the path that transformed the ancient world. 'O fortunate Britain, now more blessed than all other lands, you who first saw Constantine as Caesar!', an unknown Gallic orator proclaimed. Just as Mercury had come from the Nile, and Bacchus from the Indians, now the far west provided a new divinity – meaning Constantine himself, for the orator was a pagan. The Christian biographer of the emperor naturally had a different emphasis. God Himself, 'starting from the British sea and the land where the sun is ordained to set, repulsed and scattered by His divine might the encompassing powers of evil, to the end that the human race might be recalled to the worship of the supreme law'.

Constantine made two brief return visits to Britain, but it was nearly 30 years before another emperor came, when his youngest son Constans made a winter expedition at the beginning of 343. No details are preserved, except that he took some measures concerned with the force of *areani*, the frontier patrol units. Seven years after this, in 350, Constans was killed by the general Magnentius, who ruled the west for three years. The usurper is described by most sources as a German, but the twelfth-century Byzantine writer John Zonaras says that his father was a Briton. This statement is suspected by some but supported by a marginal note in a manuscript of the emperor Julian's speeches, which adds that he was born at Amiens and that his mother was a Frank. Certainly, Magnentius established a mint at Amiens, and, to judge from Ammianus' account of the purge which followed his death, there was considerable support for him in Britain. But his vain attempts to overthrow Constantine's surviving son Constantius II had clearly preoccupied him too much to enable him to visit the island himself. Ten years later, in 360, Constantius' cousin Julian, newly appointed Caesar, in charge of the west, contemplated an expedition to Britain, but other concerns took priority – ostensibly, he was anxious that the Germans might invade Gaul, although he may well have already decided to bid for the throne.

It was in fact nearly a quarter of a century before Britain saw another emperor, and once again it was a usurper, perhaps the most famous of them all. Magnus Maximus was a Spaniard, a distant kinsman of the emperor Theodosius; he had served in Britain with Count Theodosius, the emperor's father, in 367–368, at the time of the 'barbarian conspiracy'. When the younger Theodosius became emperor in 379, Maximus probably hoped for high office, and was evidently disappointed to be sent to Britain, probably as *dux*, commander of the northern frontier army. Early in 383 he won a victory against the Picts and Scots, and was proclaimed emperor by his army. He crossed to Gaul rapidly, and his troops put to death the young western emperor Gratian. Before long Theodosius was obliged to recognize him as a colleague, although only as one of four emperors, for Gratian's younger brother Valentinian II and Theodosius' son, the infant Arcadius, were also Augusti. Maximus never returned to Britain. His sights were set eastward, and he gained control of Spain and Gaul, and then of Italy. But then, in 388, Theodosius marched against him. Maximus was defeated, captured, and executed; the anniversary of his death was made a public holiday. Maximus' major preoccupation, other than his struggle for supremacy with Theodosius, was religious. He was a devout Catholic, who had been baptized immediately before his proclamation as emperor, and he severely purged the Priscillianist heretics. Several, including their leader, were put to death, and two were exiled to the Scillies – the only direct mention of any part of the British Isles in connection with Maximus' five years as emperor. But it can be deduced from military records that he withdrew troops from Britain, and did not replace them. It is surprising to what an extent Magnus Maximus appears to have captured the imaginations of later generations in Britain. He was claimed as an ancestor by post-Roman princes, and in the *Mabinogion* tale called 'The Dream of Maxen Wledig' the legend reached a high literary peak. Myth returned in modern times with Kipling's romanticized picture of Maximus in *Puck of Pook's Hill*.

To what extent Maximus did drain Britain of troops is difficult to decide. But increasingly the needs of the island were being neglected in favour of more important parts of the empire, as the threat from the barbarians intensified. The great Stilicho is supposed to have taken some measures to defend Britain at the very end of the fourth century, but it may be suspected that they were largely cosmetic, designed to palliate further troop withdrawals. It is not surprising that in 406 the British army produced another emperor of its own, named Marcus. They were apparently alarmed that the tribes which were poised to attack Gaul might turn against Britain as well. Marcus failed to do what the troops wanted and was replaced, this time, curiously, by a civilian, one Gratianus. He lasted only a few months, until the army produced a third emperor, who bore the magic name of Constantine. Could it be that the centenary of Constantine I's proclamation, on 25 July 406, was made the occasion for a usurpation by Marcus, and that when he and then Gratian failed to live up to their great exemplar, the troops decided that only another Constantine would fill the bill? Initially, their hopes were borne out. The new Constantine crossed the Channel, gained control of the western provinces, and defeated the invading Germans, whom he forced to make terms: and he is said to have placed the Rhine defences on a firmer footing than they had been for nearly half a century. But·unlike his namesake, he failed to extend his rule beyond the Alps. He was defeated and killed in 411, after losing the support of several of his followers, including the Briton Gerontius. In the meantime, in 409, the Britons rebelled against Roman rule and took up arms on their own behalf against the Germanic invaders. Their example was followed by some of the Gallic peoples, in Armorica and elsewhere. A few years later the Armorican rebels were suppressed, and it is clear that their movement had been a peasant revolt. It has been inferred that the British 'revolt' of 409 had been of a similar nature; but direct evidence is lacking. Furthermore, the famous letter of the emperor Honorius 'to the cities in Britain', telling them to 'look to their own defence', written in 410, may well be delusive. The rebellion of 409 had of course been against the usurper Constantine III, and it would not have been illogical for the Britons who had expelled his officials to appeal for assistance to their lawful sovereign. If so, they were perhaps rather naive to assume that he would do anything for them: Italy was herself overrun by the Visigoths, who had imposed a puppet emperor at Rome while Honorius skulked in the marshes of Ravenna. Shortly after the letter was written, to judge from where it is mentioned by Zosimus, Rome itself was sacked by Alaric. It may be that Honorius had been writing, not to the cities in *Brettania*, but in *Brettia*, or Bruttium, the toe of Italy. But it was vain for the Britons to hope in any case, whether or not they wrote to Honorius, or received a reply; their appeal a generation later to the general Aëtius was certainly ignored. The only assistance they received after 409 was spiritual.

Chapter III
High officials and senior officers

For about 170 years from the conquest, Britain was governed as a single province by men with the title *legatus Augusti pro praetore*. Literally translated, these words mean 'delegate, or envoy, of the emperor with the rank of pro-praetor', which somewhat obscures their true rank and status. By a legal fiction, originally designed to disguise Augustus' autocratic position, the emperor was technically appointed by the senate and people of Rome as proconsul of most of the provinces of the empire. Only the more civilized and peaceful areas, such as Sicily, Greece, or Cyprus, continued to be governed on the old Republican system, with an annually changing proconsul. The emperor governed his provinces through deputies, either senators, of varying rank, or, in the case of certain special areas such as Egypt and Judaea, men from the next order in Roman society, the *equites* ('knights'). The governor of Britain, although, like all legates of the emperor, called 'pro-praetorian', was not an ex-praetor, but one of the highest ranking senators, the ex-consuls, or consulars; and among the provinces assigned to consular governors, which included four or five along the northern frontiers, Britain was reserved for very senior men. Only Syria seems to have been more highly regarded as a posting. The reason lay principally in the very large size of Britain's garrison, and, certainly, among the governor's duties that of commander-in-chief must have bulked largest. The legate was also, however, the supreme civil administrator of the province, filling the role of Chief Justice and supervising the entire life of the province, with one significant exception. This was finance: Augustus carefully devised a system whereby *equites*, with the title of imperial procurator, *procurator Augusti*, were in charge of taxation, payment of the troops' wages, and fiscal matters of all kinds, in his provinces. The legate was obliged to refrain from interference in this sphere; not surprisingly, there were sometimes problems of conflicting interests.

The first 11 governors of Britain are all known, spanning the years 43–83, thanks to the writings of Tacitus, principally his biography of the eleventh, his father-in-law Cn. Julius Agricola. The length of their tenure varied: Q. Veranius died after only one year, while Trebellius Maximus had six years and Agricola, exceptionally, had seven. But the average of a little over three and a half years derived from these governors provides a reasonable yardstick with which to calculate how many governors there must have been in the succeeding 130 years. One may thus assume that from 84 to c. 213 there were about 35. It must be noted that the exact date when Britain was divided into the Upper and Lower provinces is not clear from present evidence. But even if it was as early as the year 197, as the historian Herodian appears to state, at least three of the known governors in the following decade were of the same status as their predecessors, ex-consuls who had previously governed other 'consular' provinces. Whatever minor adjustments may be made at the end of this first period, it is clear that an unusually high proportion of all the governors is known, compared with many other provinces, even after Tacitus' account ceases. One ought perhaps to allow for the possibility that the average tenure was reduced during the period 84–213, from the figure observed for the 'Tacitean' governors, say to a round three years. This would require us to postulate a total of 43: in fact some 27 are known, from a variety of sources.

Appropriately enough, Agricola himself is the first governor attested by evidence from Britain itself. His name appears on lead pipes from the legionary fortress at Chester and on a fragmentary building inscription from Verulamium. The next governor recorded in the province is L. Neratius Marcellus, whose name has been partially deciphered in a soldier's letter from Vindolanda, evidently involving an attempt to gain promotion. Apart from a handful of bronze diplomas (discharge certifications) of auxiliary veterans, which include mention of the governor as commander-in-chief, and a tiny fragment of a wooden plaque on which a few traces may be restored as part of the name of Platorius Nepos, all the other British evidence consists of inscriptions on stone. The vast majority of these come from Hadrian's Wall and its outposts, which account for 50 of them, while a further 25 or so come from the Wall's hinterland in northern England. Otherwise, apart from the items mentioned earlier, one can only point to two inscriptions from Scotland, and one each from Caerleon, Cirencester, London, and Reculver. A further important body of evidence is provided by 'career inscriptions' from elsewhere in the empire, on which the *cursus honorum* of former governors is set out. Finally, historians such as Cassius Dio supply a few names.

Little is known of Aulus Plautius' career before his appointment as commander-in-chief of the invasion force in 43 and first governor of the new province, except that he had been consul 14 years earlier, that he had suppressed a slave uprising in Italy in Tiberius' reign, and that he had been an army commander or governor of Illyricum shortly before going to Britain. But much more is known of his family, and its links over several generations help to explain why he was the man chosen to lead Claudius' greatest venture. The Plautii had their home at Trebula Suffenas, near Tibur (Tivoli), and had played a modest part in Roman politics during the last 50 years of the Republic. They almost certainly had no real connection with an earlier family of the same name prominent long before, although they may have affected descent from the censor of 312 BC, who had been a colleague of the famous Ap. Claudius Caecus. Claudius, with his antiquarian tastes may have believed this; at any rate, he may well have liked to pretend that he was following family tradition by his association with the Plautii. The family had already begun to rise rapidly under Augustus, thanks partly to the intimate friendship between Livia and Urgulania, wife of a Plautius. Her granddaughter Plautia Urgulanilla had been chosen as the young Claudius' bride, and although the marriage ended in divorce, her cousin A. Plautius would have had an excellent opportunity to become acquainted with the husband, then a despised member of the imperial household. The two were probably exact coevals. But also significant were A. Plautius' own connections. His mother was a Vitellia, and his sister was married to P. Petronius (*cos.* 19), later described as 'an old boon companion' of Claudius; and his wife, Pomponia Graecina came from a family that was influential under Tiberius. The Vitellii, in particular, in the person of L. Vitellius, consul with Claudius in 43 and 47 and his colleague as censor, dominated the scene in the first part of Claudius' reign. A curious point is that Plautius, like the Vitellii, P. Petronius, and Q. Veranius (a young man whose brilliant career was owed to his father's friendship with Claudius' brother Germanicus and to his own participation in the events which made Claudius emperor) all dispensed with a *cognomen*, and contented themselves with the old-fashioned *praenomen* and *gentilicium*. The emperor, with his archaizing tastes, will have liked this – after all, although he had several *cognomina* himself, he was known principally by his *gentilicium* alone, Claudius.

Plautius left Britain in 47, and there is no direct evidence for him being involved in British affairs again after the *ovatio* (minor triumph), a unique distinction during the principate, which he was awarded in that year. The extraordinary suggestion that the 'foreign religion' which his wife was accused of practising, 10 years later, was Druidism, picked up in Britain, may be dismissed as a curiosity of modern scholarship. It is not known how long he lived after that, although his wife survived for 40 years after the invasion of Britain, and Tacitus probably knew her. But it is worth noting that P. Petronius Turpilianus, the man who was made governor after the suppression of Boudica's revolt, was Plautius' sister's son. Nero and his advisers no doubt hoped that Petronius, who had the same mild temperament as his father, Claudius' friend – the man who had impressed the Jews with his moderation under Caligula – would calm the situation down in Britain. But it may also have been hoped that a nephew of the conqueror would enjoy unusual prestige in the island and could exert influence over the clients inherited from his uncle among the British upper classes.

There are not many cases from Britain or other military provinces where sons or grandsons of governors are known to have received the same appointment. This was partly because the son of a man who had reached this eminence would not need to go through the kind of career expected of men who were to command such a large army; they could achieve prestigious but less demanding offices almost automatically. But there are a few instances worth noting. M. Atilius Metilius Bradua, governor in the early second century, may have been the nephew of P. Metilius Nepos, governor in 95. Cn. Julius Verus, who was in Britain in 158, was certainly a close kinsman, presumably son or nephew, of Sex. Julius Severus, governor in the early 130s. An interesting possibility is the case of Ulpius Marcellus. The exploits of this redoubtable figure, who crushed the north Britons in 184, are described in a famous passage of Cassius Dio, but it is doubtful whether the three inscriptions from Hadrian's Wall recording a governor of the same name, can be assigned to this period, and a fourth inscription, now lost, from the reign of Caracalla, apparently gave the governor's name as Marcellus. It would be attractive to suppose that when Severus' sons withdrew from Scotland after his death, they left as governor a son of the man who had given the northern tribes such a battering a generation earlier, in the hope that his name would help to keep the tribes quiet.

Pompeius Falco, the first governor appointed by Hadrian, had two indirect links with men who had served in Britain. His full nomenclature included the names of Roscius Coelius, the turbulent legate of the XXth legion whom Agricola succeeded in 70 – Falco must have acquired the names by adoption or inheritance. Falco's wife was the granddaughter of Julius Frontinus, Agricola's predecessor as governor. Hence he may have had the opportunity, long before he went to Britain for the first time, of hearing about the province from men with expert knowledge. Whether the men who served in Britain in the years immediately following 98 studied the pages of Tacitus' biography of Agricola in the hope of gaining an extra insight into the province's problems is unfortunately an unanswerable question.

Family links of a different kind may be seen when governors appointed their sons or other young kinsmen to commissions as legionary tribune. The only clear case from Britain is that of Ostorius Scapula, whose son Marcus won the 'civic crown' for valour in Britain in the 40s. But governors were not generally permitted to have their kinsmen in the higher rank of legionary legate – Titus' service as legate of XV Apollinaris under Vespasian in Judaea was a rare exception. Hence it is unlikely that Mummius Sisenna Rutilianus, legate of VI Victrix some time before his consulship in 146, was holding that post as early as 135 when his presumed father Mummius Sisenna was governor. But the emperors seem to have allowed brothers to serve together, or to succeed one another in the same post. Several examples are known, or may be postulated, in Britain. Thus Vespasian and his elder brother Sabinus were both legionary commanders in the invasion army of 43. A little later Q. Petillius Cerialis, who also had the names Caesius Rufus, was legate of IX Hispana shortly after a man called Caesius Nasica had commanded it; the two could well have been brothers.

Connections of another sort may be traced. Minicius Natalis the younger served as legate of VI Victrix under Sex. Julius Severus, who had himself commanded a legion in Pannonia when the elder Natalis was governing that province and the son was tribune in Severus' legion. Lollius Urbicus was sent to govern Britain in 138 or 139 soon after he had served as a senior staff officer under Julius Severus in the Jewish war. In these two cases one may detect the influence of a highly respected general, obtaining appointments for his protégés.

Our sources rarely give us a direct insight into the emperors' motives for choosing particular men to govern provinces. The historians of Rome under the Caesars could not readily uncover such imperial secrets – these things were no longer discussed openly, as they had been when Pompey was given the command against Mithridates or when Julius Caesar became proconsul of Gaul. Tacitus gives the impression that Agricola had been selected to govern Britain almost by acclamation, with the implication that his two previous tours of duty there made him a natural choice. But it must be pointed out that out of numerous senatorial careers during the principate, no other case is known of a man who served three times, in the successive grades of tribune, legionary legate, and governor, in the same military province. It was rare enough to serve twice with the same army. Very few governors of Britain whose careers are known in any detail had ever been to the province before. Cerialis is one, but thereafter one can find only a handful of cases. Statius Priscus and Helvius Pertinax, governors 161–162 and 185–187 respectively, had each served in the British army before, but this had been much earlier in both cases, and as equestrian officers, before they had been transferred to senatorial careers. Junius Faustinus Postumianus, governor probably in the early third century, may have already been in Britain as a *comes* of Severus and his sons. Otherwise, the only case is that of Claudius Paulinus, legate of II Augusta in Upper Britain. He returned after a few years to be governor of the Lower province. Admittedly there are enormous gaps in the evidence, and a great many governors might, for all we know, have been tribune in a British legion at the beginning of their careers. But taking evidence from other provinces into account, it looks as if imperial policy was to give men variety of experience. 'British specialists', such as Agricola may be called, were probably very rare.

Very often in the Roman empire, as in all societies, nepotism, favouritism, corruption of various kinds, were a significant factor. Vespasian is known to have received his appointment to II Augusta through the influence of the powerful imperial freedman Narcissus – very likely money changed hands. Cerialis unquestionably owed his governorship to the fact that he was a close relation (perhaps the son-in-law) of Vespasian. For that matter, Agricola's accelerated promotion, culminating in the consulship at the early age of 36, with other honours, and the British governorship that followed it, for what was to be an exceptionally long tenure, may well have been owed as much to his personal friendship with Titus, his exact coeval, as to his qualifications for the job. Above all, patronage was important, and the support of an influential figure, with the emperor's ear, must often have been decisive where there was a choice to be made between rival candidates. The possible influence of Julius Severus in the 130s has already been mentioned.

Occasionally one may detect what may be a deliberate policy of choosing men especially qualified, by their previous experience, for particular problems. Thus during the 50s, when there was campaigning to be done in the Welsh mountains, a series of men were sent to Britain who had already conducted mountain warfare elsewhere – Didius Gallus in the Balkans, Veranius in southern Asia Minor, Suetonius Paullinus in the Atlas range in north Africa. But this may be no more than coincidence. In the case of Gallus, it may be noted that Britain was probably the province which he had once 'strenuously tried to obtain, only to complain when he finally got it', and once he arrived, if we may believe Tacitus, he was markedly inactive. Veranius, by contrast, was said, on his funerary monument, to have been appointed to Britain by Nero, 'even though he did not ask for it', if the inscription is correctly interpreted. Later on there are signs that, when the province had settled down, governors were regularly sent to Britain according to a predetermined pattern. Of the men whose previous careers are known, more than a handful had previously been governor of Germania Inferior, where some of the problems facing them would resemble those which they would find in Britain. Cerialis is the first such case, but as shown above, other considerations were more important with him. In the second century and early third there are five more definite examples of this pattern, and several more possible ones: Platorius Nepos in the 120s, Lollius Urbicus in the 130s, Julius Verus in the 150s, Antistius Adventus in the 170s, all went directly from the northern Rhineland to Britain, and the last case, Valerius Pudens, in Germany in the late 190s and in Britain in 205, had only a short gap at most between the two posts. Of course, other factors can be adduced. Nepos had been a friend of Hadrian for some years; it might be fanciful to speculate that his ownership of brickworks near Rome was thought to qualify him for the task of building the Wall. Urbicus may have owed the post to the patronage of Julius Severus, Julius Verus may have been chosen because he was Severus' son, and Adventus because his son was betrothed to Marcus Aurelius' youngest daughter. On the other hand, it is still reasonable to suppose that all four were sent to Lower Germany with the intention of giving them suitable experience before they took over the command of one of Rome's largest armies.

During this period, c. 120–208, some 20 governors are known, and if an average tenure of 3–4 years is assumed, there cannot be many missing names. A minimum of five and a maximum of seven may be said to have proceeded from the Lower

Rhine to Britain. The careers of five are unknown. Two, perhaps three, had previously governed the Lower Danubian province, Moesia Inferior, while each of the other five had been in a different province.

The origins and family background of the governors known to have been in Britain during the period 43–213, before the division of the province, reflects well the changing composition of the Roman governing élite. The first six, from A. Plautius to P. Petronius Turpilianus, were all undoubtedly Italian, and their home towns are known in some cases. Plautius was from Trebula Suffenas, near Rome, Didius Gallus from Histonium on the east side of Italy, Suetonius Paullinus probably from Pisaurum. But Trebellius Maximus, governor 63–69, may have come from Toulouse in southern Gaul, foreshadowing what was to come. Bolanus and Cerialis were clearly Italian, but Frontinus was probably another southern Gallic senator and his successor Agricola's home town of Forum Iulii (Fréjus) is of course proudly proclaimed by Tacitus. However, Agricola is the last known governor of provincial origin for nearly 40 years. The next five men, from Sallustius Lucullus in the late 80s or early 90s, to Atilius Bradua under Trajan, were all Italians. In two cases their precise *origo* is known – Avidius Quietus was from Faventia (Faenza) and Neratius Marcellus' family were great landowners at Saepinum in the Samnite country.

A change appears with the accession of Hadrian. His first governor Falco typifies the new cosmopolitan aristocracy which had come into being and was beginning to reach its peak under the first two provincial emperors Trajan and Hadrian, members of the colonial élite of the west. Falco's full names also neatly illustrate the practice of the period, for wealthy men to accumulate a lengthy nomenclature, commemorating the families with which they were linked by adoption, marriage, and, most significantly no doubt, by inheritance of property. He was known as Q. Pompeius Falco for short, but his full style, set out on an inscription at Tarracina in Latium, was Q. Roscius Sex. f. Quir. Coelius Murena Silius Decianus Vibullius Pius Julius Eurycles Herculanus Pompeius Falco. Rather irritatingly it proves impossible at present to discover the original home of this man's family. It might perhaps have been somewhere in Italy; but Spain, north Africa and the eastern provinces are also possible. What is clear is that he acquired the names from Vibullius to Herculanus from the last representative of the royal house of Sparta, who died in about 130, and, as mentioned earlier, Roscius Coelius (and Murena) from the family of the legate of XX Valeria Victrix, while Silius Decianus must derive from the consul of 94, son of the poet Silius Italicus. (Falco's own son and grandson added further names, and the latter may be said to hold the record, for an inscription in his honour gives him the amazing total of 38).

The origin of Falco's successor Platorius Nepos is also unknown, although his early friendship with Hadrian, combined with other slight hints, suggest that he may have been from Spain. An alternative possible home for him is Dalmatia, which was certainly the origin of Sex. Julius Severus and Cn. Julius Verus. The terrain of Dalmatia was mostly unsuitable for generating the wealth, based on the ownership of broad acres, required to obtain senatorial status, and not many senators from this province are known. Hence the fascinating examination of the family by J. J. Wilkes and G. Alföldy is all the more valuable. Its fortune was evidently founded by one of the original settlers of their home town, Aequum, in the early principate, Sex. Julius Silvanus, who held office as 'chief supervisor of

Roman citizens', *summus curator civium Romanorum*, at the place and was later a magistrate when it was made a *colonia* in 45. His *gentilicium* shows that his father or grandfather must have acquired citizenship from Julius Caesar, and his tribe, the Aniensis, little used outside Italy, is that of Forum Iulii, the home of Agricola's family. Silvanus, and Noster, the *cognomen* of another Sex. Julius at Aequum, are names favoured in Celtic areas, and it is probable that Silvanus settled at Aequum after service in the legion VII Claudia, which he will have joined from his original home, Forum Iulii, in the 20s. Within two more generations the family had produced a senator.

Other colonial Romans may be found among the Antonine and Severan governors. Urbicus, Adventus, and L. Alfenus Senecio, all came from Numidia, and Clodius Albinus was a native of Hadrumetum in proconsular Africa. Papirius Aelianus came from southern Spain, and Mummius Sisenna's home may also have been in the Iberian peninsula. The *gentilicium* of Ulpius Marcellus is sufficient to indicate that an ancestor had received citizenship from Trajan, and he must therefore have been of provincial stock, possibly from the east, unless he was the descendant of an imperial freedman. It is perhaps not surprising that very few governors of western provinces before the third and fourth centuries were from families whose first language was Greek, but one must note A. Claudius Charax, a distinguished historian from Pergamum, who is now known to have commanded II Augusta at the time when it was involved in Lollius Urbicus' campaigns in Scotland. M. Antonius Gordianus (the future emperor Gordian I), who seems to have been governor of Britannia Inferior in 216, was from an Asia Minor family and had links with several prominent Greek literary figures.

Of the 38 governors whose names are known from A. Plautius in 43 to C. Julius Marcus in 213, no more than 14 may be regarded as definitely Italian, and all but one of these served during the first 80 years of the province's existence. The exception is P. Helvius Pertinax, the future emperor, whose career is in all respects so unusual that it makes him one of the most remarkable figures in Roman history. He was born in 126, the son of a prosperous freedman, who had a textile business on the Ligurian coast. After completing his education, Pertinax became a schoolmaster, but at the age of 34 abandoned teaching because of the poor financial rewards, and tried unsuccessfully to become a centurion – a post which would have guaranteed him a steady income, with plenty of chances to earn extra money 'on the side', for life. Instead he had to accept the more highly paid but only temporary appointment as an equestrian officer, commanding a cohort in Syria. The outbreak of war shortly afterwards transformed his prospects. There were major campaigns throughout most of the following two decades, and Pertinax moved up the ladder almost without a break, from 161–182, acquiring senatorial rank midway through the period and later the consulship, ending up by governing four major military provinces in succession – all of this before he even set foot in the senate-house at Rome. After three years in enforced retirement he was recalled to service and sent to Britain in 185, where he had the difficult task of reimposing discipline on a mutinous army, whose attempt to make him emperor he resisted. He was recalled at his own request, but went on to further appointments, culminating in the prefecture of Rome and a second consulship, before the murder of Commodus catapulted him to a brief occupancy of the throne.

A few of the other governors, whose origin is unknown, may also have been Italian, but the significant aspect of the second century is that this no longer counted for much. Sir Ronald Syme has stressed that the origin of the emperor Trajan and his successors in the second century should not be given exaggerated importance; what mattered were 'education and national spirit, wealth and energy and rank'. The same applies to a large extent to the senatorial order as a whole, from which both emperors and governors derived. Even so, it must be conceded that when new evidence reveals the origin of some prominent man to have been in a backward or remote area, or in a relatively barbarous region of the empire, some insight is gained into the possibilities of social advancement during the principate. The case of Julius Severus has already been mentioned. The prime example from the later second century is M. Valerius Maximianus, from the Pannonian *colonia* of Poetovio, but he did not become governor of Britain so far as we know. No senators at all of British origin are known during the principate, not even, as was once thought, King Cogidubnus, but there are one or two men of unknown extraction whose home might have been at Britain's oldest *colonia*, Camulodunum. M. Statius Priscus, an outstanding general of the 150s and 160s, who was briefly governor of Britain before being summoned to deal with a crisis in the east in 162, could have come from Colchester; but the evidence, if such it may be called, is discussed in a later chapter.

The quality of the governors obviously varied, and one of them, at least, whose name is unknown, was caught napping by invading northern tribes and lost his life, c.182; he was the third governor known to have died at his post, for Ostorius Scapula and Veranius had both died in Britain in the 50s of the first century. But it is at least clear that some of Rome's leading military figures held the British post – Julius Severus is specifically described as 'first among Hadrian's leading generals' by Cassius Dio, who informs us that Hadrian sent for him to suppress the Jewish uprising of 132. Statius Priscus was likewise summoned from Britain to restore Roman fortunes after a disaster in Armenia 30 years later. These two cases in particular, and the senior status and long previous experience of other governors, allow one to conclude that the army of Britain was a command equalled in status only by that of Syria, if at all.

After the division of Britain, in 213 if not earlier, this doubtless changed, but very few governors of the Upper, two legion province are known and there is virtually no evidence for their careers. This change in the nature of the evidence reflects both the epigraphic sterility of the southern part of Roman Britain and, of course, the disturbed conditions of the third century. By contrast there is a series of no fewer than 13 governors of Lower Britain for the period 216–244, whose names are provided by inscriptions from Hadrian's Wall and its immediate vicinity. The list may indeed be complete, although not all may be dated more closely than to within a five- or 10-year portion of the period. Clearly the average tenure must have been less than three years, as had been the case with Agricola's governorship of Aquitania, which he held *minus triennium* in the mid-70s of the first century. Lower Britain was a province of the same rank as Aquitania, in that it was entrusted to men who had been praetor but not yet consul. However, in the absence of epigraphic evidence about the later careers of any of these men, bar one, not to mention the lack of a Tacitus for the period, it is hard to say whether they could have expected the consulship almost as of right on the completion of their stint.

Gordian is the only one known to have achieved the consulship, and this was probably under exceptional circumstances, several years after he had left Britain, where he appears to be attested in 216. It may be added that he was already in his late fifties at that time, a sign that the province may not have been one for the young and ambitious senator of the Agricolan type. Not that there were many of these about by that time. The system established by Augustus, which had reached its full fruition by the early second century, was in fact beginning to collapse, and senatorial governors were frequently replaced by equestrian 'acting governors', a practice which became standard in most provinces from the 260s. Britain, as it happens, seems not to have fallen into line until the mid-270s, for the island formed part of the breakaway Gallic empire, where senators continued to hold military posts. Octavius Sabinus, named on an inscription at Lancaster, is the last senatorial governor known to have commanded troops, and the first known equestrian *praeses* – by now the standard Latin word for 'governor' – is Aurelius Arpagius, who held the post under Diocletian and his colleagues, after the recovery of Britain from Allectus in 296.

Apart from the interesting case of Gordian, these governors are mostly mere names with which one can do little but speculate. There is a fair prospect that Modius Julius, the next governor after Gordian, was a man of humble extraction, for the slightly odd name which he bears is found on a list of craftsmen from Ostia 20 years earlier. Elagabalus, who was then emperor, was notorious for promoting persons of this type to the senate and high office, in a manner which respectable pillars of society like Cassius Dio found distressing. Other governors, Claudius Xenophon and Claudius Apellinus, have Greek *cognomina*, which probably indicates eastern origin, reflecting the circumstances at Rome, where the grandsons of Severus' Syrian sister-in-law reigned from 218–235. Xenophon may have been the son of a financial procurator of the same names, and Apellinus was probably related to the Claudii Apellini of Perge in Lycia.

But far and away the most interesting of the 13 – except perhaps for Gordian, whose significance in any case derives mainly from his subsequent history – is Ti. Claudius Paulinus. His brief tenure of the governorship fell entirely within the reign of Elagabalus, and its duration may be calculated with unusual precision. An inscription from High Rochester, an outpost fort north of the Wall, records the construction of *ballista*-platforms during his term of office, under the direction of P. Aelius Erasinus, tribune of the Loyal Cohort of Vardulli, in the year 220. Paulinus' predecessor, Modius Julius, was almost certainly in office in 219, and his successor must be Marius Valerianus, known from three fine inscriptions on and near the Wall, the first dated 30 October 221, the others being from 222. Nothing is known of Paulinus' origin, for the names are so commonplace that he could belong anywhere in the empire, but he is of particular importance for several reasons, associated with two other inscriptions. The first is from Caerwent, Venta, where the *respublica civitatis Silurum*, 'the commonwealth of the state of the Silures' set it up, presumably on a statue-base, *ex decreto ordinis*, 'by a motion of the council'. After his name it lists three of his offices, thus providing the only specimen from Britain of a senatorial *cursus honorum* inscription, albeit an abbreviated one. It lists only the command of II Augusta, the post that gave the Silures the opportunity of knowing him, then two posts as governor to which he had gone on from there, the proconsulship of Gallia Narbonensis, and the imperial legateship of neighbouring Lugdunensis. It is the latter post for which Paulinus is most remembered, for he figures largely in the grandiose inscription of Sennius Sollemnis of Vieux, the celebrated 'Marbre de Thorigny'. Late in the year 238, for reasons which may be linked to the political and military upheavals of that year, the Council of the *Tres Galliae* caused the monument to be erected in honour of Sollemnis, recording the principal events in the life of this local dignitary. He is proudly described as having been 'a friend of Tiberius Claudius Paulinus, imperial propraetorian legate of the province of Lugdunensis, and his client, and afterwards *assessor* to him when he was imperial propraetorian legate in Britain, attached to the Sixth Legion; and Paulinus sent him his salary and other gifts, many more of them'. Paulinus is thus the only governor of Lower Britain whose tenure of the post is recorded outside the province itself – interestingly enough, the title does not include the term *inferior*, but the periphrasis *in Brit(annia), ad legionem sext[am]*.

But there is more, for on one side of the monument there was carved the text of a letter from Paulinus – here described merely as governor 'of the province of Britain'. Written from an unknown place called Tampium, the letter contains Paulinus' apologies for not yet being able to offer a commission as tribune, and sending presents, 'small things, yet, since they are offered to show you honour, I would that you accept them readily', including cloaks, brooches, a British rug *(tossia)*, a sealskin – and 25,000 *Sesterces* in gold. On the other side of the monument another letter, from Aedinius Julianus, acting governor of Lugdunensis in succession to Paulinus, and later praetorian prefect, reveals why Paulinus was so anxious to please his Gallic friend. Sollemnis, as representative of his people, the Viducasses, on the Council of the Gauls, had successfully resisted a motion which, had it been pursued to the bitter end, could have led to Paulinus' prosecution at Rome and disappearance from public life, if not worse.

Far fewer of the lower ranking officials or officers are known than is the case with the governors. From 43–*c*. 273 a great many men must have served in Britain as legionary commanders. There were four legions for the first 42 years or so, and if each legate held the post for three years a total of about 56 men must be postulated, but only 10 names may be listed with any confidence, most of them provided by Tacitus and Cassius Dio. For the years *c*. 86 to *c*. 213, when the province had three legions, one ought to assume as many as 127 legates, but only 20 or so can be identified. After *c*. 213, one of the legates, the commander of VI Victrix, received a new status, as seen above, governing Britannia Inferior; for the last period, *c*. 213–273, one cannot find more than three other legates, all of II Augusta; not a single commander of the XXth is known. The situation is even worse with other posts. *Juridici*, law officers, of whom the first was probably appointed in the late 70s, are attested sporadically for just over a century, but only seven are known altogether. The military tribunes of senatorial rank, the *laticlavii*, who were, because of their social standing, second in command to the legate, probably served for much less than three years in many cases, but even if the average commission lasted for two years there will have been a good 350 of them over the 230 years in question. The definite names only amount to 18.

The position is little better with the equestrian officials. No financial procurators at all are known who definitely belong to the period after the division of the province, nor indeed are any known in the first 15 years or so after 43. Ten names can be supplied for the period 60–*c*. 213, during which over 50 may have served. As for the commanders of the fleet, the *praefecti classis*, one has the curious situation that the only four men known to have held this post may all be dated to the period *c*. 130–150. The rest is a blank.

One or two of the legionary legates have been mentioned in passing earlier in this chapter, but there is more to say about them as a group, and some individuals are worth further comment. The first eight, from the period 43–70, are all known solely from literary sources. Three, Vespasian and his brother Sabinus, and Hosidius Geta, receive mention in Dio's account of the invasion campaign, and Vespasian's command of II Augusta was frequently alluded to by Flavian and later writers. The remaining five, including of course Agricola and Cerialis, are all known from Tacitus. The case of one of these, Manlius Valens, is rather curious. Tacitus refers to him in the *Annals* because he incurred a defeat at the hands of the Silures just after the governor Scapula died, in 52. If nothing else were known about him, it would probably have been assumed that he was a young man in his early thirties who had recently been praetor; indeed, before the Flavian period legionary legates were often younger still, although the known men who served in Britain were all probably ex-praetors. So the Manlius Valens described in the *Histories* as commander of a legion in Gaul in 69 might well have been regarded as a son of the man who had fought the Silures, were it not for Dio's information that the Manlius Valens who was *consul ordinarius* in AD 96 was then aged 89. Thus Valens must already have been 45 or 46 when Claudius appointed him – and his second post as legionary legate, when he was well over 60, makes him the oldest recorded commander of a legion. In the absence of a Tacitus for the later principate, it is not surprising that only one other British legionary legate is named in the literary sources, a certain Priscus, who gets a mention from Dio only because the mutinous British army tried in vain to make him accept the purple at their hands.

Ten legates are known from inscriptions set up in Britain, mostly at the three main legionary bases. The earliest such case, and the only legate of the XXth among the 10 is a friend of the younger Pliny (whose verses he admired), T. Pomponius Mamilianus Rufus Antistianus Funisulanus Vettonianus, a Spaniard. His pompous string of names is set out on a stone dedicated by his freedmen and slaves at Chester. Three legates of VI Victrix are known. Q. Antonius Isauricus is named on a dedication at York made by his wife Sosia Juncina, and Cl. Hieronymianus built a temple to Serapis there. Both these cases must date before the division of Britain, *c*. 213, after which the legate of the VIth would have styled himself governor. The third man, L. Junius Victorinus Flav. Caelianus, is known from a dedication he made at the western end of Hadrian's Wall, 'for successes across the frontier'. The only other legionary commander thus recorded far away from his headquarters is L. Julius Julianus, whose dedication to Victory was found near Hexham; it may be assigned to the Severan period, for Julianus is also the only one of this group whose British post is attested by evidence outside Britain as well. It is mentioned on a *cursus* inscription set up at Interamna in Italy, after he had held other posts.

Of the other five legates of II Augusta attested in Britain, Claudius Paulinus has already been discussed in detail. Two more deserve brief comment. An inscription from Caerleon, now lost, had been set up by a man called Haterianus from Lepcis Magna in Africa, who described himself, not as legate of II Augusta, but 'propraetorian imperial legate of the province of Cilicia', in southern Asia Minor. The inference must be that he was making a thank-offering to some deity after receiving news of his appointment, a promotion of exactly the same type that took Agricola from his legionary command in Britain to the province of Aquitania. Another inscription from Caerleon, datable to the period 253–258, names the governor (of Upper Britain), Desticius Juba, and Vitulasius Laetinianus, *leg. leg. II Aug.* This man is the latest *legatus legionis* – that is, senatorial legionary commander – from anywhere in the empire, for shortly afterwards Gallienus was to exclude senators from army service. Although the Gallic empire of which Britain was a part did not follow this ruling, as was seen with the governor Octavius Sabinus, Laetinianus is none the less the last recorded senator to command a legion.

The largest category of known British legates is provided by inscriptions from other parts of the empire, mainly *cursus honorum*, in which command of a legion in Britain features only as one of many posts. Furthermore, these inscriptions seldom specify where the legion was, so that in a number of careers it is uncertain whether the legion in question was still in Britain, in the case of IX Hispana, or whether it had yet arrived, in the case of VI Victrix. No commanders of XIV Gemina or II Adiutrix from their British period are known with certainty. Only with II Augusta and XX Valeria Victrix, which remained here from the conquest in 43 until their disappearance over three centuries later, can one be practically certain which officers and men who served in them had been in Britain. Even so, many inscriptions are fragmentary, and sometimes the legion's number or title is conjectural.

It seems to have been exceptional for a man to command more than one legion. In most known cases special circumstances can be invoked, as with Manlius Valens, whose second appointment, 17 years after the first, when he was well over age, was a product of the civil war of 69. Hence the epigraphically recorded case of Q. Aurelius Polus Terentianus requires careful examination. This man made a dedication to Liber and Apollo at Mainz (Moguntiacum) in Upper Germany for the welfare of Commodus, and after his names describes himself only as *fetialis* (holding a priesthood), and as legate of two legions, XXII Primigenia, the Mainz garrison, and II Augusta. It seems reasonable to suppose that Terentianus made the dedication for the same reason as Haterianus at Caerleon: he had received an official letter of appointment, instructing him to go to his new base. The fact that the priesthood is also mentioned suggests that the letter had informed him also of his election to the college of *fetiales*, perhaps an honour arranged by Commodus as an earnest of imperial favour. Reasons for sending this man to Britain can be found readily enough. The legions had been mutinous, and at one point had tried to force a legionary legate to make himself emperor; and one of our muddled literary sources also tells us that during the war of 182–185 the legates had all been dismissed and replaced by equestrian commanders – a portent of what was to come in the third century. H.-G. Pflaum has detected an example of these equestrian commanders in an inscription from Dalmatia, honouring L. Artorius Castus, prefect of VI Victrix and *dux* (which before the late third century merely meant 'commander' on an *ad hoc* basis) of British legions, apparently 'against the Armoricans'. Whether or not this is the correct date (and there is no other direct evidence of trouble in Armorica at that time) it may be remarked that one might see there the origin of the Arthurian legend – Artorius Castus, 'Arthur the Chaste' commanding troops in Armorica. But it would take us too far afield to pursue that question here.

The origins of the legionary legates, explicitly recorded in a number of cases and clear enough in others, will occasion no suprise in the light of what has been seen of the governors. The first definite provincial after Agricola is C. Caristanius Fronto, who commanded the IXth in the late 70s when Frontinus and Agricola were governing the province. Fronto's tenure of the post is known from an inscription at his home town, of which he was a patron, the Augustan *colonia* of Antioch towards Pisidia, one of the handful of Latin enclaves in the Greek half of the empire. During the second century one or two men from the east who were Greek speakers may be discovered commanding legions in Britain. The origin of Claudius Charax from Pergamum has been mentioned already, and Cl. Hieronymianus was almost certainly a Greek too, judging from his name. Italians abound and were still playing a part in the third century, for it is probable that Vitulasius Laetinianus was one. His *gentilicium* is so rare that it is reasonable to regard him as a descendant of the Flavian consul Sex. Vitulasius Nepos, who had estates in the Abruzzi. Curiously, in view of the number of governors whose home was in north Africa, none of the *legati legionum* are known to derive from there and there are only a few for whom this origin is plausible. There are several Spaniards, including some fine specimens from Hadrian's reign, M. Aemilius Papus (to give only the short form of his name), son of a friend of the emperor, the younger Minicius Natalis, from Barcelona, and a polyonymous senator, most of whose names are fragmentary or missing, except for Grattius and Geminius, but with enough surviving on his inscription from Tarragona to show that he was closely linked with several members of the Spanish upper classes of that period.

Minicius Natalis, although known only from inscriptions, supplies so much information in them that a clear impression emerges of his personality as well as of his official career. Like many leading Spanish Romans – Hadrian himself above all – Natalis had a country estate at Tivoli. He was extremely wealthy, somewhat vain – both characteristics suitable for a man who won the Olympic four horse chariot-race at the Games of 129, just before he commanded VI Vixtrix – and also, in the manner of the age, a pious devotee of a number of religious cults. Several of these features – although not the Olympic victory – were shared by a man who commanded VI Victrix a few years later, Mummius Sisenna Rutilianus, another wealthy resident of Tibur, perhaps also a Spaniard. He was to become hopelessly infatuated by the notorious religious charlatan Alexander of Abonuteichos. For this he was richly satirised by Lucian; but it all happened 20 years or so after he was legate of the VIth, and he was perhaps reasonably well-balanced when he was in charge at York.

Agricola is the only legionary legate known to have been in Britain before this appointment and he and Cerialis are the only legates known to have returned as consular governor. There is also Claudius Paulinus, who came back to be governor of Lower Britain some time after service in the Upper province as legate of II Augusta. A fair number of the legates later achieved the consulship but very few are among the small category of the most senior generals, men who governed more than one consular province or who commanded a major army in war. Vespasian and Sabinus both reached the top of the tree, Vespasian as commander-in-chief against the Jews in the war of 66, his brother as legate of Moesia and then prefect of Rome. But men who were legates of legions during the invasion campaign should not be compared with those whose service came later, when the province had settled down. Natalis, Papus and Rutilianus all governed consular provinces under Antoninus Pius, but not more than one in each case. Only Curtius Justus, legate of the XXth in the 140s, looks like a true military specialist, if such men really existed, in that he governed the important province of Upper Dacia between his legionary command and the consulship, after which he governed Upper Moesia. But it is not known whether he held further office. Finally, Polus Terentianus, whose appointment to II Augusta was in any case exceptional, is found governing the vital consular province of the *Tres Daciae* in the momentous year 193. But the remaining stages in his career are unknown, and evidence for other cases in that year suggest that he may have received the Dacian post for political rather than military reasons. Overall, the impression gained from studying the known legates – which may simply reflect the gaps in our evidence – is that after the 70s command of the legions based in Britain was not given to 'high fliers'.

During the first four decades or so of Roman Britain, the legionary legates must have spent much of their time campaigning, although they may have had some civil responsibilities in their districts during the winter. There is one special case, the episode in 69, the year of the four emperors. The unpopular governor Trebellius Maximus was forced out of the province in April, the lead being taken by the turbulent legate of the XXth, Roscius Coelius. Until the arrival of a new governor, the legionary legates ran the province jointly, with Roscius exerting the main influence. When Agricola's drive north began in the late 70s, all five senior commanders must have been heavily engaged with military duties, mostly far away from the southern part of the province. This is doubtless one reason why a sixth *legatus* is found in Britain from this time, the *iuridicus*. The earliest examples, who are probably also the first two holders of the post, are well known figures in the literature of the period, Salvius Liberalis, a leading advocate, from Urbs Salvia in Italy, and Javolenus Priscus, who was to become head of one of the two 'schools' of Roman lawyers. The *gentilicium* Javolenus is of an exceedingly rare type and there is no reason to doubt that he was closely connected with Iguvium in Umbria, whence it appears to derive. But his original home may have been the place where he was honoured, Nedinum in Dalmatia, as G. Alföldy has suggested, for his other names include Octavius, and there was a family of Octavii at Nedinum. He may thus have been a colonial Roman by birth, later adopted by a Javolenus. However this may be, Javolenus is the only one among the *iuridici* to have left a record of his work in Britain. A passage in the *Digest* cites an opinion he gave concerning the disputed property of one Seius Saturninus, chief helmsman of the British fleet, whose son Seius Oceanus had died before inheriting. These names may have been fictitious, but the case was surely genuine. It is also worth noting that two rather poorly preserved inscriptions from Britain appear to mention persons bearing Javolenus' *gentilicium*, suggesting that he obtained citizenship for some of the province's inhabitants while in office.

One of the other *iuridici*, M. Vettius Valens, must certainly have made a good impression in the province, for he was its patron, indicating that the council of Britain had officially conferred this title on him. Valens served in the early 130s, at a time when the governors will have been much preoccupied with the new northern frontier. But he and the other known *iuridici* were all relatively junior men, unlike Liberalis and Javolenus: after the post had become established, it could safely be entrusted to less experienced senators. The most interesting case among them is that of Antius Crescens Calpurnianus, who was acting governor of Britain as well as *iuridicus*. The appointment is not directly dated, but Calpurnianus was one of the *XVviri* (member of the Board of priests) at the Secular Games in 204, and must have served some time before. It may have been as much as 20 years earlier, when a governor is known to have been killed in the north, and at this period too, the legionary legates were temporarily removed. Calpurnianus may have been the only senator in the province for a time.

As for the origins of the *iuridici*, the known ones may all have been Italian. The two whose names are missing are recorded on inscriptions at Tivoli and Palestrina (Praeneste), but these were both fashionable places for provincial senators to live when in Italy. Calpurnianus was evidently Italian, for he held a local priesthood at Ostia, and Vettius Valens came from Rimini (Ariminum). As for the remaining *iuridicus*, Sabucius Major Caecilianus, who was in Britain in the 170s, although his *gentilicium* is only attested in Italy, he might possibly have derived from north Africa.

Enough has been said about the origins and careers of other senatorial personnel to make detailed comment on the most junior category, the *tribuni laticlavii*, hardly necessary. They are a mixed bag, from various parts of the empire, although no easterners may be detected. None of the evidence is from Britain, with the possible exception of an inscription from Corbridge, but the man in question may have been an equestrian, and only one letter of his name survives anyway. Some of the *tribuni* had undistinguished careers, but a few went on to high rank and fortune. It will suffice to mention some of the more interesting cases. Some have been treated already – the younger Scapula, Agricola, and Titus, who are the first three known. Another early tribune is L. Antistius Rusticus, probably a Spaniard, whose career ended with the consular governorship of Cappadocia in the 90s. Immediately after the mention of his tribunate of II Augusta in the inscription from that province which lists his career, military decorations are recorded, of the grade appropriate to a legate. The explanation must be that Rusticus was serving in the IInd in 69, and was rewarded in this exceptional way for helping to swing Vespasian's old legion to the Flavian cause. It is a melancholy reflection on the paucity of our sources that we can only recover the name of one man out of the dozen *laticlavii* at the very least for whom Agricola must have obtained commissions during his seven years as governor. This is L. Roscius Aelianus Maecius Celer, and he, as it happens, left Britain with part of his legion, the IXth, to reinforce Domitian's army in the German campaign of 83. Perhaps the most interesting of the tribunes is M. Pontius Laelianus Larcius Sabinus, of VI Victrix, 'with which he transferred from Germany to Britain', as his inscription at Rome put it 50 years later. The approximate date which may be calculated from the year of Laelianus' consulship, 144, neatly coincides with the moment when Platorius Nepos moved from Lower Germany to Britain, no doubt with the emperor present also. Laelianus was to go on to a remarkable career, governing two consular provinces and serving as *comes* to L. Verus and M. Aurelius in their wars of the 160s and 170s. Finally, one may note that Septimius Severus' brother Geta began his career with a tribunate in II Augusta. If, as seems probable, he was a few years older than Severus, he will have been in Britain in the 160s, at a time of retrenchment. It may not be too fanciful to guess that his reminiscences, reflecting the views of officers who had been unhappy at the withdrawal from Scotland, may have had some slight influence in forming the revanchist policy which emerged again at the end of Severus' reign.

The very limited quantity of our evidence for the equestrian officials is to some extent made up for by its high quality. The first two procurators known are splendid specimens. First we have the rapacious Decianus Catus, helping to provoke the uprising of Boudica by his insensitive and oppressive conduct, and then ignominiously scuttling across the Channel when the rebels seemed to have swept the field. Nothing more is heard of Catus – he would hardly have won further office after that fiasco. It may be noted that Decianus was plainly his *gentilicium,* one of the rare type ending in -anus, and not a second *cognomen.* Tacitus, as he often did, inverts the names when he first mentions him as Catus Decianus; Cassius Dio puts the names in the right order. Catus' replacement, Julius Classicianus, whom modern writers portray as a figure of shining virtue, Catus' opposite, is treated equally harshly by Tacitus. This was because he quarrelled with the governor, and Tacitus clearly admired the old general, to whom Agricola had owed his first commission. Classicianus' adverse report on Paullinus, which led in due course to his dismissal (according to Tacitus) is rightly seen as a paradigm case for the way that relations between senatorial governor and equestrian procurator must often have developed in imperial provinces. Tacitus points out that Agricola, as legate of Aquitania, was careful to avoid quarrels with procurators. The dual system designed by Augustus was meant to ensure that the emperor could more effectively control his subordinates.

It is rather sad that Tacitus, who may have been of Celtic extraction himself, as Agricola certainly was, should have ascribed Classicianus' action to unworthy personal motives. The story must derive from Agricola, loyal to his chief. Classicianus would not have had much chance to defend his conduct, for he died at his post, as his funerary monument, found in London, reveals. The inscription has also made definite what the names Julius Classicianus suggest, that he was a Gaul. He had a further name, Alpinus, or Alpin(i)us, both of them largely confined to the Celtic north-west. But, more important, his wife Julia Indi f. Pacata, who commemorated him, turns out to be the daughter of the Treveran noble who had helped to suppress an anti-Roman rebellion in Gaul forty years earlier. Classicianus' credentials as a member of the loyal romanized northern Gallic aristocracy are thus well established. Agricola, from the very much more Roman southern Gaul, may have been especially prejudiced against him. However this may be, Tacitus himself repeats Classicianus' insistence that Rome should be showing clemency towards the defeated Britons, rather than the hostile and angry intolerance of a conqueror. Tacitus did not believe that the procurator was sincere, but we are justified in inferring that, as a Celt, Classicianus had a genuine fellow-feeling for those who had been implicated in the rebellion.

Only two more procurators from the remainder of the first century are known by name. Ti. Claudius Augustanus, commemorated by his daughter-in-law at Verona, where the family is well attested, was probably another Celtic noble by origin, from one of the Italian Alpine peoples north of that city. He or his father were presumably granted citizenship by Claudius or Nero, as his names indicate. Nothing else is known of him or his career, but his son entered the senate after starting his equestrian career as army officer and procurator, and is mentioned as a senator in Pliny's *Letters.* This allows us to date Augustanus' service in Britain very approximately to some time in the years 65–80. The other man, Cn.

Pompeius Homullus (to mention only his first three names), is more fully documented, by a lengthy *cursus* inscription from Rome. This records that he had been in Britain before, as chief centurion of II Augusta, from which post he proceeded to a series of tribunates in the Rome garrison, including one in the guard; and at some stage he was decorated, presumably in Domitian's northern wars. After his procuratorship in Britain, which probably fell in the late 80s or early 90s, he rose rapidly in the equestrian hierarchy, achieving the post of *a rationibus* (chief accountant – or 'finance minister' of the emperor). His origin is unknown, but one item in his lengthy nomenclature gives a clue to his connections, Aelius Gracilis. There was a senator of that name in the 50s, from Dertosa in Spain.

Of the second century procurators the most interesting case is that of Maenius Agrippa, for his total length of service in Britain was probably only exceeded by that of Agricola. His first appointment as an equestrian officer was to command a British unit on the Lower Danube, *cohors II Flavia Brittonum* in Moesia Inferior, which doubtless still had some native Britons in its ranks. He then served as tribune commanding the *cohors I Hispanorum*, at Maryport on the Solway, where his presence is attested by four out of the 16 splendid altars to Jupiter Optimus Maximus from that fort's parade-ground. This suggests that Agrippa was there for at least four years. His *cursus*-inscription from his home town, Camerinum in Italy, mentions that he was 'chosen by the deified Hadrian and sent on the British expedition' to command the Hispani. Thus he probably arrived when Hadrian did, in 122, to remain until 126. Maryport was a key site in the new frontier scheme, and Agrippa's role, albeit a subordinate one in comparison to that of his chief, Platorius Nepos, was of some importance. His third post brought him back to Moesia Inferior, as commander of a cavalry regiment. The governor of that province was then Sex. Julius Severus, who himself proceeded to Britain *c*. 130. Since Agrippa's next appointment was that of admiral of the British fleet, *praefectus classis Britannicae*, it is logical to suppose that Severus had a hand in his promotion – which enabled him to enter the procuratorial service without a preliminary post at the most junior grade. The procurators were ranked in grades which came to be known in terms of their annual salaries, the most junior receiving 60,000 *sesterces* a year and being called *sexagenarii*, followed by the *centenarii* earning 100,000, *ducenarii* 200,000, and *trecenarii* – a grade not introduced until the later second century – 300,000. The prefecture of the British fleet was evidently a 'centenary' procuratorship. Agrippa doubtless remained in Britain for much of the 130s, for his next and final post was the 'ducenary' procuratorship of the province, and it may be assumed that he received the promotion without leaving Britain. What has been said about Maenius Agrippa already would be enough to demonstrate that he enjoyed imperial favour. but the Camerinum inscription actually allows us to see a little more. It calls him 'host of the deified Hadrian and father of a senator', and, after listing his career, concludes with an expression of gratitude to Antoninus Pius for the grant of unspecified privileges to one of the communities of Camerinum, 'thanks to the intervention of Agrippa', the town's patron.

It so happens that the other three known prefects of the British fleet after Agrippa all date to the period between the early 130s and 150, and it seems logical to discuss them first, before returning to the procurators. L. Aufidius Pantera, perhaps Agrippa's immediate successor, is the only prefect to be attested as such in Britain, appropriately enough by an altar which he dedicated to the sea-god Neptune, at Lympne on the Sussex coast. All that is known about him directly otherwise is that he was prefect of a double-strength cavalry regiment *(ala milliaria)* in Upper Pannonia on 2 July 133, according to a diploma issued to one of his men on that date. The exceptionally high status, known as the *quarta militia*, accorded to commanders of these regiments at this period meant that he would automatically have been exempt from the 'sexagenary' procuratorial grade, and he probably went on to command the British fleet in 133 or soon after. The diploma gives his *origo* as Sassina, an Umbrian town where several other Aufidii are recorded. It also spells his name as Panthera, which helps to make explicit why he bore it. A tribune of the plebs named Aufidius had won passing fame in the second century BC by being the first man to exhibit panthers in the Roman arena. Over 300 years later our prefect was thus alluding to his ancestor, real or assumed, a reminder of the Roman obsession with the past.

The third prefect was also Italian, and, like Agrippa, had commanded an auxiliary unit in Britain, in his case the *cohors II Asturum*, which was his first commission. This was Q. Baienus Blassianus, a native of Trieste, where several inscriptions in his honour have been found. But the British fleet prefecture, and many of his other posts, are known from a great inscription set up in his honour at Ostia in the 160s. By then he was virtually at the peak of the equestrian career, being prefect – Viceroy – of Egypt: no senator was permitted to enter this vitally important province; its governors were always *equites*, second only to the prefects of the guard in status. A papyrus shows that Blassianus was in Egypt in 168, and his command of the Channel fleet must have been held many years earlier, perhaps *c*. 140 – in which case he may have seen active service off the Scottish coast during the campaigns of Lollius Urbicus.

Sex. Flavius Quietus, the last of the four, who may be assigned to the period *c*. 150, was a man of humbler origins than the others. In his case the prefecture was his last post, as shown by the tombstone which records it, put up at Rome by his widow and sons. He was probably considerably older than Agrippa, Panthera, and Blassianus, for he had been chief centurion of XX Valeria Victrix. This is the first appointment mentioned on the funerary inscription, and it may safely be assumed that he had risen through the ranks to the centurionate before reaching the position of *primus pilus*. In that capacity he was sent with an expeditionary force to Mauretania, presumably in the mid-140s, at the time of the Moorish rebellion. It was no doubt on his return that he was promoted to command the fleet. Nothing definite can be said about his origin. Although no more of these *praefecti* are known, it must be recalled that Carausius' responsibilities, before his usurpation, included those once carried out by the commanders of the *classis Britannica*.

The remaining procurators, after Maenius Agrippa, are a varied body of men. C. Valerius Pansa, who held the post in the mid-second century at earliest, was a local magnate at Novaria in north-west Italy; Sex. Varius Marcellus, under Severus, was a kinsman of that emperor's Syrian wife; and M. Oclatinius Adventus, later in the same reign, was – according to Dio's hostile account – a barely literate former soldier, whose previous posts had included service as a military policeman *(speculator)* and as commander of the 'secret police', *princeps peregrinorum*. Q. Lusius Sabinianus and M. Cocceius Nigrinus are known only from dedications which they made in Britain, and their names do not reveal much. Sabinianus set up two altars in Scotland, near the Antonine Wall, one of which was re-used for a second inscription. This must mean that his presence there should be relatively early in the history of Roman Scotland, during the first Antonine occupation if not in the Flavian period. Nigrinus' inscription, now lost, was from somewhere near the Wall in Cumberland, and, as it was a dedication for the welfare of Caracalla, this makes him the latest procurator known.

Oclatinius Adventus is the only procurator mentioned on an official inscription in the province. His name appears together with that of Alfenus Senecio the governor, on two building slabs, from Chesters on the Wall and at Risingham, one of its northern outposts. As none of his predecessors appear to have been involved in this kind of work, to judge from the fairly numerous stones from military sites which name the governor but not the procurator, it is difficult to avoid the conclusion that he had special instructions from Severus. He might, for example, have been asked to send his own report to Rome, independently of Senecio, to give the emperor the fullest possible information on which he based his decision about the British frontier – and as need hardly be recalled, that decision proved to be a massive expedition led by Severus himself.

Before we leave the principate, it is worth noting the presence, from time to time, of subordinate officials of equestrian rank. In particular they are recorded – in every case by evidence outside the province – as having participated in the holding censuses in Britain. Before Hadrian's reign such officials were generally army officers, with the title *censitor*. For example, T. Haterius Nepos was assigned to 'the *Brittones Anavion[enses]*', presumably the inhabitants of Annandale in south-west Scotland. At the other end of the country, Munatius Bassus dealt with 'the Roman citizens of the Victricensian colony which is in Britain at Camulodunum', i.e. Colchester. From Hadrian's day, it seems, the holders of such posts were given the rank and title of procurator, of the lowest grade, sexagenary. There is one example of a rather different kind of official. A certain L. Didius Marinus had, among other posts at a junior level, one that involved him in the recruitment and training of gladiators for the Roman arena, in a group of provinces which included Britain.

With the accession of Diocletian in 284 the new practices in provincial government and military command, that had been coming into being during the appalling crisis of the third century AD, were soon made the basis of an entirely new system. It may be that the British empire of Carausius and Allectus adopted administrative measures peculiar to themselves during the period 286–296, but if so we are left in the dark about their nature. But Allectus before supplanting his master in 293, was evidently his *rationalis summae rei* (in charge of finance) with the minting of Britain's first independent coinage since the conquest as one of his responsibilities. After the recovery of the island, Britain no doubt fell into line rapidly, with the further subdivision into four provinces being achieved at latest by 313. As elsewhere in the empire, with few exceptions, each province was entrusted to a *praeses*, as governor. The new smaller provinces were grouped together in dioceses under the supervision of an official entitled the *vicarius*, 'deputy' or 'representative' of the praetorian prefects, whose own role had changed from military to civil. Although there were new financial officials, some of high rank, stationed in the provinces, replacing the old-style procurators, under the new dispensation the governors themselves also had financial responsibilities. The old demarcation between legate and procurator had disappeared.

Instead the division was between civil and military duties. The exact steps in this development are very hard to pin down, and the division may not have been absolutely clear-cut, for in Britain at least it has been argued that the *vicarii* retained some residual military responsibility. The principal source of information on the late Roman army, the *Notitia Dignitatum*, is a notoriously controversial document, impossible to date with complete conviction and difficult to interpret in detail. Under Diocletian, a *praeses*, Aur(elius) Arpagius, was still the commander responsible for the northern frontier, for he is named as such on a building inscription at Birdoswald fort on the Wall.

But, doubtless before the end of Constantine's reign (AD 337), the military duties of the British governors, *praesides*, had been transferred to an independent general, the *dux* (from which the modern 'duke' derives). The forces of the *dux* extended through more than one of the four provinces. A further complication is the emergence in this period of the military rank of *comes*, 'Count'. *Comites* have already been encountered in another context, as aides or staff-officers accompanying the emperor on expedition – the word literally means 'companion', but the *comites* of the late empire were directly in command of troops. What is more, the men that they commanded were of superior status. The old division – discussed below in chapters on the army – between the citizen legions and the *auxilia* recruited into cohorts and *alae* among the non-citizen provincials had been gradually rendered obsolete during the continuous crisis of the third century. Under the new system which emerged in the fourth century, a selected force constituted the mobile field army, at first, theoretically at least, in attendance on the emperor, while the frontier troops were distributed around the periphery of the empire. Britain at first had no field army, although at times of emergency small detachments of 'comitatensian' troops drawn from the mobile field army were sent here, under a *comes*. Yet the system, if it deserves that name, contained anomalies. A separate frontier force was created to guard the south and east coasts against sea-raiders, and by the 360s its commander had the title *comes*, Count, of the Saxon Shore, even though he evidently had no field troops in his army. Finally, it may have been Stilicho who assigned a small field army to the island, under the *comes Britanniarum*, the 'Count of the Britains'.

After these preliminary remarks, something may be said of the men known to have served in fourth and early fifth century Britain. The earliest *vicarius* and the most precisely dated of them all is L. Papius Pacatianus, to whom Constantine I sent a rescript, preserved in the Theodosian Code, on 20 November 319. The subject was the fiscal obligations of decurions, and, as C. E. Stevens suggested, the Vicar's need to consult the emperor may have arisen from a conflict between Celtic and Roman laws of land-tenure. Pacatianus is known to have been *praeses* of Sardinia a decade earlier, and was to be one of the praetorian prefects from 332–337; and he was also *consul ordinarius* in the first of those years. It should be noted that the old division between senate and equestrian order had to all intents and purposes ceased to be meaningful, although new titles and ranks proliferated.

There is a long gap in the evidence after 319 until the period covered by the surviving part of Ammianus Marcellinus' *History*, from 353–378. At several points in his narrative Ammianus turns his attention to Britain and he also has some valuable flashbacks to the years preceding 353. Thus we learn that Gratianus, father of the emperors Valentinian I and Valens, had served as *comes* in Britain, some time before 351 when he was living in retirement at Cibalae in Pannonia, his home-town – he entertained the usurper Magnentius there in that year. Ammianus paints a lively portrait of the man, giving his nickname, Funarius, and revealing that he had made his way up through the ranks, helped not least by his physical strength and prowess as a wrestler, to commissions as *protector* and *tribunus* and then *comes*. The usurper Magnentius recurs more directly in Ammianus' account of Martinus, Vicar of the Britains, the first of two vivid episodes in British history which we owe to his pen.

After Magnentius' overthrow in 353, Constantius II, from his headquarters at Arles, ordered a thorough purge of the usurper's followers. The leading part in this grisly exercise was played by the Spanish notary, Paulus, nicknamed Catena, 'the Chain'. He was despatched to Britain to deal with the soldiers who had 'conspired with Magnentius', but exceeded his orders by arresting numbers of innocent persons. Martinus tried in vain to protect these people. Finally he drew his sword on the notary, but failed to kill him, and turned it on himself. 'Thus died a most just governor', Ammianus concludes, and, in his view, the affair was a blot on Constantius' reign.

The next Vicar, Alypius, is perhaps the most interesting of the six who are known. He was a friend and correspondent of the orator Libanius and of the emperor Julian, whose letters, in each case, were directed to him while he was in Britain, and Ammianus also refers to his tenure of the post in passing. Alypius' son Hierocles was one of Libanius' numerous pupils at Antioch, when the orator wrote to Alypius, reporting on the young man's progress and congratulating him on the magnitude of the appointment which he held and the excellence of his conduct of it. Likewise Julian, then only Caesar to his cousin Constantius, and in charge of the west, expressed his pleasure at Alypius' active administration, tempered by mildness; he also thanked him for having sent a map. The other letter was evidently written immediately after Julian's proclamation as Augustus by his troops, at Paris in 360. It is couched in veiled terms, but concludes with a summons to Alypius' to come to your friend', to join him in the venture which lay ahead. Julian may have been nervous that Lupicinus, his Master of Cavalry, who had just gone to Britain, and whose attitude was ambiguous, might intercept the missive. Alypius was later given an important task, the rebuilding of the Temple at Jerusalem, a project abandoned on Julian's death in 363. Alypius must have then gone into retirement, probably in his home in Cilicia, and eight years later was sentenced to exile on trumped up charges: This 'mild and charming man', as Ammianus calls him, was 'plunged into the depths of wretchedness'.

It is when Ammianus reaches 367, the year of the 'barbarian conspiracy' that he provides the richest detail about Britain. He describes how Valentinian, preparing for a campaign across the Rhine, received news of the devastation of Britain and in succession sent two of his senior generals to inspect the situation. Their reports revealed the desperate state of the island. The two generals had been disastrously defeated. Nectaridus, Count of the Saxon Shore (which is what Ammianus presumably meant by *comes maritimi tractus*) had been killed and the *dux* Fullofaudes had been cut off in an ambush, or trapped *(circumventus)*. It must be remarked that both these officers were probably Germans – Fullofaudes' name is certainly Teutonic, and Nectaridus may be also. The situation was restored by the despatch of Count Theodosius with a small field army. It may be, of course, that Ammianus deliberately exaggerates both the extent of the disaster and the magnitude of Theodosius' role, for he was writing in the reign of the great man's son. Nonetheless, the account is of enormous value. The course of events need not be retold in detail here. It is sufficient to note that a new Vicar, Civilis, and a new *dux*, Dulcitius, were appointed at Theodosius' request after he had set up his headquarters at *Augusta*, 'which they used to call Lundinium in the old days'. Dulcitius was delegated the task of suppressing an attempted coup by a prominent man named Valentinus, then in exile in Britain, while Theodosius himself coped with the main problem, clearing out the invaders. It may also be noted that among the officers who served under him were his son, the future emperor, then a young man in his early twenties, and another Spaniard, a client and distant kinsman of Theodosius, Magnus Maximus.

Count Theodosius, who had another successful campaign, in Africa, was suddenly executed in mysterious circumstances just after the death of Valentinian, early in 376. His son retired to the family estates in Spain, but three years later was elevated to the purple by Valentinian's son Gratian, as his colleague. Magnus Maximus may have hoped for advancement from his former comrade-in-arms; his own career had evidently proceeded steadily after 368. But by 383 he had risen no further than a military command in Britain, probably as *dux*. Whether his motives were personal or otherwise, he was proclaimed emperor in that year; the episode has already been described in the previous chapter.

With the adventure of Magnus Maximus we are approaching the end of Roman Britain. The strange trio whose usurpations marked the close of Roman rule, Marcus, Gratian, and Constantine, have also been dealt with earlier. It remains to discuss a few other men who served in Britain during its last decades as part of the empire. Not much can be said of Flavius Sanctus, a Gaul, and a kinsman of the Gallic statesman and writer Ausonius. Sanctus' career, as Ausonius reveals in one of his poems, included the post of *praeses* in Britain. But the last two *vicarii*, Chrysanthus and Victorinus, are worth pursuing more closely. The former's service is known only from a passing mention in the fifth century ecclesiastical historian Socrates, in the resumé of his career which serves as an introduction to what interested Socrates about the man. Chrysanthus' father Marcianus had been in the imperial service, and then, after a spell as tutor to the daughters of Valens, became Bishop of the Novatianist sect at Constantinople. Chrysanthus followed in his father's footsteps by serving as a palatine official, and under Theodosius I was *consularis* of an Italian province. After this he was 'Vicar of the British Isles'. By now of advanced years, he went to Constantinople in the hope of being appointed prefect of the city, but instead was forced to take up the same episcopal seat that his father had once occupied. He evidently took to the role in a commendable fashion, as Socrates reports, refusing to accept a stipend and distributing his own funds to the poor. It should be observed that in spite of his name, there is no guarantee that he was a Greek. In the Christian empire the practices of Roman nomenclature had drastically altered – and the New Rome was, after all, a Latin-speaking city.

We meet Victorinus in the celebrated work of his friend Rutilius Namatianus, *de reditu suo*, describing the poet's return to Gaul in the autumn of 417. On his journey he called on Victorinus, then living in enforced exile in Tuscany after Toulouse, his home, had been overrun by barbarians. Rutilius describes his friend's career, in which his principal post had been the vicariate of Britain. He had evidently behaved in exemplary fashion, even though it hardly mattered if one earned disfavour in that quarter. The comment is revealing, perhaps reflecting anti-British prejudice among the Gallic aristocracy – a generation earlier Ausonius had amused himself by waxing sarcastic over the British poet Silvius Bonus, whose name was incompatible with his origin. But Rutilius may be alluding indirectly to the three British usurpers, or to the Britons' remarkable expulsion of Roman officials in 409. At all events, we now take our leave of the men who governed and defended Roman Britain. The last two suitably reflect the new age, the one going on to become a schismatic Bishop at Byzantium, the other vegetating on his Italian estates while his Gallic home, like the island he had governed, was afflicted by the barbarians.

Chapter IV
Equestrian officers

We know the names of about 300 men who served as commanders of the auxiliary regiments stationed in Britain or as *tribuni angusticlavii* in its legions, in other words the equestrian officers, with the rank of 'knight', *eques Romanus*. The British section of the Roman army was exceptionally large throughout Britain's history as a Roman territory, which, apart from anything else, made it an important sphere of patronage. The consular governor of undivided Britain during the years 43–*c*. 213 had more legions at his disposal than most other governors, four from 43–*c*. 86 and three thereafter, each of them requiring five *tribuni angusticlavii*. More important still, there was a greater number of auxiliary units in Britain than in any other single province, at least during the second century, when the evidence is fullest. The governor of this province, therefore, had more patronage, more posts to be filled on his recommendation, than any other servant of the emperor (if we exclude periods when particular corrupt favourites held sway). We may take, for example, the diploma of July 122, issued to a Pannonian who had been serving in the *ala Tampiana*. The document lists all the units from which men had been discharged by the outgoing governor Pompeius Falco, and which were at that moment under the orders of his successor Platorius Nepos. There are 13 cavalry *alae*, one of them milliary, and 37 cohorts, two of which were milliary, on the diploma, to which one must add a handful of units known to have been in the province but which are not included, presumably because none of their men were due for discharge. If one adds the officers of the three legions II Augusta, VI Victrix, and XX Valeria Victrix, the total number of commissions for equestrian officers which may be assumed to have been filled by Falco is very large. In the *prima militia*, 'first grade' for prefects of cohorts, there were well over 30 posts, nearly 20 in the *secunda militia*, for tribunes, more than 12 for the third grade, the cavalry commanders, together with the single, élite appointment, the prefecture of the milliary *ala Petriana*. The latter position, of which there were never more than 10 or so in the entire army of the principate, had recently been elevated to a separate grade, the *quarta militia*, and it may well be that the governor had little say in selecting who would fill it. Equally, the choice of candidates for the third *militia* was generally restricted to men who had held positions at both the previous levels.

There is no need to suppose that nepotism was untrammelled. Few senators can have had over 60 suitably qualified clients of their own to occupy all these commands, and although the governor's friends in turn would do their best to obtain commissions for their protégés, this can hardly have filled the need either. It must have been regular practice for governors of military provinces to seek new officers by application to the emperor, whose *ab epistulis* would have files of applicants, *petitores militiae*, for all the relevant grades. But there is plenty of evidence, in the correspondence of Cicero, Pliny, Fronto, and Symmachus, to illustrate the custom for distinguished Romans to canvass their friends for positions for their clients by writing *litterae commendaticiae* ('letters of recommenda-tion'). In their published form, at least, these letters often omit detailed reference to the province or army and it is not always clear which one is in question. But Pliny was certainly dead several years before Pompeius Falco came to Britain, and the letter asking him to appoint Pliny's protégé, Cornelius Minicianus, to a tribunate must have been written when Falco was governor of Judaea. In the event this paragon had to be content with a cohort-prefecture, as an inscription from his home-town in northern Italy reveals. Either Falco had no vacancies for tribunes or he was not wholly convinced by Pliny's string of superlatives. We have already seen, in the previous chapter, how the governor of Lower Britain, Claudius Paulinus, in the early third century, failed to find a tribunate for his client Sennius Sollemnis and had to take him on his staff as a supernumerary. The one clear case from surviving literature which refers to Britain is not addressed to a governor, although it alludes to a letter written to him. Pliny writes to his young friend Suetonius Tranquillus to tell him that he will gladly arrange for the tribunate, which he had obtained for Suetonius, to be transferred to the latter's kinsman Caesennius Silvanus. The governor in whose gift the commission was is named as Neratius Marcellus; Britain is not mentioned, but the date of the letter and Marcellus' known career make it certain that this was the province. Pliny concludes with the remark that Suetonius' name had not yet been gazetted (*in numeros relatum*) and hence that it was open to him to substitute that of Silvanus. One wonders whether the superstitious man of letters was deterred from going to Britain by some bad omen; at all events he seems to have gone there eventually, as *ab epistulis* of Hadrian, and to have been sacked while in the province.

During the first two and a half centuries or so of Roman rule more than 5,000 men may have served as equestrian officers in the legions and *auxilia* of the British garrison. But these figures are very speculative. They are based on an estimated average tenure of three years for each post, and on the assumption that the average numbers of posts to be filled was about 65. The latter figure may well be too high; although it must have been exceeded at times, the strength of the garrison may well have been sharply reduced during the third century. More important is the consideration that the *tres militiae* system, which disappeared for good with the establishment of the tetrarchy, had been running down for many decades during the later third century. There may not have been very many equestrian officers anywhere in the empire from the 270s onwards. It must also be pointed out that only a handful of the known officers belong to the first 50 years of Roman Britain, and the great majority of those who are attested in the province itself may be dated after the creation of the Hadrianic frontier. Hence, while we may know only five or six per cent of the total from the whole 250 years, the figure must be nearer eight per cent for part of the period, *c.* 120–270. By no means all the men concerned are closely datable, but particular groups are instructive. For example, the milliary cohorts *I Aelia Dacorum* and *I fida Vardullorum* were stationed respectively at Birdoswald on the Wall and at the outpost fort of High Rochester only from 197, it would seem. Much of the evidence for the tribunes commanding those units derives from the two forts, and may therefore be assigned to a relatively short period of about 80 years.

Taking the known equestrian officers of the British army as a whole, about 180 names are supplied by inscriptions in the province, the great majority on stone, with the heaviest concentration being on Hadrian's Wall and the military zone

Altar dedicated to 'Jupiter Best and Greatest of Doliche and to the Imperial Divine Spirits for the welfare of the emperor . . . Antoninus Pius and of the legion II Augusta' by a centurion of the legion, M. Liburnius Fronto, at Benwell on Hadrian's Wall (RIB 1330). The same centurion, at least 10 years earlier, then serving in the XXth legion, had helped to build the Wall (see RIB 2077)

close to it. The remaining 120 or so are known from inscriptions in other parts of the empire. In some of these cases – about 30 – it is not definite whether the man concerned was in Britain. Either his unit is attested elsewhere as well as in Britain at certain periods and the inscription is not explicit on the question; or it was one of several with the same title. Thus there were evidently three distinct *cohortes III Bracaraugustanorum* stationed in different provinces, and there is no way of determining whether any or all of the small number of recorded *praefecti* commanded the unit of this name known from four British army diplomas of the second century and by stamped tiles from Manchester. The situation is even trickier, with *alae* and cohorts of Gauls and Thracians, of which there were several series. Thus the amazing career of the Pannonian general M. Valerius Maximianus, recorded by an inscription in Numidia, began with the prefecture of a *cohors I Thracum*, followed by the tribunate of the milliary *cohors I Hamiorum*. The Numidian inscription provides copious evidence for the date, and it is a reasonable hypothesis that he was commanding his Thracians in Britain in 161 or 162, when Statius Priscus arrived as governor, and that Priscus took Maximianus with him on his sudden departure to deal with the Armenian crisis a few months later. But there were at least three other cohorts with the title *cohors I Thracum*, so the possibility cannot be verified.

The length of tenure of an equestrian officer's commission does not seem to have been subject to any rules. In the early principate there are cases of men holding the same post for over 10 years, but this was undoubtedly the product of Tiberius' lethargic attitude to appointments. It is not surprising that no such cases are recorded for the army of Britain. The record is that of an unknown man from Verona, in Britain for seven years, evidently as legionary tribune, and then prefect of cavalry in Cyrenaica for six. As these officers depended on the governor for their appointment, and the governors themselves generally did not serve for longer than three to four years, there was bound to be a fairly regular turnover at lower levels. Such evidence as we have from the province in the second century supports the view that three years may have been the normal length of service for the commander of an auxiliary unit. We have three successive commanders of the *ala Augusta* at Old Carlisle: P. Aelius Septimianus Rusticus was there in 185, Ti. Claudius Justinus in 188, and P. Aelius Magnus, from Mursa in Lower Pannonia, in 191. At neighbouring Maryport there are six officers known to have been responsible for the dedication of more than one of the annual altars to Jupiter Optimus Maximus. Maenius Agrippa, tribune of the *cohors I Hispanorum*, whose career was discussed in the previous chapter, put up four altars, as did C. Caballius Priscus, while L. Cammius Maximus is known to have set up three. Both these men also commanded the *Hispani*. Two prefects of the *cohors I Baetasiorum*, T. Attius Tutor and Ulpius Titianus, respectively, have three and two altars to their credit, and Paulus Postumius Acilianus, prefect of the *cohors I Dalmatarum*, is also known to have made two dedications. Of course, the Maryport evidence for these men need not be complete, and it would be rash to assert that none of them were in command for longer than two, three, or four years. After all, several other officers from this fort are only represented by one Jupiter altar. But it does at least help to indicate that a fair number of officers probably served for at least three years.

The arrival of a new governor cannot have resulted in a general post, and, as would be expected, there are cases of men serving under successive governors.

For example, L. Vinicius Pius, prefect of the *cohors VI Nerviorum* at Bainbridge in Wensleydale under C. Valerius Pudens in 205, continued to carry out building operations there under the orders of Pudens' successor L. Alfenus Senecio. But Senecio may well have relieved him of his post within a year or so – not necessarily with the result that Vinicius Pius would return to private life. Senecio might have found him another post, in the same grade or in the *secunda militia*. This was the experience of Pertinax, the future emperor, who came to Britain in the 160s to be a tribune of VI Victrix, and, after a year or two in this position received the command of one of the milliary cohorts of Tungrians. Both these posts were in the same grade, the *secunda militia*, although the independent command of a milliary cohort was evidently reserved for especially selected officers. One may also trace cases of men promoted from one grade to another within the province. The clearest example is that of an unknown man from Ilipa in the southern Spanish province of Baetica, whose *tres militiae* were all in Britain. He was successively prefect of the second cohort of Vascones, tribune of II Augusta, and prefect of the first *ala* of Asturians. It is apposite to comment, in this case, that the two units he commanded were both Spanish – Basques and Asturians – albeit from the other end of the peninsula. It must be added, however, that this officer had already served elsewhere, for the inscription which records his posts in Britain also states that he was honoured by the armies in which he served. This means that we cannot be certain whether the military decorations listed on the stone were gained during a campaign in Britain or elsewhere.

There are a few cases where it may be postulated that young men of equestrian rank whose home was in Britain itself were given their first commission in the province, after application to the governor. M. Statius Priscus is a faint possibility – he might have come from Colchester. His first *militia* was served as prefect of the *cohors IV Lingonum*. In this case we may detect the hand of Sex. Julius Severus as the governor to whose patronage Statius Priscus owed the start of this career – whatever his origin – for he went on from his cohort-prefecture to service as a legionary tribune in the Jewish war of Hadrian. There seems no doubt that Julius Severus took Priscus with him when he himself was made commander-in-chief against the Jews.

The system of the equestrian *militiae* was in fact just becoming regularized at the time of the invasion by Claudius, who is known to have attempted to reorganize it by making the tribunate the senior post. But not long after his death the career familiar from hundreds of inscriptions in the Flavian, Antonine, and Severan periods, was already firmly established. At its height in the mid-second century there were about 270 posts in the *prima militia*, for cohort-commanders, less than 200 tribunates, mainly in the legions, 90 or so cavalry prefectures, with a further nine or 10 posts, the *quarta militia*, for prefects of double strength cavalry regiments. Thus, manifestly, about one-third of the men who commanded quingenary cohorts dropped out when their term ended, and returned to civilian life; likewise, only half the men who had been tribunes went on to command an *ala* – and only about 10 of the *praefecti alae* could hope to achieve the *quarta militia*. It was not uncommon, of course, for men to hold several appointments in the same grade, and some skipped the *prima militia*: a few seem to have gone from first to third *militia*, omitting the tribunate. But a high proportion of equestrian officers must have served for a maximum of 10 years, and many for much less.

These officers might be almost any age when first commissioned. Some are

An altar dedicated to Jupiter, Best and Greatest, and the other immortal gods, and the Spirit of the *praetorium* (commander's house) at Vindolanda by the commander of *cohors IV Gallorum*, the unit stationed there in the third and fourth centuries. The dedicator, Q. Petronius Urbicus, specifies that his home was in Italy, at Brescia. The erasure in the sixth line from the bottom is of the names of an emperor whose memory was condemned after his overthrow. The crane depicted on the side of the altar might represent the regimental emblem (RIB 1686)

known who were in their teens, as the senatorial tribunes (*laticlavii*) generally were, but most were in their twenties or thirties, with a few older men, some of them special cases. Their background was varied too, but at any rate until the third century they were generally men of some standing in society, who, if they did not already possess the necessary property qualification to be classed as *equites Romani*, had wealthy patrons who could supply this want if they sought a commission. Along with local 'gentry', the *domi nobiles*, who held office in the chartered towns of Italy and the provinces, we find sons of centurions and descendants of imperial freedmen.

Those who had no wish to return home after a few years with the army had two choices. They could seek entry to the procuratorial service – we have seen some examples of these men in the previous chapter; alternatively, they might take a drop in salary and enter the centurionate. A major attraction of this course must have been that a lifelong career was virtually guaranteed, as was not the case with the *tres militiae*; and the centurionate itself could lead to high administrative office. It is not surprising that a fair number of *equites Romani* opted for the centurionate in the first instance, without entering the equestrian career – we shall meet some cases in the next chapter.

The majority of the officers who served in Britain are known by a single inscription only. This kind of evidence is often evocative enough in its way. The tribune C. Cornelius Peregrinus, recorded at Maryport, was surely homesick and ready to return to private life when he dedicated an altar jointly 'To the Spirit of the Place, to Fortune the Home-bringer, to Eternal Rome, and to Good Fate', adding after his names and rank that he was 'From the province of Mauretania Caesariensis, at home at Saldae, a town-councillor'. An altar found near Piacenza in Italy shows us another officer, L. Naevius Verus Roscianus, already back home fulfilling the vow to Minerva that he had made in Britain as prefect of the *cohors II Gallorum*. For men like these, service in Britain must have been the main, or the only adventure in their life. But there are a good many for whom it was only an early episode in a life of active service that took them from end to end of the empire, to high office, and even, for Pertinax, to the throne. Eight or nine, at least, were later enrolled in the senate and 15 or more others entered the procuratorial service, including one prefect of the guard. T. Furius Victorinus, while Q. Baienus Blassianus, his contemporary, achieved the prefecture of Egypt. Both these men, at their peak in the 160s, had started their careers commanding cohorts in Britain under Hadrian, but it will give a better impression of the variety of persons who served in Britain if we look at a further selection. Taking the officers who happen to be attested on the Antonine Wall in Scotland, and then a few of the third-century garrison-commanders on Hadrian's Wall, we can examine the differing geographical and social origins of all the known officers of the British army.

It is reasonable to deduce that the half-dozen or so officers whose presence is recorded at forts on the Antonine Wall may be dated to the relatively brief spell in the second century when that frontier was occupied – though it must be conceded that the second period of that occupation is still difficult to pin down, nor can it be excluded that one or two of them might belong to the time of the Severan expedition. This latter date has been proposed for Publicius Maternus, prefect of the *cohors I Baetasiorum* when his unit, under the temporary charge of a legionary centurion, dedicated an altar to Jupiter at Old Kilpatrick. The centurion, Julius

Candidus, gives his legion as I Italica, stationed on the Lower Danube. This could be an indication that Severus had brought troops from Moesia for his northern campaigns; but other explanations are possible, for example that Candidus had received his appointment to I Italica just before he supervised the dedication. At all events, there is little doubt that the other men belong to the Antonine period. Caristanius Justianus, prefect of the Syrian *cohors I Hamiorum*, who dedicated an altar to Silvanus at Bar Hill, almost certainly derived from the same colonial family as the legionary legate Caristanius Fronto, in Britain in the late 70s, whose home was in Asia Minor, at Antioch towards Pisidia. The other prefect of this cohort known at Bar Hill was buried there. This was C. Julius Marcellinus, whose names are much too commonplace to tell us anything about his origin. The same might be said of the tribune Caecilius Nepos, who dedicated an altar to Fortune at Balmuildy. Two of the others are rather more interesting in that respect. L. Tanicius Verus, prefect of an unnamed cohort, who set up an altar to Silvanus at Cadder, was surely descended from the centurion of the same names attested in Egypt in AD 80, whose home was Vienne in southern Gaul. The rarity of the *gentilicium* makes the inference very probable. Likewise Q. Pisentius Justus, prefect of the *cohors IV Gallorum*, who made a dedication to the gods of the parade-ground, the Campestres, and to Britannia, at Castlehill, has a sufficiently rare *nomen* to make it virtually certain that he was an Italian.

The final example from the Antonine Wall is Trebius Verus, in command of the *cohors I Fida Vardullorum*, a milliary unit – although he has the title prefect, not tribune, which is odd – when the unit made a dedication to Neptune at Castlecary. It is tempting to suppose that the Vardulli wished to propitiate the sea-god because they were about to sail for the south – perhaps when the Romans evacuated most of Scotland either in the late 150s or at the close of the second period of the Antonine Wall (whenever that was). It is tantalizing that the Colchester diploma, issued to a soldier of the Vardulli, is fragmentary. The commander of the cohort was called Verus, but his *nomen* is not preserved, and of the governor's name only the last three letters survive; other items in the diploma's wording show that it cannot be earlier than 149, but further precision is impossible.

It is natural to suppose that major redeployments of units was infrequent, after the creation of the artificial frontier, and that these only took place when there was a major change of policy – for example, the move from Hadrian's Wall to the new Antonine Wall, or vice versa. But caution is required. The British garrison was very large; if there were outbreaks of trouble elsewhere in the empire, *auxilia* might be withdrawn from the empire, temporarily or even for good, and the governor would then need to reorganize. Trebius Verus might have been commanding the Vardulli with the rank of prefect because the cohort had been temporarily reduced in size – and the dedication to Neptune might have been made on behalf of the men who were sailing off overseas. A good example of a unit that was frequently moved about within Britain is the *cohors IV Gallorum*. In the first century it was at Templeborough in south Yorkshire, and tiles also attest its presence a little further north at Castleford. It was later moved to the Antonine Wall, as shown by the inscription of Pisentius Justus. Under Marcus Aurelius it was at the Northumbrian outpost fort of Risingham on Dere Street, but it had also had a spell at Castlesteads on Hadrian's Wall, where two of its prefects made dedications to Jupiter. But it has left more traces of its presence at Vindolanda than anywhere else, for it was there that it must have been transferred in the Severan reorganization, and it is listed there, with the units *per lineam valli*, in the *Notitia Dignitatum*. Five of its commanders from this last period are recorded, all of them probably of third-century date, three on inscriptions from the fort, the others on stones which probably also came from Vindolanda. The two best-preserved inscriptions are particularly valuable, for they show that two of the third-century prefects were Italians. The first made a dedication 'to Jupiter Best and Greatest and the other immortal gods and to the Spirit of the commander's house *(Gen(io) Praetor(ii))*', followed by his full name, Q. Petronius Q. f. Fab. Urbicus, his rank and unit, and then his origin: 'From Italy, his home Brixia' (Brescia). (The Fourth Cohort of Gauls was given an extra title, subsequently erased, which must have derived from an emperor who later suffered *damnatio memoriae*.) An earlier Petronius Urbicus was procurator-governor of Noricum in the year of the four emperors, AD 69. The Vindolanda prefect was doubtless a remote descendant. It is only an inference that Pituanius Secundus, who put up an altar to the *Genius Praetorii*, was also an Italian; but the exceedingly rare *nomen* is enough to suggest derivation from Reate in the Sabine country (the native place of the emperor Vespasian), where a handful of Pituanii are on record.

The origin of the equestrian officers of the Roman army is a subject of long recognized interest, and it is worth attempting a brief analysis of the large cross-section furnished by the army of Britain. A variety of evidence, explicit in some cases, circumstantial in others, as has been seen already, shows that virtually every part of the empire contributed some men to this service. As would be expected, there are not many from the eastern provinces. Less than 20 have Greek names, for example, although this is not a conclusive test, as the case of Caristanius Justianus has indicated already. Justianus indeed belonged to the relatively restricted breed of Latin-speaking settlers from the eastern provinces. But men from those parts of Greek family not infrequently bore completely Latinized names. A man like L. Domitius Proculus, prefect of the *cohors I Cugernorum* and then tribune of II Augusta, in Britain, among other posts, might well have been regarded as a westerner, were it not that he is known from his tombstone, in Greek, at his native Prusias in Bithynia. The other side of the coin is that Greek *cognomina* were sometimes borne by westerners, particularly those of freedman origin. Thus P. Aelius Erasinus, one of the third-century commanders of the Vardulli, may be assumed to have been a descendant of a freedman of Hadrian of the same names. It is possible, too, that Claudius Epaphroditus Claudianus, tribune of *cohors I Lingonum* at Lanchester, was descended from the notorious imperial freedman Epaphroditus who assisted Nero to commit suicide in AD 68 and was later the patron of Josephus. At any rate, these two officers of the British army could hardly be said to have been Greek in the normal sense of that term if imperial freedmen were indeed their ancestors. As for P. Licinius Agathopus, if he had been attested in Britain, with no further details except his rank, he would probably have been regarded as a Greek of some sort. But it is on an inscription at Gadiaufala in Numidia, which was his home, that he recorded that he had been 'prefect of cavalry in Britain serving at *Brauniacum*' (Kirkby Thore). Why he had a Greek *cognomen* (meaning 'fair of face') must be a matter of conjecture – but his date is evidently mid-third century, and fashions in nomenclature were by then changing. Two Greeks are known to have accompanied

Claudius to Britain in 43 with the rank of equestrian officer, Ti. Claudius Balbillus and C. Stertinius Xenophon, the emperor's doctor. But these were special cases. It must have been a long time before Greek-speakers regularly found their way to the westernmost part of the empire. With the gradual penetration of Greeks into all levels of public life during the second century – Greek legionary legates and governors from this period and from the third century have been referred to in the previous chapter – it was only to be expected that there would in due course be men from the eastern provinces among the equestrian officers as well. There are two clear cases from the reign of Elagabalus, M. Claudius Menander, tribune of the *cohors I Aelia Dacorum* at Birdoswald in 219, and Septimius Nilus, prefect of the *ala II Asturum* at Chesters two years later. Given that the governors of Lower Britain in this period included at least three men of Greek origin, and that the emperors Elagabalus and Alexander were Syrians, this is in no way surprising.

Several of the men with Greek *cognomina*, including most of those just mentioned, had imperial *gentilicia*, witnessing their descent from men enfranchized by the Caesars; and this is generally a pointer to provincial origin. But the test is not infallible, of course, for, apart from Nerva (Cocceius) and Trajan (Ulpius) none of the emperors bore especially rare family names. It is clear, for example, that L. Septimius Petronianus (as his names may be restored), prefect of the *ala Agrippiana miniata*, did not derive his citizenship from a grant by Severus, for he can be dated to the mid-second century. Again, a number of the Julii – the best represented of the imperial *gentilicia*, with 18 examples – may have been Italians whose families had gained citizenship before the dictator Caesar. But, with this proviso, it is fair to regard a high proportion of the 60 or so men in this category as the descendants of new citizens from the provinces. There are some 13 Claudii, including nine with the *praenomen* Tiberius; their ancestors must in most cases have been enfranchised under Claudius or Nero. The grants made by the next dynasty are represented by 10 Flavii, including four with the *praenomen* Titus. Of this group the earliest must be Flavius Cerialis, named on several of the Vindolanda tablets, evidently the officer commanding the Vindolanda garrison early in the reign of Trajan. Twelve have the name Aelius and the same number Aurelius, attesting the further spread of citizenship under Hadrian and the Antonines respectively – but Aurelius was to become the 'universal' *nomen* in the third century with Caracalla's granting of citizen status to all free inhabitants of the empire in 212. Two of the Aelii belong unequivocally to the late second century, the prefects of the *ala Augusta* at Old Carlisle, Septimianus Rusticus and Magnus, mentioned earlier in this chapter. A third-century date is either definite or probable for the rest and for all 12 Aurelii. In other words, this sample indicates what other evidence also shows, that it generally took several generations for the family of new citizens to climb to equestrian rank – what Roman status Ti. Claudius Cogidubnus enjoyed, apart from the citizenship granted by Claudius or Nero, and his title of 'Great King', remains uncertain.

There is a similar number of men with what one might call 'colonial' *gentilicia*, that is, non-imperial names that were particularly common in the provinces, reflecting the activities of certain great families in the last century and a half of the Republic. The Valerii, Caecilii, Cornelii, Domitii, Aemilii, and Fabii are the best represented, ranging from eight to five examples each, all of them names high up in the 'top twenty' *nomina* in Spain and southern Gaul. Some of the other common names are curiously under-represented – only one Calpurnius, one Pompeius, and two Antonii, for example – but this merely reflects the random nature of the sample.

In some cases new citizens preferred to adapt their peregrine name, sometimes already Latinized, into a 'fabricated' *gentilicium*, instead of taking the family name of their patron, whether imperial or otherwise. Several instructive cases will be noted later among the legionaries of the British army, but there are a number of equestrian officers with this type of nomenclature too. The practice was particularly widespread in the Celtic north-west, and there is little doubt that men with names like Paternius Maternus, M. Peregrinius Super, and M. Simplicius Simplex, were Romanized Celts, perhaps even Britons. These *nomina* are adapted from Latin *cognomina*, which slightly obscures the process; but it is plain enough that Sex. Adgennius Macrinus, tribune of VI Victrix commemorated at Nimes, was a Gaul whose original name was the Celtic Adgennus, converted by an ancestor. There are some cases of the same kind of thing from other parts of the empire too, as a British example illustrates. L. Minthonius Tertullus, who dedicated an altar at Cramond on the Forth as prefect of the *cohors V Gallorum*, must have been an African. Another Minthonius Tertullus is recorded at Mactar in Tunisia, which exhibits three other Minthonii; the only remaining examples also come from north Africa – the name is an adaptation of the Punic Mintho.

We have already seen several specimens of rare Italian names, whose bearers seem to be confined to the peninsula, such as the Pisentius and Pituanius who commanded the Fourth Gauls, or, in the previous chapter, Baienus Blassianus of Trieste who began his career of prefect of the Second Cohort of Asturians. Rare names otherwise found only in Italy do.not always guarantee Italian domicile, of course. Some families emigrated during the Republic, leaving few traces in Italy – a good example being the Ulpii of Italica in southern Spain. The Sittii are not represented very strongly in the homeland but occur in large numbers in the Cirta region of north Africa, reflecting the activities of the late Republican condottiere P. Sittius of Nuceria. A Sittius is known from an inscription at Numidian Thibilis to have commanded the Vardulli, while Q. Sittius Caecilianus, prefect of the *cohors I Aquitanorum*, who dedicated an altar to a local 'brewing-god', Braciaca, in Derbyshire, may also be regarded as a Numidian. One more example of an Italian recognizable by his rare nomenclature may be cited. A third-century tribune of the *cohors I Aelia Dacorum* was called Funisulanus Vettonianus and must have been a descendant, perhaps collateral, of the prominent first-century senator of this name. It will also be recalled that the legate of XX Valeria Victrix recorded at Chester included these items in his lengthy nomenclature. But the most instructive case is that of A. Cluentius Habitus, one of the prefects of the Batavians who worshipped in the Carrawburgh Mithraeum. Cluentii are fairly uncommon, although half a dozen crop up in the provinces; but there is no doubt about Habitus' extraction. On his altar to the god he states his *origo* in a slightly curious fashion: *domu Ultin(i)a colon. Sept. Aur. L.*, 'his home being, in the Voltinian tribe, the Septimian Aurelian colony L.'. He did not need to spell out what the initial letter stood for, since his fellow-worshippers, educated men, would have known their Cicero. The defence of Habitus' homonymous ancestor, packed with juicy scandal about life in Apulian Larinum, was probably more appetising to the Roman reader than many of the orator's works. Habitus did however indicate by the words *Sept. Aur.* that his home town had been given the rank of *colonia* by Severus and Caracalla.

Men like Habitus are important for their reminder that even in the third century men of old families in the Italian towns were still entering the imperial service at this level. But it must be conceded that provincial officers probably predominated during the last decades of the principate. Some of the Greeks have already been mentioned. One might add Julius Melanio, who put up an altar to Victory and Peace at High Rochester in 253; he was possibly from Ephesus, to judge from a dedication to an Ephesian deity which he later made in Spain as procurator. Africans are particularly well represented – partly no doubt because of the epigraphic fertility of that region. A particularly fine inscription from there is that commemorating Q. Gargilius Martialis, presumably the agricultural writer of that name, who died defending his native Auzia in a Moorish uprising in the 250s. His brief military career had begun as 'prefect of the First Cohort of Asturians in the province of Britain'. Sometimes the evidence is indirect, as with L. Aemilius Salvianus, tribune of the First Vangiones at the Northumbrian outpost fort of Risingham, where he put up an altar to the Unconquered God Hercules, and is also named on a building inscription of the Severan period. He is presumably the same man as the L. Aemilius Salvianus who was buried at Lambaesis, base of the Numidian legion III Augusta, and it may be inferred that he gained his commission from the governor Alfenus Senecio, a fellow-Numidian with whom he is named at Risingham. Another African, Aemilius Crispinus, prefect of the *ala Augusta* in the reign of Gordian III, specifies on his dedication at Old Carlisle that he was 'born in the province of Africa, from Tusdrus'. Tusdrus, or Thysdrus, was the scene of the proclamation of Gordian I as emperor in 238. There can be no doubt that Crispinus wanted to underline his link with the town that had, in effect, put the Gordians on the throne, in turn leading to his own commission in the *tertia militia*.

By contrast there are surprisingly few Spanish Romans detectable among the equestrian officers. No doubt several bearers of uninformative 'colonial' names, such as L. Antonius Proculus, T. Fabius Liberalis, or Sulpicius Secundianus, may have derived from there. Sir Ronald Syme has even suggested that the poet Juvenal, D. Junius Juvenalis, who apparently commanded the *cohors I Delmatarum* in Britain, may have been of Spanish colonial extraction, in spite of his residence in Italy. But there are a few men who can be described unequivocally as Spaniards on the strength of inscriptions from the Spanish provinces. C. Sempronius Fidus is known from a statue base at Tarragona, set up in his honour by the provincial council of Tarraconensis when he was its chairman (*flamen*). His origin is given as Calagurris in the Basque country, and his was an unusual career – four legionary tribunates, three in eastern legions, the fourth in XX Valeria Victrix. Another equestrian officer is known from his tombstone set up at the same city, of which he had become a decurion. This was M. Lucretius Peregrinus, who, after serving as centurion in two legions, achieved equestrian rank as prefect of the *cohors IV Lingonum*, which belonged to the army of Britain. A third man, the unknown from Ilipa in Baetica, who apparently served three separate *militiae* in Britain, has already been mentioned. T. Junius Severus of Dianium on the east coast, where he held all the local offices, held the first two *militiae* in Britain, as prefect of the *cohors IV Dalmatarum*, then as tribune of the XXth. One can add a few examples where the evidence is circumstantial. Paulus

Postumius Acilianus, attested by five inscriptions at Maryport, where he was prefect of the *cohors I Delmatarum* under Antoninus Pius, must be connected with the Trajanic procurator Postumius Acilianus of Cordova. The Maryport man was probably a son or grandson of a freedman of the procurator, since their tribes were different, the prefect being in the Palatina, in which freedmen were enrolled. Likewise, L. Caecilius Optatus, tribune of the Vardulli at High Rochester, may be regarded as the son or descendant of the retired centurion of the same names who became a local dignitary at Barcelona.

Several Gallic officers have already been referred to and men from those parts seem to have played a significant role at all periods, together with some from the Rhineland, in staffing the army of Britain. One of the earliest cases is probably A. Atticus, the only Roman officer killed at Mons Graupius in 83. Tacitus omits the *gentilicium*, but there are good grounds for regarding him as a Gallic Julius, like his commander-in-chief Agricola. Explicit epigraphic evidence supplies a number of specimens from southern Gaul: three from Nîmes, one each from Narbonne and Vienne, two more from unknown places in the same province of Narbonensis, and one from neighbouring Lugdunum. From further north one may recall C. Julius Camillus of Avenches, who served in the invasion army, T. Julius Valerianus of Geneva (although his tribunate in VI Victrix may have been before that legion went to Britain), M. Tituleius Victor of Besançon, and Attius Tuticanus, who commemorated his wife at Langres after his service in II Augusta. It is a pity that more are not directly attested, but, as indicated earlier, there are a good many whose nomenclature makes their origin in the north-west – in Britain itself if not in Gaul or the Rhineland – practically certain. One may also assume that the four men who served under the Gallic empire, Fl. Ammausius, Marcius Gallicus, and Probius Augendus under Postumus, Pomponius Desideratus under Tetricus, all came from the western provinces. There are a few equestrian officers of the British army who may have been natives of Britain; these cases are considered in later chapters.

The Danubian and Balkan lands are the last area to be considered in this geographical survey. Their contribution seems to have been small in total, but the known cases have some interest. Two men from Solva in Noricum served at the same fort as garrison-commander. L. Cammius Maximus was prefect of the *cohors I Hispanorum* at Maryport, while T. Attius Tutor, who was to rise to the *quarta militia*, began his career there in command of a later garrison, the *cohors I Baetasiorum*. Both men have left records in Cumberland as well as being well-known in their home area. Maximus was a decurion (town-councillor) of Aquileia, while a brother is known from an inscription at Solva. Tutor's family owned the finest house in the town in the second century. The Cammii and Attii were both of Celtic origin. A third Norican, C. Rufius Moderatus Junianus Juncinus, came from Celeia, where he erected a statue to Trajan, recording his own service as prefect of the *cohors VI Raetorum*, a unit of the British army, and as tribune in a Danubian legion. There are two good examples from Dalmatia. Q. Servilius Pacuvianus, who had been prefect of the *cohors I Morinorum* in Britain, was a magistrate at Salonae; although not a native of the town he may be assumed to derive from the province. The evidence in the other case is indirect. Desidienus Aemilianus, who was commanding the Housesteads garrison in the year 258, has a *gentilicium* of a rare type practically confined to Etruria and adjacent areas. The only other specimens are found, not in Italy but at Salonae, one of them a town-councillor. Aemilianus may thus be regarded as a descendant of an Italian family who settled in that place. Several other officers whose origin is unknown could well derive from this province. But it should be stressed that southern Noricum and the coastal cities of Dalmatia both had such close links with Italy from an early period that it would have been curious not to find them represented among the British army officers. It is rather more significant to find one or two men from the more barbarous provinces in the region. P. Aelius Magnus from Mursa in Lower Pannonia has already cropped up in this chapter. His career may have got under way as a result of the Danubian wars of the 170s and their aftermath. That certainly accelerated the rise of M. Valerius Maximianus of Poetovio in the same province, although his career had begun in the 160s, perhaps in Britain, it was suggested earlier. The only other case seems to be M. Valerius Speratus, who died in Britain at the age of 55 as prefect of the *cohors I Aquitanorum*, but who was commemorated at his native Viminacium in Upper Moesia. Speratus' tombstone, put up by his wife Afrodisia, carries the revealing information that he was a veteran of the Viminacium legion VII Claudia, who had become a councillor of that frontier town before achieving equestrian rank.

Valerius Speratus is one of half a dozen cases from the British army, all in the third century, of men who had served in the ranks filling posts previously given to men from the municipal élite, to sons of centurions, or to others of comparable standing. Licinius Agatopus of Gadiaufala is another: his children, who buried him there at the age of 81, described him as *veteranus praefectus in Britania*, without specifying the branch of the service in which he had been a soldier. The remaining four are all known from inscriptions in Britain, and, whether by coincidence or not, three are from the same Cumbrian outpost fort of Bewcastle, north of Birdoswald on Hadrian's Wall, where the fourth man is found. The Birdoswald man, Fl (avius) Maximianus, is the only one who can be dated closely. As tribune commanding the *cohors I Aelia Dacorum* he is named on one of the unit's altars to Jupiter. After his title he adds that he had been an *evocatus* (veteran on special service) of the first cohort of the praetorian guard, to which he gives the title of the emperor, Maximinus. The latter was the first of the Danubian soldier emperors, who had himself risen from the ranks to high command before overthrowing Severus Alexander in 235. It may readily be imagined that the Birdoswald tribune was only one of numerous long-serving guardsmen given commissions by this emperor, who was – rightly as it turned out – deeply suspicious of the old élite. The men from Bewcastle, tribunes of the *cohors I Nervana Germanorum*, had also been guardsmen. Q. Peltrasius Maximus had been on the office staff of the praetorian prefects; Aurunc. Felicissimus and Paternius Maternius were both former *evocati*.

Men of the old type continued to serve, as has been seen with Desidienus Aemilianus, for example. But by that date – the late 250s – they may have been in a minority. The Gallic Empire will inevitably have excluded, for over 13 years, the unpolished ex-legionaries or ex-guardsmen (mainly by then drawn from the Danubian legions) of the type that we have just been considering. But their places are likely to have been filled by veterans of the Rhine and British legions, along with country gentlemen from the western provinces. When Tetricus surrendered to Aurelian in 273 the principate had little more than a decade to run. The old officer-corps was on the way out, and what replaced it, is ill-recorded, in Britain at least. The latest known equestrian officer from the army of Britain must be

Aur. Verinus, tribune of the Dacians at Birdoswald under Probus (AD 276–282). As an Aurelius, his family's citizenship is unlikely to go back further than Caracalla, and the name Verinus, although nondescript enough, is found chiefly in the Celtic and German parts of the empire. No further occupants of the Birdoswald *praetorium* are known. Twenty or so years later, 'covered with earth and collapsed in ruins', it was restored, together with the headquarters building and bath-house, by the acting-commander of the Dacians, a centurion named Fl. Martinus.

A record of building on the Wall by the 'century of Julius Rufus', one of three stones with the name of this centurion from the eastern end of the Wall (RIB 1357)

Chapter V
Legionary centurions

The stern figure of M. Favonius Facilis, standing confidently in his niche, his left hand on the pommel of his sword while his swagger stick (*vitis*) dangles from his right, is a potent and expressive symbol of the army that made Britain Roman. The stylized fringe and apparently projecting ears suitably recall the portraiture of his emperor, and his name and tribe duly confirm, although his freedmen and heirs neglect to give his origin, that he was a north Italian. At the time of the invasion most of the legionaries shared this origin, and Facilis had doubtless risen from the ranks, as most centurions did. There were, to be sure, other avenues which led to the centurionate – guardsmen could become officers if they transferred to the legions, for example; and even Roman knights did not disdain to apply for direct commissions. The position was attractive, offering good, regular pay – and there was no compulsory retiring age. Cases are known of centurions who were in the army for 40 , 50, or even, in one case, 61 years. A fair number of young men of good family, with healthy parents, must have preferred to seek the centurion's baton and see some action rather than to rot at home waiting to inherit a small estate. The centurionate offered prospects with which the equestrian *militiae*, with their 'short-service commissions', could not compete. The· centurionate no less than the *tres militiae* could lead to higher things, as the case of Cn. Pompeius Homullus, *primus pilus*, chief centurion, of II Augusta and later procurator of Britain, has shown. Most centurions, naturally, did not achieve these heights. But they must have had a reasonable hope of becoming an officer in the First Cohort, one of the centurions of the *primi ordines*, if not *primus pilus*, before they retired (if they so wished) or died. We shall be meeting two of the longest-serving centurions of the Roman army later in this chapter, Flavius Virilis with 45 years and Petronius Fortunatus with 50, 46 of them as an officer. Here it may be remarked that several others of the 19 known men with 40 or more years had included a spell in Britain in their service. This is attested for M. Tillius Rufus and Varius Quintius Gaianus, both former guardsmen whose army service, including centurionates in the XXth, totalled at least 44 and 55 years respectively. One might perhaps add M. Sabidius Maximus, who was in the army for 40 years. His inscription at his home in Macedonia could be restored to include a mention of II Augusta, and the *gentilicium* is sufficiently rare to suggest identifying him with the Sabidius Maximus who dedicated an altar to Silvanus at Cirencester.

The possibility of indefinite service makes it impracticable to attempt to estimate how many men served as centurions in Britain during the period of about 250 years in which the legions formed the most important part of the garrison. Another factor, already alluded to and to be exemplified in more detail shortly, was that centurions were often transferred from legion to legion, both within a single province and overseas. This was not, it seems, a deliberate policy, to discourage men from becoming too set in their ways or too attached to their base. It was simply the product of the military system devised by Augustus and further developed by his successors, especially Hadrian, of concentrating troops in outlying areas of the empire, leaving no central reserve. When trouble flared up, reinforcements had to be taken from other frontier provinces. We have already met Sex. Flavius Quietus, chief centurion of the XXth, taking men to Mauretania in the 140s, and there are plenty of similar examples. When the troops went, their centurions went with them; and while the legionaries may sometimes have been sent back to base when the war was over, the centurions had often been transferred, gaining promotion in some cases, to another legion in the campaign army. Besides this, centurions had to be intelligent literate men (although a different impression is often gained from upper-class writers). Not all governors would be able readily to fill all 60 posts in each legion from candidates in the ranks, particularly if losses had been suffered. When these were on a large scale, as in Britain in 60, or again in the 150s, large drafts had to be called for from the German armies.

Some 300 centurions are known from evidence in Britain, most of them merely as names on building-stones or pieces of equipment, but several dozen more are recorded elsewhere, often with considerable detail, who served in the legions here. Even where only a name is known, the information to be gained can be surprisingly full. This is especially the case where they may be studied as a homogeneous group, as can be done with the centurions involved in building Hadrian's Wall. But first we may examine some of the men who were in Britain before that frontier was built. One of the early *praefecti castrorum*, camp-prefects, is on record, and may suitably be included here, as a *primipilaris*. This was P. Anicius Maximus, who was prefect of II Augusta in 43 and was decorated by Claudius. His home was at Antioch towards Pisidia, a Latin enclave which was later to provide both senatorial and equestrian officers for the army of Britain. P. Palpellius Clodius Quirinalis is known both by an inscription at Trieste, his home town, and by a mention in Tacitus. The inscription gives his career, in part at least: he had been chief centurion of the XXth before rising to become prefect of the Ravenna fleet, a post he was holding in 56 when, as Tacitus records, he poisoned himself to escape prosecution.

The other centurions who were in Britain during the first 80 years of the province's history are lay figures in comparison with Quirinalis, but not devoid of some interest. The seven from II Adiutrix, whose stay in the province can be closely dated to the years 71–85/6, have an instructive set of names – two Julii, appropriately enough in a period when two of the governors also bore this name; and most of the other names, *nomina* and *cognomina* alike, are common as well, Met(t)ius, Petronius, Pontius and Vibius, Clemens and Proculus twice each, Ferox, Fidus and Secundus. Only the *gentilicium* of Dossenius Proculus is at all rare, suggesting Italian origin. The others may have come from Italy too, particularly the north, but at this period, with names like these, they could belong to colonies anywhere in the empire. Another guarantee of early date is service in IX Hispana; even though that legion may have survived until the mid-second century, in that case it was almost certainly in the east for its last 30 years and none of its known centurions can be assigned to that period. Only two names are found in Britain itself, Babudius Severus and Cassius Martialis. Both these men must be early in date, since they are named on soldier's tombstones at Lincoln, where the IXth was based before the 70s. Babudius is a good old Italian name, but a Cassius could come from anywhere, including Italy – one T. Cassius Firmus, a magistrate at Aquileia, had had a commission in the IXth. Some provincial centurions of this legion are certainly known, for example Blandius Latinus of Geneva, who served in the XXth as well as in legions of other provinces. Finally, one may mention two men from the IXth with parallel careers, both spanning the late first and early second centuries. Ti. Claudius Vitalis, whose imperial nomenclature betrays his provincial origin, while his tribe, Galeria, suggests that he was from Spain, was a knight; he was commissioned directly into the Moesian legion V Macedonica, then served in I Italica, in the same army, and I Minervia, normally on the Rhine but at that time further east, since Vitalis was decorated at this point for service in a Dacian war. This was followed by commissions in the XXth and IXth legions in Britain, and a final centurionate in VII Claudia on the Danube. The other man, L. Valerius Proclus, began as a soldier in the ranks of V Macedonica, was commissioned in that legion, then in I Italica and XI Claudia; he too was decorated for a Dacian war, in his case in V Macedonica. Then he too, like Vitalis, went to Britain and served successively in the XXth and IXth, retiring at this point and doubtless returning home, to Moesia, where he was buried at his death, aged 75. Both men were probably sent to reinforce the army of Britain in the early second century. Their differing geographical origins and social background well illustrate the kind of men who were officering the legions at this time.

About 150 centurions' names are known from the building records on Hadrian's Wall, which allows us to consider them as a group, datable to the 120s AD. A remarkable number, some 70, come from the XXth legion, although some are known by *nomen* or *cognomen* only and half a dozen names are too fragmentary to restore. One must allow for the possibility that there are some duplicates – for example Avidius is probably the same man as Avidius Rufus and Libo is doubtless identical with Olc. Libo – and it must be recognized that a fair number are likely to have been transferred to one of the other legions or even perhaps to have been sent to another province, before the Wall was finished. Even so, we still have too many names for them all to have been on the strength simultaneously, and we can indeed detect men who had left by observing centuries which name their officer in adjectival form. Thus Socellius, a centurion in the third cohort of the XXth, is named on a stone found close to Willowford Bridge where the Wall had to cross the Irthing. By the time his men had reached the length a few miles to the east he had moved on, and not yet been replaced, for two stones are signed by the *c(enturia) Socelliana*. In some cases the promotion or transfer of a centurion within the legion may be spotted: Olc. Libo (misspelt as Obc.) was in the second cohort at Willowford Bridge, but is recorded in the first cohort at Housesteads, and had probably been promoted shortly after the Bridge section was complete, if he is the First Cohort centurion called Libo on a stone less than two miles east of it.

II Augusta is slightly less fully represented with just over 40 names, two of them very fragmentary. Once again there are some probable duplicates, such as Pompeius in the Seventh Cohort, who must surely be the same as one of the three Pompeii, Aemilianus, Albinus – known however in the Sixth Cohort – or Rufus. Again, Proculus may be the man elsewhere called Rom. Pro. for short, and Alexander is surely Fenius Alexander, given that only two other centurions from the group have Greek *cognomina*. Surprisingly, at first sight, only three men are definitely assignable to the other legion involved in the project, VI Victrix, two of them with fragmentary names. It seems that it may have arrived after the construction work had begun and that its main role may have been in fort-building. But one cannot rule out the possibility that the centurions of the VIth had not been accustomed to sign the legion's number on building stones in their previous province of Lower Germany. At any rate, there are a further 45 or so centurions whose legion is uncertain, and some of these doubtless belonged to VI Victrix.

A few of these centurions may be traced at a later stage in their careers. One may readily identify the Lib. Fro., whose century in the Fourth Cohort of the XXth is named on a building-stone slightly more elaborate than most, with M. Liburnius Fronto, attested at the nearby Wall fort of Benwell. There he dedicated an altar to Jupiter Dolichenus and the imperial *numina* for the welfare of Antoninus Pius and of II Augusta, to which legion he now belonged, 10 years at the least after the Wall-building ended. We can only guess his origin. Liburnii are found mainly in northern Italy, but legionaries of this name are also known from Galatian Ankara, and Dolichenus was an eastern god. A much less definite case is that of C. Arrius Domitianus, centurion of the XXth, who is known from his dedication of three altars at Newstead, where he evidently commanded a detachment of the legion and the *ala Vocontiorum* in the early Antonine period. The *gentilicium* is rather too common for it to be at all certain whether he can be identified with the centurion of II Augusta named Arrius known from two building-stones at Benwell and one at Rudchester. Even more tenuous, perhaps, is the possibility that Marit(imus), whose century is recorded near Housesteads, is the same man as C. Julius Maritimus of Cologne. This man, who had become a centurion in III Augusta, was buried at Lambaesis by his wife Salviena Metiliana, having reached the age of 45, and his previous service had been restricted to the three legions of the British army. The first of these was VI Victrix, and if this hypothesis has any validity one might suggest that he had enrolled in that legion when it was still based in his home province of Lower Germany. There is less doubt over a fourth man, Statilius Solon, centurion of the Sixth Cohort of one of the three legions, named on a stone near milecastle 24. He must be the same man recorded by an inscription from Brigetio on the Danube as chief centurion, *primus pilus*, of the Upper Pannonian legion I Adiutrix. That evidence incidentally confirms the origin implied by his *cognomen*, for both Greek and Latin are used on the Brigetio stone.

Only two other men among these Hadrianic centurions have Greek *cognomina*, Claudius Cleonicus, from the Third Cohort of an unknown legion, and Fenius (the name is more often spelt Faenius elsewhere) Alexander of II Augusta – for Gellius Philippus' name had long been 'naturalized' at Rome. Alexander could of course have been a Greek from southern Italy, where plenty of Faenii are attested, but Cleonicus was probably an easterner. In the light of what has been said earlier about the movements of centurions there is nothing particularly surprising about their presence in the British army. One might suggest, for example, that Pompeius Falco had brought some men with him when he moved from the Lower Danube to Britain a few years earlier.

Only a handful have rare and interesting *cognomina* which provide a clue to their origins. A few seem barbarous, Celtic in all probability, Sorio of the IInd, and Julius Subsio from an uncertain legion. This may also apply to Octavius Sebanus, although his name might be Etruscan. That is undoubtedly the case with Ulpius Volusenus, whose second name is an Etruscan *gentilicium* used as a *cognomen*. Two 'ethnics' used as *cognomina*, by Terentius Cantaber of the IInd and Flavius Noricus of the XXth, suggest origins in north-west Spain and beyond the Alps respectively, although it must be admitted, in the latter case, that the name is found in Noricum itself only once, at Salzburg. Otherwise, one may note only Verullus, which is really only a rare variant of the commoner Verulus, diminutive of Verus, and Scipio – Carius, or Carisius, Scipio of II Augusta was one of only 10 bearers of that name, made famous in the Republic, who were not senators. Finally, Ostorianus of the XXth happens to be the only known person of that name except for a man at Ostia, but it is of a straightforward type, derived from the *gentilicium*. One is however entitled to wonder whether he derived it from a British mother whose ancestor had been enfranchised by the governor Ostorius Scapula.

Most of the centurions' *cognomina* are very straightforward, common names reflecting the humble origins of men who had started in the ranks, often, no doubt, acquiring citizenship and being given a set of names 'from the book' on enlistment. Old favourites like Maximus, Priscus, Proculus, Rufus, and Verus are each represented by three or more specimens. Many of the others are among the 'top twenty' *cognomina* in the empire, Primus, Secundus, and Tertius, for example, or Crescens, Felix, Sabinus, Saturninus, and Vitalis – the latter being a name particularly favoured in Britain, it seems. Analysis of the *gentilicia* is rather more fruitful. Imperial names are the clearest guide to new citizens or their descendants and there are some 25 in this category – but one must exclude the single Aelius. Not only is it too early to find a man enfranchised by Hadrian with the rank of centurion – but this man, Aelius Aelianus of the XXth, shows by his *cognomen* that he was at least a second generation Roman, unconnected with the emperor. There are two Ulpii, Paullus and Volusenus, who probably owed their Roman status to Trajan, although Volusenus, an Etruscan name, as pointed out earlier, is unexpected for a new citizen and some other explanation may be required. But there can be no doubt about the single Cocceius, Regulus of the XXth, who must be the son of a man enfranchised in the brief reign of Nerva, if indeed he was not the recipient of the grant himself. Likewise, the seven Flavii, who reflect grants made by Vespasian or his sons, and the three Claudii, with citizenship going back to Claudius or Nero. One of the Claudii, Augustanus, known from three building-stones on the Wall and also from a lead die found at the XXth legion's base, Chester, has the same names as a first-century procurator of Britain. Claudius Augustanus, recorded at Verona, and probably of Alpine origin, may have been from the same family as the centurion, for only nine other bearers of the *cognomen* are known. Claudius Cleonicus has already been identified as a probable Greek, while Priscus, the third of the Claudii, has far too ordinary a name to reveal his origin. Finally, there are no fewer than 13 Julii, most of them with uninformative *cognominà* – Primus and Tertullianus of II Augusta, Candidus, Florentinus, Juv(enalis), Priscus, Proculus, Rufus, and Valens of the XXth, and Vitalis from an unspecified legion. Only Subsio has a clearly peregrine name; that of another man has been read as Commidi, in the genitive, giving the otherwise unattested name Commidus or Commidius, but the lettering is very messy and any one of several well-known *cognominà* beginning with Com- or Con- may have been intended. Finally, there is Janal(is), whose name is otherwise unrecorded but is of the well-known type derived from deities, of which Apollinaris, Cerialis, and Martialis are common examples. All these Julii were probably at least third generation Romans, with citizenship going back to Caesar or Augustus, although one or two might derive from grants sponsored by the governors Frontinus or Agricola. They could all perfectly well be grand-sons or great-grandsons of veterans of the invasion army settled in Britain. As will be seen in the next chapter, Julii are well represented among the legionaries and veterans in Britain, and for the most part the centurions must have come from the same background.

As would be expected, the common 'colonial' *gentilicia* are well represented, with the ubiquitous Valerii to the fore, showing five examples.

The three or four Pompeii, all in II Augusta, have already been mentioned, and there are three Caecilii. Many of the other *nomina* familiar from the provinces, particularly Spain and southern Gaul, are in the list – Antonius, Atilius, Cassius, Junius, Marcius, Marius, Octavius, Sextius, Terentius. The only surprise perhaps is the absence of a Cornelius, but specimens of this and most of the other commonest *gentilicia* are found among the British centurionate on other inscrip-tions. In complete contrast are the bearers of unusual Italian names, found only in particular corners of the country with occasional instances overseas attesting the presence of Italian traders or soldiers. Even here one must be cautious about insisting on Italian origin, as has been stressed in a previous context. But this is certainly highly probable with names like Aurunceius (or Aurunculeius), Caledonius (in spite of its north British sound), Delluius, Olc(inius), Socellius, or Turrianius. Vesnius Viator, whose century evidently built part of the bridge carrying the Wall across the Eden, may be traced with some confidence to Urbino, where a senator and knight of this name are found. The only other Vesnius is a man with a Greek *cognomen*, probably a freedman of the senator, at Rome. As for Vesuius, or Vesuvius, Rufus, of the XXth, his name, which looks Etruscan in type, seems unique. This also applies to Congaonius Candidus of II Augusta, although Congonius and Conconius are found.

The last category of names to be considered within this group is that of 'fabricated' *nomina*. It was indeed a custom that went back far in Roman history to convert a personal name into a *gentilicium*, Sextus producing Sextius, or Flavius deriving from Flavus, for example. But, as was seen with the equestrian officers, and will be noticed again with legionaries and others, the practice was especially followed in the imperial period by the Celts, among whom names like Simplicius, from Simplex, or Secundinius, from Secundinus, became popular. This Secun-dinius Verullus of II Augusta was very probably a native of the Rhineland. There are not many other clear cases in this group – they became commoner later on: the centurion of VI Victrix, L. Senecianius Martius, who dedicated an altar to Fortune at Manchester, is a good example. Celtic origin is easier to detect when the fabricated names are themselves made from a Celtic original. This seems to be so with Adauc. Pudens and certainly with a centurion of the XXth whose name, which sounds rather unsatisfactory to English ears, was Lousius Suavis.

The Antonine Wall has not provided a harvest of centurial stones like that of its southern predecessor, for it was built of other materials, and the legionary working parties marked their – much longer – sections with more elaborate slabs instead, naming only the emperor, their legion, and the distances completed, not their officers. As most of Scotland was only occupied for relatively brief periods in any case, few centurions' names are recorded here, but all nine probably belong to the Antonine period, and it may be instructive to take them together. C. Arrius Domitianus at Newstead has been mentioned already. Another centurion of the XXth stationed there is definitely recorded on the Wall. L. Maximius Gaetulicus dedicated an altar to Jupiter Dolichenus at Great Chesters and one to Apollo at Newstead. Another that he set up on the Lower Danube in A.D. 184, when chief centurion of I Italica, reveals that he had been enlisted into the XXth 57 years earlier, in A.D. 127, and that his home was Vienne in southern Gaul. A third centurion, Barrius (a rare Italian *nomen*), is merely a name on a legionary's piece of equipment found at Newstead. The origins of the other centurions found in Scotland are more readily identifable. Fl. Betto, of the XXth, acting commander of the *cohors VI Nerviorum*, who dedicated to Victory at Rough Castle, has a Celtic name. Fl. Verecundus of VI Victrix is named on an altar dedicated by his wife Vibia Pacata at Westerwood. Both these *cognominà* are found mainly in Celtic areas, so that Gallic or British origin seems probable. In view of the paucity of Greek *cognomina* among the Hadrianic centurions, it is striking that three of the Antonine centurions in Scotland have them – Sta(tilius?) Telesphorus, at Carriden, Antonius Aratus at Castlecary, and Glicon at Croy Hill. The latter might of course be an officer in an auxiliary cohort. It may be no more than a coincidence, but if an explanation is required one might recall that the governor Sex. Julius Severus had taken officers and men from Britain to Judaea in 132. Whole units or detachments that later returned to Britain may have picked up new officers in the east, who came with them. But considering that the legate of II Augusta at the time the Antonine Wall was being built was the eminent Pergamene Claudius Charax, one ought not perhaps to be puzzled at eastern centurions (and the 'Latin colonial' equestrian officer from an eastern province Caristanius Justianus at Bar Hill completes the picture). We must omit two men from Cramond from this discussion: the name of one is abbreviated to S.A., that of the other is too garbled in Horsley's eighteenth-century drawing to be intelligible. Pride of place among the centurions of Roman Scotland must go to M. Cocceius Firmus of II Augusta, justly celebrated as the dedicator of four remarkable altars at Auchendavy, on which he propitiated no fewer than 10 deities, including the Spirit of the Land of Britain, the *genius terrae Britannicae*. As E. Birley was able to show, Firmus' other dedications, particularly those to the Campestres, Hercules, Epona, Diana and Apollo, permit the inference that he was a man of Danubian or Balkan origin who had served in the *equites singulares*, the imperial horse guards at Rome. It seems legitimate to follow his further suggestion that the centurion from Auchendavy retired to Histria on the Black Sea, and that he is the Cocceius Firmus named on a dedication made there in the summer of 169. Another item about this man must be reserved for a later chapter.

Whatever the explanation for the Greek centurions in Antonine Scotland, a probable case of a man taken east for the Jewish war by Julius Severus and then sent back to Britain is C. Ligustinius Disertus of Pitinum Mergens. His career as a centurion consisted solely of two terms with XX Valeria Victrix, interrupted by a commission in IV Scythica of the army of Syria. Disertus' inscription shows that he entered the centurionate after service as a guardsman – he was a *beneficiarius* (soldier on special assignment) of the prefect – and as *evocatus*, before being commissioned in the British army. Another Italian guardsman, who had been the prefect's *cornicularius* (adjutant) was certainly made a centurii in the XXth under Hadrian. This was Q. Albius Felix of Falerii; his *cognomen* is unfortunately far too common for us to tell whether he is the centurion Felix whose men did some building near Carvoran on the Wall. Even where only one or two legions are named on a centurion's career inscription, we generally cannot tell how long his service lasted if this is not explicit. This deficiency is however made good by a number of cases, of which the most notable is perhaps that of Petronius Fortunatus. Living in retirement at his home at Cillium in the province of Africa he set out his long career on a monument erected for himself, and for his son of the same names who had died at the age of 35 while serving with II Augusta, also as a centurion. The elder Fortunatus, by then aged 80, recorded that he had served for 50 years in the army. For the first four years he had been in the ranks of the Lower Moesian legion I Italica, holding the posts of *librarius* (clerk), *tesserarius* (NCO of the watch) and *optio*, ('deputy centurion'). The centurionate, in I Italica, came 'by the vote of his own fellow-legionaries', *ex suffragio leg.*, the only published case recorded by an inscription, although Tacitus knew of this happening. He spent the next 46 years as a centurion in this and 12 other legions. Even though the dating must be conjectural, the sequence in which he held his posts allows us to reconstruct his career with some degree of probability. From I Italica he went to the Palestine legion VI Ferrata, followed by three posts in legions normally garrisoned in Lower Germany (I Minervia), Upper Pannonia (X Gemina), and Lower Pannonia (II A[diutrix], as it may be restored). He could, to be sure, have gone to those provinces after being in VI Ferrata, but it so happens that all three legions were sent to the east in the 160s for the Parthian war. What is more, the third of them, II Adiutrix, was taken over by the legate Q. Antistius Adventus, who had been commanding VI Ferrata, when it arrived. One may readily suppose that Adventus, a fellow-African, had a hand in Fortunatus' successive appointments, and may well have helped to secure him his next posting, to III Augusta in their home region. This would be a 'cushy billet', but well-deserved, since he had been decorated 'for valour' in the war. Fortunatus' next commission, his seventh, was with the Syrian legion III Gallica, but after that he moved to the north-west, successively to XXX Ulpia Victrix on the Lower Rhine and VI Victrix at York. Once again one may detect the hand of Antistius Adventus, who went from Lower Germany to Britain as governor in the 170s. Fortunatus may not have cared much for northern climes, but for whatever reason he next went east again, to III Cyrenaica in Arabia and XV Apollinaris on the Upper Euphrates. Having by now served in 11 legions, he was unusually well suited for what followed, a centurionate in II Parthica, one of three new legions formed by Septimius Severus in the late 190s – they would obviously have needed a nucleus of experienced men. Finally, he had a term in the Upper Pannonian legion I Adiutrix, taking him back to the Danube, where his military career had begun. On the interpretation here advanced he joined up *c.* 156, in his mid-twenties, and retired *c.* 206, in his seventies. His wife, Claudia Marcia Capitolina, was 15 years younger than himself, and their son had been born when she was 30, perhaps when Fortunatus was in Britain. The young man served only six years in the army – perhaps he had tried civilian life for a time without success – in the Upper German legion XXII Primigenia, and then in II Augusta. It may be suggested that he went to Britain in the Severan expeditionary force, and died in the northern campaign.

Another north African centurion of II Augusta certainly did die 'on active service in Britain', at the age of 38, for his tombstone records this: *def(uncto)*

Brittaniae in procinctu. He had previously served in XIII Gemina in Dacia and with III Augusta at Lambaesis, near his home, Castellum Arsacalitanum in Numidia. But the principal interest of this man, M. Julius Quadratus, is that he was a Roman knight, who accepted a direct commission as centurion after being on the panel of jurymen at Rome. There are enough examples of knights who became centurions to demonstrate the attraction of the permanent career that the centurionate afforded even to men of this class. Two other cases with a British connection may be mentioned. T. Pontius Sabinus of Ferentinum in Italy held commissions as an equestrian officer in the first two *militiae* before transferring to the centurionate. This ostensible demotion, however, proved the path to a distinguished career; in well under a decade he had become *primus pilus* and after a special mission bringing reinforcements to Britain in Hadrian's reign, began a series of tribunates in the Rome garrison. The third case is another African, C. Octavius Honoratus of Thuburnica who was given a centurionate in II Augusta by Antoninus Pius, *7 adlecto ex eq. R. a divo Pio in leg. II Aug*. It may have been the Numidian governor of Britain at the start of Pius' reign, Lollius Urbicus, who offered Honoratus the post, from which he went on to three other legions, in Upper Moesia, Syria, and Upper Pannonia.

The cases that we have been examining are of men who moved around a great deal. But the majority of the centurions in Britain, as in other armies of the empire, must have stayed in the province from first commissioning until retirement or death, or at most will have had one transfer. Within the province itself they may well have moved from one legion to another, as was seen with some first century examples; and many will have exchanged the routine of life at their base fortress for a spell in an out-station, from time to time. We may note a man who made a dedication to Fortune at Carvoran on the Wall, Audac. Romanus, centurion in the VIth, XXth, and IInd. A case from Lambaesis shows a slight variation. T. Fl. Virilis was centurion in the IInd, XXth, and VIth, the reverse order. However, he moved to III Augusta and then to the newly formed III Parthica, and was buried at the base of the former, Lambaesis, at the age of 70, after 45 years' service, by his wife Lollia Bodicca. Her name provides one clue, for she is certainly British. Virilis could have been a Numidian who went to Britain, married a wife there, and, after long years in the province, managed to get a transfer back to Africa, where he died after a term with III Augusta and as a training officer with the new legion. But Virilis is a name mainly found in Celtic provinces. It is more likely that he was a Briton himself, and his transfer to Numidia might equally be explained as arising from the battle of Lugdunum: Severus doubtless found it desirable to transfer some officers from the defeated British legions to other areas, and Virilis may be one of them.

We have already seen several legionary centurions away from base – the three men at Newstead, commanding a detachment of the XXth, Fl. Betto of the same legion as acting commander of a cohort on the Antonine Wall, L. Senecianius Martius at Manchester for unknown reasons, and making a dedication there. There are plenty of other examples like these, some with sufficient personal detail to give them extra interest, but it is impossible to treat them all here. One may note the records of several officers of the VIth and the XXth at Corbridge, made into a special depot manned by legionaries in the Antonine period. At Watercrook in Cumbria we find Aelius Surinus of Mursa – where he later became a town-councillor on retirement – who was in VI Victrix, attending to the burial of his colleague, also from Mursa, Aelius Bassus of the XXth; the reason for their presence there is unknown. Others are found as acting commanders of auxiliary garrisons at Wallsend, Greatchesters, and Birdoswald, on the Wall – Fl. Martinus' acting command over the Dacians at that fort was mentioned at the end of the last chapter; another man, Jul. Marcellinus, had a similar position there some time in the third century. After the division of Britain into Upper and Lower provinces, men from II Augusta and XX Valeria Victrix continued to be seconded to the other province, presumably when the resources of VI Victrix were inadequate. Thus we find M. Lollius Venator of the IInd commanding a force stationed at Piercebridge in County Durham in the reign of Caracalla. Some centurions must have been required regularly to act as 'district officers', *centuriones regionarii*. Two good specimens are recorded. T. Floridius Natalis, of the VIth, it may be presumed, made a dedication at Ribchester where he commanded a *numerus* and the *regio*, probably Ribbledale and the Fylde, assigned to a group of Sarmatians in the 170s. C. Severius Emeritus, probably from II Augusta, calls himself *c(enturio) reg(ionarius)* on a dedication he made at Bath, 'restoring a holy place wrecked by insolent people'. His *regio* may have included Bath itself, which must have made it a plum posting; but he could have gone there for private reasons, his health or his religion. These factors were doubtless what brought M. Aufidius Maximus of VI Victrix to the spa, where his freedmen paid vows to the goddess for his health and welfare. The third man, C. Curiatius Saturninus of II Augusta, could have been a district commander, although he does not say so on his altar to Sulis.

Of the centurions known at the three main bases, most are merely names on building-stones. Of the handful who speak to us a little more directly we may select two with which to conclude. Aur. Super of VI Victrix was interred in a stone coffin at York when he died at the age of 38 years, 4 months, and 13 days, by his wife Aurelia Censorina, whose spelling was slightly imperfect – *anis* lacks a letter, *possuit* has one extra. At Chester M. Aur. Nepos stands at attention, immortalized in stone, his centurion's baton in his right hand, a scroll in his left, bareheaded and with the short beard favoured in the mid-third century. His 'most devoted wife', who erected the tombstone to Nepos on his death at 50, does not give her own name. She had her own effigy carved alongside that of her husband, on a step at his side, no doubt to suggest that she was standing at a respectful distance behind him. She left a space below for her own name, and the monument was protected by the formula *sub ascia d(edicatum)*, 'dedicated under the hammer', but it stayed blank – perhaps she remarried and moved home. The two centurions, both Aurelii, reflecting their origins as new citizens of the third century, and, in the case of Super and his wife Censorina, Celtic extraction, aptly characterize the developments in the two centuries that had elapsed since Favonius Facilis was buried by his freedmen at Colchester. The province had been greatly extended, had contracted again, and settled down, although still requiring a large garrison. The native Britons had become Romans, and some were officers. If the portrayal of Nepos is less impressively realistic than that of Facilis, that may simply be a matter of taste, but even if Nepos' widow had had the funds she would have found it impossible to procure a sculptor of that quality. If she had known what the gathering storms of the age would bring, of course, she would not have bothered at all – within the next century the tombstone was to be overthrown and used in the reconstruction of the North Wall of the fortress.

Chapter VI

Legionaries

For most of the second century, the third century and beyond, three legions formed the backbone of the garrison, II Augusta at Caerleon, XX Valeria Victrix at Chester and VI Victrix at York. The latter was a late arrival, moving to Britain with Platorius Nepos in 122, while the others had come with the conquest. II Augusta and XX Valeria Victrix were to remain in Britain permanently, unlike the other two legions in the invasion force, XIV Gemina, transferred to the continent temporarily in the mid-60s, and, after a brief return in 69, leaving Britain for good in 70, and IX Hispana, which seems to have moved from Britain to the Lower Rhine early in the second century, before its still mysterious disappearance in the Antonine period. Finally, II Adiutrix, only formed early in the year 70, spent a few months in the Rhineland before coming to Britain for some 15 years. It was withdrawn in the mid-80s to reinforce the Danubian army, ultimately being stationed at Aquincum (Budapest).

Evidence for the personnel of these legions is limited. Some legionaries are of course attested outside Britain, but in several cases it is impossible to be certain whether or not the man concerned served in the legion while it was here. The inscriptions from this province are naturally the most reliable guide. A little over 100 legionaries are known from Britain, a tiny fraction, considering that there were at least three legions stationed here for over 300 years. For two of the legions, XX Valeria Victrix and II Adiutrix, a slightly higher proportion is known. In spite of this inadequate statistical sample, comparative evidence can be deployed, permitting some tentative conclusions about the men's origins during the first 200 years or so of the province's history.

Some 70 soldiers recruited in the period from Augustus to Claudius, and who served in the four legions which were to be in A. Plautius' army in 43, have known origins. Italians outnumber provincials by over four to one (57:13). Only a handful of recruits into these legions are known for the years 41–69, but of these three were Italian and four from the provinces. During the next period, 69–117, the origins of the men recruited into II Augusta, IX Hispana and XX Valeria Victrix, appear to be drastically altered: five Italians and 18 provincials. (The other legion that was here in this period, II Adiutrix, was a special case.) In the period from Hadrian onwards, although Italians are known to have been serving in the British legions, only one is known by name, a *ballista* specialist named Aelius Optatus. Where origins are specified, they are all provincial.

The first century Italian legionaries included a few men from central Italy – Samnium, Umbria, and Etruria, for example – but the overwhelming majority came from the Roman regions VIII, IX, X and XI of the peninsula, from towns such as Bologna, Faenza, Modena, Piacenza; from Aosta, Milan and Turin; and from Brescia, Cremona, Verona, Padua, Vicenza, and Aquileia. The provincials were drawn predominantly from the *coloniae* of the western Mediterranean, Merida, Cordova and Lisbon in the Spanish provinces, Lyons, Carcassonne, Arles, Fréjus, Toulouse and Vienne in Gaul being among the towns represented, together with some recruits from the Alpine provinces of Raetia and Noricum. Isolated cases are also known of men from Heraclea in Macedonia, Nicopolis in Epirus, and Berytus in Syria.

Something may now be said about the evidence for individual legionaries in Britain. Only three men from XIV Gemina are recorded, and one of these, a veteran settled at Lincoln, may well have been a native of the *colonia* whose service with the XIVth was overseas, long after it had left the province. But the other two, T. Flaminius T.f. Pol. from Faenza and M. Petronius L.f. Men. from Vicenza, may be regarded as typical representatives of the predominantly north Italian legionaries of the Claudio-Neronian period. Their nomenclature, lacking the *cognomen* which was to become practically universal after the mid-first century, bears out this dating.

Only eight men are known from IX Hispana, six buried at Lincoln, the legion's base in the 60s, the other three from York, where it remained from the early 70s until its departure from Britain soon after the year 109. Five of these men have a recorded *origo*. C. Saufeius, who died at 40 after 22 years' service, and was buried at Lincoln, was from the colony of Heraclea in Macedonia. L. Sempronius Flavinus, 10 years younger at his death, with only seven years' service, came from Clunia in Spain. The *signifer* (standard-bearer) L. Duccius Rufinus, from Vienne in Narbonensis, died at 28 and was buried at York. The other two, whose names are not preserved, were from Italy. A man from Novaria – who might of course have been a veteran, or perhaps a centurion – was commemorated by his freedmen at York, and a man from Pisaurum was buried at Lincoln. There remain three other men from the IXth, C. Valerius, who died at 35 after 13 years' service, was enrolled in the Maecia tribe, not found outside Italy. Not much can be deduced about Q. Cornelius Q. f. Cla., who died at 40 after 19 years' service, except that his lack of *cognomen* points to an early date. But L. Celerinius Vitalis, *cornicularius* (adjutant), who made a dedication to Silvanus at York, has a 'fabricated' *nomen* of the kind favoured in the Rhineland and the Celtic north-west. He could even have been a Briton.

II Adiutrix may conveniently be taken next, since its stay in Britain falls so definitely within the first century. Sixteen tombstones, all of them at Chester except for two at Lincoln and one at Bath, commemorate men from this legion. All presumably died before their unit was transferred to the Danube *c.* 85. The fact that two of them had had more than 15 years' service – C. Juventius Capito had done 17 years and Q. Valerius Fronto had done 25 – must indicate that they had been transferred to II Adiutrix from other legions when it was founded. This legion was one of two mainly composed of marines from the Ravenna fleet, who had gone over to Vespasian's side in the autumn of 69. Their ranks were clearly stiffened by the addition of seasoned men from elsewhere; the ex-marines were *peregrini*, non-Romans, given citizenship when they entered legionary service. No fewer than four out of the 14 whose *gentilicia* are preserved were called Valerius, and three out of 14 were called Pudens, two from Savaria in Pannonia and one from Noricum. But by way of compensation there are a few rare *nomina*: Calventius, Epidius, Juventius, and Murrius. The latter, C. Murrius Modestus, from Forum Iulii – hence a fellow-townsman of Agricola – who died at Bath at the age of 25, may have been sent there in a vain effort to let him recuperate from wounds. Most of the 16 may be regarded as casualties of Agricola's campaigns, or those of his two predecessors. Three died after 13 years' service, pointing to Agricola's last season.

Not surprisingly, II Augusta and XX Valeria Victrix, with several hundred years of continuous service in Britain, are better represented than other legions, the former by two dozen or so stones, while thanks mainly to the rich epigraphic yield from the North Wall at Chester, some 60 men may be definitely or very probably assigned to the XXth. Just over half of the II Augusta men are recorded at Caerleon, its base from the Flavian period onwards. There are no cases of the manifestly early type, men without a *cognomen*. By contrast, there are four Julii, three Flavii, an Ulpius, an Aelius and an Aurelius, names which derive from imperial grants of *civitas* to provincials. One or two of the Julii might conceivably be descendants of Britons enfranchised under the governors Julius Frontinus and Julius Agricola, taking their patron's *gentilicium*. However this may be, if the *nomen* of a II Augusta man at Bath may be read as Jav[olenus], it is plausible to suppose that his family owed this rare *nomen* to a grant of *civitas* obtained through the good offices of the Flavian *iuridicus* Javolenus Priscus. Only a few of the men from II Augusta are given an *origo* on their tombstones. Q. Julius Severus was from Dinia in Narbonensis, C. Valerius Victor from Lugdunum, and T. Flavius Candidus from Traiana, probably Xanten on the Lower Rhine. One man, Tadius Exuper(a)tus, who died 'on the German expedition', was certainly born in the settlement outside the fortress, where his mother and sister commemorated him. More than two-thirds of these men are known from tombstones, in most cases being the person commemorated, by family or heirs, with a few cases represented by comrades who erected the memorial. A couple of men are known from rough inscriptions on the rock in quarries used for building or repairing Hadrian's Wall, Ael(ius) Lucanus, whose name suggests citizenship derived from Hadrian himself, and the *optio* Agricola, in charge of a working party. Another *optio*, Oppius Felix, made a dedication to Mars Cocidius close to the Wall. A veteran of the legion named Ulpius Silvanus, at London, and a serving soldier named Justus at Caerleon, made dedications in Mithraea. At Bath a freedman made a dedication for the health of a standard-bearer – the Jav-[olenus?] mentioned above – and the accounts-clerk (*actarius*) Ursus was responsible for erecting a fine inscription, nine feet high, at Caerleon on the legion's 'birthday', 23 September, in the year 244.

The XXth is too well represented for more than a few of its men to be mentioned individually. A very wide range of origins is demonstrated both by specific attribution and by nomenclature. There are half a dozen Valerii with indistinctive *cognomina* – Justus, Latinus, Martialis, Pud[ens] – five Julii, two Flavii, one Ulpius, two Aelii and two Aurelii. A high proportion are given filiation, tribe and *origo*, indicating that they are relatively early, from the period *c.* 85–125. The earliest man from this legion is probably C. Mannius C.f. Pol. Secundus, from Pollentia, *beneficiarius* of the governor, buried at Wroxeter at the age of 52 after 31 years' service. There are three others from Italy, from Turin, Cremona and Brescia, three from Spain, four from Gaul, two from the German provinces, three from Noricum, two from Upper Pannonia, one each from Syria, Thrace, Epirus and Africa – and a single Briton. There are some others for whom origin in particular parts of the empire may be deduced from their nomenclature. The [*ima*]*ginifer* Aurelius Diogen[es] was probably from the east and Con-drausisius, whose name was scratched on a rock near Hadrian's Wall, was probably from the Rhineland, certainly from a Celtic province. Likewise L. Ecimius Bellicianus Vitalis, buried at Chester, has a string of Celtic names including a 'fabricated' *gentilicium*. The two Flavii, Aelius Claudianus, and the legionary trooper, *eques*, Aurelius Lucius, were pretty certainly provincials. One man, the armourer Julius Vitalis buried at Bath, is described as a *Belga* – pretty certainly he was from the British Belgae, whose chief town was Winchester.

Only a dozen of these men are recorded elsewhere than at Chester. Three are recorded on tombstones at Bath, two at London and one at Wroxeter (already mentioned). Three, including Condrausisius, are known from rock-inscriptions in the Cumberland quarries, and a man named Julius Quintilianus made a dedication at Corbridge. C. Valerius Tullus, from Vienne, was buried at Carvoran, one of the Wall forts. Finally, one Compitalicius (a unique Latin *cognomen*) is known to have served in the detachment at Newstead in the second century. In 13 cases details are preserved of the soldier's age and length of service, giving an interesting conspectus of the age on enlistment. Three were rather young – two 14 and one 15 – one was 17, one was 19, five were 20, one each was 21, 22 and 23. The cause of death is generally not stated. Disease is as likely as death in battle, although the warlike character of the decoration on the tombstones occasionally suggests death on the field of glory. An exceptional case is the tombstone of an unknown *optio* in the century of Lucilius Ingenuus, who 'died by shipwreck', *naufragio perit*. At the bottom of the inscription are the letters *S.E.*, with a space left for an *H.*, in the hope that the body might be recovered.

VI Victrix, the last legion to arrive in Britain, is disappointingly poorly attested. Only a dozen or so men may be confidently assigned to it. Three or perhaps four of these are veterans and only seven serving soldiers. None the less, as with II Augusta and the XXth, the legion is represented at London and Bath and in the frontier district, as well as at its base. A man named Flavius Agricola who died at the age of 42, was buried at London by his wife Albia Faustina. The dead man's names evoke the Flavian governor Julius Agricola, and it is tempting to suppose that an ancestor had been enfranchised when the great Agricola was in the province, taking the imperial *gentilicium* and giving the governor's *cognomen* to a son, to pass on to later generations. Albia Faustina, on the other hand, has names which suggest descent from a veteran. A man called Forianus – who might, however, have been an officer, for his stone is fragmentary – dedicated to the 'Spirit of the Place' (*Genius Loci*) at Bath. Three men had homes in the north-western provinces, C. Julius Calenus from Lyons, L. Bebius Crescens from Augsburg in Raetia, and C. Julius Speratus, apparently from Upper Germany. But the presence of men from Africa and Italy, as well as Gaul, is demonstrated by the dedication at York to the 'African, Italian and Gallic Mother-Goddesses' by a helmsman (*gubernator*) of the VIth, M. Minu(cius) Audens – whose duties presumably involved river-traffic on the Ouse-Humber waterway. One north African, at least, is attested by a tombstone from Birdoswald on Hadrian's Wall, C. Cossutius Saturninus of Hippo Regius. There remain only a man who supplies no more than his uninformative *nomen*, Valerius, on a little altar to the 'Spirit of the Garrison' and the local god Cocidius, at Housesteads; C. Jul(ius) Fl(avius) Ingen[uus] – with two imperial *gentilicia* – buried at High Rochester, north of the Wall; and L. Val(erius) Justus, buried at Corbridge.

A fair number of other men, whose status is not recorded on their dedications or tombstones, may well have been legionaries too. At Corbridge, for example, while L. Val Justus is the only certain case, it is likely that his two heirs, Egn(atius) D(i)onisius and Surius Justus, were fellow-soldiers in VI Victrix. If so, the Greek *cognomen* of the former is a little unexpected. At all events, Corbridge housed legionary detachments over a long period, from the VI and XXth legions in the later second century, with men of II Augusta replacing those from VI Victrix in the third century. One other man at Corbridge may be regarded as a legionary, the book-keeper (*librarius*) T. Tertinius – his *cognomen* is missing. The *gentilicium* is of the 'fabricated' type, and one may note a homonyn, T. Tertinius Virilis, dedicator of an altar to the goddess Nehalennia at Domburg on the Dutch coast. The Corbridge clerk very probably came from the Rhineland. It is clear that most of the men in these detachments were craftsmen, whose skills were put to use in military workshops in this frontier town. Once Britain was divided into two provinces, it would be logical to suppose that the detachments of the IInd and XXth were withdrawn, for these legions belonged to the Upper province, while Corbridge was at the further end of the Lower. None the less, detachments from these two legions continued to operate in Britannia Inferior. A joint force was carrying out building work at Netherby, north of Hadrian's Wall, in the year 219 under the governor Modius Julius, and men of the XXth made a dedication to the god Cocidius on the line of the Wall itself in the 260s. These two legions were also called upon to supply troops for campaigns on the continent. During the third century these demands became more serious than had been the case before, and some detachments may never have returned. The soldier of II Augusta, Tadius Exupertus, mentioned earlier, 'died on the German expedition', but other men may have been prevented from returning to Britain when political changes supervened – as with the creation of the secessionist Gallic empire in the years 260–273. These factors also worked in reverse, for it looks as if Carausius was able to take over detachments of II Parthica, IV Flavia, and VII Claudia, when he made himself independent. There is a delightful record of one of these 'field-service brigades' now preserved in the Cabinet de France. It is evidently the badge of an officer, Aurelius Cervianus, whose name appears below a splendid Roman eagle and between confronting rows, five in each, of soldiers. Above the left hand row is a flag standard with the letters LEG XX V. V. and a wild boar, emblem of the XXth, while the right hand row has a similar standard, the legend LEG SECUNDA AVGVS, and the sea-horse of the IInd. Below the soldiers are the words *utere felix*, 'Good luck as you use this!' and a charming assortment of beasts, two peacocks, dogs chasing a hare and a stag, and a startled-looking lion. Cervianus, whose own name perhaps derived from *cervus*, 'stag', was doubtless the commander of an Upper British task force sent to assist the armies of the Rhine or Danube during the third-century invasions.

Further evidence of continuing contact between the divided provinces comes from two inscriptions, one from Vindolanda, close to the Wall, the other from Greta Bridge, a fort on the Stainmore road. At each of these sites altars were dedicated by *beneficiarii* – legionaries on special assignment – 'of the consular (governor) of the Upper province'. Aurelius Modestus, who set up his altar to Silvanus at Vindolanda, names his legion as II Augusta; the names of the man at Greta Bridge are fragmentary. Whether these two were merely transient visitors – who had, for example, been taking messages from the governor of Upper Britain to his junior colleague in the Lower province, and had had to follow him north from York towards his frontier – or were stationed permanently

for some purpose at these Lower British auxiliary forts, is open to conjecture. But there are a number of 'beneficiarii of the governor' whose location suggests that they were carrying out regular supervisory duties at key points. The earliest case is C. Mannius Severus, referred to earlier in the chapter, at Wroxeter, still an important part of the military system at the time. There are two of these men recorded in the civil zone of Britain, where their function was presumably to act as police and to protect traffic on major routes. The first, [A]ntonius Lucretianus, dedicated an altar to the 'Italian, German, Gallic, and British Mother Goddesses' at Winchester – presumably indicating, by his choice of deities, something of the origin of his fellow-soldiers. The other man, M. Vari(us) Severus, 'put up an altar with screens at his own expense to Jupiter and the divine imperial powers' at Dorchester-on-Thames.

The other governor's beneficiarii are all from the northern frontier area. At Housesteads, a man with a rare gentilicium, Litorius Pacatianus, dedicated an altar 'to the unconquered Sun god Mytras Lord of Ages', while at Risingham on Dere Street, north of the Wall, another beneficiarius worshipped a local deity, Mogonitus Cad. (the second name presumably an abbreviation). The Risingham man, whose cognomen was Secundinus, abbreviated not only his praenomen,

M(arcus) but his family name as well, G., which no doubt stood for one of the commoner *gentilicia* beginning with that letter, such as Gabinius or Gavius. Secundinus adds that he made the dedication 'on his first tour of duty at Habitancum' (*Habitanci prima stat.*) thus providing evidence not only of the Roman name for the fort but of the nature of his presence there. Another five of these men are found at forts on major routes. Vibenius Lucius, at Lancaster, has a fairly rare *gentilicium*, but uses Lucius, one of the standard *praenomina*, as his *cognomen*. The remaining four, all from Dere Street south of Hadrian's Wall, on the Corbridge–York route, afford a good variety of nomenclature: M. Didius Provincialis at Lanchester, Pomponius Donatus and Tib. Cl(audius) Quintianus at Binchester, and Q. Varius Vitalis at Catterick. Not much clue to their origins is supplied, although the name of the Lanchester man might appear to exclude Italian origin, while the dedications by the two men at Binchester, both to the Mother Goddesses named Ollototae, given the additional epithet 'from across the sea' (*transmarinis*) by Donatus, should indicate that they were not natives of Britain. The final case of a governor's *beneficiarius*, Q. Varius Vitalis at Catterick, is dated to the year 191. Q. Varius Vitalis restored, in that year, an altar which another man, perhaps a predecessor with the same function, had dedicated 'to the God who invented roads and paths', a curious conception, otherwise unattested, which perhaps reflects the nature of Vitalis' duties: Catterick lies just to the south of the convergence of Dere Street and the Stainmore road, and he must have had to supervise a great deal of traffic of various kinds.

A few more men seconded for special duties also deserve mention. Two were *stratores consularis*, 'grooms', assigned to look after the governor's horses. One of them, Anicius Saturn(inus) is known from his tombstone at Irchester in Northamptonshire. This town lies away from any major routes. It is possible that Saturninus was there on official duties – but it might of course have been his home. The second *strator*, Ol. Cor[. . .] Vict(or), is attested by his dedication 'to the Italian Mother-Goddesses' at Dover. It is easy to see why he was there, escorting a departing governor, for example, or awaiting the arrival of a new one. His nomenclature is a little unusual, for the *praenomen* Ol(us) is a rare form of Aulus, normally abbreviated A. His *gentilicium* was probably the very common Cornelius, abbreviated Cornel., and the dedication suggests Italian origin. A third category, *speculatores*, military police, is attested by a tombstone in London. The names are rather fragmentary, but the dead man was called Celsus, son of Lucius, and was enrolled in the Claudia *tribus*, which makes it very possible that he was a native of Colchester; his legion was II Augusta. His three or four comrades who put up the stone, all *speculatores* evidently, may be presumed to have been drawn from the same legion, the nearest to the provincial capital.

A handful of other *beneficiarii* may be noted, who owed their appointments to officers of lesser rank. The most interesting, perhaps, is a man buried at London, C. Pomponius Valens. On his tombstone – which should be no later than the early second century, for *dis manibus* is written out in full – his origin is given as *Victricens[is]*; in other words, he came from Colchester, the *colonia Victricensis*, which took its title from the names of the two 'victorious' legions which defeated Boudica. He was, if the inscription is correctly restored, [*bf.*] *t[r]ib(uni)*, in the service of a tribune. Another man attached to a tribune is found at Chester, where there is also an example of a *beneficiarius* of the legionary legate. It was, after all, at the legionary bases that most of the men spent not only their 25 years in the army but most of their lives, and it is appropriate to conclude this chapter with an examination of some of the remaining epigraphic evidence from two of the three main bases, Caerleon and Chester; York, which became a *colonia*, is considered in a later chapter.

On most of the private inscriptions from both Caerleon and Chester, the people recorded are probably legionaries, veterans, or their families, even where this is not explicit. At Caerleon, Fl(avia) Veldicca, Amanda, and Julia Secundina, were married to men in II Augusta. Tadia Vallaunius, who had a son in the army, may have had a liaison with a legionary, rather than a marriage, for her son had the same *gentilicium* as herself. Several of the other women called Julia may have been the daughters of legionaries – Nundina, buried by her husband Agrius Cimarus at the age of 30, Veneria, commemorated by her husband Julius Alesander and son Julius Belicianus, Senica, who died at 60 and Belismicus, wife of Cornel(ius) Castus. The predominance of the *nomen* Julius is certainly very marked at Caerleon, both with legionaries and with women. It is also striking that while several of the names are standard and colourless – Julia Secundina, Flavius Natalis, or Cornelius Castus would pass without notice anywhere in the western provinces – others combine not particularly common *gentilicia* with Celtic names used as *cognomina* – Tadia Vallaunius and Agrius Cimarus. As for Caesoria Corocca, both names look non-Latin, Caesoria being perhaps a 'fabricated' *gentilicium*.

At Chester there are rather more Greek names. A woman named Curatia Di(o)nysia was commemorated on her death at the age of 40 by an elaborate tombstone, erected by an unnamed heir. Another stone was set up by Thesaeus to his brother Fl(avius) Callimorphus and son Serapio, who died aged 42 and three respectively. These people may all have been ex-slaves, for Greek names were regularly given to slaves, and several other inscriptions from Chester reveal the presence of freedmen and slaves (discussed in a separate chapter). In two cases, however, Greek names were borne by Greek-speakers, as the language of their inscriptions shows, Antiochus and Hermogenes. Furthermore, their dedications, to 'the Saviour Gods Asclepius and Hygieia ('Health')' and 'the mighty Saviour Gods' respectively, show, they were doctors. Both were probably attached to the legion, although one might ask whether Hermogenes was the same man as Hadrian's doctor of that name. Not much can be guessed about the origin and status of Aur(elius) Timot[heus], except to note that he died at the age of 90. Of the handful of other women and children, none looks out of place as the daughter of a legionary. Two are called Saturnina, Domitia and Flavia; there is a Tiberia; Fesonia Severiana; and two little girls called Restita and Martia. Finally, one may note a man and woman who jointly dedicated an altar to the Ollototae, found at Heronbridge, less than two miles from Chester. The relationship between Jul(ius) Secundus and Aelia Augustina is not stated, but they may be regarded as a very typical couple.

Chapter VII

Auxiliaries

At the time of the invasion of Britain the *auxilia* of the Roman army were beginning to reach the form which became standard throughout the principate. No details of the *alae* and cohorts that came over with A. Plautius are recorded, but it is not long before we hear of auxiliary units, as well as legions, engaged with the enemy of Wales and the north. Outstanding in the Julio-Claudian period were the eight cohorts of Batavians, withdrawn from Britain by Nero in the 60s, along with the legion XIV Gemina. New Batavian units were formed after the Rhineland revolt in which those eight had played a leading role on the enemy side, and some were present, along with two cohorts of Tungrians, at Agricola's last battle, Mons Graupius. The difficulties of identifying some of these units has been alluded to in the chapter on equestrian officers. Curious though it may seem at first sight, the Romans were content to raise successive series of regiments in the same area and duplicate the numbering. This is particularly troublesome with the Gauls, Spaniards, and Thracians. It seems virtually certain that there were two *cohortes I Hispanorum* in Britain at the same time; and the same could apply to *cohortes I Thracum*. The evidence of the diplomas provides valuable assistance in determining which units were in Britain, but it is restricted to a relatively short period of about 60 years. Otherwise one must rely on occasional references in inscriptions from elsewhere, such as that of Gargilius Martialis, which is the only clear evidence for a *cohors I Asturum* having been in Britain; on tile-stamps bearing the unit's name, generally much abbreviated and therefore often ambiguous; and on inscriptions set up by personnel from the *auxilia*. The commanding officers, who have been discussed separately, are better represented than their men, for obvious reasons. Even though they were here for a short time only, while the men served for 25 years (more in the first century) and often retired near by to their bases, wealth made the difference. Only about 80 inscriptions refer unambiguously to auxiliary soldiers of the *alae* and cohorts, mostly tombstones or religious dedications. Almost half of those named are junior officers, cavalry decurions and infantry centurions. They are, of course, mentioned on tombstones of their men as well and on building-stones, in a few cases (very much less than the legionary centurions), which inflates their total. But they are still relatively over-represented in the very small epigraphic record, again because, with their higher pay, they were better able to afford the luxury of a stone inscription. Rather frustratingly, there are many other men named on inscriptions at or near forts of auxiliary regiments, whom one cannot readily include because they do not reveal their status – they could have been civilians. There are indeed over a dozen inscriptions, all certainly third century if not later in date, which mention Germans, and even if no unit is mentioned, one may be certain that they were soldiers. This adds more than 30 names.

We can trace a small number of the auxiliaries who were in Britain during the decades immediately following the invasion. A fine tombstone at Colchester portrays a *duplicarius*, 'double-pay trooper', or NCO, of the *ala I Thracum*. Longinus Sdapeze, son of Matygus, came from Sardi(ca), the modern Sofia; he died at the age of 40 after 15 years' service. Another Thracian is Rufus Sita, trooper in a *cohors equitata*, (infantry regiment with some cavalry attached to it) *VI Thracum*, who also died at 40, after 22 years' service. His heirs did not supply his origin on this stone, found just outside Gloucester, but Sita is a name borne by a Thracian king. Two further tombstones name troopers of the 'Thracians', both of them Roman citizens. This is clear enough with Tib. Claudius Tirintius, *eques* of the *cohors I Thracum*, commemorated at Wroxeter on his death at the age of 57. Tirintius' name is Greek – a simplified form of Tirynthius – but he was doubtless a Thracian as well. His length of service was at least 20 years – the stone breaks off after *XX* — and probably over 30. Not until the Trajanic period could auxiliaries expect discharge after 25 years, although Claudius had made it standard for them to receive citizenship at that point. Sextus Valerius Genialis, trooper of the *ala Thracum* buried at Cirencester, whose troop-commander was also called Genialis, is more interesting, for his heir describes him as *civis Frisiaus*, a 'Frisian', or, more probably, a 'Frisiav(on)ian citizen' – the Frisiavones, whose territory lay between Aachen and Cologne in the Rhineland, were soon to contribute a cohort to the army of Britain. Genialis who died at 40 after 20 years' service could have come to Britain with a draft of men sent from Lower Germany after the revolt of Boudica, to make good the losses the army incurred then.

The names and origins of these men will illustrate the development of the *auxilia* in the early period of the occupation. Sdapeze and Sita are easily recognizable as Thracians. But they had taken additional, Latin names, perhaps to suit their officers; and it would not be long before many auxiliaries dropped their native names – becoming, when citizens, indistinguishable from their colleagues in the legions. The process is already complete with Valerius Genialis: without the label *civis Frisiaus*, his origin would be undiscoverable. On the other auxiliary's tombstone from Cirencester one may observe the variants. The dead man, Dannicus, a Raurican (from Upper Germany), in the *ala Indiana* ('Indus' Horse'), troop of Albanus, has a Celtic name and died still not a citizen. His heirs, Fulvius Natalis and Fl[av]ius Bitucus, were both citizens; Natalis, like Valerius Genialis, has a name that would pass for Roman anywhere. Bitucus has kept his Celtic name as a *cognomen*, while his imperial *gentilicium* reveals him as a man awarded citizenship by Vespasian or his sons. Of course, it is not impossible that Natalis was a citizen before enlistment. A good case of a clearly non-Roman cavalryman of the later first century is provided by the massive tombstone found re-used in Hexham Abbey: Flavinus, trooper and standard-bearer of the *ala Petriana*, would certainly have been given his full style if he had been a *civis Romanus*. His decurion, Candidus, might have had the *tria nomina* – but in his case it would not have been appropriate to give the full name.

Another citizen auxiliary from the early period is L. Vitellius Tancinus, son of Mantaius, trooper of the *ala Vettonum c(ivium) R(omanorum)*, buried at Bath; he had served 26 years and died aged 46. He was a Vettonian himself, from Caurium, one of their towns, in Lusitania – *Hisp. Caurie(nsis)*. The *ala* had received a block grant of citizenship, probably for valour on the field, as shown by the letters *c.R* But Tancinus himself had almost certainly been a citizen before this – his names L. Vitellius must derive from Claudius' friend, his fellow-censor in 47, who died in 51. Tancinus was probably at Bath for health reasons, one of several military men recorded at the spa, unless his unit was stationed there in the early period. It is found later at Brecon Gaer in Wales, where two more of its troopers were buried. Later still it garrisoned Binchester in County Durham, where several of its men are recorded.

Two other peoples whose territories were close to those of the Vettones, and who, like them, had been fierce adversaries of the Romans before the pacification of the Iberian peninsula was completed, also contributed units to the army of Britain; the Celtiberi, with a cohort, and the Astures, with two *alae* and two cohorts. The Asturians are better attested on Hadrian's Wall, where they formed an important part of the garrison, than elsewhere in Britain, but there is a particularly interesting record from Ribchester(Bremetennacum). Their presence as garrison at this fort is attested by an altar to the Mother Goddesses erected by a decurion of the *ala II Asturum*, M. Ingenuius Asiaticus, whose fabricated *gentilicium* suggests an origin in northern Gaul or the Rhineland. It must have been a trooper in this unit who owned the famous parade helmet found at Ribchester, for the name *Caravi*, 'property of Carav(i)us', incised on it is clearly Spanish.

The junior officers commanding cavalry troops were often citizens; this was certainly the case with Ingenuius Asiaticus, and probably with Genialis in the *ala I Thracum* and Albanus in the *ala Indiana*. This was less often so with auxiliary centurions. The pay differential presumably attracted legionaries to try for the post of decurion in an *ala* or *cohors equitata*. Auxiliary centurions were not paid enough to make the post attractive. Hence it is not surprising to find centurions of the *cohors I Frisiavonum*, named on building-stones at Manchester, who are manifestly non-Roman, or who have retained native names as *cognomina*, Masavo and Cudre(nus). On the other hand, Val. Vitalis, another centurion of this unit on a stone found at nearby Melandra, and two more centurions at Manchester, Candidus and Quintianus, all have Latin names, and Vitalis was a citizen – but probably a Frisiavonian for all that, like his men, and like Sex. Valerius Genialis.

It is probably no coincidence that the early tombstones of auxiliaries which we have been considering are those of cavalrymen – with their higher pay they were better able to leave sufficient funds for their heirs to commemorate them in permanent form than were their infantry colleagues. The earliest tombstones of auxiliary infantrymen found in Britain seem to be two from Templeborough in South Yorkshire of men from the *cohors IV Gallorum*. Cintuṣmus, a serving soldier, was commemorated by Melisus, presumably a comrade. Both names are Celtic, as is that of the other man, Crotus, son of Vindex – and his father's name, although Roman-sounding, is really the Celtic word for 'white' in a Latin guise. Crotus, who was 40 when he died, was described by his wife, Flavia Peregrina, as *emeritus*, indicating that he had served his time. Since this was never less than 25 years for auxiliaries, either he had joined up at 15 or he had misled his wife about his age – or, more charitably, it may be recalled that 'age-rounding' on tombstones is common throughout the empire. The other oddity is that Peregrina, a citizen herself – perhaps a veteran's daughter – does not give her husband the *gentilicium* he ought to have assumed on discharge. Perhaps he died so soon after receiving it that she regarded it as inappropriate. A third tombstone at Templeborough commemorates a woman, also apparently a citizen, Verecud. Rufilia. Her husband, Excingus, describes her as *cives Dobunna*, a Dobunnian. He may have been a soldier in *IV Gallorum*, (although he does not say so) who had married a British girl that he had met at Cirencester; but he may have been British himself, and at Templeborough as a trader or sutler. Another British woman buried at the site of a fort away from her home territory is the Cornovian at Ilkley, whose name began with the letters *Ved*. No husband or other heir is named, and one can only speculate about the reasons which took her from the Upper Severn Valley, or the Wirral, to Wharfedale, where she died at 30.

The most vivid insight into the life of an auxiliary unit in Britain is that afforded by the writing-tablets found at Vindolanda in 1973 and 1974. Mention of the governor Marcellus in one letter, combined with the archaeological context, allow this material to be dated to the beginning of the second century, about 20 years before the building of Hadrian's Wall. Virtually the whole of Scotland is known to have been abandoned at this time, and the Vindolanda men may thus be regarded as serving on Rome's northernmost frontier. Several of the men have Celtic names, others are Latin. In one letter the recipient, presumably a soldier, is told that his correspondent has sent him some 'pairs of socks, two pairs of sandals from Sattua, and two pairs of underpants . . .'; the writer concludes with greetings for several individuals, and 'all your messmates, together with whom I pray you may live a most prosperous life'. Only two of the persons to be greeted have decipherable names, Tetrecus and Elpis, or Elpides. The first is Celtic, recalling the last of the third-century Gallic emperors, Tetricus. The other name is Greek, and if the form in the nominative was Elpis, it was a name usually born by women (meaning 'Hope'). A Greek serving in an auxiliary unit in the north of Britain may appear unlikely at this period, and perhaps Elpis was a woman camp-follower. Yet a centurion of the *cohors I Hispanorum* buried at Ardoch in Scotland, probably more than 10 years before this letter was written, had the name Ammonius, son of Damio, which is certainly eastern.

The fullest evidence for the composition of the auxiliary garrison of Britain comes from the first half of the second century. A series of diplomas issued to men in the province's army, the first dating to 98 and the last to some time in the 150s, provides the names of most of the units stationed in Britain. The largest number of regiments appears on that of 17 July 122, found at Brigetio in Upper Pannonia, where it must have been taken by its recipient, a native of that province: Gemellus, son of Breucus, a Pannonian, formerly *sesequiplicarius* [trooper who received 50 per cent extra pay] in the *ala I Pannoniorum Tampiana*, commanded by Fabius Sabinus. The *ala Tampiana* was one of 13 cavalry regiments from which men were discharged by Pompeius Falco; and no fewer than 37 infantry cohorts also figure in the list. The *ala Tampiana*, as it happens, was shortly after this transferred to Noricum, never to return. It had already been away once to reinforce the Danubian army, probably in the 90s. One of its troopers of that period, T. Flavius Crensces (an idiosyncratic version of Crescens), from the Rheims area, was buried at Carnuntum in Pannonia by his decurion Flavius Silvanus: the *ala* is described on the tombstone as part of the *vex. Brit.*, the 'British detachment'. In spite of this unit's relatively brief stay in Britain, at most about 75 years, it was here long enough, and within the province at one particular place, to make a permanent mark. It was from a place called *Tampium* in Lower Britain that the governor Claudius Paulinus wrote his celebrated letter in the early 220s, just a 100 years after the *ala Tampiana* left. Its location is unknown but the inference seems inescapable that one of the forts in the north of England must have taken this name from that regiment. There are parallels from other parts of the empire, the best known being the place where the legion VII Gemina was stationed, which became *Legio* – Leon. There is one in Britain too, for the only milliary *ala* in the province was stationed at a place which the *Notitia Dignitatum* calls Petriana. This must be Stanwix on Hadrian's Wall, on the outskirts of Carlisle, and it must have taken its name from the *ala Augusta Gallorum Petriana bis torquata milliaria civium Romanorum*, known to Tacitus as the *ala Petriana*, 'Petra's Horse', for short.

The *ala Petriana*, although unique in Britain as the only double-strength cavalry regiment, is typical of the *auxilia* stationed here in having been raised originally in Gaul. Of the units on the 122 diploma, five out of 13 *alae* and 13 out of 37 cohorts may be classed as Gallic; and one may add a half-share in the mixed *ala Gallorum et Thracum Classiana*. Other regions contributed much less: next come Spain, with nine, three *alae* and six cohorts, and Germany with the same number, one *ala* and eight cohorts. Pannonia, with the *alae Tampiana* and *Sabiniana* and the *cohors IV Breucorum*, Dalmatia and Thrace with three cohorts apiece, can be seen to have contributed far fewer units to the army of Falco and Nepos. The remaining five units are a mixed bag, two *alae*, the mixed Gallic-Thracian *Classiana*, and the *Agrippiana miniata*, 'Agrippa's Red Horse', possibly a regiment of German or Thracian origin once in the service of the Jewish king Herod Agrippa; and three cohorts, *I Afrorum* and *V Raetorum*, from north Africa and the Alps respectively, and the Syrian archers, *cohors I Hamiorum sagittariorum*. As has been mentioned previously, there are a few other units known to have been in Britain at this time which are not listed on the 122 diploma, but even if they are taken into account the basic proportions of the auxiliary garrison are not significantly affected. Three-quarters derived originally from the western provinces, Gaul, Germany, and Spain, about one-fifth from the Danubian and Balkan lands. The Africans, whose presence was very brief anyway, and the Syrians, were in a tiny minority.

If we take the principate as a whole, a grand total of about 70 regiments is reached, 16 or 17 *alae* and 54 cohorts. The overall proportions differ slightly from those of 122: 20 Gallic regiments, 12 each from Germany and Spain, and 18 from the Danubian-Balkan lands, including Raetia, and the Sarmatians from outside the empire, in this category. There was even one British unit stationed here eventually, the *cohors I Cornoviorum*. This will be discussed in the next chapter, where it will be seen that at any rate the *alae* and cohorts of Britanni or Brittones raised in the province were mainly sent to the Danube region. Thus, whether by chance or otherwise, there was some degree of reciprocity. But until local recruitment became the norm, which cannot be assumed to have happened before the later second century, far more men were apparently sent to Britain from elsewhere than she provided for other frontiers. What may have balanced the equation is the uncertain number of men conscripted into *numeri Brittonum*, attested on the Upper German frontier from the 140s and probably present there from the early second century. This category of troops must be discussed next.

Numerus means simply 'number' or 'unit' and it may be misleading to use it as a blanket term, for analogous formations are found that do not carry it in their title, and old-style *alae* and *cohortes* are sometimes referred to in that way as well. It was pointed out earlier how the 'allied' troops of the republic gradually became standardized; the *alae* and *cohortes* of the principate settled down into regular units which, even in the mid-first century often had men from diverse regions in their ranks, whatever their place or origin. Beginning in the early second century new contingents of soldiers were formed, taken from outlying regions or sometimes from beyond the frontiers, retaining their native chiefs as leaders in some cases, and their own weapons and style of fighting. The *numeri Brittonum* of the Upper German army are one example. In the second- and third-century army of Britain we find several good specimens. There are the *Raeti gaesati*, the Alpine spearmen, stationed beyond Hadrian's Wall. There were two *cunei* ('wedges'), irregular cavalry formations, of Frisians, at forts on the Wall, Burgh and Housesteads, and the latter fort also had the *numerus Hnaudifridi*, 'Notfried's unit'. Other such forces whose provenance is known include the *Mauri*, Moors, at Burgh in the mid-third century, but formed in the second, the 'Tigris barge-men', *numerus barcariorum Tigrisiensium,* which the *Notitia Dignitatum* places at South Shields, and the unit of cavalry from Stratoniceia in Caria, attested by an inscription at Brougham in Westmorland. As the *auxilia,* once barbarous, became increasingly Roman in their ways and Latin in their speech, it was clearly found preferable to create these separate units for peoples who could not readily be absorbed in *alae* and *cohortes.* At the same time, Hnaudifridus and his men at Housesteads foreshadow Crocus and his Alemanni who played such an important role in the proclamation of Constantine at York in 306. The Roman army in Britain was remarkably stable and uniform in many ways during its first 250 years in Britain. But several features in it point the way to the very different army that was here in the last century of Roman rule.

It was a long time before the *auxilia* in Britain had a real chance to settle down. Throughout the first 80 years there was frequent movement, and during the period from Hadrian to Caracalla (AD 117–217) the changes of policy over Scotland resulted in several major redeployments of auxiliary units. It is to one of the spells when Scotland was held that we may date the service in the *cohors II Thracum* of Nectovelius, son of Vindex, a 'Brigantian by nation', buried at Mumrills on his death at the age of 29. We have seen, at the beginning of the chapter, Thracian units manned by men from their Balkan homeland, but also a Rhineland German serving in one. In the second century local recruitment must have gradually become normal, limited though our direct evidence is – it is discussed in detail in the chapter on Britons in the Roman army. The presumption must really be that men with Celtic, or colourless Latin names, were British, from the second half of the second century onwards, unless the contrary is stated. Thus another soldier of *cohors II Thracum*, at Moresby on the Cumberland coast in the third century, was called Smert[ri]us, son of Mac[er]. The name is Celtic in type and he was probably another Brigantian. It is no surprise to find Frumentius, a German name, in the *cohors II Tungrorum* at Birrens in the Antonine period, but to find another, Hurmio, son of Leubasnus, in the sister First Cohort at third century Housesteads might seem unexpected. One could also cite an *optio* of the Frisiavonians, called Maus, who dedicated to Coventina at neighbouring Carrawburgh at this period. That name need not be German – and could be misspelt or abbreviated. But there are two known Germans at Carrawburgh, probably serving in the *cohors I Batavorum*, Aurelius Crotus and Maduhus, who specify their origin as *German.* and *Germ.* respectively. Several comments are required. First, the fact that these two felt it necessary to state their origin implies that it could no longer be assumed that men in the Batavians were all, or mainly Germans. Secondly, the arrival in Britain of units like that of Hnaudifridus and the *cunei* of Frisians may have led to some of their men being transferred, if suitable, to existing 'regular' *auxilia*, if need arose. Finally, since soldiers' sons tended to follow their fathers into the army, a process fostered by the emperors, it may be imagined that traditional names were perpetuated from generation to generation. Hurmio and his father Leubasnus, for example, although bearing German names, may have been descended from a Tungrian who had married a British woman in the second century. The question cannot be resolved easily. One may note, in conclusion, two further cases from the third-century garrison of Hadrian's Wall which suggest continued links between the units and their original homeland. A child buried at Birdoswald, where the *cohors I Aelia Dacorum* was stationed, appears to have been called Deciba[lus], the name of the famous Dacian king defeated by Trajan. Does this mean that his father was a Dacian born in Dacia – or was the name popular among service families at Birdoswald for sentimental reasons? A less ambiguous case is that of a woman buried at Carvoran, where the *cohors II Delmatarum* was based in this period: Aur. Aia, 'who lived 33 years without a blemish'. Her husband, Aur. Marcus in the century of Obsequens, names her home as Salonae, the chief city of Dalmatia.

The colourless nomenclature of Aur. Marcus typifies the third-century auxiliaries. There are several Julii, with common *cognomina* for the most part – Augustalis, Candidus, Carantus, Firmus, Gr[ati]nus, Pastor, Rufinus, Victor. One or two other imperial *gentilicia* are represented, for example by Fl. Hilario and Ael. Gemellus, and Aurelii appear, beneficiaries of Caracalla's grant of universal citizenship. One may mention, in addition to Crotus and Marcus cited earlier, Armiger, a decurion at Castlesteads, Campester, a soldier in the *Cohors I Cubernorum*, and Januarius, a veteran at Chesters. A high proportion of the other persons from garrisons or their attendant *vici* do not record their status, and generally only give one name on their dedications to the gods. The reason is plain enough – after a generation at most, Caracalla's Edict had placed all free persons on the same level. All were citizens, and there was no need to advertise the fact by including *gentilicium* as well as *cognomen*. A list of 13 names, one of which is repeated, on two sheets of lead found in the bath-house of the large fort at Leintwardine, strategically placed to control the central part of the Welsh Marches, provides a suitable note on which to terminate this chapter. Probably 13 individuals are intended – for what purpose we cannot say – although one might make two pairs into persons with *gentilicium* and *cognomen*, Maslorius Cunittus and Motius Comitinus, both, in that case, thoroughly Celtic combinations. Six of the names are Latin; Carinus, Comes, Comitinus, Consortius, Similis, and Tiberinus. The remainder are probably Celtic: Ceanatis, Cunittus (repeated), Enestinus, Maslorius, Motius, and Senorix, even if only the last is otherwise known. They may serve as specimens of the kind of men serving in the army of the late second or third centuries.

Chapter VIII

Veterans

Veterans were a privileged class in the Roman empire, exempt from taxation – at least into the later second century, if not into the third – and from other burdensome obligations. Legionaries, originally granted land on their discharge, were regularly receiving a cash bounty by the time Britain was incorporated in the Empire, although land grants must have been made in connection with the *deductiones* (settlements) at Colchester, Lincoln and Gloucester. Auxiliaries, although they are not known to have received a bounty on discharge, did obtain other privileges, including citizenship if they did not already possess it. Besides this, if not rich by some standards, all army veterans were likely to be among the better off members of society after receiving regular pay over 25 years, from which they were able to make savings, with sporadic donatives as well. By the time of Nero the tendency for veterans to prefer to settle near their old base, rather than at a site selected by the authorities, was becoming marked. Equally, large numbers preferred the settlements, called *vici* and *cannabae* respectively, outside their forts and fortresses, rather than a return to their original home. This preference increased as the provincial garrisons stabilized and troop transfers became less frequent. The growth of local recruitment went hand in hand with this.

Hence one would expect to find evidence from Britain for army veterans, other than those at the *coloniae* (of which only Colchester is described by a Roman writer), and 42 can be counted, 20 from the legions and 22 from the *auxilia*. If the findspots of their inscriptions or *diplomata* can be taken as evidence for their place of residence, which is only doubtful in one or two cases, their distribution within the province presents a reasonably varied pattern. One, a legionary, whose status is rather doubtful, is recorded on the Antonine Wall, and 11 others, all auxiliaries, are known in the northern frontier area. Fifteen legionary veterans are found at the three legionary bases, Caerleon, Chester, and York. Of the remaining four legionary veterans, two are attested at Lincoln, one at London, and one at Bath. Hence none of them was demonstrably settled on the land or engaged in agriculture. But of the remaining 11 auxiliaries – apart from one each at the colonies of Lincoln and Colchester – nine are found in what might be called country districts. Three seem to have settled among the Cornovii, one at the *civitas*' chief town, Wroxeter, and two in Cheshire; one at Cirencester, centre of the Dobunni; one in the territory of the Belgae, near Bath; one in Kent; two in southern Brigantia; and one among the Parisi.

Of the legionaries, an *origo* is supplied for half a dozen at the most. Two, perhaps three, were from southern Gaul, one from Lugdunum, one probably from Nicopolis in Epirus, and one possibly from the Taunus region of Upper Germany. Many if not all of the others may have been natives of this province originally recruited in the *coloniae* or the *cannabae* of their legion. Even fewer of the auxiliary veterans have a known origin. One of the men who settled in Cheshire was a Spaniard, the man at Wroxeter was a Treveran, and one of the two from southern Yorkshire was a Sunucan, from the Lower Rhineland. But the man whose presence is attested at Colchester was from another British *colonia*, Gloucester, and the majority of the remaining 18 known veterans are likely to have been Britons.

Two other pieces of evidence, one direct and one indirect, reveal veteran settlement in the province. Ribchester, on the western fringe of the Pennines, was known, at least in late antiquity, as *Bremetennacum veteranorum*, which must indicate that the surrounding area, no doubt including the Fylde, had been allocated for one or more 'land settlements', *missiones agrariae*, thereby depriving the Brigantes of part of their territory. On the other hand the area in question might have been taken over as an imperial estate during the conquest in the 70s and only allocated later. It is interesting to note that a unit of Sarmatians was stationed at Bremetennacum, Ribchester, for the Sarmatians came from the Hungarian plain, beyond the Danube. When 5,500 soldiers from this people were sent to Britain in AD 175, there was nowhere in the military zone of Britain where they could have felt more at home than in the Fylde. Other veteran settlers in Brigantian territory, particularly its southern heartland, may be deduced from the Aurelii, including two T(iti) Aurelii whose citizenship must stem from grants by Antoninus Pius, attested sporadically in south-west Yorkshire. But, for that matter, a high proportion of the individuals recorded on inscriptions outside forts in northern Britain, whose status is not specified, must have been descendants of soldiers or veterans.

The earliest of the legionary veterans may be the man at Bath, who died there at the age of 45 – which suggests that he had gone there in the hope of improving his health soon after discharge, rather than that he was a permanent resident. His name was Antigonus, and his *origo* is given as *Nic.*, probably Nic(opolis) in Epirus. His legion, the XXth, is not given the titles Valeria Victrix which it bore after its part in suppressing the rising of Boudica, and the tombstone looks early from the formula *H.S.E.*, rather than *Dis Manibus*. The next earliest case from the XXth is unlikely to belong much before the end of the first century, a man called L. Ecimius Bellicianus Vitalis, buried at Chester. All his names suggest a Celtic origin and he may indeed have been British. The funerary formula, *Dis M(anibus)*, is not fully abbreviated, to *D.M.*, as was the practice later. Similarly, one of the veterans at Lincoln, C. Julius Calenus, whose original home was Lugdunum, has a tombstone prefaced *Dis Manib*. But in his case, as his legion was VI Victrix, he can hardly have settled at Lincoln until after 122, when the VIth came to Britain. C. Valerius Crispus, veteran of II Adiutrix, who was buried at Chester, must have been discharged *c*. 85 at latest, when that legion left Britain for good, unless he chose to make his way back to its old fortress after the move. His tombstone lacks the formula *Dis Manibus*, so he probably precedes Ecimius Bellicianus.

There are five other cases of legionary veterans at Chester, two of them specifically stated to have belonged to the XXth, and the others probably from the same legion. Three of these men lived to be 80 or over. One was a native of Arelate in S. Gaul, while no origin is preserved for the others. They could have been natives of Chester or one of the British communities. Six veterans are recorded at Caerleon, five of them explicitly discharged from II Augusta. Only in one case is *origo* given, Dinia in S. Gaul. The others could well have been born and bred at Caerleon or elsewhere in Britain. Two of them were Julii, and another was a T. Flavius, whose wife, Fl. Veldicca, has a very Celtic – or British – name. Genialis, a former *signifer*, was buried by one Se . . . ius [Se]necianus, whose names sound Celtic. The best known of these veterans of II Augusta is Julius Valens, who lived to the age of 100, according to his wife and son. His wife, Julia Secundina, also buried at Caerleon, by their son C. Julius Martinus, only reached 75. Of the others, C. Julius Decuminus died at 45, very soon after discharge, T. Fl. Natalis at 65, Valerius Verecundus at 70.

There are only two cases from York, both tombstones for veterans of VI Victrix. One, a fragmentary inscription, was for a man called Cresces. The other is the fine family tombstone put up for himself in his lifetime and for his deceased wife and infant children by C. Aeresius Saenus. His wife, Flavia Augustina, died at the age of 39, his son at the age of only one year and three days, the daughter at one year, nine months and five days. It is noteworthy that the son's name was not Aeresius but Saenius Agustinus, illustrating the Celtic practice of fabricating *nomina*. Saenus preferred to convert his *cognomen*, doubtless his real personal name, into a *gentilicium*, giving the child the mother's *cognomen*. The daughter's names are unfortunately not preserved.

One of the two veterans at Lincoln has already been mentioned. The other is recorded there as heir to a freedman. His own names are fragmentary, but interestingly enough he was a veteran of XIV Gemina, which is not known to have been stationed at Lincoln during its relatively brief stay in Britain. He may have been a Lincoln man who joined XIV Gemina long after it had left Britain, and who returned home later after his discharge. Finally, there are two cases at opposite ends of the province. Ulpius Silvanus, retired legionary of II Augusta, who had some link with Arausio in south Gaul, made a dedication at the London Mithraeum. His *nomen* shows him to be from a family whose *civitas* derived from Trajan. C. Jul(ius) Speratus, apparently a Mattiacan (from Upper Germany), dedicated an altar to an unknown god at Castlecary on the Antonine Wall. In neither case can we be certain where they had made their permanent home – and Speratus may not even have been a veteran at all, but a *ve[x(illarius)]*, (standard-bearer).

There are 12 auxiliary veterans recorded on stone inscriptions, and the presence of another 10 men as settlers in the province may be inferred from the discovery of their *diplomata*, certificates of *honesta missio* ('honourable discharge') and other privileges, within the province. Four of the inscriptions refer to ex-officers. One, whose names are lost, a former decurion of the *ala II Astor(um)*, died at Lincoln at more than 70 years of age. There is no particular reason to doubt that he was a native of Lincoln, possibly even a descendant of a legionary veteran colonist. Such men were quite content to enlist in the *auxilia*, particularly the cavalry, where prospects of a commission were more favourable than in the legions. The other three inscriptions of officers are in the north, although none from the frontier itself. One, a mile north of Lancaster, is a dedication to the local deity Jalonus Contre(bis) by Jul(ius) Januarius, ex-decurion, perhaps of the *ala Sebosiana*, stationed at Lancaster in the third century. A third ex-decurion, Aurel(ius) Romulia[nus], was buried at Greta Bridge on Stainmore at the age of 60. Finally, there is the interesting tombstone from Ambleside at the head of Lake Windermere, commemorating Fla(vius) Fuscinus, former centurion, who died at 55, and also his son 'killed by the enemy in the fort', *in cas(tello) inte(rfectus) ab hosti(bus)*.

At least two other officers are attested among the recipients of the 10 diplomata found in Britain. Reburrus, son of Severus, a Spaniard (who presumably became M. Ulpius Reburrus), ex-decurion of the *ala Tampiana*, was discharged in 103. His *diploma* was found at Malpas in Cheshire, not far from the road linking Chester and Whitchurch, and it is reasonable to suppose that he had settled there. The other officer's *diploma* is very fragmentary – it is not even clear whether the man was a [*centu*]*rio* or [*decu*]*rio*, or to which unit he belonged. It was found in Kent, and had been issued in 105, at a time when no auxiliary regiments are likely to have been stationed among the Cantii.

The earliest of the ranker veterans appears to be Crotus, son of Vindex, who served in the *cohors IV Gallorum*. He was commemorated, on his death at the early age of 40 – showing that he must have joined up at 14 or 15 – at Templeborough in south Yorkshire, by his wife Flavia Peregrina. The stone ought not to be much later than the end of the first century, since the formula *Dis Manibus* is written out in full. But it is curious that Peregrina, herself a citizen whose status derives from a grant by Vespasian or his sons, does not supply a *gentilicium* for her husband, who should certainly have received the franchise on discharge.

The other eight *diploma* holders all received their discharge in the first 60 years of the second century, in 105, 124, *c*. 130, 135, 146, two probably from the 140s, and one *c*. 160. As it happens, the officer Reburrus is the only one among the total of 12 whose name is complete and legible. The trooper from the *ala Classiana*, discharged in 105, whose diploma was found at Middlewich in Cheshire, was the son of Ramm(i)us and his wife was called [A]mabilis ('lovable'). The Sunucan infantryman discharged in 124, who seems to have settled in south Yorkshire, was the son of Albanus, but his own name, perhaps a rather outlandish one, seems to have defeated the engraver, who rendered it as CNTI ГꓱNT. Finally, the Treveran discharged in 135 from the *cohors II Dalmatarum*, who settled at Wroxeter, was probably called [Ma]nsuetus, son of Lucius, and the Gloucester man from the *cohors I fida Vardullorum*, discharged *c*. 160, was probably called [Satu]rninus.

Of the remaining seven rankers, three are nameless, an ex-trooper from an unknown *ala* at Corbridge, a man of unknown service at Kirkby Thore, and an *em (eritus) al (ae) Petr (ianae)* whose original home was Ulpia Traiana (presumably Xanten in the Lower Rhineland) and who was buried at Old Penrith a few miles to the south. The four named men include three Aurelii, indicating that they are certainly second century at earliest and may well be later. M.Aur[el(ius)] Januarius, *emeritus*, made a dedication to an unknown deity at Chesters on Hadrian's Wall and Aur(elius) Tasulus *vet (eranus)* set up a little altar to the local deity Belatucadrus near the fort of Old Carlisle. The third, Aur(elius) Macrinus, *ex eq (uite) sing (ulari) Au[g (usti)]*, an 'ex-trooper in the imperial horse-guards', was buried at Malton in Yorkshire. He had probably started his military career as a trooper in one of the *alae* of Britain, perhaps the *ala Picentiana* which is known to have been stationed at Malton. Finally, there is a man called Sigilius, *emeritus*, probably of the *ala Augusta*, who made an offering to Hercules outside the fort at Old Carlisle.

Chapter IX
British soldiers in the Roman army

The first Britons to have served in the Roman army must have been men recruited as auxiliaries, very probably immediately after the conquest in some cases. Definite evidence is not available for this early period, but a cavalry regiment called the *ala Britannica* is mentioned by Tacitus among the forces with Vitellius in AD 69. In the *Agricola,* Boudica is made to complain of the levy among other evils brought by servitude to Rome, and Tacitus himself comments directly that 'the Britons put up with the levy and the tribute and the burdens imposed by imperial rule'. Some of these men were doubtless shipped overseas, in units of Britons, while some selected men would fill gaps in the auxiliary units stationed in this province. The latter category is referred to in Calgacus' speech before the battle of Mons Graupius.

A variety of evidence from different parts of the empire records the existence of two cavalry regiments, the one mentioned above, which was later doubled in strength, and was stationed on the Danube in Lower Pannonia, and the *ala I Brittonum,* probably raised by Agricola and sent to the Danube in the mid-80s, to remain in that region. In addition, 12 infantry units are known, and the existence of at least two more may be postulated. Eleven of these cohorts were part-mounted, and three of these are double strength, 'milliary' units – as were the three purely infantry cohorts. Three of the cohorts may have been formed before the civil wars of 69–70, the *cohortes I, II* and *III Britannorum milliariae equitatae,* the first cohort also being recorded under the name *coh. I Britannica eq.* The remaining cohorts, like the second *ala,* were evidently units of *Brittones* rather than *Britanni.* It must remain obscure why the Romans differentiated thus with the titulature of the units raised in this island. One possible explanation is that those formed in the original province were called *Britanni,* while the ones created among the peoples overrun by the Flavian governors Cerialis, Frontinus, and Agricola were called *Brittones.* At least, it may be noted that the third type of unit raised in Britain, the *numeri,* which were certainly drawn from the more barbarous peoples of the far north, were *numeri Brittonum,* not *Britannorum.*

Most of these *alae* and cohorts were to form part of the garrison of the Danubian provinces – Raetia, Noricum, both Pannonias, Upper Moesia and Dacia, all had British units in their armies. Several of them gained battled honours for distinguished service, notably the *coh. I Brittonum Ulpia milliaria equitata torquata civium Romanorum,* decorated for its part in winning Trajan's second Dacian war. Two British units have a rather puzzling title, *coh. I* and *II Augusta Nervia Pacensis Brittonum. Nervia* is clearly a title derived from the emperor Nerva, but *Pacensis,* otherwise found only with the meaning 'inhabitant of [city called] Pax', remains unexplained. The exception among the British units was *coh. II Brittonum equitata,* which was based, for a long time at least, in Mauretania Caesariensis. But its stay there may only have been temporary, as was the case with the *ala Britannica,* assigned to Mauretania to reinforce the province's garrison in the mid-second

As has been seen in the section on the *auxilia* of the British garrison, the *alae* and cohorts raised in the provinces of the empire bore a variety of names to indicate their original provenance, in some cases that of a single tribe or state, *civitas*, such as the Vocontii or Astures, in other cases a wider title, of a whole nation, such as Galli or Hispani. The units raised in Britain were all Britanni or Brittones, with a single exception, the *cohors I Cornoviorum*. What is more, the Cornovii were stationed in Britain itself, at *Pons Aelius*, Newcastle upon Tyne, near the eastern end of Hadrian's Wall. The sole clear evidence for this unit's existence, and for its station, comes from the fifth-century *Notitia Dignitatum*, but there is good reason to believe that the section of that document which concerns the Wall garrison reflects the situation in the third century. The cohort may possibly have been stationed in Wales earlier on, but the tile-stamp, *C.I.C.*, might belong to another unit. However this may be, the *cohors I Cornoviorum* is an anomaly requiring explanation. It may be that it was raised during a period of emergency, when the *juventus*, the young men of fighting age, had been called up by the governor and had acquitted themselves particularly well. The fact that no other British *civitas* provided a cohort ot its own may have been because none had a sufficiently large population. But the Roman authorities may have preferred, for political reasons, to mix together elements from the different peoples of Britain.

Evidence for the composition of the British units is hard to come by, but there are a few cases known from the second century. A diploma found in Pannonia was issued in 105 to Lucco, son of Trenus, a Dobunnian, and his wife and children. He had been serving in the *cohors I Britannica milliaria civium Romanorum*, and had married a woman from a Pannonian people, the Azali; she had already borne him three children. They are also named on the *diploma*, his son Similis, and his daughters Lucca and Pacata. Lucco and his children presumably became Ulpii, taking the emperor's *gentilicium*. M. Ulpius Lucco would have a half-Roman sound to it, but M. Ulpius Similis is a nomenclature which could be called featureless – a man with those names might come from anywhere in the empire. To judge from the find-spot of the diploma, Lucco and his family settled, after his discharge, close to his old place of garrison. Another Briton, M. Ulpius Novantico son of Adcoprovatus, whose original domicile is given as Ratae, Leicester, received citizenship in 106 before his discharge. His unit was the *coh. I Brittonum Ulpia torquata civium Romanorum*, decorated and rewarded with *civitas* for its conduct in the second Dacian war. Another man from this cohort, M. Ulpius Longinus, son of Sacc(i)us, a Belgus, in other words from the British Belgae of Hampshire and Somerset received his diploma, which also names his son Vitalis, in 110. It is worth noting that Longinus, from a more southerly *civitas*, already had a Latin name, and he may thus be classified as a specimen of 'first stage Romanization'. Unrepresentative though this evidence may be, it does at least demonstrate that men from the Belgae, Dobunni and Coritani were being recruited into British units in the early 80s. It is safe to infer that other British *civitates* also supplied men.

Recruitment from the province of origin seems to have died out with many auxiliary units at an early stage in their history, but it continued with at least one of the British units as late as *c.* 130 AD, when one Ivonercus, son of Molacus, a Briton was recruited. On the diploma issued to him in the mid-150s, he is designated simply *Britt*. He had presumably settled in Dacia, where the diploma was found, and where his unit, the *coh. I Ulpia Brittonum* mentioned earlier, was by then stationed. But Ivonercus may have been one of a special batch of recruits brought from Britain to meet a particular need. Other British units had already begun to enrol men from the area surrounding their stations. Sepenestus, son of Riv(i)us, discharged from the *cohors I Britannica* in 133, hence recruited *c*. 108, was described on his diploma as *Pannon.*, Pannonian, emended to *Cornac*. Although it has been argued that the emendation was an attempt to render the name of a British people or town (Coritani, Cornovii, Corinium, for example), the man's own name, with its characteristically Illyrian termination in -estus, shows that he was from the Cornaces of Pannonia. No conceivable doubt can attach to Mog. Ursus, a soldier in the *coh. I Aelia Brittonum milliaria* of the army of Noricum, for he is known by an inscription from the province, which was set up by his parents – the family was Norican.

There are obvious difficulties in determining the origin of men with Celtic or Latin names attested by undated inscriptions. They might have been enrolled into British units almost anywhere in the northern frontier areas of the empire. But for the record one may list the small number of other men from these units who could possibly be British. Fidelis, son of Saturio, a soldier in the *coh. I Fl. Brittonum,* was buried at Salonae in Dalmatia after 18 years' service – his inscription is thought to be not later than the early second century. M. Ulpius Faustinus, *librarius* of the *ala Britannica,* was buried by his 'fiancée' at Portus Magnus in Mauretania after 12 years' service. If his presence in Mauretania may be explained by the transfer of troops there from the Danube and elsewhere in the mid-second century, he might be a Briton. But if the inscription is from the second century, the *sponsa* would have had to wait at least 13 years before the betrothal could become a legal marriage. Soldiers were not permitted to have wives before the time of Septimius Severus. Catavignus, son of Ivomagus, a soldier in the *coh. III Britannorum equitata* of the army of Raetia, was commemorated in northern Italy on his death at the age of 25, after six years' service, by his fellow-soldier Paternus. Virssuccius, a cavalryman and standard-bearer in the *cohors I Britannica milliaria civium Romanorum equitata,* who died at 35 after 15 years' service, was buried by two comrades, Bodiccius, another standard-bearer, and Albanus, at Acumincum on the Danube, in Lower Pannonia. All three may have been British, and the two standard-bearers at least have thoroughly Celtic names. By contrast, there can be no certainty about the origins of five men named on the tombstone of a trooper in the *ala I Flavia Brittonum* at Vindobona (Vienna) in Upper Pannonia. The dead man was called T. F(lavius) Verecundus, his troop-commander was Italicus and his heirs were Pro(bus?) or Pro(culus?), Priscinus and Ingenu(u)s, all standard Latin names of an uninformative nature.

There is a single example only of a Briton serving overseas in a non-British auxiliary unit. This is a man called D. Senius Vitalis, described as *civis Brit.* on his tombstone at Cologne. His case is rather unusual on several counts. He died at the age of 55 after 19 years' service, revealing that he must have joined up at the relatively advanced age of 36. The auxiliary unit in which he served was the *cohors VI ingenuorum civium Romanorum,* one of the small number of *auxilia* formed from Roman citizens. Vitalis' own *gentilicium* is of the 'fabricated' type favoured in the Celtic north-west of the empire, and S(a)en(i)us is found several times in Britain – where Vitalis was also particularly popular as a *cognomen*.

None of the small number of known sailors or marines from the *classis Britannica* appears to have been a Briton, but there is a man from south-west Britain, A *civis Dumnonius*, called Aemilius son of Saen(i)us, who served in the *classis Germanica*, and was buried at Cologne. Hence, it is worth remarking, the first recorded British sailor was a man from Devon who served in the German fleet.

Finally, there are four known Britons who served in the imperial horseguards, the *equites singulares Augusti*, who were based at Rome with the praetorians, and like them accompanied the emperor on expedition. They were recruited from auxiliary cavalry regiments in the provincial armies, and most of those whose origin is known were from the Rhine, Danube and Balkan regions. The name of one of the Britons, who died at Rome aged 48, is missing. Two of the others were also buried there, M. Ulpius Justus, *natione Britto,* who died at 45 after a full 25 years' service, was commemorated by his friend M. Ulpius Respectus, who was already a veteran. Nig(rius?) Marinianus, *natione Britanicianus,* who died at 38 after 18 years' service, was buried by his son of the same names. The fourth man, Aur(elius) Macrinus, was buried at Malton in Yorkshire. He had perhaps returned to the place where he had served in an *ala* before being picked for the *equites singulares Augusti.*

As for Britons serving in the province itself, in other units, there are only two specific examples. One is Nectovelius, son of Vindex, a Brigantian, *nationis Brigans,* who served in the *coh. II Thrac(um)* in the second century and was buried at Mumrills on the Antonine Wall. The other is a man whose name ends . . . *rninus,* almost certainly the very common *cognomen* [Satu]rninus, who was from the colony of Glevum, Gloucester and thus may have been of immigrant – legionary veteran – descent, in part at least. He was discharged from the *coh. I fida Vardullorum* in the 150s, as revealed by a fragment of his *diploma,* found at Colchester.

This is rather scanty evidence on which to base the generalization that by the later second century most auxiliary units were manned by natives of the province. But there is no reason to believe that Britain was an exception among the armed provinces of the empire, and in all those where there is evidence it points to local recruitment. Of course, the practice of recording *origo* begins to die out in the second century, for the good reason, it could be argued, that it became unnecessary to specify this when most members of a community, whether civil or military, were native to the place. One would feel more confident that the argument was conclusive, and not merely circular, or an *argumentum ex silentio*, if there were more cases of soldiers' parents or sisters on record. There is an army clerk or adjutant, *cornicularius*, at Greatchesters on Hadrian's Wall, Ael(ius) Mercurialis, commemorated by his sister Vacia. One may be encouraged to regard a case like this as typical – the two should be the son and daughter of an army veteran, born and bred in the *vicus* outside the fort, with the son entering the cohort. Yet there is a family tombstone from Chesters, also on the Wall, on which a soldier called Lurio commemorated his sister Ursa, his wife Julia and his son Canio – but Lurio was a German, hence manifestly born elsewhere. His sister must have followed him to Britain.

The first Britons, or permanent residents of Britain, that one would expect to find serving in the legions would naturally be from the first-century *coloniae,* and there is indeed evidence for legionaries from all three cities. It has even been suggested that it became imperial policy to ensure that each major military province had as many *coloniae* as it had legions, so that there would be a regular supply of citizen recruits from a conveniently close quarter. To take first the evidence for men serving overseas: T. Statius Vitalis of Camulodunum, who was buried at Carnuntum on the Danube, legion not specified, probably died in the first century, to judge from the funerary inscription. He was only 23 and had had three years' service. He could well have been born in Britain, as son of one of the first colonists and have entered XIV Gemina just before it was summoned to Italy in the late 60s; but he might equally have gone in one of the drafts called for by Vitellius in 69. (His *cognomen* Vitalis was, as has been noted already, one that seems to have been favoured in Britain.) Lincoln provides two examples. M. Junius Capito, a soldier in X Gemina, which was stationed for most of its history at Vienna on the Danube, died in Africa after 10 years' service. He had presumably gone there with a force sent during one of the Moorish revolts, in the second century. The second Lincoln man, M. Minicius Mar[ce?]l[linus?], apparently rose to become chief centurion of XXII Primigenia, based at Monguntiacum (Mainz) on the Upper Rhine. The names of both men are thoroughly 'colonial' in type.

Gloucester cannot provide quite the same kind of evidence, but there is a legionary from the city who died while serving at Rome, as a *frumentarius*, 'commissary agent' – the euphemistic name for a secret policeman. His name was M. Ulpius Quintus, which is enough to show that he was not a descendant of one of the original veterans settled at the *colonia* under Nerva. An ancestor of his must have been admitted to membership of the *colonia*'s citizen body after gaining the franchise from Trajan, and he was probably an auxiliary veteran. Finally, there is another man whose home town is not known but whose origin in Britain is indicated by his dedication at Vetera (Xanten) in Lower Germany to the 'British mother-goddesses', the *matres Brittiae*. This was L. Valerius Simplex, a soldier in XXX Ulpia Victrix.

There are, however, several other *frumentarii* recorded at Rome, nominally on the books of the three legions which formed the backbone of the British garrison from Hadrian's time onwards. One or two have origins specified outside Britain, but one might be from Lincoln, [P. A]elius [. . .]ogont[ius?], unless . . . ogont should be restored as [M]ogont[iaco], Mainz, and [. . .]ndo represented his *cognomen* rather than [Li]ndo, his *origo*. If [Li]ndo is right, then it should be observed that this man, like Ulpius Quintus, has a *gentilicium* which indicates descent from a man enfranchised after the foundation of his *colonia* rather than from one of the original settlers. Of those whose *origo* is not specified, T. Flavius Verecundus and P. Aelius Urbicinus of II Augusta, T. Aurelius Pius of VI Victrix and his heir Aurelius Verecundus, could all, with their imperial *gentilicia*, be descendants of enfranchised Britons or auxiliary veterans settled in Britain. Some of them, such as L. Aemilius Flaccus and his friend T. Sempronius Pudens of XX Valeria Victrix, and Ulpius Quintus' *collega* Calidius Quietus, could be descendants of legionary veterans settled in Britain. One should also note Q. Aemilius Marinus, a *singularis* of II Augusta, and Val(erius) Paternus, *speculator* of the British army, legion unspecified, buried by Sempronius Pudens, who may also fall into this category.

The explicit evidence from Britain itself for natives of the province serving in legions here is rather scanty, not surprisingly – as has been stressed already, few would bother to specify their *origo* if it was local, from the second century onwards. A first-century legionary buried at London, C. Pomponius Valens, came from Colchester, described as the *colonia Victricensis*. Julius Vitalis, armourer, from the XXth legion, who died at Bath at the age of 29 after nine years' service, is described as *natione Belga*. This must mean that he was one of the British Belgae, considering that Bath was within the territory of that *civitas*. Tadius Exuperatus, commemorated by his mother and sister at Caerleon by a tombstone placed alongside that of his father, after his death in 'a German expedition', was clearly born in the *cannabae* of II Augusta. What is more, his *nomen* is that of his mother, indicating either that she was his father's freedwoman or that his parents' union had not been a legal marriage. The latter explanation is the more likely. Serving soldiers were not permitted to marry until the time of Severus, but the illegitimate sons of legionaries provided a steady flow of recruits, to judge from the evidence of other provinces.

Apart from these cases, there is an apparent reference to British soldiers of the VIth and XXth legions serving at Castlecary on the Antonine Wall. But the inscription is now lost and the reading is disputed. Among the legionaries at Chester are one or two men with the tribe *Cla(udia)*, in which Camulodunum was enrolled, but several other towns in the empire are equally likely homes for them. One of the veterans from Chester apparently came from a place of which the name ended *--va*, which could perhaps be [De]va, Chester itself; but in that case one would have expected *castris* ('born in the camp') to be given. The veteran L. Ecimius Bellicianus Vitalis, also recorded at Chester, has a very Celtic type of nomenclature, but origin in Gaul or Germany is rather more probable than in Britain. A number of other legionaries whose origin is not specified could perfectly well have been natives of Britain. Some of them are referred to in the chapter on legionaries. One should also note that there are several centurions of the British army who look as if they were natives of the province, as well as a few officers of higher rank, serving in Britain and elsewhere, who may have been born in Britain.

A record of building on the Wall by the 'century of Gellius Philippus', found near Housesteads (RIB 1572)

Chapter X
People of the frontier

A strange deity, unknown elsewhere in the empire, is recorded on well over 50 little altars found in the frontier region. There are more than a dozen variants of the name. It appears often in a plural form, 12 times as *veteribus* or *dibus Veteribus*, as if the devotees thought that they were dedicating 'to the Old Gods', and a similar number are to *deo Veteri* in the singular. The varying spellings of the name are remarkable: *vitiribus, hveteribus, hvitiribus*, even perhaps *vicribus*, in the plural, *vetiri, vetri, viteri, vitire, vitiri, votri, hveteri, hvitri, vheteri*, in the singular. The worshippers' own names, where they are given – and a third of the altars do not name their dedicator – certainly suggest that they were humble folk, perhaps barely literate. But the variety of forms, especially the rarer ones with *hv-* (or *vh-*), indicates rather that the deity's name could not readily be expressed in the Latin alphabet. This may be a local spirit, originally worshipped before even the Celts came to the north, ill-defined as to number – and to sex, for two altars, from Chester-le-Street, honour the Vitires as female deities.

Of the 30 or so named worshippers only two were definitely soldiers, Julius Pastor, a standard-bearer (*imaginifer*) of the *cohors II Delmatarum* at Carvoran, and a senior auxiliary centurion (*princeps*) at Lanchester, whose name was apparently Unthau[s]. Only one altar was certainly dedicated by a woman, Romana, at Greatchesters, although two other devotees, Ivixa and Mocuxsoma might perhaps have been female. Mocuxsoma, it must be noted, is a rarity in any case, for this person's dedication, a silver plaque rather than an altar, was found in a temple at Thistleton Dyer in Rutland, and not in the frontier zone. Otherwise, except for an altar at York, every example comes from the frontier and the great majority have been found in the central sector of the Wall. It is reasonable to conjecture that whatever Mocuxsoma was doing in the East Midlands he or she had close connections with the frontier people. The nomenclature of the dedicators repays study. Only five have *gentilicium* and *cognomen*. Apart from Julius Pastor, there are two Aurelii, Mucianus and Victor, Aelius Secundus, and Menius Dada. Another 12 have single Latin names, one *gentilicium*, Deccius and 10 *cognomina* which are all common, Fortunatus, Longinus, Maximus, Primulus, Regulus, Romana, Senilis, Superstes, Tertulus, and Vitalis, while the remaining one, Senaculus, at Vindolanda, is a Celtic name with a Latin suffix, otherwise unattested. The other 13 dedicators have names that are manifestly barbarian, for the most part Celtic, although one or two, such as Aspuanis and Duihno, look German. But the lettering on several of the altars is so crude, and the apparent readings so curious, that one must suspend judgement over cases such as Ivixa, Suadnus, Uccus, Unthaus, and Viasudri(us). One of these people, Necalames, was responsible for three altars: on two, set up to *deo Veteri*, his name is clear enough; the third was to *deo Vitiri*, and his own name appears as Ne[ca]limes.

Some have supposed the deity's origin to be Germanic, adducing the ancient north German epithet for Odin, *vithrir*, 'the weather-god' – in that case, perhaps this would be no bad presiding deity for the northern borderlands. But the derivation has not commended itself to specialists. An alternative is the Old Nordic *hvitr*, 'white' or 'shining', or *hvethr-ung*, 'son of a giantess', an epithet of the Teutonic fire-god Loki, equivalent to the Roman Vulcan. An attraction of this view is that Vulcan was certainly worshipped in the *vici*, the settlements outside the forts. At Vindolanda, where numerous altars to the Veteres have been found, the villagers, *vicani Vindolandesses*, made a communal dedication to Vulcan: the god of fire was also the god of smiths, whose work was of vital significance in the frontier settlements. There can be no certainty at present about the Veteres, except to note that nearly half the deity's worshippers addressed their vows in a form which shows that they regarded it as a primaeval spirit. Likewise, the identity of these people may fairly be taken as representative of the population of the frontier zone, extending from the northern Pennines to Hadrian's Wall.

It is unfortunate that even where we possess more than one inscription of one of these humble frontier people, we can learn so little about them. The centurion M. Cocceius Firmus at Auchendavy on the Antonine Wall, or the trader Barathes of Palmyra, attested at South Shields and Corbridge, whose stories are examined in other chapters, come alive as real individuals, but the three altars of Necalames do not tell us much more about him than a single inscription would have done. As for bearers of Latin names, the commoner ones conceal origins, and it is hazardous to assume identity between homonyms. A simple tombstone found at the outpost fort of Risingham on Dere Street, 15 miles north of the Wall, records the death of a man of 22. The inscription is fragmentary, but it is clear that the deceased had been 'entrapped', *deceptus*, presumably by some of Rome's enemies beyond the frontier. He had died on a day in May of a year when an emperor was consul for the second time – the emperor's name is missing, but there is space only for a short one, such as Decius, Gallus, Probus or Carus, making a date in the mid- or later third century fairly certain. The stone was put up by 'his uncle [A]ure[l]ius Vict[or] as heir'. There is no means of telling whether the uncle is the same man as the Aure(lius) Vict(or) who dedicated an altar to the Veteres at Housesteads. There are two other specimens of the name. At Haltonchesters, close to where Dere Street crosses the Wall, Aurel(ius) [Vic]tor buried his daughter Aurelia Victor[i]na, and at Chesters there is a tombstone, with a relief showing a mounted trooper, commemorating M. Aurelius Vic[t]or, who died at the age of 50.

The historical novelist could reconstruct, from these items, the life of a cavalryman serving on the Wall, at Chesters, dedicating an altar to a local deity at nearby Housesteads, marrying and having a daughter. Then Aurelius Victor lost his daughter, named after himself, and buried her at Housesteads, and had to go north to Risingham when his sister's son, serving no doubt in the Vangiones or the *exploratores Habitancenses*, the 'Risingham scouts', died in action during an enemy foray in the spring. Finally, our man dies, buried presumably by his comrades or former comrades in the Second Asturians at Chesters. He might be tempted further to identify as Victor's sister the lady named Aurelia Lupula, buried at Risingham by her son Dionysius Fortunatus – who would himself be the nephew that Victor was to bury one day in May in the third century; and Aurelius Quartinus, who buried his daughter Quartilla there on her death at the age of 13, might be another kinsman. The historian must unfortunately recognize that Aurelius had, after the Edict of Caracalla in 212, become the commonest *gentilicium* in the empire, and there is no need to assume any kinship between Aurelii unless it is explicitly stated. As for Victor, that too is exceedingly common: it is the tenth most frequently recorded *cognomen* in the empire. In the frontier zone of Britain, if we exclude from consideration the centurions whose names are recorded on the building stones of the Wall, and the equestrian officers, Aurelius is found in far more cases than any other name. Most of them, if not all, look third century in date. There is a nice clutch of Aurelii on a tombstone from the fringe of the frontier district, found at Burrow-in-Lonsdale. It commemorates a soldier named Aurelius Pusinnus, who died at the age of 53, having apparently been in the army for 36 years, and his wife, aged 37 at her death, Aurelia Eubia: it was set up 'to the spirits of the departed and their everlasting calm' by their loving son Aurelius Pr[o]p[inquus] (as the name may be restored). In each case, the *gentilicium*, now so widespread, is abbreviated Aur. The dead man's name is Celtic – two examples of the female form are known in the region. His wife's name was Greek (meaning 'respectable'), but there is no need to infer that she was a Greek-speaker by origin. She might have been a freedwoman, for such persons commonly had Greek names at all periods; but in the later empire they were gradually adopted by westerners of all sorts. The son, Propinquus, on the other hand, has a Latin *cognomen* of a standard type. Aurelia S[abin]illa, and her 'dearest sister' Aurelia Caula, whom she commemorated on her death at the age of 15, at Greatchesters on the Wall, and two more sisters, the Aureliae Romana and Sabina, who put up a tombstone to their father at Greta Bridge, may perhaps be earlier in date than the third century, before the name became common enough to abbreviate as *Aur.* A curious case at Carlisle is of a woman called Aur. Aurelia. Rather than suppose that she really had Aurelia as both *nomen* and *cognomen*, not a Roman practice, it has been suggested that the second name was intended for Aurelia(na). Her husband, Ulpius Apolinaris, incidentally, also has an imperial *nomen*, in his case going back to the emperor Trajan. It must be added that bearers of other imperial *gentilicia* are also very numerous in the region: over 20 Julii, a dozen each of the Flavii and Aelii, and a handful representing the family names of other emperors. The Julii, of course, are in a somewhat different category, as far as Britain is concerned, for the island did not enter the empire until after the death of Caligula, last of the Julian emperors. Hence the British Julii must be of immigrant derivation, in many cases Gaulish, unless it be supposed that the two Flavian governors Frontinus and Agricola, both of them Julii, had encouraged Britons enfranchised through their patronage to assume the name. At all events, if the Julii are included, the imperial *gentilicia* exceed all the other *gentilicia* in the frontier region put together. Some of them were no doubt legionaries, immigrant traders, and equestrian officers or members of their household, a consideration which must also apply to a number of the bearers of non-imperial *gentilicia*. Thus Vettia Mansueta and her daughter Claudia Turianilla, who jointly dedicated a small altar with good quality lettering to the Nymphs, may well have been the wife and daughter of the commanding officer of the Carvoran garrison. L. Arruntius Salvianus, who buried his nine-year-old son at South Shields, is unlikely to have been an ordinary soldier in the garrison, and may himself have been the prefect. But other explanations are possible. On the other hand, Baib(ius) Duvianus, who buried his wife Mamma, daughter of Victor, at Carvoran, on her death aged 24, looks more like a trader – an officer's wife would surely not have had a name like Mamma. Yet Duvianus could have been a soldier, especially if the tombstone is third century in date.

There are only a handful of 'fabricated' *nomina* of the Celtic type. Amatius Ingenuus, buried at Old Carlisle at the age of 60, and Venustinius Lupus, who set up an altar to Mars at Castlesteads, are two good specimens formed from adjectives, and another case, also at Castlesteads, is C. Verecundius Severus, whose altar was to Jupiter and the Spirit of the Place (*genius loci*). A man called M. Senecianius V . . . reveals his origin by his dedication to the 'German Mothers' on an altar thought to come from Hadrian's Wall. His *gentilicium* is certainly typical of the Rhineland. The only example from the whole region of a totally Celtic nomenclature borne by a Roman citizen, comes from Risingham, on a tombstone set up by one Blescius Diovicus to his infant daughter. The same place also yields a Greek fabricated *gentilicium*, the Dionysius Fortunatus mentioned earlier in this chapter. It would be rash to infer that he, or his father, derived from the Greek-speaking part of the empire, given the apparently third-century date suggested by his mother's name Aurelia Lupula. An interesting case which ought to be much earlier, perhaps Hadrianic, because the funerary formula *dis manib(us)* is scarcely abbreviated, is the tombstone of a man called L. Novell(ius) Lanuccus. Novellius could be an authentic *gentilicium* – there are examples in southern Italy – but it might have been invented by its bearer, or an ancestor, from the *cognomen* Novellus. At any rate, the *cognomen* Lanuccus seems not to be Latin, yet the man's daughter Justina, who set up the stone, specified that he was a Roman citizen, *c(ivis) R(omanus)*. Since his age is given as 60, yet he is not described as a veteran, it looks as if he must have been a trader of some kind.

Whether or not a Germanic origin be postulated for the *di Veteres*, Germans were certainly present in force among the garrison from an early stage. In the first century, before the Wall was built, there were Batavians, Tungrians, and Frisiavonians in the northern army, and cohorts of these and several other Rhineland German peoples are found on and close to the Wall in the second and third centuries. In the third century, too, more barbarous units are found, the *cuneus* ('wedge-formation') of Frisians, and the *numerus* ('unit') of Hnaudifridus, who worshipped their Teutonic Mars, Thincsus, and his Valkyrie-like attendant spirits the Alaisiagae, Beda and Fimmilena, Boudihillia and Friagabis, at Housesteads. More than 60 persons of German origin may be identified in the frontier area, some of whom explicitly describe themselves as Germans, others identifiable by their names – but some Germans, it must be noted, had adopted Roman names, such as Gratus, son of Fersio, Romulus, son of Alimahus, and Similis, son of Dailus. These three appear, with at least four others, on a tombstone set up at Housesteads by Delfinus, son of Rautio, 'from Upper Germany'. Another group of Germans is found at Old Penrith, in the hinterland of the Wall, making a joint dedication 'to all the gods', *omnibus dibus*: Unsenis, Fersomeris, Burcanius, Arcavius, Vagdvarcustus, and a sixth person whose name began Pov- and ended – arus. An altar found somewhere in northern Cumbria to the local deity Maponus and to the 'divine spirit of the emperor' was set up by four *Germani*, Durio, Ramio, Trupo, and Lurio. The last of these might be the same as the Lurio, *Germ(anus)*, who erected a tombstone to his sister Ursa, his wife Julia, and their son Canio, at Chesters. Another family group is revealed at Old Penrith by the tombstone set up to Crotilo, a German, aged 26, and Greca, aged four, by Vindicianus, brother – presumably of Crotilo. Another evidently German child was buried at

Corbridge, Ahtehe, daughter of Nobilis, aged five. Pervica, buried at Greatches-ters, has a name which recalls Pervinca, one of the people on the German tombstone at Housesteads.

Apart from these Germans, the other soldiers and their officers, who have already been discussed in earlier chapters, there are a few examples of people in the frontier area whose non-British origin is either made explicit or may legiti-mately be inferred from their name. Salmanes who buried his son of the same name on the Antonine Wall, is a good specimen of the latter category, since the name is Semitic. If he had been a soldier he would surely have stated the fact. The Palmyrene Barathes, apparently a dealer in ensigns, is discussed in the chapter on slaves and freedmen. It is generally difficult to be certain, in this area, whether individuals named on tombstones or altars were soldiers or not. Only in the case of women is their civilian status unambiguous, and in many or indeed most cases they were probably soldiers' wives. This is explicit in the case of Aurelia Aia, from Salonae, buried at Carvoran, and it is likely enough in the case of Titullinia Pussitta, 'citizen from Raetia', buried at Netherby on her death at 35, even though her tombstone does not state who set it up.

There is a handful of persons with Greek names in the frontier area. As already stressed in the cases of Aurelia Eubia and Dionysius Fortunatus, this need not always mean the person was from the Greek-speaking part of the empire. But this is certain with the tombstone of the 16-year-old Hermes, from Commagene, which formed part of the province of Syria, and the epitaph is in passable Greek verse. The stone comes from Brough-under-Stainmore, where a large number of lead sealings have been found, suggesting that the place was the depot to which important packages, possibly including products from the lead-silver mines near Alston, were despatched. One need not suppose that Hermes was a relative or friend of a Greek clerk in the administrative bureau here, for he might easily have been the son of a trader attracted by the good prospects which such an establish-ment offered. As for Fla(viu)s Antigonus Papias, 'Greek citizen', as he is described on his Latin tombstone at Carlisle, recording his death at the aged of 60, he probably was a trader – he might have been a Christian, too, some have supposed, from the language of his epitaph, giving his age as 'more or less 60' (*plus minus LX*), in striking contrast to the frequently observed pagan concern for exactitude in these matters. Hermione, daughter of Quintus (her *gentilicium* is missing), who was responsible for two fine altars at Maryport, to Juno and 'the Valour of the Emperor', may have been an officer's wife, and was certainly a freeborn citizen as the filiation shows. A Greek speaking Roman citizen is on record at Maryport in the person of A. Egnatius Pastor. His Latin nomenclature would have concealed his origin, except that his altar, with a dedication in Greek to Asclepius, reveals him as a Greek doctor. Finally, there is a third possible Greek at Maryport, a woman named Sotera, buried by her husband Julius Senecianus – whose own name is typical for a Romanized Celt – 'in accordance with the condition of the place' (*pro condicione loci*) as the epitaph somewhat ambiguously states. Sotera, which is fairly common – it is the female form of *Soter*, meaning 'saviour' – might of course have been a slave's name, irrespective of origin, and Sotera might have been a freedwoman. There are certainly several examples from the frontier area of persons of servile or libertine status with Greek names; most are discussed in a later chapter, but attention must be drawn here to one case. An altar to an unknown deity, abbreviated by the letter E, from

Netherby, *castra exploratorum*, 'the Scouts, Fort' north of the western end of the Wall, was dedicated by a woman whose second name was Monime ('steadfast' in Greek). Her *gentilicium* is very hard to decipher, but the reading Javolena seems possible. If so, it must surely reflect a grant of citizenship arranged by the Flavian *iuridicus* of Britain, Javolenus Priscus, for the name is inordinately rare. It could then be postulated that Monime was a freedwoman of a Briton whose ancestor had obtained citizenship by this means in the early 80s of the first century. One final case of a person with a Greek name, Diodora the priestess of Astarte, attested at Corbridge, is reserved for discussion in a later chapter.

The largest category of persons in this area is that where only a single name is given. There are plenty with common Latin *cognomina* – names like Januarius, Maximus, Victor and Rufinus are represented by several specimens. But there are a good many examples of more outlandish names, definitely Celtic in some cases, presumably so in others; but several are unique; and there are likewise some rare Latin – or apparently Latin – *cognomina*. A tombstone at Maryport commemorated a 20-year-old man called Morirex, set up by 'heirs appointed in place of his sons' – a surprisingly technical Latin legal formula. A much simpler stone from the same place records the death of Rianorix. Both these names are Celtic, with the familiar suffix. No doubt it was because the termination -rix normally indicated a male name that a tombstone from Old Carlisle specified that the person commemorated, Tancorix, was a woman (*mulier*). There are some other good examples of Celtic compound names. A man called Enemnogenus was responsible for a crudely lettered altar to Mars, found at Greta Bridge on the Stainmore road. At Birrens an enigmatic slab reads: *Cistumuci lo. Mabomi*, which may perhaps mean 'Cistumucus' (gift) at the place of Mabomus', the latter name being a blundered version of Maponus. Half a dozen other dedications to this Celtic deity, in four cases equated with Apollo, all from the frontier district, combined with a place name in the Ravenna list, suggest that the cult-centre was probably in Dumfriesshire, at Loch*maben*. The other worshippers included the four Germans mentioned earlier in this chapter, the camp-prefect of the Sixth legion and two centurions, and a person rich enough to pay for a silver *lunula* found at Vindolanda. Cistumucus' crude inscription seems a little out of place in this group. Even more cryptic is a stone found somewhere in Northumberland, reading *Sucabo Cunovindus*. The latter is an acceptable compound name, but it is not clear whether Sucabus (?) is a deity or another person.

Two tombstones from Cumbria provide a good mixture of names. At Moresby, someone called Clanova was commemorated by a woman whose second name, Fontia, may perhaps have been intended as a Latin one. At Papcastle a single stone commemorates three dead, Apullio, aged 35, Sabina, aged 17, and Huctia, aged 47. Sabina is an ordinary Latin name, while the other two seem to be Celtic, although unattested in this form. Apullio and Huctia were doubtless Sabina's parents, the mother outliving the father by some years and her name and age being added to the stone last. A graffito on an early fourth-century cooking pot containing a cremation, found at Beckfoot in this same part of Cumbria, reads *Vrocatae*. The name is attractively interpreted as a derivation from the root *brocco-*, 'badger'.

One of the best samples of the humbler strata of the population is provided by the inscriptions from Brougham, where the main road south from Carlisle met routes running south-westward to Lakeland and east across Stainmore. Half a dozen little altars found here honour a local deity, whose name appears in various forms here and in the examples – over 20 of them – from other frontier sites, among which the version Belatucadrus, thought to signify 'bright shining one', predominates. His named votaries at Brougham were Audagus, Baculo, and Julianus: the last of these is straightforward enough, but it is hard to tell whether the first two were Celtic or aberrant versions of Latin names (Audacius, Baculus). A fourth person from Brougham may be identified with some probability as a fellow-worshipper of Belatucadrus. This is a man called Lunaris, whose name appears on the tombstone he set up to 'his dearest wife Pluma'. The wife's name, apparently the Latin word for 'feather', is unexampled but seems acceptable. Lunaris happens to be very rare, with less than 10 examples from the whole empire, three of them British. The best-known is the *sevir* of York and Lincoln recorded by the famous altar at Bordeaux from the year 237 (discussed in a later chapter). Apart from the Brougham stone, there is an altar set up at Carrawburgh on the Wall, honouring, not the nymph Coventina, to whom 14 dedications have been found at that place, but the god Belleticaurus, surely an idiosyncratic form of the god favoured at Brougham. In that case the men from the two places may be identical. Two other married couples from Brougham display unashamedly barbarian nomenclature on their simple Latin inscriptions. Annamoris and Ressona, father and mother of an unnamed boy, depicted him in a carved relief, cloaked and barefooted. A man called Talio commemorated his wife Nittiunis, on her death aged 40 years and seven months. Further stones from Brougham are unfortunately too fragmentary to give complete names. A man whose name began with M commemorated his brother Tittus M-, which can hardly be a misspelling of the *praenomen* Titus. On another stone the termination – orix survives, while Aur. C . . . vinda on another may have been a female form of the name cited earlier, Cunovindus, borne by a woman with the standard third-century *gentilicium* Aurelia. Finally, one may note Crescentinus, a young man of 18 commemorated by his father Vidaris: the latter's name is thought to be Germanic.

Other inscriptions from Brougham reflect the military character of the place, as would be expected – dedications to Mars and Victory, or to Mars alone, for example, one made by a soldier named Januarius from the Stratonician Cavalry. There is one inscription of an officer, whose name is missing, recording his promotion from commanding a cohort of Gauls to a military tribunate in the Upper German legion VIII Augusta. Another dedication to Mars is an elaborate inscription, now barely legible, but the man responsible had some connection with VI Victrix, and the words *ex Africa* probably give his origin. But in some ways the most interesting stone is the milestone honouring the emperor Postumus, misspelling three of his names but revealing, in the last two lines, that it was set up by the 'republic of the state of the Carvetii', *r.p.c. Car.* The abbreviated name *Car.* can be expanded with confidence on the basis of a tombstone from Old Penrith nearby, naming a local *senator* (councillor) *in c(ivitate) Carvetior(um)*, Fl(avius) Martius. Thus the civilian population at least of the western part of the frontier hinterland had acquired full local self-government by the later third century. The Carvetii, a name which seems to mean 'stag-people', perhaps had their administrative centre at Carlisle, and their territory may have comprised the Solway plain, Edenside, and Stainmore, if not Lakeland. Within the frontier districts the writ of the army no doubt continued to run, although the exact details of the relationship between the fort-garrisons and their commanders on the one hand and the *vicani*, or the council of the Carvetii, on the other, elude definition. The camp-followers from outside and the indigenous population, had from an early stage, it is clear, become inextricably entwined with the soldiers by ties of mutual interest and above all by intermarriage. It is fitting to terminate this chapter by reference to the earliest of the handful of inscriptions which attest to the corporate existence of the *vicani*. It comes from Carriden on the short-lived Antonine frontier in Scotland and is a dedication to Jupiter, Best and Greatest, by 'the *vikani* living at the fort of Velunias (*consi[s]tentes castel[lo] Veluniate)*'. The man who supervised the dedication was called Ael(ius) Mansuetus. A more fitting name would be hard to imagine, for his *gentilicium* is that of the emperor who had conceived the first linear frontier, Hadrian, while his *cognomen* means, in Latin, 'tamed'.

A record of work done on Hadrian's Wall by the 'century of Sorio'. The rough figure scratched below the name looks like a shrew-mouse, Latin *sorex*, presumably the centurion's personal 'trade-mark' (RIB 1821, Carvoran)

Chapter XI

The curial class and the urban population

The existence of at least four *coloniae* and one *municipium* in Britain is well attested, and other towns, such as Leicester, Chester, and, above all, London, probably acquired this status sooner or later as well. But the institutions of local govern-ment found in the Roman chartered towns were in due course installed, in the pacified areas, among the peregrine communities as well. Leading British *civi-tates*, (tribes, or states) in the lowland zone of the province, such as the Cantii, Coritani, and Dobunni, were probably released from direct military rule within a few years, and large parts of the military districts in the highland zone seem to have acquired the right to administer their own affairs in the end. Not all the territory of the province away from the vicinity of garrisons was handed back. Considerable areas were clearly taken over as imperial estates from the start, and these were added to by confiscations from time to time, for instance when client kingdoms were absorbed, and, of course, after political upheavals such as the rising of Boudica and the usurpation of Albinus. But, in the main, it suited the emperors to allow the provincials to administer themselves. In practice this meant government by the wealthy, upper classes of the provincial communities. They resumed the responsibility, away from the military districts, of maintaining internal law and order, and were now given the task of collecting one of the main sources of imperial revenue, the property tax.

To help to ensure the loyalty of these classes in the peregrine (non-Roman) *civitates*, the emperors, no doubt on the recommendation of the governors and other officials in most cases, but perhaps in response to direct petition in some, granted privileges, of which the most obvious and sought after was the citizen-ship. Only Verulamium, described as a *municipium* by Tacitus, may be regarded as a community that received this as a bloc grant; and, if his language is technical, this may mean that the city, or perhaps the people whose chief town Verulamium was, the Catuvellauni, received Latin status. In that case, only the annually elected magistrates would acquire full Roman franchise and the right to wear the toga, the *tria nomina*, and the full benefits of being a member of the ruling people. Unfortunately there does not appear to be a single member of the curial class of the Catuvellauni attested in the epigraphic record, although the fragments of commemorative slabs of Purbeck marble, on which a few letters only survive in each case, make it clear that some of them acquired the 'epigraphic habit'. It may be that the great inscription from the forum there, set up in the year 79 or 81, when Julius Agricola was governor, named one or more of the magistrates. It is so fragmentary that certainty is impossible, but in the last line the letters VE might refer either to Ve[rulamium] or to the [Catu]ve[llauni], and NATA could be part of a local official's name, such as Nata[lis]. There is very slightly more to be gleaned from the inscriptions of the four *coloniae* and a few of the peregrine *civi-tates* which were eventually to become Roman with the rest of the empire in 212.

There must have been considerable variation in the origins of the population in the four *coloniae*. At Camulodunum the first settlers were legionary veterans recruited by the 20s of the first century AD, who will have been predominantly Italian. A limited number of natives may have been enfranchised and admitted to citizenship of the *colonia*, and there may have been a fair sprinkling of resident aliens, *incolae*. Equally, the wives of many veterans were probably provincial, even if necessarily Roman citizens. But it must be remembered that the place had to be refounded after its destruction in 60 and the later citizen body of Camulodunum would be descended from settlers brought in in Nero's reign, presumably veterans of the XIVth and XXth legions. There may have been a rather greater number of provincials, from the western provinces, among them, than was the case at the first settlement, *deductio*, in the 40s. At Glevum, founded *c*. 97, and Lindum, where the *colonia* was created a little earlier, the veterans would have been men recruited into the army in the early 70s, some perhaps in the disturbed conditions of AD 68–70, when large numbers of provincials joined the legions. Hence the Italian element in the population would have been less dominant. In any case, since large numbers of the Italian legionaries came from the Celtic region of Italy, the former province of Gallia Cisalpina, the distinction between them and the legionaries drawn from the communities of the western provinces is perhaps rather artificial. The fourth *colonia*, Eburacum, evidently did not acquire this status until the early third century. By then the term had a diminished significance: the creation of a *colonia* did not involve actual settlement of veterans in a specially founded city, merely the grant of the title and rank to an existing town, in this case the community across the River Ouse opposite the fortress of VI Victrix. By this time, a high proportion of the legionaries had probably been recruited in Britain, not least from the other three *coloniae*, but also from the *civitates*. With the grant of universal Roman citizenship in 212, which coincided almost exactly with the grant of colonial status to Eburacum, the remaining free-born *peregrini* in the British province became Romans.

Given the overall paucity of epigraphic evidence from the civilian region, it is fitting that such scanty evidence for members of the curial class as there is comes mainly from the *coloniae*. Colchester, indeed, has not yet supplied a single example of a decurion or magistrate, but there is a fine tombstone there of a man who was probably a member of the colony's upper class, for he was a Roman knight, the only firmly recorded specimen from the island. His names are not even complete, but one of them was Macr-, Macer, Macrinus or Macrinius. His tombstone was erected by his widow Val(eria) Frontina and two men named Flor. Cogitatus and Flor. Fidelis, presumably his sons or freedmen, although their relationship to the dead man (who was apparently only 20) is not specified. If Cogitatus and Fidelis were connected with him in this way, his *gentilicium*, or his main one – he could well have been polyonymous – will have been Flor(ius), Flor(idius) or Flor(onius). At any rate, this name, and that of the widow, could perfectly well indicate descent from first-century veteran colonists. Another tombstone from Colchester might just possibly refer to another man of equestrian rank, but it is too fragmentary to determine whether he had commanded the auxiliary unit mentioned on the stone or was only a ranker in it. It is right to mention the possibility, however remote, that three prominent generals of the later Antonine period may have been natives of Colchester, M. Statius Priscus and the two Macrinii Vindices. All three were enrolled in the *tribus Claudia*, to which

Camulodunum belonged. Priscus and the younger Macrinius served as equestrian officers in Britain early in their career (and Priscus was governor of the
province for a brief spell in 161–162). The *gentilicium* Statius is attested for
Camulodunum in the first century, while the *eques Romanus* discussed above may
have been a Macrinius – and in any case, the nomenclature Macrinius Vindex
suggests origin in a Celtic region. It may be noted, further, that a third-century
equestrian officer, Q. Florius Maternus, who commanded the *coh. I Tungrorum* at
Housesteads, might perfectly well derive from a family of Florii at Colchester. At
all events, there is no reason to doubt that this *colonia* had the potential to generate
a few families with equestrian census by the second century, and such men, if they
proved useful officers in the wars of the 160s and 170s, could have obtained
senatorial rank by adlection (special enrolment). *Equites Romani* in Britain ought
to have been unusually well placed to obtain commissions in the army, in view of
the province's exceptionally large garrison.

At Lincoln, the only recorded decurion Aur(elius) Senecio has names which
indicate that his family's *civitas* could not have been earlier than the reign of
Antoninus Pius – the inscription is probably third century, in view of the
abbreviation *Aur.* and the absence of *praenomen*. An ancestor of his presumably
acquired membership of the colony's citizen body well after its foundation.
However, his wife Volusia Faustina (specifically described as a Lincoln woman,
c. Lind.) could well have been descended from a first-century veteran colonist.
Less certainty attaches to another woman named on the same stone, Claudia
Catiotuos, perhaps Senecio's second wife or his mother. The *cognomen* is Celtic,
and she might therefore be of British descent. But by the third century such
distinctions were probably long forgotten, and the families of the original settlers
may have been Celticized to a considerable extent. Other potential members of
the curial class at Lincoln may be noted. M. Minicius Mar[ce]l[linus?], chief
centurion of the Upper German legion XXII Primigenia, would certainly have
enjoyed a leading position in his colony if he chose to return to it. It is worth
noting that a man of the same names is now known to have been prefect of the
First *ala* of Britons in Dacia in the year 123. If he was an ancestor of the chief
centurion, the latter would be an example of a man entering the centurionate with
a direct commission. But the names are a little too common for certainty. C.
Antistius Frontinus, who describes himself as *curator ter*, 'supervisor for a third
time', on an altar which he dedicated at his own expense, may confidently be
regarded as a member of the colonial upper class, although it is impossible to say
what kind of curator he was. Both Minicius and Antistius, it should be noted,
have typically 'colonial' nomenclature.

There is a tombstone recorded at Bath of a decurion of Glevum, who died at the
age of 80, but unfortunately his names are missing. However, the names of several
magistrates appear to be recorded on building-tiles stamped by the council of the
colony, 'the republic of Gloucester', *r(es) p(ublica) G(levensis)*. One stamp has been
read as RPGQQIVLFLORETCCRSM. This can be interpreted as referring to
the *duoviri quinquennales* who took office every fourth year, as the equivalent of the
ancient censors of Rome, and were responsible, *inter alia*, for letting out contracts
for public works. The first name is clearly Jul(ius) Flor(us) – or some longer
cognomen such as Flor(entinus), or Flor(ianus). The last five letters CCRSM are
not readily intelligible. They might be an abbreviation of his colleague's names,
as they stand, but perhaps are a botched attempt at CORSIM, representing

e.g. Cor(nelius) Sim(ilis). Julius Florus and Cornelius Similis are certainly names of the type one expects to find in veteran colonies in a western province. Both could perfectly well be regarded as descendants of late first-century veterans. This does not apply to a third magistrate whose name is partially preserved on another Gloucester stamp as PAELFI . . . , P. Ael(ius) Fi[rmus], or perhaps Fi[dus], or Fi[delis]. The combination P. Aelius proclaims unequivocally the receipt of Roman citizenship from Hadrian. An ancestor of this man must have been admitted to the colony in the second century, as is the case with the Gloucester legionary M. Ulpius Quintus, from a family enfranchised by Trajan. Finally, there is a stamp reading RPG . . . ATTO . . . This may represent a magistrate called Attus, a rare *cognomen* probably adapted from a Celtic original. But it might equally be an abbreviation for At(ius) To(rquatus).

Three or four decurions are known at York, all presumably of the third century, and there is a satisfactory variety of nomenclature. Cla(udius) Florentinus is recorded on the tombstone which he erected to his father-in-law, Ant(onius) Gargilianus, who died at the age of 56 and was a Roman knight, ex-prefect of the VIth legion. Gargilianus himself, as he evidently retired at York, may conceivably have derived from there. Flavius Bellator is attested by his own tombstone, giving his age as 29. His *cognomen*, meaning 'warrior' in Latin, looks at first sight rather appropriate for a town like York, dominated by its legion, but it was probably a Latinized version of a Celtic name. The status of a third decurion has to be deduced from the description of his widow, Ael(ia) Severa, as *honesta femina* 'honourable lady', which appears to have become an unofficial title for women of the curial class. Her own name indicates descent from someone enfranchised by Hadrian. A fourth inscription, a fragmentary dedication to Hercules, evidently recording the restoration of a temple, may have been set up by two officials of the colony, one named T. Perpet[uius? . . .] and the other Aetern[ius . . .]. Both these *nomina*, if that is what they are, are of the 'fabricated' Celtic type, in contrast to those of the other decurions.

This certainly applies to the nomenclature of T. Tammon[ius] Vitalis, *Saeni Tammon[i fil.*], 'son of Saen(i)us Tammon(i)us', possibly a decurion or magistrate of the Atrebates at Silchester. He had clearly converted his native name Tammon(i)us to a Roman style *gentilicium*, instead of adopting the *nomen* of the emperor, governor, or other patron, when he received the franchise. The latter course had been taken by M. Ulpius Januarius, the aedile who paid for the stage of the theatre at Brough on Humber in 139 or soon after. His first two names demonstrate that he or his father had been enfranchised by Trajan. However this may be, he was aedile not of the *civitas* of the Parisi, but only of one of its communities, Petuaria.

The only clear case of a decurion of one of the *civitates* comes from the very fringe of the province, close to the frontier, at Old Penrith in Cumbria. Here Martiola buried her father Fl(avius) Martius, councillor of quaestorian rank in the *civitas* of the Carvetii, *sen(atori) in c(ivitate) Carvetiorum qu(a)estorio*, who died at the age of 45. The Carvetii, originally part of the Brigantes, it would seem, may not have been relieved from military rule until the third century, after the division of Britain. The name Flavius might indicate descent from a native of the area enfranchised during the conquest of northern England in the 70s, or from an auxiliary veteran who had settled near his old station. Martius and Martiola, names derived from the war-god Mars, seem appropriate for this part of the province.

A sprinkling of other individuals could be mentioned, who might have been members of the province's upper class. The two Tammonii at Silchester, one of whom has already been mentioned, and M. Sabinius Victor at the same town, were certainly well off to judge from their inscriptions. Flavia Victorina, the wife of T. Tam(monius) Victor, may also be included in this group. A number of those attested by inscriptions of superior quality at Bath must also have been *curiales*. Some of the individuals recorded by inscriptions or graffiti at villa sites surely fell into this category also. Discussion of these name is reserved for the chapter on country-dwellers. Other townspeople are treated below.

One cannot do a great deal more than list the known cases of other town-dwellers, so limited is the evidence. Some of those attested by inscriptions in urban contexts have already been treated in their capacity as soldiers or veterans, and others will be mentioned in the chapters on merchants and craftsmen, and elsewhere. But it will help to give some impression of the composition of the literate class, at any rate, in the main centres of population, if we examine some of this evidence here. Many cases may be dealt with summarily. Exeter and Winchester, for example, are effectively blanks on the map, apart from a soldier on special assignment at the latter. Yet Dorchester, the chief town of the Duro-triges that lay between these two, demonstrates what may have been lost and remain to discover, with its single fine, if now poorly preserved, marble tomb-stone of a man called Carinus, whose widow Romana and children Rufinus, Carina, and Avita proudly call him *civi* [*R*]*omano*, suggesting that he had acquired citizenship relatively early, when it was still prized. Canterbury, which was in one of the richest areas of Britain, is even more unrewarding, although the fragmentary marble tombstones indicate what was once there. None is complete enough to supply a name, and the graffiti are meagre: one supplies the name Agessilus, possibly Greek, as is the other, Nican[or?]. Chichester offers a little more. The inscription of the 'guild of craftsmen' is discussed in a later chapter, and there are a few informative tombstones, albeit still fragmentary, one with two Roman names, Catia and Censorin . . ., another with the imperial *gentilicium* Aelia and the enigmatic Cauva, either a barbarous name or an ethnic. There is also an instructive altar to the 'Spirit (of the place)', set up by Lucullus son of Ammin(i)us. Lucullus, ostensibly Roman, is probably a Celtic name derived from that of the god Lug, disguised in Latin form, while his father's name is that of a British prince from the pre-conquest period. In other words this is an example of the first stage in the Romanizing process. Further north, three of the chief towns of *civitates* on the fringe of the military zone, Caerwent of the Silures, Wroxeter of the Cornovii, and Aldborough of the Brigantes, offer a poor harvest. At Caerwent there is the mid-second century dedication by M. Nonius Romanus, perhaps an immigrant, but no trace of the Silures; at Wroxeter the family tombstone of Placida and Deuccus is the only clear specimen of the civilian population; and at Aldborough there is a very modest tombstone of a woman called Felicula whose husband conceals his identity behind the initials C.M.P., and part of a more elaborate funerary monument to an Aurelius or Aurelia. Caistor, Venta of the Iceni, Boudica's people, offers only Jovinus and Justus. Leicester, chief town of the Coritani, makes a slightly better showing, with its soldier Novantico, enfranchised to become a M. Ulpius, and a few graffiti revealing the presence there of persons called Civilis, Martina, Primus and Bitudacus – a satisfying mixture of Celtic and Roman nomenclature, the old and new. A little more exciting is the four lines scratched on a piece of pottery: *Verecunda ludia Lucius gladiator,* 'Verecunda, actress, Lucius, gladiator'.

The remaining *civitas*-capitals, Silchester and Cirencester, are somewhat more informative. Silchester's known inhabitants have mostly been treated earlier in the chapter, as possible *curiales*. Two names remain to be mentioned. First there is a lady named Venusta, owner of a pewter bowl (*vas*), bearing her name. The second was a certain Senicianus, whose name is found on a gold-signet ring. The stone has a female bust, labelled Venus, the pagan goddess of love, but Senicianus himself seems to have been a Christian, for the ring bears the motto 'Senicianus, mayst thou live in God!' (*Seniciane vivas in de(o)*). The name is not uncommon in Celtic areas of the empire, but it is reasonable to suppose that the Silchester man may be the same person as the Senicianus cursed as the suspected thief of a ring on a lead *defixio* tablet found at Lydney, dedicated to the god Nodens by the ring's irate former owner Silvianus. Cirencester offers, apart from the military tombstones discussed in an earlier chapter, a small selection of civilians. Sabidius Maximus, bearer of a fine rare Latin *gentilicium,* might be a centurion of II Augusta on leave. There are several common Roman names, Julia Casta on a tombstone, Lucanus, Martia[lis], [Mi]nervalis, Valerius, and Vitalis furnished by graffiti. Philus, son of Cassavus, is an immigrant from Gaul buried here, perhaps a trader. Aurelius Euticianus, who buried his small son Igennus, might be another, of Greek or freedman origin. There are several Celts, who may be assumed to be Dobunnian, Nemmonius Verecundus, who died at 75, Cast. Castrensis, named on another tombstone, Comitinu[s] who buried someone called Petronius, and Attius Ch[. . .]vus, dedicator of a statue to a Genius. P. Vitalis, and his wife P. Vicana whom he buried, seem to flout the rules of Latin nomenclature, but P. perhaps stood for a common *gentilicium.* Finally, there is the sculptor Sulinus, also attested at Bath, discussed in the chapter on craftsmen.

There is a little more to say on some of the towns examined at the beginning of this chapter, although nothing can be added in the case of Gloucester. Nor is there much more to offer on Lincoln apart from its military tombstones and its handful of possible *curiales*. Graffiti provide a few informative names – the Celtic Eberesto and the Latin Lucret[ius] and Flavinus. The Greek Fl. Helius buried by his wife Fl. Ingenua was perhaps a trader, and so too may Sacer, son of Bruscius, a Senonian Gaul, have been, who was buried with his wife Carssouna and son Quintus. Their tombstone, with *Dis Manibus* written out in full, presumably dates to the early second century, soon after the *colonia* was founded. York, where civil town and legionary fortress long co-existed, affords a good number of inscriptions which may well belong to men from VI Victrix and their families, even where this is not explicit. One can only indicate the presence of Julii, Ulpii, and Aurelii, common imperial *gentilicia,* to go with the Claudius, Flavius, and Aelia attested among the *curiales* mentioned earlier, and mention some of the other less common specimens. The total number is not large, admittedly, compared with cities like Aquincum. But it is satisfying to note several Greeks, or bearers of Greek *cognomina,* Vol. Iren[aeus], [V]al. Theodorianus and his mother (A)emi(lia) Theodora, from Nomentum, near Rome, Andronica, wife of Ulpius Felix, Anto(nius) Step(h)anus and his wife Eglecta. Celtic names are present too, M. Aurinius Simnus along with Mantinia Maerica and Candida Barita on an elaborate tombstone being the best, but one should not neglect the simple *cognomina* Brica and Velva borne by two women called Julia. Finally, there are a few less common Italian *gentilicia*, Agrius, Corellius, Crepereius, and Rustius. One suspects that these four may have been legionaries or veterans.

Verulamium may conveniently be taken next, since it has fewer names by far than the remaining towns. All are supplied by graffiti. There is one possible Greek name, Andoc . . . and a few Latin ones, Julius Primus being the only definite Roman citizen. Nothing much can be said about the rest, Lupinus, Marcus, Marinus, Karinus, Similis and two women, Sabina and Tacita. Only Octobrianus is at all uncommon. Finally, there is a name on a pewter plate, presumably fourth century in date, Viventia Victorici (wife of Victoricius). Bath is in a different category from the other towns, as a spa and cult-centre, which inevitably means that a high proportion of the persons on record here were visitors. The military men among them have mostly been discussed in an earlier chapter, and other persons will be dealt with under slaves and freedmen, and craftsmen. Of the few that remain one may single out Rusonia Avent[i]na, a woman of the Mediomatrici in Gallia Belgica, whose tombstone was erected by her heir, L. Ulpius Sestius. There is also a group of men particularly associated with the goddess Sulis, and something more needs to be said about them.

Most pagan cults did not require full-time priests, set apart from other worshippers of the gods. Men and women of all ranks could combine the holding of a priestly office with their secular role. A senator who governed Britain might in the course of a varied career of public service become, for example, a *pontifex* or *augur* of the Roman people. Some of the decurions of the British communities must have been *flamines* of the imperial cult. But there were some major shrines which attracted devotees in greater numbers and these were provided with priests and priestesses to administer them, conduct sacrifices, and interpret the will of the deity. Several such temples can be detected in Britain, but only at Bath is there evidence for the priesthood. C. Calpurnius Receptus is described on his tombstone as *sacerdos deae Sulis,* priest of the goddess Sulis, and L. Marcius Memor who made a dedication to the goddess, is called *harusp(ex)*. The *haruspices,* originally an Etruscan priesthood, whose task included the examination of sacrificial entrails, had become a regular feature in Roman communities all over the empire. Marcius Memor might therefore have been a *haruspex* of one of the *coloniae,* but since he does not specify this it may be presumed that he was attached to the service of Sulis Minerva. Two other men are named on fragments of an elaborate inscription recording rebuilding, [C]laudius Ligur and C. Protaciu[s . . .]. They might have been priests, but it is more probable that they were officials of the *col(l)egium* or guild also mentioned on the inscription. It is striking that all four men associated with the cult of the goddess have thoroughly Roman names. Claudius Ligur might theoretically have been descended from a Briton enfranchised under Claudius or Nero, but the *cognomen* is characteristic of southern Gaul and northern Italy. The *gentilicia* Calpurnius and Marcius were fairly common and it is just possible that the ancestors of these two were Britons who had obtained the franchise through the good offices of Roman officials with these names. But Protacius is a rare *nomen* of Etruscan derivation and this man at least should be the descendant of an Italian immigrant, presumably a first-century legionary veteran or trader.

A brief digression, at this point, is convenient, to review other evidence for pagan priests in Roman Britain, for it is sparse indeed. Priests of a different type from those of Sulis were the proselytising votaries of eastern deities. Jupiter Dolichenus, a Syrian god, was one such, as may be seen from a few dedications set up 'by the god's command'. The god's will was no doubt transmitted to the worshipper by a priest, but no British examples are on record. At Corbridge two fine altars bear Greek inscriptions. One has a hexameter verse recording its dedication to the goddess Astarte by Pulcher. The other also has a verse inscription, in honour of Heracles of Tyre, the Phoenician Melqart, by Diodora, 'high priestess', ἀρχιέρεια. Pulcher's name is of course Latin and as he is not called priest he may simply have been a worshipper. But it must be assumed that Diodora presided over a temple of the deities of Tyre and Sidon.

A few other altars include the letters SAC in their dedication, but in each case this probably means *sac(rum)* 'sacred to' rather than *sac(erdos)* 'priest'. The only other pagan priest firmly attested in Britain is on a little altar found somewhere on the line of Hadrian's Wall, dedicated to the goddess Nemesis by Apollonius. His name too is Greek, although the brief inscription is in Latin, and calls him *sacerdos*. Elsewhere in Britain this deity seems to have been worshipped in her capacity as goddess of the gladiatorial arena. But during the later empire she began to acquire a wider role as a universal goddess, 'queen of the Cosmos', regarded with particular dislike by Christians. How she was presented to the frontier people of Britain by the priest Apollonius must remain uncertain.

Before we turn to the last two towns, one further example of the epigraphy of Bath may be cited, a leaden curse tablet found in the reservoir of Roman date under the King's Bath of the Georgian Spa. The unknown who flung it in the water was perhaps a jilted lover, the person he was deprived of was called Vilbia, an otherwise unknown name, presumably Celtic, and no fewer than nine individuals are cursed as possibly responsible: three women, Velvinna, Germanilla, and Jovina; and six men, Exsupereus, Severinus, Agustalis, Comitianus, Catus, and Minianus. Of course, neither they nor Vilbia nor the aggrieved unknown were necessarily inhabitants of Bath itself. None the less, they provide a useful insight into the mixture of nomenclature, with Latin names slightly dominant, that was probably common in southern Britain of the third century.

We have already had a look at some members of the upper class at Colchester, other persons recorded here have been dealt with in chapters on the military, and others again are more appropriately reserved for treatment in later chapters. Here it only remains to note some of the different categories of nomenclature at the colony. There is an incomer or visitor from the Cantii, Similis, son of Attius, and other Celts include Aesubilinus, patron of a freedman; Vassedo, from a graffito; most of the Colchester potters of the second century; a coppersmith, Cintusmus; and a Caledonian, Lossio Veda, in the third century. Only three Greek names are known so far, Hermes, who dedicated to Silvanus, and two from bronze signets, Pomp(eius) Nic. and P.F. Hyginus – but one may note a man whose names are missing, the centurion of the XXth buried at Colchester, who had served in at least three other legions earlier, and was a native of Nicaea in Bithynia. Finally, there is a small selection of straightforward Latin names, Attic[us], Cata, Lucianus, Paratus, Aur. Sat(urninus), Cominius Familiaris, and, choicest of them all, P. Oranius Facilis.

Last among the towns comes London, appropriately the best endowed with inscriptions. There is a wide range, including official and private dedications, tombstones, both civil and military, and a good range inscribed on materials other than stone. The latter range from the famous graffito, 'Austalis has been wandering off on his own every day for a fortnight' to the more modest statement on a pot, 'I belong to Gaius' (*Gai sum peculiaris*). Two lead tablets curse T. Egnatius Tyranus and P. Cicereius Felix, in a restrained way, and Tretia Maria (perhaps really called Maria Tertia) in the most virulent fashion. The writing-tablets provide a small insight into the business life of the city, as does a leaden consignment tag. The persons named on these, and the craftsmen known from tools and other objects found in London, are dealt with in later chapters. Pride of place among the stone inscriptions must go to the tombstone of the famous procurator Classicianus, discussed in Chapter II, and to the dedication by the governor M. Martiannius Pulcher, consular legate, presumably of Upper Britain, who restored a temple of Isis in the third century. His remarkable otherwise unmatched *gentilicium* is an excellent specimen of the fabricated Celtic type, derived from the *cognomen* Martianus. Several of the civilian tombstones of London must commemorate immigrants, presumably traders of some kind. A. Alfid. Pomp. Olussa, who died at 70, was apparently 'born at Athens', if that is what *na. Atheni.* means. His first two names are clear enough, A. Alfid(ius); but the remainder is less straightforward. It may be *Pomp(tina tribu)*, with *Olussa* as a *cognomen*; but *Pomp,* might be a second *gentilicium*, Pomp(eius); or the *cognomen* might be Pompolussa. At all events, the lettering and the formula *H.S.E.* combine to date his presence in London to the first century AD. Another presumed expatriate settled in London is T. Licinius Ascanius. His funerary formula, *dis manib(us)*, although found on the monument of Classicianus who died in the 60s, did not become common in Britain until the end of the first century, after which it was soon abbreviated to *D.M.* Grata, daughter of Dagobitus, and her husband Solinus who buried her with this formula, probably belong to the second century, and they are very probably Britons. The woman's name is Latin (meaning 'welcome'), her father's Celtic, as that of her husband may also be. Two final stones will suitably illustrate Roman nomenclature of the third century. On a slab of imported marble a woman called Aur. Eucarpia commemorated her six year old son, M. Aur. Eucarpus; and on an impressive oolite sarcophagus Valerius Superventor and Valerius Marcellus honoured the memory of their father Valerius Amandinus. The Aurelii are presumably Greeks, who have the 'universal' *gentilicium* distributed to all peregrines by Caracalla. The origin of the other people is unclear – Amandinus comes from Amandus, 'worthy of love', Marcellus is one of the commoner *cognomina,* and Valerius the commonest of all non-imperial *gentilicia.* Superventor, however (if it is really one name, and not two persons, Super and Ventor) is otherwise only known to have been borne by a bishop in late antiquity. In the fourth-century historian Ammianus the word denotes a variety of shock troops.

Chapter XII
Merchants

According to Caesar, on the eve of his first invasion in 55 BC Britain was largely unknown, even to the Gauls: no one had occasion to go there except for merchants, *mercatores*, and even they did not penetrate inland; and those that he summoned for cross-examination could not tell him much. However this may be – and one suspects that many avoided the conference and that some who came were reticent – there is plenty of evidence for lively contact between the island and the mainland in the century between the invasions. With the Claudian conquest large new markets were opened; merchants were needed not only to sell Roman or Gallic goods to the natives, but to supply the great army of occupation. Britain had always had goods to export in return. But the identification of individual traders, or firms, is not easy. Not many individuals can be found who may be securely labelled as *mercatores* or *negotiatores*, 'businessmen' even though their presence is certain from the mass of imported goods, notably pottery, and containers for wine and oil. One can, of course, locate the sources of supply for samian pottery and amphoras, but it would be beyond the scope of the present work to attempt an analysis of the Gaulish makers of *terra sigillata* or the Spanish oil producers. On the other hand, the potters who made mortaria within Britain are best dealt with in a later section, as craftsmen, even if they may reasonably be regarded as businessmen too.

Another group difficult to categorize is the oculists, whose names and prescriptions are found carved on small stones, in reverse, to impress on salves or ointments. It is impossible to tell whether these *signacula* can be taken as evidence for the men there named being apothecaries or pharmacists, selling their wares. The names may merely represent the man who originally made up the prescription. Still, the examples found in Britain – well over 20 – indicate that these preparations were advertised under names that mostly have a thoroughly western ring to them. There are eight Julii, several other colourless names, such as L. Val(erius) Latinus, Fl. Secundus, and M. Vitel(lius) Cres(cens), and two very Celtic specimens, C. Silvius Tetricus and T. Vindac(ius) Ariovistus. There are only a few Greek ones, surprisingly enough, since the Greeks rather dominated medical practice in the Roman world. It may be mentioned, in parenthesis, that the great Greek doctor of the Antonine period, Galen, praises an eye-salve prescribed by a doctor in the British fleet named Axios (or 'a British doctor named Stolos') – even he need not have been Greek, since Axius was a good old Italian *gentilicium* as well as a Greek adjective used as a name.

If Britain were epigraphically more fertile, one might hope to have copious evidence for *negotiatores* of all sorts from abroad, both before and after the conquest, of the kind found at sites like the Magdalensberg in Noricum. As it is, one is merely tantalized by hints, like that provided by three inscriptions at Silchester set up by the 'guild of immigrants resident at Calleva', *collegium peregrinorum consistentium Callevae*. One of them preserves the name of a man called

Atticus, whom we may no doubt think of as a wealthy incomer, engaged in trade. Various persons named on the more elaborate non-military tombstones and sarcophagi at London may also belong to this category; and one inscription from there may refer to [*navi*]*cular*[*ii*], 'shippers'. In AD 60 London was already, 'not marked, to be sure, with the title of *colonia*, but exceedingly busy with large numbers of merchants and shipments of goods' (*copia negotiatorum et commeatuum maxime celebre*). Not many of these *negotiatores* have left a trace, although the early potters, to be considered presently, must be included among them. A generation later, in the reign of Domitian, a writing tablet refers to a sum of money owed by one Crescens, who seems to have been a client or business associate of the writer. A lead tag found at London evidently represents a seal on a consignment of goods, that had been checked and found to be 'undamaged', *illaesi*; *Cillentici*, written after it, could represent the name of an employee of the shipper, the place of origin, or a description of the goods. A hint of a slave-market is provided by the writing-tablet in which Rufus, son of Callisunus, instructs Epillicus to sell a girl. But it is really only when we reach the early third century that we come across a group of merchants whose names and identity have something to tell us. Two inscriptions from York name the shipper M. Verec. Diogenes, a Biturigan, from central Gaul, south of the upper Loire; his wife, Julia Fortunata, was from Sardinia. He himself, while having a Celtic *gentilicium*, and using a Celtic word to describe his profession, *morit*(*ex*), was probably a freedman, to judge from his Greek *cognomen* and his membership of the *seviri Augustales* of York. Although he might have been in business shipping goods from Bourges to north Britain it is perhaps likelier that he was trading with the Rhineland. The only other man to call himself a *moritex*, C. Aurelius Verus, 'shipper in the British trade', *negotiator Britannicianus moritex*, is found at Cologne, where he made a dedication to Apollo. Persons engaged in trade called Verecundinius, Verecunius, and Vercund(ius) are attested both at Cologne and at Voorburg in Holland. Further down the Rhine, at Kastel opposite Mainz, a merchant from Britain, *ex* [*provinc*]*ia Bri*[*tannia*], named Fufidius, is recorded.

The best evidence comes from Domburg on the Dutch coast, where seamen and traders, among others, paid vows to a deity called Nehalennia. Several of the altars found there refer to trade with Britain. M. Secund. Silvanus is known from two identically worded dedications to the goddess, made 'for the safe consignment of his wares' – which were breakable, for he was a 'pottery exporter', to or from Britain, probably the former, a *negotiator cretarius Britannicianus*. Several other men attested at Domburg may be connections of his, L. Secundinius Moderatus, for example, and T. Calvisius Secundinus. He was pretty clearly from a trading family, either of Secundii or Secundinii. These men have the fabricated *gentilicia* so characteristic of the region. Both sets of names derive from Latin originals, but the Domburg dedications include a fine set of purely Celtic Roman nomenclature, of which Ascattinius Rascua is perhaps the prime example. For direct links with Britain the best case is that of Placidus, son of Viducus, a Veliocassian – from the people whose centre was at Rouen. He calls himself a 'British trader' on his altar to Nehalennia, but, interesting though that may be, he would not have stood out had it not been for the discovery of the fine inscription, set up in AD 221, at York; 'L. Viducius Placidus, of the Veliocasses', paid for the construction of 'an arch and a temple' in the city. Once again he calls himself 'merchant', *negotiator*, although what comes after – perhaps specifying the commodity he dealt in, is lost. Of particular value is the fact that he is another case of the idiosyncratic Celtic practice of nomenclature. On his altar at Domburg he calls himself Placidus, son of Viducus; at York, where he needed to describe himself in more formal terms, his father's name is converted into a *gentilicium*, Viducius. We cannot tell what the father's *gentilicium* had been, and if Placidus had a son, he may well have called himself Placidius rather than Viducius. Some of the merchants recorded at Domburg were doubtless shipping goods from the coast – such as salt from the lands of the Morini and Menapii – up the Rhine; others presumably traded with London and the south-eastern ports of Britain. Another *negotiator Britannicianus* at Domburg was apparently a freedman, called Arisenius Marius. But the Viducius Placidus inscription illustrates graphically the links between York and the Rhineland which archaeology had already detected. The frequent liaison between Lower Germany and Britain, seen in the careers of governors like Nepos and Urbicus and Antistius Adventus, and rein-forced by frequent movements of troops, must have made trade between the two areas fruitful.

There were, however, other routes in operation at this time. An altar found at Bordeaux dated to AD 237 is described as one 'that he had vowed when he set out from Eboracum' by its dedicator M. Aur(elius) Lunaris. He calls himself a *sevir Augustalis* of the colonies of York and Lincoln in the province of Lower Britain' on the inscription, to the goddess Tutela Boudig(a), whose second name has an unmistakably British ring to it, recalling the rebel Queen; and the altar is made of millstone grit. Since he does not specify an origin – and M. Aur. is too common, Lunaris too rare, to provide clues – it may perhaps be assumed that he was a Briton by birth and domicile; as a *sevir* he is likely to have been a freedman, as was suggested for Verec. Diogenes. The other 'merchant dealing with Britain' named at Bordeaux was a Treveran, from the Moselle valley, L. Solimarius Secundinus, who was buried there. In neither case can we be at all certain what the merchan-dise carried was. It is natural to think of claret, or its ancient equivalent, going from Aquitaine to York, but there is no evidence.

Two other cases, from the frontier region, may be mentioned. [Ba]rathes of Palmyra, who died at Corbridge at the age of 68, and is presumably the Pal-myrene Barates who buried his British wife at South Shields, is described on his tombstone as *vexila(rius)*. It is reasonable to suppose that he was a 'trader in ensigns' rather than a 'standard-bearer', for otherwise his unit's name would have been given; or if he had retired – and at that age he would have – he should be called *ex vexila(rio)*. *Vexilla*, flags, may have been only part of his stock in trade; but he should have had plenty of customers for them in the Wall area. The other man's name is only partly preserved as well; the termination -onianus is rather too common to allow restoration. He is known from a dedication-slab at the western end of the Wall, Bowness on Solway, with six lines of verse, praying the deities whom he had honoured to confirm his prayers by granting him a pro-fit – in which case he will gild the lettering of his poem. Presumably he was trading across the frontier, perhaps even across the Irish Sea. Tacitus tells us that the means of access to Ireland, and her harbours, were known to Agricola from merchants who had traded there. A curious piece of evidence, suggesting a Roman merchant ship swept off course in a storm, came up in a fishing net 150 miles off the west coast of Ireland, a Roman cooking pot with a graffito on it, C. PISCI FAGI. The name Fagus recurs on a little altar at Lugdunum Convenarum in Aquitania, dedicated to the local god Bonxus; Piscius was doubtless a fabricated *gentilicium*. Piscius Fagus may have been a Roman merchant seaman, improbable though the name may sound.

Although the men so far discussed constitute the sum total of identifiable merchants in Britain during the Roman period, one may infer that a good many other known persons were traders of some kind. This is particularly the case with immigrants who do not specify that they are soldiers. Philus, son of Cassavus, a Sequanian (from the Besançon area), who died at 45, is portrayed on his tombstone, found near Cirencester, as a civilian, in a hooded cloak. Other men, apparently civilians, who could be traders, include the Treveran Peregrinus, son of Secundus, dedicator of an altar at Bath, and M. Nonius Romanus, probably also a Treveran, to judge from his choice of *Lenus* as an epithet for Mars on the altar he set up at Caerwent in 152. Men who are described as Greeks, such as Fl. Helius at Lincoln and Fl. Antigonus Papias at Carlisle, may be regarded as likely to have been engaged in trade. The same consideration applies to Salmanes, who buried his 15-year-old son, also Salmanes, at Auchendavy on the Antonine Wall. It is easy to believe that a bearer of this name, clearly Semitic, was in Scotland as a trader. The Hamian archers, a Syrian cohort, were stationed on the Scottish Wall at this time; but if the elder Salmanes had been in their ranks he would be expected to have said so – it could more plausibly be suggested that he had followed the Hamii to Britain to cater for their tastes in food or other commodities. Some of the fairly numerous other persons with Greek or eastern names may also have fallen into the category of traders; but the above examples will suffice to make the point. As a final example of a possible immigrant merchant one might take, instead, Lossio Veda, grandson or nephew (*nepos*) of Vepogenus, the Caledonian whose dedication, on a bronze plate, to 'Mars Medocius of the Campeses and the Victory of Our Emperor Severus Alexander', was found at Colchester. That he gives, not his filiation, but the name of the person whose *nepos* he was, suggests that this *Caledo* was Pictish; Vepogenus would be his mother's brother. No reason for his apparent presence at Colchester is given, but since he paid for the dedication himself, *de suo*, perhaps he was a merchant (a slave-trader, for example). But he might equally well have been a mercenary in Roman service, or a noble hostage.

Other persons who were undoubtedly engaged in trade are best dealt with under the category of craftsmen, for it is as makers rather than sellers that they are recorded. One further category of businessmen which deserves a mention is dealt with more fully in the discussion of slaves and freedmen, namely the contractors who worked the lead-mines. One should note, too, the solitary but not very informative stamp from a copper ingot found in north Wales: SOCIO ROMAE, and, in smaller letters between the two words, NAT.SOL. This may be taken to represent a partnership, *socii*, based at Rome; and *Nat. Sol.* might be the local agent – Nat(alius) Sol(lers), for example. But numerous other interpretations are possible.

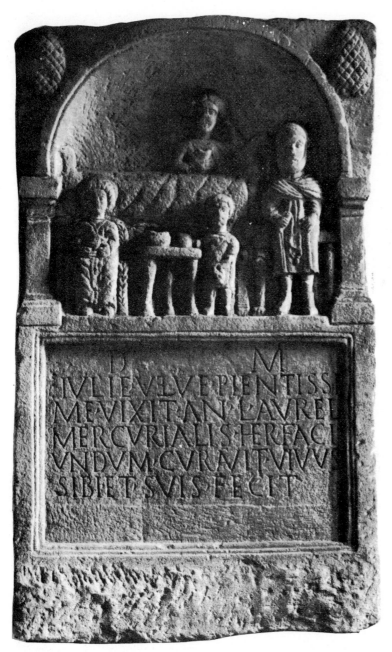

Tombstone of Julia Velva.

The dead woman Julia Velva, 'lived most dutifully for fifty years' and was commemorated by 'her heir, Aurelius Mercurialis, who made [the tomb] for himself and his family in his own lifetime'. Mercurialis, whose relationship with the dead woman is not specified, is presumably the bearded man wearing tunic, cloak and boots, while the smaller figures will be the members of his family, portrayed in front of Velva, who reclines on the couch with a cup in her hand. (RIB 688)

Centurial stones from Hadrian's Wall.

Five examples are known of the centurion Lousius Suavis' working party. His *nomen* is a good specimen of a Celtic 'fabricated' name. (RIB 1499)

The name of the second centurion, Sorio, is otherwise unrecorded and may be Celtic, but the rough drawing below appears to be intended as a shrew-mouse, Lat. *sorex*, perhaps Sorio's 'trade-mark'. (RIB 1821)

A·PLATORIO·A·F
SERG·NEPOTI
APONIO·ITALICO
MANILIANO
C·LICINIO·POLLIONI
COS·AVGVRI·LEGAT·AVG
PRO·PRAET·PROVINC·BRI
TANNIAE·LEG·PRO·PR·PRO
VINC·GERMANINFERIOR
LEG·PRO·PR·PROVINC·THRAC
LEG·LEGION·I·ADIVTRICIS
QVAEST·PROVINC·MACED
CVRAT·VIARVM·CASSIAE
CLODIAE·CIMINIAE·NOVAI
TRAIANAE·CANDIDATO·DIVI
TRAIANI·TRIB·MIL·LEG·XXII
PRIMIGEN·P·F·PRAET·TRIB
PLEB·III·VIR·CAPITALI
PATRONO
D   D

For translation of Platorius Nepos inscription see page 213.

Above A centurion of the XXth legion.

M. Aurelius Nepos died at the age of 50 and was buried by his wife, who does not give her name. The space left below her figure shows that her intention was that her own details should be added after her own death. (RIB 491)

Left A centurion from the invasion army.

M. Favonius Facilis was buried at Colchester in the years immediately following the conquest of AD 43. His name and tribe, Pollia, indicate that he was an Italian. He was presumably unmarried, since it was his freedmen who set up the tombstone. (RIB 200)

An NCO of the XXth legion.

Caecilius Avitus of Merida in Spain, died at the age of 34 after 15 years' service, holding the rank of *optio* (deputy centurion). (RIB 492)

A veteran of the VIth legion and his family.

C. Aeresius Saenus commemorates his wife Flavia Augustina and infant children. In the Celtic fashion his son's *nomen* is 'fabricated' from the father's *cognomen* Saenus. (RIB 685).

A building inscription from Hadrian's Wall.

This stone from milecastle 38 records that this work 'of the emperor Hadrian' was constructed by the IInd legion under the orders of A. Platorius Nepos, the governor, here referred to by his first three names only, in contrast to the marble statue base from Aquileia. (RIB 1638).

A fourth-century mosaic from Hampshire.

The god Bacchus, depicted in the centre, indicates that the owner of this villa at Thruxton was a pagan. His name, Quintus Natalius Natalinus, is a good specimen of the 'fabricated' nomenclature favoured in the Celtic regions. The last two words 'et Bodeni' are probably an extra name, or *signum,* rather than a reference to a group of people (as implied by the restoration *fecerunt* at the bottom left).

Opposite above left A Thracian cavalryman.

As was common with non-citizen soldiers, the dead man had two names, a Roman one, Rufus, and a native – Thracian – one, Sita. He died after 22 years' service at the age of 40, and was buried at Gloucester in the first century AD. (RIB 121)

Opposite below A Thracian cavalryman at Colchester.

Longinus Sdapeze, son of Matygus, had two names, a Roman and a native one, like many non-citizen soldiers. He came from Sardica – the modern Sofia – and was buried in the years immediately following the conquest of AD 43. (RIB 201)

Above The wife of a civil servant.

The 19-year-old Claudia Martina is commemorated at London by her husband Anencletus, who reveals his status by the expression *provinc.*, meaning 'slave of the province', or of the 'provincial council', the body to which each of the British states sent representatives to conduct annual ceremonies of emperor-worship. Anencletus, whose name is a Greek word meaning 'blameless', was not necessarily of Greek origin – it was traditional to give slaves Greek names. The fact that his wife was a free woman and a citizen indicates the superior status of slaves whose owners were not private individuals (slaves of the emperors were naturally of even higher status). (**RIB** 21)

An altar from Bordeaux.

This stone was made of millstone grit, presumably from Yorkshire, and would have travelled as ballast on the voyage which took Lunaris to Aquitania in the year 237. Lunaris was a *sevir* of two colonies in Lower Britain, Lincoln and York – the *seviri* were organizations for the promotion of emperor-worship, most of the members of which were freedmen.

Opposite A cavalryman at Cirencester.

Dannicus, a trooper in the ala *Indiana*, who died after 16 years' service (in the first century AD) was a native of the Raurici (on the Upper Rhine). (RIB 108)

DANNICVS EQES ALAE
INDIAN TVR ALBANI
S P XVI CIVIS RAVR
C IVL FVLVIV NATALIS ET
FL BITVCVS TH HAM E
H S E

A legionary from Gloucester at Rome.

M. Ulpius Quintus, a *fr(umentarius)* – soldier on special 'secret police' duties at Rome – of the VIth legion, came from Gloucester, Glevum. His first two names show that his family obtained citizenship from Trajan (reigned AD 98–117) and were not original settlers in the *colonia*, which was founded under Nerva (AD 96–98), as the tribe *Ner(via)* given here indicates. (ILS 2365)

Below An altar from Somerset.

The dedicator, C. Indutius Felix, has a throughly Celtic *gentilicium*. The words on the bottom line, *con. vic. Ga.*, may indicate that he was a *conductor*, 'tenant-in-chief'. (RIB 181)

A town-councillor's wife at Lincoln.

Volusia Faustina, portrayed on the left, is described as *c. Lind.*, 'citizen of Lincoln', by her husband Aurelius Senecio, who was a councillor, *dec(urio)*. The relationship of the other woman, Claudia Catiotuus (?), to these two is obscure. (RIB 250)

Altars from the Antonine Wall.

Two of the four altars set up at Auchendavy by the centurion of II Augusta M. Cocceius Firmus. These two honour 'the Spirit of the Land of Britain' and a series of military deities. (RIB 2175, 2177)

A re-building project is dedicated.

This slab from Risingham in Northumberland, an outpost north of Hadrian's Wall, was set up in the years 205–207, recording the reconstruction of a gate and walls, 'which had collapsed from age' – perhaps a euphemism for enemy attack. The work was done on the order of the governor, Alfenus Senecio, 'the right honourable ex-consul' (*v.c. cos.*), under the supervision of the imperial procurator Oclatinius Adventus, together with the officer commanding the First Cohort of Vangiones, Aemilius Salvianus. The name of Severus' younger son Geta was later erased, after his murder by his brother Caracalla a few years later. (RIB 1234)

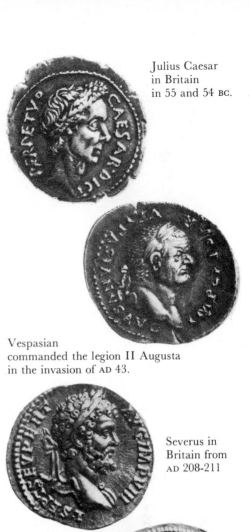

Julius Caesar
in Britain
in 55 and 54 BC.

Vespasian
commanded the legion II Augusta
in the invasion of AD 43.

Severus in
Britain from
AD 208-211

with his son
Caracalla

A worshipper of Mithras.

This altar from Carrawburgh on Hadrian's
Wall was set up by Aulus Cluentius Habitus,
prefect of the First Cohort of Batavians. He
abbreviated the name of his home-town
Larinum by the letter L., confident that
future worshippers would recognize him as
the descendant of a client of Cicero,
immortalized in a famous speech some 300
years earlier. (RIB 1545)

Right Julia Domna, wife of Severus.

A standard-bearer of the *ala Petriana*.

Flavinus, who died at the age of 25 after seven years' service, served in this regiment in the late first century, presumably when it was based at Corbridge, whence the stone was taken to Hexham Abbey. His single name shows that he was a non-citizen. (RIB 1172)

Below An immigrant from Gaul at Cirencester.

'Philus, son of Cassavus, aged 45, lies here, a Sequanian' – from the Besançon region. The date is first century AD. (RIB 110)

Gordian I, emperor for a few weeks in AD 238; had been governor of Lower Britain in AD 216.

Carausius ruled Britain and part of the Gallic coast AD 286–293.

Magnus Maximus proclaimed emperor in Britain in AD 383.

A lady's slipper from a frontier fort.

This high quality piece of footwear bears the name of its maker, L. Aeb(utius) Thales. It is not clear how T.F. should be interpreted. The date is early second century AD.

Below left Constantine III proclaimed emperor in Britain in AD 407.

Below Constantine the Great proclaimed emperor at York in AD 306.

Claudius, reigned AD 41–54. The unusual background and dramatic accession of the emperor made it imperative for him to obtain military prestige. The conquest of Britain afforded the ideal opportunity.

Hadrian, reigned AD 117–138, was the second emperor to visit Britain, in AD 122, at the time when the building of the Wall was being started.

Chapter XIII
Craftsmen

A famous inscription at Chichester, now walled into the west face of the Council Chamber, honours Neptune and Minerva. It records the establishment of a temple to these deities, 'for the welfare of the Divine House' (the imperial family), 'by authority of' the client-king, or puppet-ruler as he might uncharitably be called, '[Ti.] Claudius [Co]gidubnus'. The site was presented by [Pud]ens, son of Pudentinus, and the building was erected and paid for by the 'guild of craftsmen and its members from their own resources'. One may well understand that the craftsmen, *fabri*, who must have been benefiting from lucrative contracts in the construction and ornamentation of the king's sumptuous palace at Fishbourne; had organised themselves into a guild, *collegium*, and that they wished to ensure the continuing support of Neptune, to protect the import of their materials from across the sea, and Minerva, the patron goddess of skilled workers. The guild's members, perhaps largely expatriates, would include not just smiths, but building-workers, masons, carpenters, makers of tiles and bricks, mosaicists, glaziers, furniture-makers. Other categories of craftsmen may have had their own organizations – one thinks of soft furnishings of various kinds, requiring spinners and weavers, of basket-work; the list is lengthy. Of all this we have only a few traces. The son of Pudentinus, [Pud]ens, if that was his name, may not even have been a *faber* himself, but a local magnate. Nor, of course, do we have the name or names of the master-architects and engineers involved in the project.

For undertakings of this kind in Britain one is entitled to suppose that military technicians were made available on occasion. Some of these army craftsmen are on record, but none in a civilian context. The *architecti* Quin[t]us and Amandus who made dedications at Carrawburgh and Birrens respectively, for example, will have been involved in the construction or maintenance of military buildings. Likewise, the men known to have worked at the legionary tilery at Holt were soldier-craftsmen of the XXth, producing building-materials for the use of the army. Such cases must be excluded from the present survey. Nor can anything be said about the nameless artists and craftsmen whose identity can sometimes be traced in sculpture and ornamental masonry, or in mosaics, at a variety of sites. Above all, there is a great host of nameless potters, particularly those from areas such as the Nene valley, whom one can do no more than mention, with a passing sigh of regret at their anonymity. Fortunately, up to the end of the second century, one group, the makers of mortaria, stamped their products; and there are a few other named potters. Hence, taken as a whole, the British potters make up one of the largest and most informative groups of people from this island in the Roman period, second only to the military, and they will be considered separately in the second half of this chapter.

First it is convenient to examine such cases as are known of other craftsmen. A few are known from inscriptions which make it certain, or virtually so, that they were at work in Britain itself. In several other cases, particularly with small objects, there is no absolute guarantee that the craftsmen themselves were not working overseas. This is indeed made explicit with some items, such as the statuette from Lancaster made by Servandus of Cologne. The bronze dishes of P. Cipius Polybius are certainly imports too. But the knife inscribed Victor V.F. found at Catterick is less definite: V.F. might mean *V(iennae) f(ecit)*, 'made it at Vienne', for which there are parallels. Equally, the shoe found at Vindolanda with the maker's name on it may be an import. L.Aeb(utius) Thales was clearly the shoemaker, but T.F., which follows, could mean that he made it *f(ecit)* at a place beginning with T., or that he was 'son of Titus'. Since the name Thales is Greek, and Roman citizens with Greek names were generally freedmen who would not be entitled to the filiation, *f(ecit)* is perhaps rather more probable.

Among the most definite cases are the stone-carvers. Sulinus, son of Brucet(i)us, dedicated two altars to the *matres Suleviae*, one at Cirencester, the other at Bath, and on the latter he calls himself *scultor*. His name suggests that he was born at Bath, where another Sulinus, son of Maturus, is found. At Bath also is another dedication, to the goddess Sulis, by the stonemason, *lapidarius*, Priscus, son of Tout(i)us, a Carnutenian – from the Chartres region. Little can be said about the other two, Civilis, whose name appears as the carver on a little gabled panel depicting four figures, found in Wiltshire, or Juventinus, who carved a relief figure of the God Romulus found in Gloucestershire. There is no saying what the origin and status of these two men was. Priscus, at least, was an immigrant, from a region later famous for its carved stone. However, at any rate, in the early fourth century, Britain, after the reconquest by Constantius, provided many craftsmen to rebuild old houses, public works, and temples in a Gallic city, for, as the grateful local orator remarked to the Caesar, 'those provinces abounded' in such men (*plurimos, quibus illae provinciae redundab-ant . . . artifices*). This was Autun, which was to produce superb stone-carvers in the Middle Ages.

Smiths of various kinds are relatively well represented. The only goldsmith, apart from the anonymous slave at Malton, is Helenus, whose name is on a piece found near Birrens. There is no guarantee that Vassinus, who paid six *denarii* to Jupiter and Vulcan for bringing him safe home, in fulfilment of a vow, was the maker of the silver plate found in Buckinghamshire on which this is recorded. But as Vulcan was the patron of smiths it is a reasonable hypothesis. Other men named on silver are in a different category. (But *Viribonis* is probably not a name; it could just mean that the owner is 'a good man'). Patricius, Curmissus, and Fl. Honorinus, named on silver ingots, were evidently mint-workers or officials, from the late period. Blacksmiths, who must have abounded, are represented only by a few makers' names on tools, Bonos(us), Maenalis, Martial(is), Olondus, and P. Pas.Lib., from London, for example. Two smiths who worked with lead are known, Cunobarrus, responsible for a great rectangular basin found at Caistor in Lincolnshire, and Doccius, who worked at Lydney in Gloucestershire. Both men have good Celtic names. Best represented are the coppersmiths. Cintusmus, *aerarius*, made a dedication to Silvanus Callirius found at Colchester; he has the same Celtic name as a veteran of the *cohors IV Gallorum* buried at Templeborough. A bronze vessel found in the Fenland bears the name of another native smith, Boduogenus; and Celtic origin, whether insular or continental, may similarly be assumed for Sangus, maker of a bronze pan found at London, perhaps the same man as Sagus, whose name appears on a handle from Caernavon. Glaucus, who made a bronze statuette of a native deity, Corotiacus, otherwise unknown but identified with Mars, has a Greek name himself, and may therefore be an immigrant; his client, who dedicated the piece, was a woman named Simplicia, which is certainly a name favoured by Romanized Celts. Another artist with Celtic clients was Celatus, who also made a statuette of Mars, dedicated to that god and 'the imperial deities' by *Colasuni Bruccius et Caratius*, presumably two brothers with the fabricated *gentilicium* Colasunius. Celatus' own name, although a Latin word (meaning 'concealed'), is thought to be Celtic. This certainly applies to the last man whose work does not appear to be an import, Dubnus, named as maker on a bronze ansate plate found at Catterick.

London supplies almost all the coopers and tanners so far attested. One cooper, with the Celtic name Verctissa, is found at Silchester, but the rest come from the capital. Q. Vet[tius] Catullus has a thoroughly Italian sound to his name; he may have been a veteran or the descendant of one. Half a dozen or more names branded on staves are abbreviated, some of them so drastically that it is fruitless to attempt expansion. Va(lerius) Gemellus is straightforward, Galvisius is an acceptable variant of the common Calvisius, and T. C. Paca(tus) also looks colourless. But T. Senbon. looks fabricated; if the Avitus found on the same barrel goes with it, we have a cooper called T. Senbon(ius) Avitus. Of the London tanners or leather-workers Verus is clear enough, as is P. Jul(ius) Sur(us) or Sur(a). The others, including Anavill., are too enigmatic to interpret with confidence. Also in this category, one may note the name Victo(r?) on leather found long ago at Carlisle. One may add here a solitary name, Veluvi(us), which sounds Celtic, on a salt-making container found at Northwich in Cheshire.

Much of the good quality glass found in Britain was probably imported, but there is no reason why the phials bearing the name of Briginus *Ingenui l(ibertus)* found in the south of England should not have been made there. Before turning to the domestic potters, one should note some of the tileries attested by stamps. Cabriabanus was evidently active in Kent, Juc. Dignus in Wiltshire, and Arveri(us) or Arver(us) in Gloucestershire. Smaller numbers of examples by other makers include Patendinus, whose work is found in Surrey, Silvius from Richborough, Avienu[s] from Buckinghamshire, and Bellicianus at Caerwent. At Cirencester a tile bears the graffito *Can[d]idus f(ecit)* [*teg*]*ulas*, and similarly, one at Silchester reads *fecit tubul(um) Clementinus*, recording that Candidus and Clementinus made, respectively, 'tiles' and a 'box-tile'. Finally, there are copious specimens from Lincoln and Gloucester, the former bearing the initials L.V.L., the latter T.P.F., thought to stand for the *tria nomina* of their producers, with a variety of additional letters in each case representing particular kilns.

We know the names of at least 250 potters who worked in Britain in the Roman period. The vast majority were makers of mortaria, and almost all belong to the first or second centuries AD. It seems that it was as worthwhile for mortar-makers as it was for the Arretine potters and their successors in Gaul, the makers of samian ware, to stamp their pots. Mortaria, used for mixing and crushing food, were doubtless relatively expensive items to purchase, expected to receive heavy use. The great variety of potters' names suggests that there was fierce competition for markets, not least among the military; but it must be said that groups of makers can be shown to have worked together at the same potteries. From the early third century onwards, although archaeological evidence allows us to locate kilns and trace the distribution of their products, most notably the colour-coated wares produced in the Nene Valley (which had begun in the second century), hardly any pots bear the name of the potter. It may be that after the Severan reorganization of Britain had been carried through the economic situation changed markedly. A smaller number of firms may have cornered the market, and they may have found it unnecessary to stamp their wares, for example because of some change in the military supply and ordering system – but this is merely speculation.

The potters' names make an interesting study. Not many have the *tria nomina* which mark them unequivocally as Roman citizens, and these men are probably expatriates, from Gaul or further afield, taking advantage of the new British markets. One of the latest of these citizen potters, C. Attius Marinus, migrated twice in his working career, which began at Colchester in the late Flavian period; from there his products reached London, Caerleon, and Leicester, among other places. Then he moved to Radlett in Hertfordshire, where he used the kilns of Castus, active *c*. 110–140, before becoming established finally at the important Midlands centre, Hartshill-Mancetter. One group of citizen potters which evidently worked at Colchester in the first century consisted of five men who were all called Sextus Valerius. Two had Latin *cognomina*, Eclectus and Saturninus, a third's *cognomen* began IVS-, probably Justus, that of a fourth was abbreviated by the letter C., followed by what seems to be *F.*, probably *f(ecit)*. Only the fifth potter, Sex. Valerius Viroma, looks like a Romanized Celt. The probability is that they were all the freedmen of an entrepreneur called Sex. Valerius – or that the patron himself was one of the five potters. Other Valerii include the prolific Q. Valerius Veranius, and two of his associates, both Quinti and perhaps his freedmen, Suriacus and Esunertus, of whom the latter has a splendid Celtic name as *cognomen*. Other citizens associated with Veranius are T. Ju(lius?) Af(er?) and C. Jul(ius) Pri(mus?). A third man, Mottius Bollus, may be a Celt who had adapted his name to Roman conventions – 'fabricating' a *gentilicium* – on receiving citizenship. Further potters who were clearly citizens include Q. Rutilius Ripanus, active at Brockley Hill from the mid-60s to the mid-90s, and A. Terentius Ripanus who perhaps worked at Gloucester, and is datable to the Flavian period. Given the rarity of the *cognomen*, one might suggest that Terentius was a kinsman, perhaps nephew, of Rutilius. A link of some kind may also be suggested between Q. Justius Cico, whose work is only known at Ribchester, and Q. Jus(tius) Cres(cens), who probably worked in Lincolnshire, certainly in the first part of the second century.

A few other potters may be citizens, such as the two Junii, the first of whom worked at Brockley Hill *c*. 100–140, while the other was at Hartshill-Mancetter, *c*. 135–195. There is a third Junius, with the additional name Loccius, but the relationship between this man and the Junii on the one hand, and the Hartshill-Mancetter potters Locc(ius) Pro(culus) and Loccius Vibius, can only be guessed at. All three may, however, be taken as citizens and this is also likely for the second-century potters Metilius, and Messorius Martius. Much more doubtful are names such as Bruc(c)ius, Bruscius, Decmitius, Mossius, Sarrius, and Sennius. Sennius may appear acceptable as a Latin *gentilicium*, but names beginning Sen- are common among the Celts; it may be a fabricated name, and this may apply to the other names in -ius, but all those in that category could simply be peregrines. Finally, a small number of potters who stamped mortaria with initials may have been citizens: C.C.M. or T.M.H., for example, could stand for *tria nomina*.

The categories so far discussed account for less than 15 per cent of the total number of named potters. The remainder may be divided into two groups, those with Latin names, numbering over 60 – some of whom may of course have been citizens – and those with Celtic or definitely barbarous names, of which there are almost twice as many. It must be added that some of the latter are too implausible to count as names at all, and must either be abbreviations of some kind, not capable of being interpreted as initials of Roman names – such as R.O.A.; or may be presumed to have been devised by illiterate potters, such as IMEMITVO-BON. Some of the 'Latin' potters have exceedingly common names, found in great numbers all over the Roman world, commonest of all being Saturninus, borne by two separate British potters. The favourite name among the potters themselves, if one may put it like that, was Vitalis, for there seem to have been five different men called this. Other common names include Candidus, Fronto, Martialis, and Secundus. There are several names which are past participles, favoured among the Celts (although to a lesser extent than by the north Africans), such as Cupitus and Dubitatus, and some are clearly converted Celtic names, such as Bellicus, Messor, and Senilis. Then there are some which happen to be rare elsewhere, Amandinus, Austinus (perhaps a contraction of Augustinus), Baro (which means 'stupid' in Latin and may really be Celtic), and Docilis, for example.

The last category offers a rich harvest for the student of Celtic philology, but even the non-specialist in this field can readily distinguish several characteristic types. Aesico and Aesuminus – like Esunertus – recall the Celtic deity (A)esus, Camulacus and Moricamulus the war-god Camulos and, of course, Camulodunum. Amminus is essentially the same name as that of the British prince who fled to Caligula, Adminius or Amminius. Several names have the common termination -acus – Malliacus, Matuacus, Vediacus. There are some fine specimens of compound names. In addition to those already mentioned, one may cite Litugenus and Matugenus, Cacumattus, Cintugnatus, Cunopectus, and, two resonant names that purchasers will not readily have forgotten, Setibogius and Tamesubugus. The latter, as it happens, is a rare example of a late named potter, known from a graffito scratched before firing on a mortarium found near Oxford: *Tamesubugus fecit*. The first element in his name is eminently appropriate to a potter working in the Thames valley.

A number of potteries have already been alluded to, and something more may now be said about them, for, thanks above all to the researches of Mrs K. F. Hartley, a picture is beginning to emerge of groups of potters, whose periods of activity may be closely dated. Furthermore the areas where they worked are also being more precisely identified and in some cases their kilns located. The earliest include the Sexti Valerii of Colchester and another one, possibly working in Kent, and deriving inspiration from the Atisii, potters of Aoste in Gaul. Summacus son of Arontuis, whose own name is presumably Celtic, although it could conceivably be Greek (a version of Symmachus), was formerly linked with the Atisii. Other mortaria produced by the same 'firm', if this concept is permissible, have stamps with Latin names, one of a citizen, Q. Val. Se., and Fronto and Paullus, while the other two intelligible ones are Celtic, Buc(c)us and Orgillus. Q. Val(erius) Se. seems to have been the major potter in this group, judging from the number of stamped examples found. Their period of activity runs from the reign of Nero to the end of Agricola's governorship, and they evidently distributed their products by sea, reaching a wide area of the coastal regions of Britain.

A few years after this group became established, a second and larger group of potters started production somewhere in the same part of Britain, perhaps at a place in Kent called *Dogaeria*, for this name appears on one of the stamps of its leading potter Q. Valerius Veranius, followed by the word *fac(tum)*; This presumably means 'made at Dogaeria'. Veranius was not only a citizen but the son of a citizen, for he has the filiation *C(ai) f(ilius)* on one stamp. He seems to have migrated across the Channel after first working at Bavai or somewhere in Gallia Belgica. In Britain, where his activity dates to the years *c*. 65–100, he is associated, by style and fabric, with over 15 other potters, including four or five other citizens, two more Quinti Valerii, Esunertus and Suriacus, C.Jul(ius) Pri(mus?) and T.Ju.Af., and Mottius Bollus; some with single Latin names, Gracilis, Alb. and Ruf.; and perhaps as many as 10 with Celtic names, of which one may mention Cacumattus, Litugenus, and Orbissa. Their mortaria, like those of the first group, seem to have been distributed by sea, for they are rarely found at sites far inland, away from waterways.

Other potters were of course working in Britain in the pre-Flavian period, notably at Colchester, but it may have been the change of direction marked by the accession of Vespasian in 69, and the revival of a forward military policy, that encouraged a new group to set up at Brockley Hill, in Middlesex, which they called Sulloniacae, and at other sites between London and Verulamium, particularly Radlett in Hertfordshire. Outstanding among these potters was Albinus, whom Mrs Hartley has described as 'by far the most prominent mortar maker in Britain'. It had, indeed, been assumed that Albinus was a Gallic producer, as his stamp *f(actum) Lugudu(ni)*, 'made at Lugudunum', suggests. In fact there is no evidence that he had ever worked anywhere on the continent, at Lyons, Leyden, or elsewhere. One might suppose that he coolly decided to make his customers think they were buying imported pots. But it is more likely that, as Mrs Hartley suggests, there was a place somewhere in the home counties called Lugudunum; after all, as the place-name for Roman Carlisle, Luguvallium, shows, the element Lugu- , from the deity Lug, was common all over the Celtic regions. Albinus' own period of productivity spanned three decades or so in the later first century, *c*. AD 60–90, but potters continued producing in or near Verulamium on into the mid-second century. Albinus' son was also a potter, and, curiously, had an unambiguously Celtic name, Matugenus. Definite citizens among these men are few. There are only Q. Rutilius Ripanus, a contemporary of Albinus, and C. Attius Marinus, who moved there from Colchester in the same period. Junius is another possible Roman, and there is a mixture of Latin and Celtic names among the others: Castus, Marinus, Saturninus, and Secundus are matched by Doinus, Driccius, Moricamulus, and Sollus. The most exotic name among the Brockley Hill potters is perhaps Dares, who made amphorae as well as mortaria there in the Flavian period. This name was borne by a Trojan priest in Homer's *Iliad* and by a comrade of Aeneas in the *Aeneid*. Names like this were frequently given to slaves, and this potter may have been a slave or freedman employed by one of the Brockley Hill 'firms'.

It may have been the restless C. Attius Marinus who took the lead in establishing a major new centre, in the Midlands. A great volume of pottery was produced from the new kilns at Hartshill and Mancetter throughout the second century, particularly from the mid-130s to *c.* 190 – the dating being of course dependent on the chronology of the northern frontier sites where much of their market was. But, it must be stressed, these potters, and the potters of Brockley Hill and Hertfordshire, penetrated the whole of Roman Britain more effectively than the Kentish groups discussed previously. Some of those who worked there have already been referred to – one of the Junii, the Loccii, and Mossius. Another good Celtic name is Bonoxus. But the most prolific of them all was Sarrius, who later moved to, or established a branch at, Rossington Bridge in South Yorkshire, where Setibogius also worked.

In the meantime other potteries were being established and flourishing. Austinus, Docilis (or Doccius), and others worked at Wilderspool, near Warrington in Cheshire; these two may also have had kilns in the Carlisle area. Q. Jus(tius) Cres(cens), one of the five potters called Vitalis, and perhaps Atepacius, were producing in Lincolnshire in the first part of the second century, and Aesico, Crico, and a potter with the stamp BILCE were among those who worked in the same area later in the century. Sulloniac(us) – once taken to represent the place-name Sulloniacae (Brockley Hill) – is now thought to have been a potter working at Corbridge, where he would have had an excellent market among the soldiers. Even more enterprising were a few potters who seem to have worked in Scotland, Invomandus and two men whose names are abbreviated Emi. and Brigia. York, with its legionary garrison, not surprisingly had its own potters, or so it appears, including Agripp(a?), Mercator, and Muco. But throughout this period potters continued to work at Colchester, and towards the end of the second century some of them tried their hand at samian, as the discovery of their kilns reveals. Their sales seem to have been largely confined to the south-east, although over a dozen, perhaps 20, potters were involved. Most of them had Celtic names, including Cunopectus, Litugenus, Malliacus, and Viducus, and the few with Latin, or apparently Latin, names such as Littera, Regulus, and Senilis, need not have been citizens. Their production did not survive the civil wars of 193–197, which also seem to have put a virtual end to the main Gallic *sigillata* kilns.

In the third century, sadly, potters ceased to stamp their pots. New centres developed, with recognizable styles, but their potters are nameless. Much more could be said about the potters of Roman Britain, before and after AD 200, than is possible here – as a case study for the ancient economic historian they are rich in possibilities. Apart from the political and military changes which brought men like Summacus and Q. Valerius Veranius to Britain, and the continuing military markets and urban development, which kept them and their successors in business, questions of distribution, of raw materials (not only clay but the timber needed for firing), the stimulus represented by imports – all these and other aspects are now beginning to be better understood. For the purpose of the present study, the potters must be left behind, with Sarrius and his fellow-workers in the kilns, their successors almost totally unknown. Happily, there is a faint gleam of light. Apart from the evocative name of the Oxfordshire potter Tamesubugus, we do at least have the names of two men who worked in the richly productive Nene Valley. A colour-coated mortarium made there bears the stamp CVNOARDA FECIT VICO DVROBRIVIS ('Cunoarda made (this) at the settlement of Durobrivae' (Water Newton) – and a large buff mortarium found at Water

Newton itself has the inscription *Sennianus Durobrivis uri*[t], 'Sennianus fired (this) at Durobrivae,' painted round the rim. Both names are Celtic, as is fitting, even if Sennianus is disguised in Latin form. Potters had been at work before the Romans came, and would continue after Roman rule ended; and most of the coarse pottery used in the island in the Roman period was made by Britons.

Chapter XIV
Country dwellers

It is a commonplace that the distinction between townsman and countryman is rather artificial when applied to Britain during the Roman period. A good deal of the land was farmed by men who lived in towns; and a large proportion of villa-owners must have had town-houses. Since most of the towns in the lowland zone are very poorly represented in the epigraphic record anyway, this does not create complications; but it multiplies our ignorance. For any society, in any period of history the ownership of the land and the system of land-tenure are matters of vital significance. The answers are still obscure for Britain, and will doubtless remain so, although the questions are much studied and much debated.

As with other parts of the Empire, imperial estates must have taken up considerable portions of the province. There is a little direct evidence and rather more indirect evidence for their presence in Britain. Mines are the first and most obvious example – in the Mendips, the Welsh mountains and the Pennines, in particular. But farming land was also taken over. There are a number of obvious occasions in the history of Britain when it can be assumed that land was confiscated for the emperor, to become part of the *patrimonium Caesaris*, or later of the *res privata*. Much doubtless was seized at or soon after the conquest in 43, and more was certainly taken over as client kingdoms were absorbed – estates of Prasutagus in East Anglia in or shortly before 60 and of Cogidubnus in southern England after his death, perhaps in the late 70s. Likewise, after the downfall of the Brigantian monarchy in 69, the estates of Cartimandua, of Venutius, and of other Brigantian notables, may well have passed, in the main, into the *patrimonium*. In addition, outbreaks of rebellion were generally followed by confiscation. Supporters of Boudica will have lost their lands in 60–61, and, much later, when the legions of Britain put up their own candidate for the imperial throne, landowners who were compromised must have paid the penalty; for, with one exception – Constantine the Great in 306 – these attempts were unsuccessful. Thus active supporters of Albinus in 195–197, of Carausius and Allectus from 287–296, and of various other usurpers or would-be usurpers in the third and fourth centuries, must have lost whatever they had. It is not surprising that the *Notitia Dignitatum* records an official, the *rationalis rei privatae per Britannias,* whose office administered the emperor's land in the island.

Direct evidence for the operations of this department, or of its early third-century equivalent, comes from Combe Down near Bath, where the imperial freedman Naevius supervised the reconstruction of what was presumably an administrative centre (*principia*) of such an estate. At Bath itself a *centurio reg(ionarius)*, C. Severius Emeritus, is attested; he may have been the officer in charge of a subdivision of the same estate. Another such *regio* is recorded by an inscription in north-west England, at Ribchester, called *Bremetennacum veteranorum* in a late source: the legionary centurion T. Floridius Natalis is described as *praep(ositus) n(umeri) et regi(onis)*. In this case, it is clear that the land was used for veteran settlement. Elsewhere, notably in the Fenland, the existence of imperial estates can be deduced with some plausibility.

After the conquest, the Roman authorities must have looked to the tribal aristocracies to assist them in the task of government. Those who made their peace rapidly, 'turncoats', or 'quislings', they could even be called, must have continued to hold land, even if the imposition of Roman law altered the nature of their tenure – and they now had to pay a land-tax. Some fairly large portions would be taken up for military use, and, in the case of Camulodunum, for the territory of a *colonia*. The two *coloniae* of the later first century, Lindum and Glevum, perhaps did not require the sequestration of significant tracts of good farming land – some would have been taken already, for the needs of the legions stationed at those places. The conquest clearly saw an influx of traders, merchants and money-lenders, as well as tax-collectors. The Celtic notables, and indeed independent farmers of any kind, must have been affected. Many would have managed to improve their property by adopting new building techniques and new farming methods, both involving the need for capital. Debt would soon be a problem, exacerbated by heavy rates of interest. When the burden of debt became too harsh, the desperation that resulted drove Rome's subjects to rebellion, as happened in several provinces. Britain was no exception. But for this and other reasons immigrants who wished to invest in British land must have found plenty of opportunities; some will, of course, have been absentee landowners.

The fact that Britain's closest neighbours were also Celtic – the Rhineland, Gaul, and north-west Spain – and that a high proportion of the garrison was drawn from these areas, from the start, means that it is almost a hopeless task to distinguish between Britons and immigrants, on the basis of their nomenclature, in most of the recorded instances. The number of named 'country-dwellers' is very small in any case; but only with one or two of them can it be asserted with confidence that they could not have been Britons. (This consideration even applies to the veterans, to some extent – but they have been treated separately.)

The evidence is most conveniently presented geographically, starting with the south-east and south, then looking at the south-west, and gradually moving northward. Kent, the most civilized region of Britain according to Caesar, offers a few names. The place-name Vagniacae, apparently near Dartford, may derive from a villa-owner called Vagnius or Vagionius, a rare *gentilicium*, of which Vagnius might be an alternative form; but it might equally be Celtic. Bel. Januaris, a name found on a silver spoon at Eccles villa near Aylesford, is certainly Celtic – Bel(lius), Bel(licius) and other names beginning Bel- are common in Celtic areas. Another name found at this site is Fausta, a straightforward Latin *cognomen*. A graffito from Springhead has provided Maecius, Maxima and Ing(enuus), and Chilham can offer Ant(onius?) and Campana, all standard items of Latin nomenclature. These people could all be immigrants. Not much can be made of the enigmatic Sas- on a graffito at Lullingstone, but one from Poulton, near Folkestone, has Alpinianus, a *cognomen* of a type favoured in the north-western provinces. The place-name Sulloniacae, Brockley Hill in Middlesex, ought to derive from an estate owned by a person called Sullonius. An inscription at Beauport Park near Battle in Sussex offers tantalizingly incomplete information, evidently referring to rebuilding on what may have been part of an imperial estate at the time. The fragments of names which survive – Bassi . . . ti.. . . . – are insufficient to make any deduction about origin. The same place had produced a tile inscribed with the name Julius. Two names are recorded at Wigginholt in the same county, the mundane Sabi(nus) and the otherwise unknown Ferna.

There is almost no evidence from the Dumnonii in the far south-west. A pewter dish from Cornwall, dedicated to Mars by Aelius Modestus, may be a stray, and the name is uninformative. The man could be a Briton, but he might have come from any part of the empire. For what it is worth, however, it may be noted that there was a prefect of the *cohors I Tungrorum* at Housesteads called P. Aelius Modestus. There is no reason why a third-century equestrian officer should not have owned land in Cornwall. A graffito found at Topsham in Devon gives the name of Jun(ius) Ve . . . Turning to the lands of the Durotriges, Belgae, and Dobunni, we meet a relatively large cluster of names. Tiles from Wiltshire with the name Iuc. Digni suggest an estate owned by a Juc(undius) Dignus, producing building material – some of his products are found quite far afield. There are some interesting dedications at West Kington in Wiltshire, by Decimius, Corotica, daughter of Jutus, and [A]ur(elius) Pu . . . Graffiti from the same site record the names Paet(us) and Abe . . . At Colerne a fragmentary inscription preserves the name Ing. Fabill . . . ; which may be interpreted as Ing(enuius) Fabill[us], a typically Celtic nomenclature. Ausonius Avitus, evidently the owner of an iron tool found at East Winterslow, has names which evoke fourth-century Gallic notables. An Ulpius, whose name must derive from a grant of *civitas* by Trajan, is found at Cricklade. Two contrasting names are attested at Wanborough. Tamm. may be Tamm(onius), known at Silchester, where it is clearly a 'fabricated' *gentilicium*. The other name, Termo, perhaps an abbreviation of the Greek T(h)ermo(don), appears to be the recipient of an invitation: *mane Termo veni*, 'come in the morning, Termo'. Three names are found at Gadebridge Park villa in Hampshire, Ingenti – either Ingens or Ingentius – Ann(ius) and Tare, perhaps Tare(ntinus). Cupit(us), a Latin *cognomen* favoured in Celtic areas, is recorded at Basingstoke, and Vitalis, popular all over Britain, is found at Rockbourne. From Neatham comes a fine Celtic name, Matugena.

Most interesting of all in this group is Q. Natalius Natalinus, a name found on a fourth-century mosaic pavement at Appleshaw. Natalius Natalinus is an excellent example of a 'fabricated' *gentilicium*, with *cognomen* from the same root. This name is followed by the words *et Bodeni*, thought to be a reference to some group, 'and the Bodeni', whoever they might be. But it is perhaps likelier that Bodenus or Bodenius was Natalinus' *signum*, or extra name, a custom which became common in the fourth century. He would thus be styled Q. Natalius Natalinus *(qui) et* Bodenius, 'also known as Bodenius'. Bodenius is a Celtic name, cognate with Boudica, Bodicca, and many others in Bod- or Boud-.

At Godmanston in Dorset there is a dedication to J(upiter) O(ptimus) M(aximus), 'best and greatest', by Tit . . . Pin . . ., perhaps Tit[ius] or Tit[inius] Pin[us] or Pin[na], who may have been a legionary or veteran. Finally, two estate names have been detected in this part of Britain, Anicetis and Coloneas, both in Dorset. The latter, deriving from Colon, Colonus, or a similar form, might suggest a Celtic landowner, but Anicetis points to an immigrant, for the name is Greek. Applebaum has made the attractive suggestion that the Q. Pompeius Anicetus who made a dedication to Sulis at Bath may have given his name to the property. He notes the further possibility that Anicetus may have been

conductor – tenant-in-chief or lessor – of imperial domain in Cranborne Chase. The Greek *cognomen* certainly points to eastern, or perhaps freedman, origin.

One such *conductor* may perhaps be attested by another inscription, from the villa at Somerdale, near Keynsham in Somerset. It is a dedication for the 'imperial spirits', *num(inibus) Aug(ustorum)*, to the god Silvanus, by a certain C. Indutius Felix. The last line of the text, reading CON. VIC. GA., had been interpreted as a reference to the consulship of C. Aufidius Victorinus and M. Gavius, in AD 155. But this seems highly unlikely. Dating by suffect consuls was extremely rare in this period, especially in the provinces; to describe a consular pair by the *cognomen* of one consul and the *nomen* of another would be an odd procedure anyway; and the normal abbreviation for *consulibus* was *cos.* or *coss.* after the names, rather than *con.* before them. A possible alternative solution would be *con(ductor) vic(i) Ga ..*', in other words 'lessor of a *vicus* (village)', the name of which began with the letters GA. However this may be, the *gentilicium* is an excellent specimen of the 'fabricated' type, recalling the Treveran chief Indutiomarus, defeated and killed by a lieutenant of Caesar in 53 BC. Another example of Indutius from Britain is known on a graffito at Maryport in Cumbria.

Iventius Sabinus, whose name appears as dedicator on a bronze plate in honour of Mars Rigisamus found at a villa site at West Coker (near Yeovil), is not such a clear case. The spelling of the *nomen* could most readily be explained as a slight abbreviation for J(u)ventius; but I(n)ventius is not impossible, and this would be explicable as a fabricated *gentilicium*. The Celtic god Rigisamus is otherwise attested only at Avaricum, the chief town of the Bituriges in central Gaul.

Apart from three stones with incomplete or illegible names (two tombstones at Pitney and a dedication at Camerton), the only other named 'country-dweller' from Somerset is attested by the Chew Stoke writing tablet, recording a land sale. The purchaser's name appears to have been something like M. Aurelius Riespetecus, a good specimen of the kind of nomenclature that must have been very common after the Edict of Caracalla.

A little further north, in Gloucestershire – prime 'villa country' – there are a number of inscriptions which, from their find-spots in the countryside, may reasonably be associated with 'country-dwellers'. *Censorine gaudeas*, engraved on a silver spoon at Chedworth, might indicate that one of the people who lived at that villa was called Censorinus. Likewise, *Firmini* on a building stone at Barnsley Park might give the name of one of the owners of that villa – but it might equally well be that a mason or building contractor was called Firminus. *Saini* is another name attested at this site. It might be the same as Saenus or Saenius, recorded at Silchester and York, and for the father of a Dumnonian serving in the German fleet. A name which appears to be Gulioepius on a dedication to Romulus found near Bisley sounds Celtic, and is certainly not Latin. A young woman called Sulicena, buried near Wotton-under-Edge, carries a thoroughly Celtic name, but Jul(ia) Ingenuilla, buried near Nailsworth, has a nomenclature which might occur virtually anywhere in the empire. Not much can be said about the enigmatic tombstone from Sea Mills, where SPES C. SENTI . . . is all that survives of the inscription. Spes might conceivably be the name of the wife or daughter or slave of a C. Sentius, but it might mean that Sentius was commemorating a child who had been his *spes*, 'hope'. Mettus, 'Getan by nation', i.e. a Dacian, buried by an unknown heir near Tetbury, might have been a slave employee of a villa-owner. There are a few names from the northern part of Dobunnian territory. Bellicus, dedicator of an altar to the otherwise unknown and presumably Celtic god Tridam[us], was doubtless of Celtic origin. Two possible proprietors of land in this area have been deduced by Applebaum from the place-names Ariconium and Beroniacum. The first – Weston-under-Penyard in Herefordshire – is discussed in the next chapter, while Beroniacum, known only from a mediaeval estate name, possibly at Ludlow, is thought to have derived from a Roman landowner called Beronius or Veronius. These cases are rather doubtful.

A number of names from what may be regarded as Catuvellaunian territory require consideration next. Vassinus and Vernico, from two sites in Buckinghamshire, are clearly Celtic, likewise Lovernianus, found together with the Latin Pacata and three other, more puzzling names, Somia, Narina, and Melluna. By contrast, Veneria, found on a pewter dish from the same county, with the slogan *vivas*, is a standard Latin *cognomen*, as is Concess[us] or Concess[a], on a graffito from Sanderton. Bellicia, Mina and Satavacus, from a villa in Oxfordshire, all look Celtic.

Dum. Censorinus *Gemelli fil(ius)* and Ti. Claudius Primus Attii *liber(tus)*, the dedicators named on silver plaques in honour of Mars found at Barkway in Hertfordshire, are rather more interesting. The former might have been a citizen, with a fabricated *nomen*, such as Dum(nius), but, in spite of his own and his father's Latin *cognomina* Censorinus and Gemellus, he might have been peregrine, with two names, one Celtic – such as Dum(norix) or Dum(nogenus) – and one Latin. The freedman Primus, whose patron was evidently called Ti. Claudius Attius, might have come from anywhere, but his former master could have been an enfranchised Briton, whose *cognomen* had been adapted from a Celtic original form in Ati-. A third name from Hertfordshire, a woman called Tacita who features as the object of a curse on a leaden *defixio*, has an apparently Latin name which seems to have been more popular among the Celts than in Italy. Further north, there are two splendid Celtic names, Vatiaucus at Godmanchester and Mocux[s]oma at Thistleton in Rutland on the borders of the Coritani. Both these persons were worshippers of non-Roman deities.

There are not many names on the east side, in Trinovantian and Icenian territory. Another curse tablet – from Old Harlow in Essex – names a women called Etterna, which might be a shot at Aeterna, and a man called Timotheus, misspelt Timotneus. There are a few other names from Essex, all evidently Latin. *Amati* at Wickford might be either Amatus or Amatius. Secunda (Billericay) and Postimia (Stebbing) are equally uninformative. Quietus Remus, found in an apparently rather illiterate scrawl at Great Dunmow, has some interest, since *Remus* might be an ethnic, indicating a Gaul from the Rheims area. Finally, there is Ael. Titul . . . from Canvey Island, an undistinguished name in itself, but it is worth noting that one P. Aelius Titullus was prefect of a cohort at Rudchester on Hadrian's Wall, where he dedicated an altar to Mithras. It could have been the same man, since, although Aelii were very common, Titullus was not.

A bronze statuette base found near Ipswich records a woman named Simplicia as dedicator, honouring a Celtic version of Mars called Corotiacus. Simplicius is one of the commonest of fabricated *gentilicia*. Of particular interest is the place-name in the Antonine Itinerary, *villa Faustini*, perhaps identifiable with Scole in Norfolk. Faustinus is a fairly common Latin *cognomen*, but C. E. Stevens' attractive conjecture, that the man who had owned the villa was the governor of Belgica of that name who rebelled against the Gallic emperor Tetricus in the early 270s, deserves to be registered. Stevens' point is that the place-name, which is 'unique in the Itinerary, should imply that the villa had been confiscated' – if so, it is legitimate to look for a man called Faustinus whose property would have been seized. A graffito from this site names a woman called Tertia. Five names are found on a pewter dish from Icklingham in Suffolk: Isarninus (also spelt Ixarninus), Florenti(us), Licinius, Curati(us), Martinus. Their intention is not clear. Two names found on another pewter dish from Suffolk, Flaetio and Fidelis, may indicate successive slaves responsible for looking after it. Then there is the interesting name Rubrius Carinus Orientalis, found on an intaglio at Akenham But whether this man had any connection with Suffolk must remain uncertain.

There are several interesting names in Coritanian territory, some of them to be regarded as citizens of the *colonia* at Lincoln. This must surely apply to Q. Neratius Proxsimus at Nettleham and Aurel(ia) Con[ce]ssa at Branston, both very close to the city, and to the Claud[ius] (or Claud[ianus]) buried at Greetwell, all bearers of thoroughly Roman names, although Con[ce]ssa's *nomen* suggests descent from a second- or third-century new citizen. Proxsimus' *nomen* derives from the Samnite country of southern Italy, but he, or rather an ancestor, may have owed the franchise to the patronage of the Trajanic governor L. Neratius Marcellus. At all events, he was a worshipper of a thoroughly Celtic deity, Mars Rigonemetes, 'king of the sacred grove', otherwise unattested.

A slightly odd combination of names occurs on a limestone roundel found near Sleaford: Donatus and Saturninus are clear enough, but Adalma and Lopiscallus are not readily explicable. The two men who dedicated a bronze statuette to Mars found at Torksey on the Foss Dike, Colasuni Bruccius et Caratius, are throughly Celtic. Colasuni(us) may be a fabricated *gentilicium*, but the two men may have been non-citizens. Trenico, the dedicator of an arch to the Celtic god Viridius at Ancaster, was presumably a *peregrinus* too, although if his inscription is of third-century date he might have omitted *praenomen* and *nomen*. Canius (?) Dignus, named on a curse-tablet found at Ratcliffe-on-Soar, may have had a pair of respectable Latin names, and thus have been an immigrant; but he could equally well have been an itinerant trader, judging from the *defixio*, which mentions a sum of money.

Further west, the evidence for settlers in the Cornovian territory is extremely scanty, apart from the Spanish cavalryman Reburrus, whose diploma was found at Malpas in Cheshire, perhaps his home after discharge. The couple who made a dedication to the Matres at Heronbridge, Jul. Secundus and Aelia Augustina, are just as likely to have been inhabitants of the *cannabae* of XX Valeria Victrix as farming people, for the place is less than two miles from the Chester fortress. Two names found at Holditch, Staffs. may perhaps be regarded as evidence for Cornovians, Curatio and Senuacus.

There remains only the vast tract stretching from the southern Pennines to Hadrian's Wall, ascribed to the Brigantes by writers of the Roman period, except for the lands of the Parisi in the Yorkshire East Riding. Although there is ample evidence for villas among the Parisi, no named country-dwellers can be produced. Much of the Brigantian territory is properly regarded as within the military district, and the relatively ample documentation of the inhabitants of the northern parts – deriving from inscriptions in the *vici* outside military stations – have been considered separately (in Chapter X).

The southern Brigantian region, in the West Riding of Yorkshire, yields a few names, some of them perhaps of descendants of veteran settlers. This probably applies to the Aurelii, Aurelianus, Quintus and Senopianus, attested respectively at Greetland near Halifax, Longwood near Slack and in the Calder valley near Castleford – the first two of them having the *praenomen* Titus, deriving from a grant of *civitas* under Antoninus Pius. All three were devotees of the eponymous Brigantian deity, as was Cingetissa, evidently a *peregrinus*, who made a dedication at Adel, on the northern outskirts of Leeds. The same place provides two other names, Priminus, the object of a salacious graffito, and a girl or woman named Candiedinia Fortunata who was buried there. Her *gentilicium* is otherwise unrecorded in the Roman world, but probably formed from the Celtic name Candiedo.

Finally, two fine stone coffins from north of York may represent rare specimens of the wealthier class of country dweller. One from Eastness, near Hovingham, now lost, was made for his wife Titia Pinta and sons Adjutor and Varialus by one Val(erius) Vindicianus. The' other, found near Thirsk, once contained the remains of a lady named Cosc(onia?) Mammiola, buried by her husband Aur(elius) Serenus. These people may have been the descendants of legionary veterans.

Chapter XV
Slaves and freedmen

Chattel-slavery, far from being a 'peculiar institution' was an entirely normal feature of ancient society. Before the conquest the British had supplied slaves to the empire and some archaeological evidence has been detected for the existence of slave-labour in the Roman period, but the epigraphic record for individual slaves is sparse. A handful of inscriptions preserve slaves' names. One, a tomb-stone at London, was set up to Cl(audia) Martina, who died at the age of 19, by her husband Anencletus, *provinc*. This must be expanded either to *provinc(ialis)* or *provinc(iae servus)*, in either case meaning 'slave of the province'. In other words, Anencletus belonged to the *concilium provinciae*, the provincial council to which each of the British communities must have sent annual representatives. Their principal task was to conduct emperor-worship at an annual ceremony designed to promote loyalty to Rome. The temple at Colchester doubtless remained the main centre, but the *concilium* probably set up an office in London when the governor's residence was established there, and this would explain Anencletus' presence in the city, as a member of the council's permanent staff. This slave may thus be described as the first known British civil servant. His name is Greek, meaning 'blameless' or 'irreproachable', but this does not necessarily indicate Greek origin. Greek names were frequently given to slaves irrespective of their nationality. One of the other named British slaves and several of the freedmen also had Greek names. Another slave official of the British provincial council appears to be attested by a bronze seal found at the other end of Britain, at Cramond on the Firth of Forth, the Antonine Wall. It bears the inscription TERTVLL PROVINC, which, on the analogy of the inscription of Anencletus, ought to mean *Tertull(us) provinc(iae servus)*. Whether the seal may be taken to demonstrate operations of the *concilium Britanniae* in the far north, for example, endeavouring to secure representation from the northern tribes – and financial contributions – is another matter. The seal may have found its way to the Forth by chance, with a consignment of goods sent by sea from London.

Anencletus was in a very different category from the ordinary household slave. His superior position is emphasized further not only by the stylishness of his wife's tombstone (which was probably surmounted by a statue of the dead woman), but by her status as a free woman, and a Roman citizen into the bargain. She might have been a freedwoman, although this is not indicated; but it is unlikely as she was well below the statutory minimum age for manumission. In any case, by a senatorial decree of AD 52 a free-born woman who cohabited with a slave with the consent of the slave's owner – in this case the Council of Britain – was reduced to the status of a freedwoman. If consent was not forthcoming, she herself became a slave. From the formula *h(ic) s(ita) e(st)* at the end of the inscription, combined with the abbreviated *D(is) M(anibus)* at the beginning, a late first-century date looks probable.

Three other named slaves appear together on a tombstone at Chester, set up by their master (*dominus*) Pompeius Optatus, who does not state his occupation. He put the stone up to Atiliana, aged two, Atilianus aged eight and Protus aged 12. The implication must be that they were *vernae*, children born to a slave-woman in the household of Optatus, who was probably a military man: the funerary formula *Dis Manibus* is written out in full, not abbreviated, indicating a date soon after the arrival of the garrison at Chester. Another tombstone from Chester commemorating two brothers named Hermagoras and Felicissimus may record further slaves of Pompeius Optatus.

Another inscription referring to slaves also comes from a military context, the fort of Haltonchesters on Hadrian's Wall. It appears to be a tombstone erected to a slave named Hardalio by the *collegium conser(vorum)*, 'the guild of fellow-slaves'. Hardalio, which means 'busybody', a typical slave-name, presumably belonged to an officer or soldier of the garrison. Several other tombstones, from various parts of Britain, commemorate *alumni*, 'foster-children', or 'foundlings'. Their status seems to have varied. The term could refer simply to adopted children, but could mean 'foundling', an abandoned child rescued and brought up, sometimes as a slave. Finally, it could cover favourite slave-children, treated as playmates for the master's own family. There is no way of deciding how Ylas, his 'dearest foster-child' who died at 13, first entered the household of the tribune Claudius Severus who buried him at Old Penrith; and Honoratus, tribune at High Roches-ter, was even less informative on the tombstone of his *alumnus* Hermagoras. But it is unlikely that Merc. Magnil(la), who died at the age of one year, six months and 12 days, at Bath, could have been either a foundling, since her exact age was known, or a slave, since she appears to have been a citizen. She was presumably an adopted child.

The sources of slaves were various. Many were no doubt brought to Britain with their masters, and others would be born in the household. But new slaves were undoubtedly imported from the regions beyond the frontier, a practice indirectly attested for Britain by a passage in the *Digest*. A second-century jurist is quoted for a case where 'a woman condemned for crime to hard labour in the saltworks and later captured by foreign brigands was sold by them in the course of trade; and by repurchase she reverted to her original condition. The price had to be refunded by the imperial treasury to the centurion Cocceius Firmus', whose service on the Antonine Wall in Scotland is attested by several inscriptions. In this case the slave in question had been kidnapped from within the province – which was to be the fate of St Patrick in the late fourth century – but the peoples of the unconquered parts of north Britain were no doubt happy to supply captives from rival tribes as well. Many officers and men serving on the frontier would have had the opportunity of purchasing slaves in this way, as well as to acquire them by capture on punitive expeditions. Slave-dealers were probably active in the region as well. Certainly, the existence of a slave-market at London is implied by a letter found there in which a man named Rufus, after other remarks, instructs his correspondent Epillicus (who has a typically Celtic name) to 'take care to turn that girl into cash'.

Inscriptions recording freedmen are slightly more numerous. This is indeed natural. Most slaves would be unable to afford the cost of an inscribed stone, and few masters were likely to have laid out more cash to record the loss of a piece of property, or capital, a *res mortalis*, 'mortal object'. But, besides this, it appears that in Roman times a fair proportion of slaves were given their freedom on attaining the minimum age for manumission, 30. Economic considerations no doubt played a part. Life expectancy was short, and after the age of 30 a slave's usefulness may have been limited. In any case, freedmen were self-supporting but could still be called upon to perform services for their former masters. A further factor may have been widespread in some parts of the empire, particularly the Celtic regions. Circumstantial evidence strongly suggests that it was a common practice for parents to sell children into slavery, often for a fixed period. By this means poor parents reduced the number of mouths to feed (and, when the master was of citizen status, they could hope that their child would eventually attain citizenship on manumission). There is one example from Britain which may be evidence of this practice here, Regina the freedwoman and wife of Barates of Palmyra. She died at South Shields at the age of 30 and received an ornate tombstone from her husband, inscribed in both Latin and Palmyrene. In the Latin text she is described as *natione Catvallauna*, in other words from one of the most civilized of the peoples of southern Britain, whose chief town, Verulamium, enjoyed the rank of *municipium*. It is difficult to see how a Catuvellaunian girl could be sold into servitude except by a voluntary act on the part of her parents. Regina seems not to have acquired citizenship on manumission. But another British freedwoman, Calpurnia Trifosa obtained this status from her former master C. Calpurnius Receptus, priest of Sulis at Bath, whom she married, and to whom she erected a tombstone on his death at the age of 75. Her *cognomen* is surely a Latinized spelling of the Greek Τρυφῶσα, meaning 'dainty' or 'delicious' – which does not necessarily mean that she came from the Greek-speaking part of the empire. Slave-traders would be likely to give such a name to an attractive girl-slave, whatever her origin.

As with slaves, the position of freedmen varied enormously according to the rank of their patron. Naturally, the most favoured were the imperial freedmen, a number of whom must have been regularly employed on the emperor's business in the province. The senior of these had the title procurator of Britain, making him the chief deputy of the equestrian *procurator Augusti*. For Britain, the only recorded example comes on an inscription from Tricomia in Phrygia honouring M. Aurelius Marcio. He was *proc. prov. Britanniae* in the middle of his career, after being in charge of state marble quarries and before going on to manage the scenery and stage props for the theatres of the capital (*proc. summi choragii*). The freedmen and equestrian procurators had a considerable staff of imperial slaves and freedmen working under them, and several of the latter are attested in Britain. Naevius, *Aug. lib., adiutor procc.*, 'assistant to the procurators' restored a headquarters-building (*principia*) at Combe Down near Bath in the reign of Caracalla. The building in question was presumably the centre of an imperial estate in the west country of which Naevius was the administrator. At York, another imperial freedman whose name cannot be read with confidence made a dedication to the goddess Holy Britannia. He too may have had responsibility for imperial property, or alternatively may have worked in the office responsible for army pay. The imperial freedman Aquilinus who restored a temple at London was presumably attached to the procurator headquarters in the provincial capital. The three men named on the inscription with him, Mercator, Audax and Graec(us) whose status is not recorded, may have been imperial slaves.

Roman officials of all ranks, from the governor downwards, army officers and many ordinary soldiers, would have their own slaves. Tacitus specifically notes that Agricola did not use his freedmen and slaves for official duties. No governor's household happens to be recorded, but there is a fine inscription from Chester set up by the *liber(ti) et familia*, 'the freedmen and slave-household' of the legate of the XXth legion Pomponius Mamilianus. It is a dedication to Fortuna Redux, 'Fortune that brings men home', and to Aesculapius and Salus, deities that preserved health, indicating that the legate's household may have been suffering from the effects of their stay in Britain. Freedmen of equestrian officers commanding the garrisons at three outpost forts north of Hadrian's Wall, Risingham, High Rochester and Birrens, also dedicated altars. Theodotus, freedman of Arrius Paulinus, made a dedication to an unknown deity for the health of his patron (whose status is not explicitly recorded). At High Rochester, the freedman Eutychus, together with his family (*c(um) s(uis)*), fulfilled his vow to Silvanus Pantheus for the welfare of the tribune Rufinus and the latter's wife Lucilla, and the *libertus* Felicio, buried at the same place, had presumably gone there in the household of a commanding officer. At Birrens, the freedman Celer paid his vows to Fortuna on behalf of the prefect Campanius Italicus.

Several other inscriptions record freedmen of centurions. The *liberti*, unnamed, of Sempronius Sempronianus, set up a tombstone to him and his brothers at London. At Bath the freedmen Eutuches and Lemnus dedicated altars to Sulis for the health and safety of their patron M. Aufidius Maximus, centurion of the VIth legion, who was no doubt taking the cure there. The famous tombstone at Colchester of M. Favonius Facilis, centurion of the XXth legion, was put up by his freedmen Verecundus and Novicius. P. Aelius Bassus, another centurion of the XXth, from a later period, who died at Watercrook in Cumbria, left two freedmen as his heirs. Ordinary legionaries and veterans must be assumed to have had slaves and freedmen too in many cases, although the direct evidence in Britain is rather fragmentary. But a fine tombstone at South Shields shows that a cavalryman in the *ala I Asturum*, one Numerianus, had a freedman named Victor, 'by nation a Moor', who died at the age of 20 (well below the official legal minimum age for receiving his freedom). Numerianus might have purchased Victor in a slave-market in Britain, although he could have acquired him on campaign in north Africa.

The name of another freedman recorded in Britain has been read as Imilico, which looks like a variant spelling of the Punic name Himilcho. He set up a marble dedication near Colchester to the imperial *numina* and to a Celtic version of Mercury. His patron's name, Aesubilinus, is thoroughly Celtic and this man might have been a prosperous Trinovantian who had acquired an African slave. Ti. Claudius Primus, freedman of Attius, dedicator of a silver votive plate found in Hertfordshire, was more fortunate than Imilico, having had a citizen master. Ti. Claudius Attius himself was perhaps one of the early recipients of citizenship among the Catuvellauni, adopting the *praenomen* and *nomen* of the Claudian imperial family.

Apart from the record of an unnamed slave-goldsmith at Malton, there is virtually no hint in the British inscriptions of any specific work carried out by slaves and freedman for their masters and patrons. It is probably too fanciful to suppose that the freedman Caec(ilius) Musicus who commemorated his former master's widow Ael(ia) Severa on a tombstone at York had originally been named Musicus when a slave with the hope or intention that he should be some kind of entertainer. But undoubtedly some slaves and freedmen would be engaged in trade, as is the case with two men whose status as freedmen is not stated, although it is probable, for they were *seviri Augustales* – the *seviri* (board of six men) who conducted emperor-worship in the chartered towns of the empire, were overwhelmingly composed of freedmen. It is therefore likely that the merchants M. Aurelius Lunaris, *sevir* of York and Lincoln, and M. Verec(undius) Diogenes, *sevir* of York, a Gaul by origin, fell into this category.

Diogenes and Lunaris, if they were indeed freedmen, might have begun their careers as businessmen as slaves and have carried on after manumission as agents for their patrons, later perhaps setting up on their own. It was certainly a common pattern in the ancient world for traders, craftsmen and manufacturers to use slaves and freedmen, and evidence from Britain strongly suggests that some of the producers of mortaria exemplified this pattern.

The prime example is the five potters from the same workshop at Colchester or somewhere in south-eastern England, in the mid-first century AD, all called Sex. Valerius, with different *cognomina*, mentioned in Chapter XIII on craftsmen. One more instance may be given, the glass-maker Briginus Ingenui *l(ibertus)*. Briginus' name is typically Celtic, while his patron Ingenuus has a Latin name, meaning 'free born' (although it may have been adapted from a Celtic original).

An interesting group of possible freedmen in Britain are the five lead-mining contractors. Four of them have Greek names as *cognomina*, and the fifth, L. Aruconius Verecundus, has a *cognomen* commonly found in the servile class. The earliest of them is C. Nipius Ascanius, whose name is found on a lead pig at Stockbridge in Hampshire dated to AD 60 and on another found at Carmel, Flintshire. He may have leased the mines in Mendip soon after the conquest, then have followed the army northwards. Although Ascanius is a Greek name, its association with Rome's legendary Trojan origin makes it possible to regard it as 'Latin by adoption'. Nipius is an extremely rare *gentilicium*, possibly an alternative form of the Etruscan Nepius, and is only attested twice elsewhere. One bearer is an imperial procurator, who made a dedicator at Rome, C. Nipius Flavianus, the other an equestrian officer commanding a cohort in Pannonia in the Flavian period, Nipius Aquila. Ascanius' servile origin must be regarded as rather doubtful, but he is likely to have been connected in some way with the other two Nipii.

The other four contractors were all associated with a company, the *soc(ii) Lutudarens(es)*, which evidently leased mining rights in the Peak District in the first century. They may have been successive managers, but one of them is also known to have operated in Mendip. This was Ti. Cl. Trifer., whose *cognomen* is presumably Triferus, a Latinised spelling of the Greek Τρυφερός. As a Tiberius Claudius, he ought to be either an imperial freedman, of Claudius or Nero, or a freedman of a new citizen who obtained the franchise from either of those emperors. The latter alternative is perhaps more likely, since an imperial freedman ought to have signed *Aug. lib.* Equally, it is not excluded that he was an independent contractor of Greek origin, not a freedman at all.

This last possibility is less likely with the other two contractors with Greek names, C. Julius Protus and P. Rubrius Abascantus. Protus is a typically servile name, and the man may be regarded as the *libertus* of a family enfranchised under Caesar or Augustus. As for Rubrius, this is not a likely *gentilicium* for a native Greek-speaker – unless he were from southern Italy.

The final case is that of L. Aruconius Verecundus. The *nomen* is only found in one other instance, an L. Aruco[nius Cen]sorinus on an inscription from Rome. This person may himself have been a freedman, but there is no guarantee, from the nomenclature, that the lead-contractor was from this class. Verecundus is a name given to slave and freedmen, but there are 10 times as many cases where it is borne by persons of free birth. Aruconius may be a 'fabricated' *gentilicium* and Verecundus could well have been a free born businessman from the Celtic lands. One further item deserves mention, Applebaum's ingenious suggestion that the place-name Ariconium (Weston-under-Penyard) derives from an estate owned by this man. It was the centre of an iron-smelting industry in the Forest of Dean, and it is attractive to speculate that Verecundus retired from lead-contracting to become an iron-master.

Chapter XVI
The Last Century of Roman Rule

Two events separated by exactly a century conveniently delimit the last age of Roman Britain. On 25 July 306 Constantine the Great was proclaimed emperor by the troops at York. In 406 the British army elevated Marcus to the imperial power, to replace him in rapid succession, first with the local aristocrat (*municeps*) Gratian, then with Constantine, known for convenience as the third emperor of that name. It is perhaps mere coincidence that both Constantine I and Constantine III launched their very different imperial careers from Britain. But, if the 'British tyrant' was a far lesser figure than the first Christian emperor, his effect on history was not negligible – not least in that he may be said to have caused indirectly the fall of Stilicho in 408 and thus to have made possible Alaric's sack of Rome in 410. More significant for Britain itself was the fact that after his usurpation – brought to an end in 411 – the emperors never regained control of the island.

There were profound changes, in Britain no less than in the rest of the empire, during the 100 years which elapsed between the accessions of the two Constantines. That Christianity became the religion of the Roman empire was undoubtedly the most striking single consequence that flowed from the reign of Constantine the Great. Within a short time of his victory at the Milvian Bridge (AD 312), he began to take an active role in the affairs of the Church. At Arles, in August 314, a Council was convened to which the churches in the provinces under his control were invited to send delegates to debate the Donatist controversy. Five men are listed as coming from Britain, three bishops, each evidently representing the capital of a province, while the other two, a priest and a deacon, were presumably the substitutes for a fourth metropolitan bishop. The bishops' names admirably illustrate the diversity of possible nomenclature: Eborius, bishop of Eboracum, has a Celtic name, perhaps derived from that of his church; Restitutus, bishop of London, has a Latin name of a type favoured in the Celtic provinces; Adelphius' name is Greek, while his town, described as *colonia Londiniensium*, is presumably a scribal error for *Lindensium*, Lincoln. The priest and deacon, called Sacerdos and Arminius respectively, both have Latin names, which may both conceal Celtic originals. Their church is not mentioned, but may be presumed to be the chief town of the fourth British province, probably Cirencester.

There is every reason to believe that these men were merely the representatives of a much larger number of churches in Britain. The discovery of a second British specimen of the SATOR word-square, generally regarded as Christian, in a second-century level at Manchester, is a welcome reminder that the constant influx of people from the Mediterranean world, both military and civil, is bound to have included some Christians. The specimens at Cirencester, on painted wall-plaster of second- or third-century date, can be taken to show that the new religion made some progress among the settled population as well as among the transient element. Hence Tertullian's statement that parts of Britain inaccessible to the Romans were under the sway of Christ, if perhaps a little exaggerated, may not be totally implausible. A generation later, in the 230s and 240s, Origen three times mentions the Britons among the far-flung adherents of Christianity. The earliest named British Christians are shrouded in the mists of hagiography, but five may be produced who may be assigned to the third century with varying degrees of confidence. The first four were martyrs, and since the persecutions terminated in the west with the accession of Constantine, all of them ought to be earlier than 306. Further, since his father Constantius is said to have stopped short of carrying out the death penalty in his interpretation of Diocletian's edict of persecution in the years 303–305, there is good reason to argue that the late, post-Roman sources which assign the martyrdoms of Albanus, Aaron, and Julius to this 'Great Persecution' were mistaken, and that they died earlier.

The death of Alban, Britain's first martyr, is described in the earliest manu-script in circumstantial detail which has allowed John Morris to date it with some plausibility to the year 209. It is said to have taken place at the time of Severus' visit to Britain, and 'the wicked Caesar' who condemned Alban to death, and then, appalled by the miracles which at once followed, ordered the persecution to end 'without the orders of the emperors', may be identified as Severus' younger son Geta. He is specifically said by Herodian, in his near-contemporary account of the campaigns, to have been left behind in the province while Severus and Caracalla campaigned beyond the northern frontier. Since Geta himself was raised to the rank of full emperor, Augustus, at the end of 209, the account fits this context admirably. Since Albanus was beheaded, rather than crucified or thrown to the beasts in the arena, he must have been a Roman citizen. This circumstance, and his entirely Latin name, make it likely that he was a member of the upper class at Verulamium and thus a very rare specimen among the Christians of the European provinces of the Latin west at this time, where most known Christians were immigrants from the east.

Aaron and Julius are first mentioned in the sixth century, by Gildas, the British monk, who calls them 'Legionum urbis cives', 'citizens of the city of the Legions', and assigns their death to Diocletian's persecution, the only one about which he knew. We may infer that they came from Isca, the Welsh Caerleon, and, in the light of what was said about Constantius, it seems probable that their martyrdom took place in the third century, if not in 209 during the presecutions of Decius (250–251) or Valerian (257–258). The name Julius is of course uninformative, for it is the commonest Roman *gentilicium* at Caerleon as in Britain in general. But the Jewish name Aaron, with which one may compare Salmanes attested on the Antonine Wall, clearly indicates an immigrant civilian.

Quite different evidence supplies two further names. A fourth British martyr, Augulus or Agulus, is listed in the *Martyrologium* mistakenly attributed to St Jerome, and in later martyrologies. These all list a number of other supposedly British martyrs who can easily be shown to belong to other parts of the empire, being assigned to Britain by textual corruption of various kinds (e.g. by confusion between *Bithynia* and *Britannia*). But Augulus – if that was his name – cannot be so readily explained away. For one thing, several manuscripts of pseudo-Jerome locate his martyrdom *in Brittaniis*, the correct plural form for the subdivided Britain of the third to fifth centuries. His death is more specifically assigned to the town of Augusta, *civitate Augusta*, the name borne by London in the later fourth century, if not earlier; and he is called 'bishop and martyr'. It is thus at least a possibility, which deserves to be registered, that this man is the earliest known British bishop, martyred during one of the third-century persecutions. Unfortunately the variant spellings of his name make it impossible to comment on his origin.

The last of the five earliest Christians is known only from very late post-Roman tradition. Mellonus, first bishop of Rouen, is said to have been born in 'Great Britain' – distinguished thus from Brittany – 'of no mean parents, a citizen of the town of Cardiola', which is otherwise unknown. The Saint's *Life* continues with the story that he went to Rome in the reign of Valerian (253–260) in connection with the payment of taxes by his *patria*, home town presumably, rather than the whole province, being meant. Here he was converted by Stephanus, the bishop (known to have been martyred under Valerian in 257). After baptism, he sold all that he possessed, 'including his weapons, with which he served as a soldier' ('etiam arma, quibus militabat'); and later went to Rouen to be bishop. At all events, there is little doubt that his name, although otherwise unattested, is Celtic rather than Latin in origin.

However shadowy or mythical these first named Christians associated with Britain may be, it is legitimate to postulate that the first four, the British martyrs, are merely the tip of the iceberg. Although doubtless only a small minority among the population of Britain before the conversion of Constantine and for several decades thereafter, the British Christians were sufficiently numerous to send fully-fledged representatives to the Council at Arles in 314. Their churches assented to the decisions of the Council of Nicaea, at which the Nicene creed was formulated, in 325. At the Rimini Council in 359 British bishops were probably present in force. Three of them (unnamed) are singled out by Sulpicius Severus for mention, for their refusal to follow the decision of their British and Gallic colleagues to reject the state's payment of expenses. 'Three alone from Britain, who were especially poor', thought it better to burden the state than individuals.

Some Christians in Britain at this period were certainly wealthy, as shown by the treasure found at Durobrivae (Chesterton). Three of the pieces supply us with names. Two women, Innocentia and Viventia – characteristically Christian names – dedicated a silver cup for religious use. Another has the name Publianus, a standard old-style Latin *cognomen*, on the base, while the words 'Relying on you, Lord, I honour your altar' (or 'sanctuary', *altare*) in verse attest both the faith and the culture of its dedicator. A silver plaque records that a woman worshipper 'fulfilled the vow which she promised.' Her name was at first read as *Ancilla*, interpreted as 'handmaid (of the Lord)'. Anicilla, a Latin *cognomen*, has been proposed, but the most recent reading produces Iamicilla, which is certainly not Latin and may be Celtic.

A handful of other names on objects of fourth-century date may be identified with some probability as those of Christians – on bowls or spoons of silver, for example. Desiderius, whose name appears on a silver bowl found near Corbridge on Tyne, with the *chi-rho* monogram and the word *vivas*, 'mayst thou live!', is in some ways the most interesting. He might be the same as the official of that name who held office as *vicarius* of one of the three western dioceses (Britain, Gaul, or Spain) in 385, during the usurpation of Magnus Maximus. The usurper, it will be recalled, had been baptised in 383, in Britain, immediately before his proclamation as emperor. Of the others, one may note Censorinus at Chedworth villa in

Gloucestershire, Aeternus at Colchester, Augustinus at Dorchester, and Papittedo and Pascentia on 'christening spoons' in the treasure from Mildenhall, on the edge of the Fens. All of these are regarded by Jocelyn Toynbee as possible Christians. One may add, perhaps, Viventia, wife of Victoricus, whose name appears on a fourth-century pewter dish from Verulamium, and there is also the intriguing case of the Silchester ring bearing the legend '*Seniciane vivas in deo*', 'Senicianus, mayst thou live in God'. Senicianus had not been the first owner of the ring, for the name of Venus, pagan goddess of love, was inscribed on it earlier. Curiously, a 'curse tablet' found at the shrine of the god Nodens at Lydney, was dedicated to that deity by one Silvianus, who denounced Senicianus and prayed Nodens to help him find a ring. It is attractive to infer that the Silchester Christian had stolen his ring from the pagan Silvianus. Some of these names, Aeternus, Augustinus, Censorinus, and Senicianus are of standard Roman type, and might have been found in Britain or other western provinces at any period. Others, Desiderius, Pascentius, Victoricus and Viventia, seem to have been favoured by Christians, Pascentia exclusively so, while Papittedo is clearly non-Latin.

It is typical of our limited sources that while we have no direct record by a contemporary, British or otherwise, of the last age of Roman Britain and the circumstances under which the island's allegiance to Rome ended, we have a graphic portrayal from the pen of a British writer of the sack of Rome itself in 410. An aristocratic refugee named Demetrias, from the great family of the Anicii, who had fled to north Africa, astonished her relations in 413, when she was 14, by taking vows of chastity and receiving the veil from the Bishop of Carthage. Her mother and grandmother asked two great teachers to send her letters of advice on her new life, Pelagius and Jerome. Both were then in the Holy Land, but while Jerome had been there for nearly 30 years, Pelagius had been a resident of Rome until the eve of the city's sack, leaving in 409 first for Sicily and then Africa, before going to Jerusalem. His letter to Demetrias was the opportunity for Pelagius to reiterate his already controversial message, that human beings could, after all, be perfect, by their nature, and that perfection was therefore obligatory. 'I do not wish to be called a monk', he tells Demetrias ' – what I wish is that you should be a Christian'. He paints a terrifying picture of the Last Judgement, with which, to make it more vivid, he compares the sack of Rome: 'The event is recent, and one which you yourself heard. At the strident trumpet's blast, at the shouts of the Goths, the mistress of the world, Rome, was oppressed with mournful fear, and trembled. Where then was the rank of the nobility? Where the sure and distinct grades of that order? Everything was turned upside down and confused, through fear, in every house there was lamentation, all alike were in equal panic. Slave and noble were one. The same picture of death faced everyone.'

The activities of Pelagius and his supporters, and their writings, occupy a crucial role in the development of Christian doctrine. Two of the Church's greatest names, Augustine and Jerome, spent several years attacking Pelagius and Pelagianism. Jerome, in particular, and Augustine's young follower, the Spanish priest Paulus Orosius, stoop to venomous personal denigration. Jerome seems to have known Pelagius when they were both at Rome, and it may be assumed that Pelagius had gone there from Britain at the latest by the early 380s, the period of Jerome's residence at the capital. Perhaps Pelagius had crossed the Channel at the time of Maximus' usurpation. At any rate, Pelagius is evidently the unnamed monk, a man of weighty eloquence, whom Jerome attacks in violent terms in a letter written in the 390s: a big man, 'handsomely fleshy, with the flanks and strength of an athlete' and with 'a tilted and pointed head'. Some 20 years later the tone was to become even more hostile: 'thoroughly stolid, weighed down by Irish porridge' – *Scottorum pultibus*: by referring to the diet of the Britons' primitive and aggressive neighbours, the Scotti, Jerome was, by implication, blackening Pelagius as a barbarian. There is in fact no doubt that Pelagius was British, not Irish. He is uniformly, except for this passage and a similar one elsewhere in Jerome's writings, referred to as 'a Briton', 'a monk of British race', or the like, by contemporaries, including Orosius. The latter took his cue from Jerome, to whose insults already quoted we may add the comparison to a huge 'Alpine hound' – which evokes the picture of a St Bernard dog – or to a tortoise, because of his slow and ponderous gait. Orosius describes Pelagius as 'a monstrous Goliath', . . . who dispensed with a hat, which no doubt emphasized his 'bulging forehead', and dwells on his massive physique, 'nourished by baths and banquets, his broad shoulders and thick neck.'

Pelagius' name, it must be noted, is Greek, meaning 'of the ocean', but this is no way surprising. Greek names were by this date commonly adopted by all classes in the Latin west. Jerome himself, Hieronymus, is one example – and from Britain we may cite Constantine III's general Gerontius, not to mention Ambrosius Aurelianus, 'last of the Romans', whose names echo those of the great Bishop of Milan. Pelagius will undoubtedly have had other names, but speculation is fruitless. It is worth remarking only that there is no need to assume that he was (for example) the son of a Greek doctor who had emigrated to Britain; nor that his name was a translation of the British ('Welsh') name Morgan. His own writings amply attest to his excellent education. He shows familiarity with a wide range of pagan classical literature, including less obvious writers than Virgil and Horace, and he had some knowledge of Greek philosophy. His moral teaching displays some affinities to the Stoicism traditionally favoured by the Roman aristocracy for centuries. What brought him to Rome is unknown – it is mere speculation to suppose that he was a lawyer, hoping for preferment, but it is not implausible. At all events, he acquired powerful patrons and supporters among the Christianized aristocracy of Rome. His links with the Anicii have already been mentioned. More significant may have been the friendship of Paulinus of Nola, a Gallic aristocrat who was converted to asceticism in the 390s, and with the family of the younger Melania. The vast estates of that young heiress included lands in Britain. She was born in the 380s, but it may be suggested that her parents, or whichever relation of Melania it was from whom she inherited the British property, would have been obvious persons for the young Pelagius to have sought out when he first went to Rome.

Pelagius had attracted the attention, and hostility, of Jerome in the 390s, as we have seen. What caused Jerome's crude and violent outburst then was the public criticism of Jerome's very negative teaching on marriage. But the nameless object of Jerome's onslaught might have remained unidentified for ever had it not been for what followed. In about 405 Pelagius was stirred to anger by reading the tenth book of Augustine's *Confessions*. The phrase, 'Command what You will: give what You command', seemed to him to exhibit excessive tolerance to sin. Over the next few years he actively propagated his own view that man possessed freedom of choice and could be without sin. The Church would have to remain a small and compact group. This conflicted with Augustine's vision of Christianity as a universal, Catholic, religion, to which all could belong, thanks to the divine grace. Several of Pelagius' writings survive, including his *Commentaries on the Thirteen Epistles of St Paul*, the first substantial written work by a native of this island. He gained a number of passionately loyal followers, one of whom, Caelestius, has sometimes been regarded as an Irishman, on mistaken grounds. For a time Pelagius was able successfully to defend the orthodoxy of his position, in spite of the vigorous opposition by Augustine, Jerome, and others. But eventually he was roundly condemned, and his teachings denounced as heretical, by both Pope and Emperor, in 418. Nothing further is known of him after this time, but it seems possible that he quietly returned to his native Britain. Certainly, as will be seen at the end of this chapter, there is striking evidence for the revival of Pelagianism in Britain a little later in the fifth century.

In the meantime Christianity had undoubtedly made further progress in Britain, but not without controversy. The vigorous Bishop of Rouen, Victricius – himself thought by some to have been of British origin, like his distant predecessor Mellonus – came to the island towards the end of the fourth century at the request of the Britons themselves. The question at issue seems to have been the impact of St Martin's reforms. Martin's vigorous campaign to stamp out paganism and introduce monasticism had aroused opposition in Gaul. Victricius, as a fervent disciple, is likely to have fostered these aims on his visit to Britain. In a letter to Ambrose and others he explained that he had taken to Britain the precepts of the martyrs. He sums up his mission with a trenchant statement: 'I filled the sensible with the love of peace, taught those who could be taught, subdued the ignorant, and attacked the opposition.' Victricius' name, although found as a *gentilicium* centuries earlier in Italy, is not otherwise known at this period, except on a pewter vessel, found with others, one of them bearing the Chi-Rho symbol, near Andover in Hampshire. This might be coincidence, but a connection with the bishop need not be ruled out. One or two results of his mission may be deduced. At least one British monk happens to be recorded, a few years later: Constans, son of the British usurper Constantine III, had to abandon his calling when his father appointed him Caesar, evoking a cry of horror from Orosius. It is impossible even to guess where his monastery was – it could be, of course, that he had joined one in Gaul. As for the other element in Martin's programme, the conversion of the pagans, it may be that Victricius' visit inspired the mission of Ninianus or Nynia, St Ninian, to the southern Picts, which there are some grounds for dating to the beginning of the fifth century. Ninian may have been Bishop of Carlisle.

The other great Christian teacher produced by Roman Britain was a person of a very different stamp from Pelagius, and the nature of the sources is also totally different. We have the precious evidence of St Patrick's *Confession* and *Letter* to provide insight into his personality and considerable information about his origin and background. But his date of birth, and the chronology of his mission to Ireland, remain uncertain and disputed. Even so, it seems clear from his own writings that he was born before Roman control over Britain was severed. He was the son of a man named Calpurnius, who was not only a deacon of the church but a decurion, in other words a member of the provincial upper classes. Calpurnius' own father, Potitus, was a priest. The names are conventionally Roman, of the traditional kind, Calpurnius a *gentilicium* that was widespread all over the empire, while Potitus is a standard Roman *cognomen*, as Patricius is also – although much less common and particularly favoured by Christians. The family's home was at a place which the manuscripts call Bannavem Taberniae, with some variants in the spelling. A possible corruption of Bannaventa, Daventry, seems unlikely, as being too far inland, for it was while Patrick was on his father's estate nearby that he was captured by raiders from Ireland and sold into slavery there. He was then aged about 16 and remained a slave for six years until he managed to escape and return to Britain. For a few years he remained with his family, then spent a long period preparing for his ministry, being ordained deacon and priest, including evidently some time in Gaul, before going back to Ireland as a missionary bishop. The traditional date for his return to Ireland is 432. Such is the bare outline of his early life. Discussion of his mission in Ireland falls outside the scope of the present work, but his writings have something to tell us about the last years of Roman Britain.

Patrick shows himself continually conscious of his lack of education and inability to express himself fluently, of his provincialism (*rusticitas*) compared to the 'skilled master-rhetoricians'. But, it must be stressed, this is not evidence for the overall backwardness of Britain. It is simply the product of his circumstances, for he was kidnapped and sold into slavery at just the age when he might soon have hoped to begin the study of rhetoric. Six years as a slave in a foreign and barbarous country gave him a handicap in this respect which he was never to overcome. Even though he had the opportunity, after his escape, to devote years to the study of the Bible and devotional literature, he never had any higher education, unlike Pelagius. Besides, at the time when he was writing his *Confession* and *Letter* he had been back in Ireland for a long time, cut off from the society of educated men. His rule of faith is conservative and completely orthodox, betraying no awareness of doctrinal controversies such as Pelagiansim. He was living in expectation of the end of the world, preaching the Gospel to people who lived at that world's furthest limit. The one work he had certainly read was the Latin Bible. His own religious experience was intense and may fairly be called mystical. Imperfect and clumsy though his Latin was, his honesty shines through. Unlike the rhetorically trained Latin Fathers of the Church, from Tertullian to Augustine, unlike Jerome and Pelagius, he expresses his meaning directly with no trace of artifice. 'Perhaps the most honest of all who ever wrote Christian Latin. His *Confessio* . . . is the writing of an unlettered genius, unique in the Ancient World (and rare outside it). It combines tremendous power with a sort of trance-like quality that places it nearer to Thomas à Kempis than to Gibbon or Rousseau'.

It was stressed earlier that the triumph of the Church was the most obvious result of the accession of Constantine I. His nephew Julian, the Apostate, who tried, during his brief reign (361–363) to turn back the tide, and naturally took a hostile view of his uncle's conversion, coupled with this criticism another charge. He denounced Constantine for showing excessive favours to barbarians in Rome's service. Certainly, there were now numerous German troops, on which the imperial armies came to rely to a dangerous degree. This was of course far from being an innovation. We have only to recall the mutinous cohort of Usipi in Agricola's army. Men like the chieftain Hnaudifridus, worshipping his Teutonic Alaisiagae with his men at Housesteads in the early third century, and other Germans mentioned in Chapter VII are an even clearer reminder – or the 5,500 Sarmatians sent to Britain in 175 (by Julian's hero Marcus Aurelius). In the later third century the practice was increasing, in Britain as elsewhere. When the emperor Probus defeated the Burgundians and Vandals under their king Igillus in 277 or 278, he sent the survivors to Britain, where not long afterwards, loyal to their new master, they helped to suppress an attempted coup by a governor. When the Saxons first appeared within the empire, harassing the Channel coasts in the early 280s, the man appointed to repel them, Carausius, made himself emperor in Britain – where he and his successor Allectus made copious use of Franks in their own army. It is therefore no suprise to hear that the principal role in proclaiming Constantine emperor at York in 306 was assumed by the king of the Alamanni, one Crocus, who had been in Constantius' service. Some 60 years later the commanding general of the British frontier troops, the *dux*, was a German, Fullofaudes. We hear from Ammianus of another Alammanic king, Fraomarius, being posted to Britain in 372 to command a unit of his fellow-tribesmen, with the rank of tribune.

Some of the earlier groups of barbarians may, perhaps, have been sent to Britain not so much to reinforce the island's garrison as to prevent them from causing trouble elsewhere. Britain was certainly chosen as a place of exile for a number of individuals in the fourth century, some of them prominent. The former *magister officiorum* ('master of the offices' or senior co-ordinator of the palace bureaucracy), Palladius, a native of Antioch, was banished to Britain under Julian in 361; his subsequent fate is unknown. During Count Theodosius' mission in Britain in 367–368 a serious internal crisis was created when a Pannonian named Valentinus, brother-in-law of a very senior official, who had been sent to Britain 'for a serious offence', was detected plotting a coup d'état involving fellow-exiles and some of the troops. The affair was dealt with by the general Dulcitius. But only two years later another political offender was sent here, one Frontinus, who had been on the staff of a proconsul of Africa convicted of treason. The last cases recorded belong to the reign of Magnus Maximus, and they were religious offenders, two supporters of the heretic Priscillianus. Both men, Instantius, a bishop, and a high ranking Spanish layman named Tiberianus, were sent to the Scilly Isles, where opportunities to propagate their views must have been limited.

The emphasis placed so far in this chapter on the Christian community in the last generations of Roman rule should not obscure the fact that paganism survived and indeed flourished for much of the fourth century. Little is known of individual pagans, not surprisingly, given the overall decline in the epigraphic evidence. Some of the persons mentioned in the chapter on frontier people may indeed belong to this period, but there is no sure criterion by which most can be dated to the third or to the fourth centuries. But there is no doubt of the fourth-century date of the mosaic pavement at Appleshaw in Hampshire, and the presumably opulent villa owner who commissioned it, Q. Natalius Natalinus, was probably a pagan: the subject depicted is the god Dionysus. (Natalinus' nomenclature has been discussed in the chapter on countrydwellers.) Pagan and Christian may have co-existed peacefully for a time; and, certainly, the brief pagan reaction under Julian did not revive the persecution of the Church. Some have seen an illustration of this flicker of renewed paganism in an inscription at Cirencester. It records the restoration of 'a statue and column erected by the ancient religion' by a governor of Britannia Prima (the title of one of the fourth-century provinces), L. Septimius – his other name is missing. There is further evidence for the vigour of pagan cults in this part of Britain during the middle and later part of the century, with shrines flourishing at Uley in the Cotswolds and at Lydney on the Severn. At Lydney the god Nodens not only received the vow made by the irate Silvianus, but a mosaic dedicated by an official of the Roman fleet, T. Flavius Senilis. It may be remarked that the conservatism in religion exhibited by Natalinus, Septimius, and Senilis is matched by that in their nomenclature, all three retaining the old-style *tria nomina*.

At Uley a whole series of leaden curse-tablets have been found, not many of which have yet been deciphered. On one, a woman named Saturnia appears to be seeking the assistance of Mercury in recovering some linen that she had lost. On another, a certain Senacus – a thoroughly Celtic name – refers to the loss of an ox. Two other names on this tablet are particularly interesting. Natalinus evokes the pagan villa-owner from Hampshire, while Vitalinus is a name associated with the fifth-century 'tyrant' Vortigern, who is linked with Gloucester in the genealogies.

Few other British names can be gleaned from the fourth-century evidence. One should mention the Eutherius whose name appears on one of the platters in the Mildenhall treasure, already referred to. But it has been suggested that this person could be the eunuch Eutherius, who was chamberlain to Julian when the latter was Caesar in Gaul, during the years 356–361. He was a pagan, of Armenian origin, and his presence in Britain, if he came at all, can only have been temporary. It should, however, be remembered that the purge conducted in Britain by the notary Paulus, 'the Chain', after the fall of the half-British usurper Magnentius in 353, may have considerably weakened the ranks of the British upper classes. The confiscated lands of Paulus' victims may have been sold off, in some cases, allowing opportunites for officials or wealthy senators to acquire them – this could explain, for example, the British estates of St Melania.

Britain has made no surviving contribution to the secular literature of Rome, but it would be wrong to omit mention of the solitary British poet, Silvius Bonus. His name and origin were savaged by Ausonius, the poet, professor, and ultimately consul, from Bordeaux, in his *Epigrams*, evidently published in 382. Bonus, 'good', is an impossible name for a Briton; he should be called Malus:

What? Silvius Good?
No Briton could
Be – better he had
Been Silvius Bad!

It is difficult to avoid the conclusion that there was a certain amount of anti-British prejudice in Gaul, particularly when one compares the remarks of Rutilius Namatianus a generation later (cited at the beginning of Chapter I).

Epigraphic evidence can at least provide three names of men involved in the defence of Britain in the fourth century. A building inscription found at Robin Hood's Bay in Yorkshire records the officers Justinianus, the commander, and his subordinate Vindicianus, who had been constructing a signalling tower. From Hadrian's Wall we may cite a stone which also seems to belong to this period and to refer to reconstruction, giving the name of Vindomorucius. This is unashamedly Celtic, well illustrating how Celtic nomenclature maintained its identity throughout more than three centuries of Roman rule, during the last half of which all the Britons had been Roman citizens, *cives Romani*. It may have been largely a matter of family preference whether native Britons gave their children Celtic or Roman – or indeed Greek – names. The three British usurpers, Marcus, Gratianus and Constantinus, all had standard Roman names. Constantine's sons were called Constans and Julianus, while his British general, Gerontius, had a Greek name. As Geraint the latter was to remain popular with the descendants of the Roman Britons, as was that other Greek name, Ambrosius – Emrys.

The genealogies of the kings who ruled in the lands between the Walls in the post-Roman period make a revealing subject of study. The dates and interpretation must remain rather uncertain, but Cunedda, chief or king of the Votadini, or Manau Gododdin, may be regarded as having led his people from their homes in north-east England and south-east Scotland, to defend Wales against attacks from Ireland, in the early or mid-fifth century. His name is thoroughly Celtic, but he was the son of Aeternus, grandson of Paternus, and great-grandson of Tacitus, all standard Latin *cognomina*. The last of these, indeed, happens to be recorded epigraphically in the right area for the Votadini: a seal was found in Midlothian bearing the name Tullia Tacita. More interesting is the additional name given to Cunedda's grandfather Paternus, Pesrut, 'man of the scarlet robe', suggesting that it referred to his possession of authority conferred by Rome – in the fourth century. However this may be – and it might simply be a case of a man who had both Celtic and Roman names – there is justification for the hypothesis that the Romans granted some kind of special status to the traditional rulers of tribes beyond Hadrian's Wall, in return for the commitment to share in the defence of Britain. Such a practice is attested elsewhere, and of course was in some ways merely a revival of the client-kingship conferred on men like Cogidubnus and Prasutagus, and on Queen Cartimandua of the Brigantes, in the first century. The equivalent territory further west, between the Clyde and the Solway, shows a similar picture. The ruler Ceredig, son of Cynloyp, can probably be identified with the king Coroticus whose soldiers Patrick denounced in his *Letter*. While Ceredig's father had an apparently Celtic name, his grandfather and great-grandfather had Latin ones – Cinhil, Quintilius or Quintillus, and Cluim, Clemens. Either Ceredig or another man, Coel Hen, is the ancestor of all the 13 lines of northern kings of the sub-Roman period in the genealogies. Coel Hen ('Old King Cole') himself is thought to have been born *c*. 380 and his first name is regarded as the Latin Coelius or Caelius. 'Hen' meaning 'the old' might be a version of the Latin Senex, but he appears to have had another name, Guotepauc, perhaps the same as Voteporix attested in a post-Roman inscription from Wales.

In 409, while Constantine III was struggling to maintain his position in Gaul, the Britons, left defenceless by his withdrawal of troops two years before, had no option but to rebel when the Germans – particularly, no doubt, the Saxons – attacked. 'They took up arms, and, braving the danger for themselves', the historian Zosimus records, 'liberated the cities from the attacking barbarians . . . they expelled the Roman officials and set up their own state, on their own authority'. Armorica, which followed the British example, was to be the scene of peasant revolts; with their suppression in 417 that part of Gaul returned to Roman rule. But Britain was never recovered after the usurpation of Constantine III – who himself fell in 411 – as the sixth-century Byzantine historian Procopius stresses. From that time onwards, it remained under 'tyrants', usurpers like Constantine himself, not recognized by Rome, but claiming the title of emperor in some form. One such man may have been the father of Ambrosius Aurelianus, whose parents are said 'to have worn the purple', presumably in the early fifth century. Another was clearly Vortigern, the 'proud tyrant' as Gildas calls him, evidently punning on the meaning of the name. He is called son of Vitalis or Vitalinus, of Gloucester, in the genealogies. Vortigern is the ruler said to have taken the fatal step of granting land to Saxons, under Hengest. Vortigern may, for a time, have been sole ruler of what had been Roman Britain, from the Channel to the Wall, but he had rivals – a quarrel with Ambrosius is mentioned, the man who was much later to win a notable victory against the barbarians.

During the years after the revolt of 409, Pelagianism revived, or rather, perhaps, started up for the first time, in the land of Pelagius' origin. Whether or not Pelagius had returned home is speculation. The man named as responsible for spreading the heresy was a bishop named Agricola, himself the son of a Pelagian bishop named Severianus. Another British prelate of this period thought to have been Pelagian was Fastidius. The strength of the doctrine was such that the orthodox appealed to the bishops in Gaul for assistance. Germanus and Lupus came over in 429, and not only successfully overcame the leading Pelagians in public debate, but inspired the British army to victory over a joint force of Saxons and Picts. Germanus is said to have returned to Britain nearly 20 years later, once again to combat the tenacious Pelagian heresy. The tangled skein of British history in this period cannot readily be unravelled. It may merely be noted that at about this time an appeal was also made for secular – military – assistance, to the general Aëtius. It went unanswered, and the settlements of Saxons and other Germanic peoples continued. The Britons were to have their successes, none the less, under Ambrosius, 'last of the Romans', for example, in the third quarter of the fifth century. In the following generation – so it may be argued – they found another great leader, Artorius, a good old Roman *gentilicium*, more familiar as Arthur.

Subjected to pressure on all sides, from the three enemies that had been attacking her since the late third century, Scots, Picts and Saxons, Britain was gradually transformed and fragmented. Large numbers of the Britons left to recreate their way of life in Armorica, which became 'little Britain', Brittany. But, it is important to remember, as late as the 530s or 540s, when Gildas wrote his fierce tract on *The Ruin of Britain*, he and his contemporaries could regard themselves as *cives*, 'fellow-citizens', cut off from Rome, ruled by tyrannical kings and ungodly and corrupt governors. He denounces five rulers by name, Constantine of Damnonia, Aurelius Caninus, Vortipor of the Demetae, Cuneglasus, and Maglocunus. The names of the last three might not have seemed out of place in the time of Cunobelinus, but Constantine and Aurelius Caninus aptly reflect – as does the language in which Gildas wrote and the faith that he preached – the lingering influence of Rome.

Principal abbreviations

This list comprises works cited frequently throughout the work (mainly Brit., CIL, RIB). Other items cited solely or mainly in the notes to particular chapters are explained in the notes to those chapters (e.g. Ch. II, Mack; Ch. XIII, various publications of potters; Ch. XIV, Applebaum; Ch. XVI, Bartrum).

AE   *L'Annee épigraphique* (Paris, 1888–   ): cited by year and number of inscription.

Brit.   *Britannia*. A Journal of Romano-British and kindred studies published by the Society for the Promotion of Roman Studies, London (Vol. I, 1970–   ): cited by year only, in most cases; the reference in each case is to the section 'Roman Britain in 19 , II. Inscriptions'.

CIL   *Corpus Inscriptionum Latinarum* (Berlin, 1863–   ). Sixteen parts to date, of which II covers the Iberian peninsula; III the Danube, Balkans, and Greek-speaking provinces; V, IX, X, XI, XIV various parts of Italy (and Sicily and Sardinia); VI Rome; VII Britain (now partly but not wholly superseded by RIB); VIII north Africa; XII Gaul; XIII north Gaul and the Rhineland; XV *instrumentum domesticum* of Rome and suburbs (graffiti, etc.); and XVI military diplomas. Cited by volume and inscription number.

CP   H.-G. Pflaum, *Les carrières procuratoriennes équestres sous le Haut-Empire romain* (Paris, 3 vols., 1960–1961): cited by career number.

EE   *Ephemeris Epigraphica*, I–IX (Berlin, 1872–1913). Inscriptions from Britain are in III (1877), IV (1881), VII (1892), IX (1913); not wholly superseded by RIB: cited by volume and inscription number.

Evans   D. Ellis Evans, *Gaulish Personal Names. A Study of some Continental Celtic Formations* (Oxford 1967).

Holder   A. Holder, *Alt-celtische Sprachschatz* (Leipzig, 3 vols., 1891–1913): cited by volume number and column.

ILS   H. Dessau, *Inscriptiones latinae selectae* (Berlin, 3 vols., 1892–1916): cited by inscription number.

JRS   *The Journal of Roman Studies* (London: Society for the Promotion of Roman Studes, Vol. I, 1910–   ): cited by year only, in most cases; the reference is to the section 'Roman Britain in . . . , II. Inscriptions' (up to 1969, after which this section was transferred to Brit.).

Kajanto   I. Kajanto, *The Latin Cognomina* (Societias scientiarum Fennica, Commentationes humanarum litterarum 36.2, Helsinki), 1965.

RBRA   E. Birley, *Roman Britain and the Roman Army* (Kendal: Wilson, 1953 and reprints).

RIB   *The Roman Inscriptions of Britain* I, ed. R. G. Collingwood and R. P. Wright (Oxford, 1965).

Schulze W. Schulze, *Zur Geschichte lateinischer Eigennamen* (Berlin: Abhandlungen der königlichen Gesellschaft der Wissenschaften zu Göttingen, phil.-hist. Klasse, n.F. V, 2, 1904).

Note on the listing of names:

Roman citizens in almost all cases are listed by their *nomen gentilicium*, e.g. Cn. Julius Agricola under Julius. Some cross-referencing should alleviate difficulties of consultation.

Notes to Chapter I

A useful introduction to Roman nomenclature is given by E. Birley, RBRA, pp. 158 ff. For studies of other provinces where the greater volume of epigraphic evidence allows a more scientific approach, cf. A. Mócsy, *Die Bevölkerung von Pannonien bis zu den Markomannenkriegen* (Budapest, 1959), and *Gesellschaft und Romanisation in der römischen Provinz Moesia Superior* (Budapest, 1970); and G. Alföldy, *Bevölkerung und Gesellschaft der römischen Provinz Dalmatien* (Budapest, 1965), backed up by his *Die Personennamen in der römischen Provinz Dalmatia* (Heidelberg, 1969). On the spread of citizenship see A. N. Sherwin-White, *The Roman Citizenship*, 2nd ed. (Oxford, 1973). On social groups see P. D. N. Garnsey, *Social Status and Legal Privilege in the Roman Empire* (Oxford, 1970). A. R. Burn, *The Romans in Britain* (Blackwell, 2nd. ed. 1969), provides a delightful introduction to the study of Romano-British inscriptions. An interesting attempt at a systematic evaluation of the epigraphic evidence has been made by the Hungarian scholar M. Biro, 'The Roman inscriptions of Britain', in the *Acta Archaeologica* of the Hungarian Academy of Sciences, 27 (1973), pp. 11 ff. The warning (quoted on p. 17) against the incautious use of Holder was given by K. H. Jackson, JRS 1948, p. 54; I have endeavoured to take due heed. On local preferences for particular *cognomina*, see Kajanto, pp. 54, 75. R. Syme, *Tacitus* (Oxford, 1958), pp. 783 ff., analyses the 'colonial' nomenclature of Gaul and Spain.

Names mentioned in this chapter (references are to the notes of the later chapters).

Addedomaros	*Ch. II*	Julius Classicianus	*Ch. III*
Aemilius	*Ch. IX*	Julius Frontinus	*Ch. III*
C. Aeresius Saenus	*Ch. VIII*	C. Julius Quartus	*Ch. VI*
Alfenus Senecio	*Ch. III*	C. Juventius Capito	*Ch. VI*
Albinus	*Ch. XIII*	Lollius Urbicus	*Ch. III*
Ammin(i)us	*Ch. XI*	Longinus Sdapeze	*Ch. VII*
Antistius Adventus	*Ch. III*	Lousius Suavis	*Ch. V*
Arthur	*Ch. XVI*	Matugenus	*Ch. XIII*
Boudica	*Ch. II*	Neratius Marcellus	*Ch. III, cf. XIV*
Calgacus	*Ch. II*	A. Plautius	*Ch. III*
Calpurnius Receptus	*Ch. XI, XV*	Rufus Sita	*Ch. VII*
Caracalla	*Ch. II*	Saenius Augustinus	*Ch. VIII*
Caratacus	*Ch. II*	Saen(i)us Tammon(i)us	*Ch. XI*
Claudia Rufina	*Ch. II*	C. Saufeius	*Ch. VI*
Ti. Claudius Cogidubnus	*Ch. II*	Secund(ii)	*Ch. XIII*
M. Cocceius Firmus	*Ch. V, XV*	M. Simplicius Simplex	*Ch. IV*
Constantine III	*Ch. II, XVI*	Statilius Solon	*Ch. V*
Cunobelinus	*Ch. II*	Tammonius Vitalis	*Ch. XI*
Dagobitus	*Ch. XI*	M. Ulpius Longinus	*Ch. IX*
Gerontius	*Ch. II, XVI*	M. Ulpius Novantico	*Ch. IX*
Gratian	*Ch. II*	C. Valerius	*Ch. VI*
Grata	*Ch. XI*	Q. Veranius	*Ch. III*
C. Indutius Felix	*Ch. XIV*	Victorinus	*Ch. III*
Javolenus Priscus	*Ch. III*	Viducius Placidus	*Ch. XII*
Julius Agricola	*Ch. III*	Volisios	*Ch. II*

Notes to Chapter II

The most detailed general narrative history of Roman Britain is by S. S. Frere, *Britannia* (2nd. ed., London, 1974). Different parts of the period from Caesar to the fifth century AD are covered in more detail in the following:

B. W. Cunliffe	*Iron Age Communities in Britain* (Routledge, 1974)
D. W. Harding	*The Iron Age in Lowland Britain* (Routledge, 1974)
D. R. Dudley and G. Webster	*The Roman Conquest of Britain* (2nd ed., Pan, 1973)
G. Webster	*Boudica* (Batsford, 1978)
D. J. Breeze and B. Dobson	*Hadrian's Wall* (Allen Lane, 1976)
A. Birley	*Septimius Severus. The African Emperor* (Eyre & Spottiswoode, 1971)
J. Morris	*The Age of Arthur. A History of the British Isles from 350 to 650* (Weidenfeld, 1976)

The following special abbreviations are used in the references for this chapter:

D. F. Allen, Coritani	D. F. Allen, *The Coinage of the Coritani* (Society of Antiquaries of London, 1964)
Mack	R. P. Mack, *The Coinage of Ancient Britain* (3rd ed., Spink, 1975)
PLRE	A. H. M. Jones, J. R. Martindale, J. Morris, *The Prosopography of the Later Roman Empire*, Vol. I, AD 260–395 (Cambridge, 1970)

Addedomaros	Mack 266–274A; D. F. Allen, Brit. 1970; Holder I 39; Evans, pp. 218 ff.
Adminius	Suetonius, *Caligula* 44.2; D. F. Allen, Brit. 1976, showing that he struck coins in Britain, with the name Amminus. Mack 313–5. See also Ch. XI, n. to Ammin(i)us.
(A)esico	Mack 434A; D. F. Allen, Brit. 1970
Aesu	Mack 432; D. F. Allen, Brit. 1970; Holder I 53
Aesubilinus	RIB 193; see also Ch. XI, n. to this name
Aëtius	See Ch. XVI, n.
Alaric	See J. F. Matthews, *Western Aristocracies and Imperial Court A.D. 364–425* (Oxford, 1975), pp. 270 ff., esp. 287–300
Alban	See Ch. XVI, n.
Albinus, D. Clodius	See Ch. III, n.
Allectus	PLRE I, p. 45 collects the ancient references. See further N. Shiel, *The Episode of Carausius and Allectus* (B.A.R. 40, 1977)
Anted(ios) (Dobunni)	Mack 385–7; Evans, pp. 136 ff.
Antedi(os) (Iceni)	Mack 418–22; D. F. Allen, Brit. 1970
Antoninus Pius	For a discussion of the literary, epigraphic and numismatic evidence for this emperor's dealings with Britain, see A. Birley, *Marcus Aurelius* (1966), pp. 66 f., 72 ff., 145 f. The archaeological evidence is controversial: for a recent view, see D. J. Breeze and B. Dobson, *Hadrian's Wall* (1976), esp. pp. 76 ff.
Arcadius	PLRE I, p. 99

Aregwedd Foeddawg   See T. E. Casson, *Trans. Cumb. & West.*², (1944), p. 71 f.

Argentocoxus   Dio 76.16.5. The name means 'silver leg': see
K. H. Jackson, in F. T. Wainwright (ed.), *The Problem of the Picts* (1955), 237. See also Wainwright, ib., p. 27, on the possibility that the north Britons – ancestors of the Picts – practised polyandry at this period.

Arviragus   Juvenal 4.127

Asclepiodotus, Julius   PLRE I, pp. 115 f.

Q. Atrius   Caesar, *B.G.* 5.9–10

Augustus   Strabo 4.200 and Tacitus, *Agr.* 13 are key ancient sources. See also the classic discussion by C. E. Stevens, in W. F. Grimes (ed.), *Aspects of Archaeology in Britain and Beyond* (1951), pp. 332 ff.

Boduoc   Mack 395–6; cf. the Nervian leader Boduognatus in Caesar, *B.G.* 2.23; Holder I 461; Evans, p. 151

Boudica   Tacitus, *Agr.* 16; *Ann.* 14.31 ff.; Dio 62.2–7. See now above all the monograph by G. Webster, *Boudica* (Batsford, 1978), passim; p. 15 deals with the name, more familiar once as Boadicea, then as Boudicca; see also Evans, pp. 156 ff.

Britannicus   Suetonius, *D. Claud.* 27.1; Dio 60. 12.5, etc.

Caesar   His own account is in *B.G.* 4.20–36, 5.4–23. See T. R. S. Broughton, *The Magistrates of the Roman Republic* (Cleveland, Amer. Philol. Ass. 1952, repr. 1968), II, pp. 219, 224, for a convenient conspectus of the ancient sources. For a recent brief account, see G. Webster, *Boudica* (1978), pp. 34 ff.

Calgacus   Tacitus, *Agr.* 29–38; Holder I 698 f. renders it as 'sworded'

Caligula   Tacitus, *Agr.* 13.2. See further C. E. Stevens, op. cit. (under Augustus, above)

CAN DVRO   Mack 434

Caracalla   See A. Birley, *Septimius Severus* (1971), pp. 269 ff.

Caratacus   Mack 265; Tacitus, *Annals* 12.33 ff.; *Hist.* 3.45; Dio 60.20.1, 33.3; Holder I 771 f.; Evans, pp. 162 ff.

Carausius   PLRE I, p. 180 f. collects the ancient references. See further N. Shiel, op. cit. (under Allectus, above)

Cartimandua   Tacitus, *Hist.* 3.45; *Annals* 12.36, 40. The name means 'sleek filly', according to I. A. Richmond, JRS 1954, p. 43; Evans, p. 166

Cartivel.   Mack 468; D. F. Allen, Coritani

Carvilius   Caesar, *B.G.* 5.22.1; Holder I 820; Evans, pp. 329 f.

Cassivellaunus   Caesar *B.G.* 5.11.8 F., 18.1, 19.1–3, 20.1 ff., 22.3–5; Dio 40.2.3; Holder I 833 f.; Evans, pp. 65 f., 167 ff.

Castor   Dio 76.14.1 ff.

Catti   Mack 391; Evans, pp. 171 ff.

Cerialis   see Ch. III n., under Petillius

Cicero   see Tullius

Cingetorix   Caesar, *B.G.* 5.22.1; for a Treveran prince of the same name, ib. 5.56–7, 6.8; Holder I 1018; Evans, pp. 73 f., 177 ff.

Claudia Rufina   Martial 11.53

Claudius	See especially D. R. Dudley and G. Webster, *The Roman Conquest of Britain*, 2nd ed. (Pan), *passim*.
Ti. Claudius Balbillus	AE 1924. 78, discussed by H. -G. Pflaum, CP no. 15.
Ti. Claudius [Co]gidubnus	RIB 91; Tacitus, *Agr.* 14.1 (where he is called Cogidumnus). See now J. Bogaers, Brit. 1979, 243 ff.
Commius	Caesar, *B.G.* 4.21.7–8, 27.2–4, 35.1, 5.22.3, 7.75.5, 78.1 ff., 79.1, 8.6.2, 7.6, 10.4 f., 21.1, 23.2, 7, 47.1–3, 48.1 ff.; Frontinus, *Strat.* 2.13.11; Dio 40.42.1–3, 43.2; etc. Mack 92. G. Webster, *Boudica* (1978), p. 37, gives a useful sketch. See also Holder I 1074 f.; Evans, pp. 335 f.
Commodus	Dio 72.8–9; HA Commodus 6.2, 13.5. Coins and inscriptions show that he took the title Britannicus in AD 184.
Comux.	Mack 392; Holder I 1085 f.
Constans	Libanius, *Or.* 3. 320; Ammian. 20.1.1, 27.8.4, refer to his British expedition in the winter of AD 343; *Cod. Theod.* 11.16.5 shows that he was at Boulogne on 25 January of that year.
Constantine I	*Epit. de Caes.* 41.3. The quotations in the text are from *Panegyrici Latini veteres* 6 (7).9 and Eusebius, *v. Const.* 2.28
Constantine III	Orosius 7.40.4 ff.; Zosimus, 6.2 ff., etc. See J. F. Matthews, op. cit. (under Alaric, above), esp. 308 ff.
Constantius I	Eutropius 9.22.2 among many other sources refers to his reconquest of Britain in 296; for his death at York: *Panegyrici Latini Veteres* 6 (7). 7, *Anon. Vales.* 2.4, Victor, *de Caes.* 40.4; *Epit. de Caes.* 41.3; Eutropius 10.1.3
Constantius II	see under Magnentius, below
Corio	Mack 393–4; Holder I 1126
Cunedda	Ch. XVI, n.
Cunobelinus	Mack 201–61; Suetonius, *Caligula* 44.2; Dio 60.20.1, 21.4; Holder I 1193 ff.
Diocletian	W. Seston, *Dioclétien et la tétrarchie* (I, Paris 1946 – no more published) remains the only accessible modern study. See also A. H. M. Jones, *The Later Roman Empire* (Blackwell, 1964), pp. 37 ff.
Dubnovellaunus	Mack 275–91A; Augustus, *Res Gestae* 32.1; Holder I 1361 f.
Dumnovellaunos	Mack 466–7; D. F. Allen, Coritani; Evans, pp. 196 f.
Dumnocoveros	Mack 463–5; D. F. Allen, Coritani; Holder I 1357 f.
Ece/Ecen	Mack 424–31; D. F. Allen, Brit. 1970; Holder I 1405
Eisu	Mack 388–9
Epaticcus	Mack 262–4; Holder I 1443 f.; Evans, pp. 197 ff. (*ep-* means 'horse')
Eppillus	Mack 107–8, 300–12; Holder I 1445 ('little horseman')
Florus	*HA Hadrian* 16.3–4
Gerontius	Zosimus 6.2.4 f.; Orosius 7.42.4 ff., etc. See J. F. Matthews, op. cit. (under Alaric, above), esp. pp. 309 ff.
Geta	see Ch. XVI, n. to Alban
Gordian I	see Ch. III, n. to Antonius Gordianus
Gratian, emperor	J. F. Matthews, op. cit. (under Alaric, above), esp. pp. 69 ff. 89 ff., 173

Gratian, usurper   Orosius 7.40.4; Zosimus 6.2.1 f.

Hadrian   *HA Hadrian* 11–12 is the main evidence
Honorius   The letter to the cities 'in Britain' is reported by Zosimus 6.9.2. I am attracted by the arguments of A. L. F. Rivet (see his *The Place-Names of Roman Britain*, Batsford, 1979 that *Brettania* is a textual error. For Honorius generally, see J. F. Matthews, op. cit. (under Alaric, above), esp. pp. 279 ff.

Julia Domna   Dio 76.16.5, and see under Severus, below
Julian   see pp. 171 (Alypius) 173 (Lupicinus)
C. Julius Avitus Alexianus   AE 1921.64, cf. 1963.42, discussed in A. Birley, *Septimius Severus* (1971), pp. 298 f.
C. Julius Marcus   Ch. III, n.
L. Junius Silanus   ILS 957; Tacitus, *Ann.* 12.3.2; Suetonius, *D. Claudius* 24.3; Dio 60.21.5, 31.7
Q. Laberius Durus   Caesar, *B.G.* 5.15.5
M. Licinius Crassus   Caesar, *B.G.* 5.24.3, etc.
M. Licinius Crassus Frugi   Suetonius, *D. Claud.* 17.3.
Lugotorix   Caesar, *B.G.* 5.22.2; Holder II 303; Evans, pp. 98 f.

Magnentius   PLRE I, p. 532
Magnus Maximus   *Panegyrici Latini Veteres* 2 (12). 23, 31, etc.; *Epit. de Caes.* 47.7; Claudian, *de iv cons. Honorii*, 72–9; Orosius 7.34.9; Zosimus 4.35.3–4, etc. See PLRE I, p. 588; J. F. Matthews, op. cit. (under Alaric, above), esp. pp. 173 ff., 223 ff.; R. Bromwich, in H. M. Chadwick et al., *Studies in Early British History* (1954), esp. pp. 107 ff. See also P. C. Bartrum, *Early Welsh Genealogical Tracts* (Cardiff 1966) index, s.v. Macsen Wledig, p.201

Mandubracius   Caesar, *B. G.* 5.20.1–4; Holder II 404 f.; Evans, pp. 100 ff.;
Marcus   Olympiodorus, frag. 12; Sozomen, *Hist. Eccles.* 9.11.1 ff.; Zosimus 6.2.1 f., 3.1
Maximian   see under Diocletian

Narcissus   Suetonius, *D. Vesp.* 4.1f.; Dio 60.19.2

Papinian   Dio 76.14.5 f. See H. -G. Pflaum, CP no. 220
Pertinax   see Ch. III, n., Ch. IV n.
Q. Petillius Cerialis   Ch. III, n.
A. Platorius Nepos   Ch. III, n.
A. Plautius   Ch. III, n.
Ti. Plautius Silvanus
  Aelianus   ILS 986
Cn. Pompeius Magnus   Dio 60.21.5
Posides   Suetonius, *D. Claud.* 28.1
Postumus   PLRE I, p. 720. There is still some uncertainty over the exact chronology, which I take to be AD 260–269, following J. Lafaurie, in H. Temporini (ed.) *Aufstieg und Niedergang der römischen Welt*, II 2 (Berlin, 1975), p. 907
Prasutagus   Tacitus, *Ann.* 14.31. See D. F. Allen, Brit. 1970, and G. Webster, *Boudica* (1978), passim; Holder II 1041
Priscus   Ch. III, n.
Probus   Zosimus 1.66.2, 68.3, etc.

Rufrius Pollio	Dio 60.23.2
Sabina	*HA Hadrian* 11.3
Sabinus	see Ch. III, n. to T. Flavius Sabinus
Saenu.	Mack 433; Holder II 1284
Segovax	Caesar, *B.G.* 5.22.1; Holder II 1451; Evans, p. 375
Cn. Sentius Saturninus	Eutropius 7.13, now indirectly confirmed by a wax tablet found in the outskirts of Pompeii, showing that he received an honorary triumph: see A. Degrassi, *Memorie dell' Accademia dei Lincei* 14 (1969), pp. 136 f.
C. Septicius Clarus	*HA Hadrian* 11.3
Severus	Dio 76.11–15; Herodian 3.14–15; *HA Severus* 18.2, 22–24, etc. See A. Birley, *Septimius Severus* (1971), esp. pp. 244 ff.
C. Stertinius Xenophon	Ch. IV, n.
Stilicho	Ch. III, n.
Subidasto-Esico	Mack 434A (reading Subippasto); D. F. Allen, Brit. 1970
C. Suetonius Tranquillus	*HA Hadrian* 11.3. See H. -G Pflaum, CP no. 96 + add.; R. Syme, *Tacitus* (1958), pp. 788 ff.
Ser. Sulpicius Galba	Suetonius, *Galba* 7.1
Tasciovanus	Mack 149–196; Holder II 1744 f.; Evans, pp. 263 ff.
Taximagulus	Caesar, *B.G.* 5.22.1; Holder II 1778; Evans, pp. 116 f.
Tetricus	PLRE I, p. 885
Theodosius, Count	Ch. III, n.
Theodosius, emperor	See esp. J. F. Matthews, op. cit. (under Alaric, above), pp. 88–252
Tiberius	Tacitus, *Agr.* 13.2, and see under Augustus, above
Tigirseno(s)	Mack 461–2; D. F. Allen, Coritani; Holder II 1842 ('old prince')
Tincommius	Mack 93–106A; Augustus, Res Gestae 32.1
Titus	see Ch. III, n. to T. Flavius Vespasianus jr.
Togodumnus	Dio 60.21.1
C. Trebonius	Caesar *B.G.* 5.17.2
M. and Q. Tullius Cicero	Cicero, *ad Q. fratrem* 2.13.2, 15.1, 3.1.10,25, 3.3.1; cf. *ad Atticum* 4.15.10, etc.
Valentinian II	PLRE I, pp. 934 f.
D. Valerius Asiaticus	Tacitus, *Ann.* 11.3.1
Sex. Varius Marcellus	Ch. III, n.
Vellocatus	Tacitus, *Hist.* 3.45
Venutius	Tacitus, *Hist.* 3.45; *Ann.* 12.32, 36, 40; Evans, pp. 277 ff.
Verica	Mack 109–131B; Dio 60.19.1 ff.; Evans, pp. 286 ff.
Vespasian	see Ch. III, n. to T. Flavius Vespasianus
Victorinus	PLRE I, 965; cf. p.213 (Zosimus)
M. Vinicius	AE 1929. 166, discussed by R. Syme, *Class. Q.* 27 (1933), pp. 142 ff.
Volisios	Mack 463–8; D. F. Allen, Coritani; Holder III 442
C. Volusenus	Caesar, *B.G.* 4.21, 23
Vortigern	Ch. XVI, n.

Notes to Chapter III

For details on all senatorial officials, equestrian procurators and fourth century *duces*, *comites*, etc., cf. my *The Fasti of Roman Britain* (Oxford, 1981). There has been a little new evidence since then, e.g. the discovery that the Mummii Sisennae came from southern Spain (their home town being Osset, near Seville); or that the legate of II Augusta, Haterianus, was one of the Plautii of Lepcis Magna. One new *praefectus* of the British fleet has come to light, again from the Antonine period, a man called Varius from Celeia in Noricum. A number of other works which deal with the governing élite of the empire are listed below:

E. Birley	'Senators in the emperors' service', *Proceedings of the British Academy 39* (1953), pp. 197 ff.
R. Syme	*Tacitus* (Oxford, 1958)
H. -G. Pflaum	*Les procurateurs équestres sous le Haut-Empire romain* (Paris, 1950); and see the same author's CP (p. 162, above)
A. H. M. Jones	*The Later Roman Empire* (Oxford, Blackwell, 1964)

The following special abbreviations are used in this chapter:

Inscr. Ital.	*Inscriptiones Italiae* (in progress, 1936– , Rome, Libreria dello Stato)
IGR	*Inscriptiones Graecae ad res Romanas pertinentes* (Vols. I, III, IV, ed. R. Cagnat *et al.*, Paris, 1901–1927)
PIR²	*Prosopographia Imperii Romani*, 2nd ed. by E. Groag, A. Stein, L. Petersen (Berlin, De Gruyter, 1933–
PLRE	see p. 165, above
M. Aedinius Julianus	see under Claudius Paulinus, below
P. Aelius Erasinus	Ch. IV, n.
M. Aemilius Papus	by his full names M. Cutius M. f. Gal. Priscus Messius Rusticus Aemilius Papus Arrius Proculus Julius Celsus: British legionary command is known from CIL II 1283, 1371. AE 1934. 146, Rome, shows that he was known as Aemilius Papus for short
Albinus	see Clodius
L. Alfenus Senecio	RIB 722–3, 740, 746, 1234, 1337, 1462, 1909; Brit. 1977
Alypius	Libanius, *Ep.* 327 (324F); Julian, *Ep.* 402D–404B, Ammian. 23.1.2, 29.1.44
Q. Antistius Adventus	RIB 1083, cf. ILS 1091, 8977 (he was also called Postumius Aquilinus)
L. Antistius Rusticus	AE 1925. 126
M. Antius Crescens Calpurnianus	ILS 1151
M. Antonius Gordianus	RIB 590, 1049, 1279 (also Brit. 1970?)
Q. Antonius Isauricus	RIB 644
L. Artorius Castus	ILS 2770 + add.; H. -G. Pflaum, CP no. 196 + add.
M. Atilius Metilius Bradua	ILS 8824a
L. Aufidius Panthera	CIL XVI 76; RIB 66; H. -G. Pflaum, CP no. 133
Aur(elius) Arpagius	RIB 1912

Q. Aurelius Polus
  Terentianus
T. Avidius Quietus

AE 1965. 240; discussed in A. Birley, *Septimius Severus*
(1971), p. 338
CIL XVI 43

Q. Baienus Blassianus

AE 1974. 123; *Inscr. Ital.* x iv 37–40; discussed by
H. -G. Pflaum, CP no. 126 + add. (who lacked a little of the
evidence)

Caesius Nasica
Carausius
C. Caristanius Fronto

Tacitus, *Ann.* 12.40.4
Ch. II, n.
ILS 9485. See B. M. Levick, *Roman Colonies in Southern Asia
Minor* (Oxford 1967), p. 111 for this family

Chrysanthus
Civilis
Cl(audius) Apellinus
Ti. Claudius Augustanus
A. Claudius Charax
Ti. Claudius [Co]gidubnus
Cl(audius) Hieronymianus
Ti. Claudius Paulinus

Socrates, *Hist. Eccles.* 7.12.1
Ammian. 27.8.10
RIB 1281
CIL V 3337; discussed by H. -G. Pflaum, CP no. 68
AE 1961. 320
RIB 91; Tacitus, *Agr.* 14.1. See also Ch. II, n.
RIB 658
RIB 311, 1280; CIL XIII 3162, with detailed discussion by
H. -G. Pflaum, *Le marbre de Thorigny* (Paris, 1948).

Cl(audius) Xenophon

RIB 1706, 2299, 2306 (spelt Xen*e*phon on two out of three
inscriptions)

D. Clodius Septimius
  Albinus

Dio 73.14.3, 15.1; 75.4.1 ff.; Herodian 2.15; 3.6 ff.;
HA Severus 6.9–10; 10.1 ff.; *Clod. Alb.* (largely fiction);
etc. See further A. Birley, *Septimius Severus* (1971), esp.
pp. 189 ff., 324 f.

M. Cocceius Nigrinus

RIB 2066 (the inscription is now lost and the reading is
rather uncertain)

C. Curtius Justus

CIL III 1458

Decianus Catus

Tacitus, *Ann.* 14. 32, 38.3; Dio 62.2 For Decianus as a
gentilicium, see CIL VI 1056, AE 1915.22

Desticius Juba
A. Didius Gallus
L. Didius Marinus
Dulcitius

RIB 334
Tacitus, *Agr.* 14; *Ann.* 12.40, 14.29.1
ILS 1396; discussed by H. -G. Pflaum, CP no. 295 + add.
Ammian. 27.8.10

Sex. Flavius Quietus
T. Flavius Sabinus

AE 1960.28; discussed by H. -G. Pflaum, CP no. 156 *bis*
Dio 60.20.3, where, as pointed out by G. Vrind, *De Cassii
Dionis vocabulis . . .* (1923), 90, better sense is made by
inserting a sigma at the end of the word *hupostrategounta*:
thus both Sabinus and Vespasian would be legates under
Plautius, rather than Sabinus under Vespasian

T. Flavius Vespasianus
  (Vespasian)

Josephus, *BJ* 3.4, Tacitus, *Agr.* 13.3; *Hist.* 3.44; Suetonius,
D. Vesp. 4.1–2; Dio 60. 20.3, 30.1; 65.8.3, etc. A useful
discussion by D. E. Eichholz, Brit. 1972, 149 ff.

T. Flavius Vespasianus jr.
  (Titus)

Suetonius, *D. Titus* 4.1

Fullofaudes

Ammian. 27.8.1

Geta
Gordian
Gratianus
Grattius . . . Geminius . . .

see Septimius
see Antonius
Ammian. 30.7.2–3
CIL II 6084; improved reading in G. Alföldy, *Die römischen
Inschriften von Tarraco* (Berlin, 1975), no. 149

Haterianus	RIB 335
T. Haterius Nepos	ILS 1338; discussed by H. -G. Pflaum, CP no. 95; on the link with the R. Annan, I. A. Richmond, *Archaeologia* 93 (1949), p. 22
P. Helvius Pertinax	Dio 72.9.2²; 73.5.1; *HA Pertinax* 1–4; see also Ch. IV, n.
Hosidius Geta	Dio 60.20.4; ef. ILS 971
L. Javolenus Priscus	by his full names C. Octavius Tidius Tossianus L. Javolenus Priscus. ILS 1015 + add. gives the British post, cf. *Digest* 36.1.48
Cn. Julius Agricola	ILS 8704a (lead pipes); JRS 1956 = AE 1957.169 (the Verulamium inscription – note that the date of this could be AD 81 instead of 79, as pointed out by W. Eck, *Senatoren von Vespasian bis Hadrian* (1970), p. 127, n. 68: Tacitus, *Agr.*, *passim*; Dio 39.50.4; 60.20.1–3. I hope to show, in the forthcoming *Fasti*, that the governorship probably began in AD 77.
C. Julius Alpin(i)us Classicianus	RIB 12; Tacitus, *Ann.* 38.3. See PIR² J 358, 685; E. Birley, *Ant. Journ.* 16 (1936), pp. 207 f.; and (on the name Alpin(i)us), H. -G. Pflaum, *Archivo Espanol de Arqueologia* 39 (1966), pp. 5 ff.
Sex Julius Frontinus	Tacitus, *Agr.* 17.2
L. Julius Julianus	CIL XI 4182; RIB 1138
C. Julius Marcus	RIB 739, 905, 976 (? – see Ulpius Marcellus (II), below), 977, 1205, 1265, 1550 (?), 2298
Sex. Julius Severus	had the additional names Cn. Minicius Faustinus. RIB 739, 1550 (? – may refer to Julius Verus); ILS 1056 + add.; Dio 69.13.2. On the family, see G. Alföldy, *Epigraphische Studien* 5 (1968), pp. 116 ff.
Cn. Julius Verus	RIB 283, 1132, 1322, 1550 (?), 2110; ILS 8974 – 1057 + add.
C. Junius Faustinus	had the additional names [Pl]a[ci]dus Postumianus. CIL VIII 597, cf. 11764.
L. Junius Victorinus	had the additional names Flav(ius) Caelianus. RIB 2034
Q. Lollius Urbicus	RIB 1147–8, 1276, 2191–2; *HA Antoninus Pius* 5.4; cf. CIL VIII 6706 = *ILAlg.* II 3605 for his earlier career
Q. Lusius Sabinianus	RIB 2132; Brit. 1977
Lupicinus, Fl(avius)	Julian, *Ep. ad Ath.* 283A; Ammian. 20.1.1–3, 4.3, 4.6, 4.9, 9.9
M. Maenius Agrippa	had the additional names L. Tusidius Campester. RIB 823–6; ILS 2735. Discussed by H.-G. Pflaum, CP no. 120. On the date, see M. G. Jarrett, Brit. 1976, pp. 145ff.
Magnus Maximus	Ch. II, n.
C. Manlius Valens	Tacitus, *Ann.* 12.40.1; *Hist.* 1.59, 64; Dio 67.14.5.
Marius Valerianus	RIB 978, 1060, 1465
Martinus	Ammian. 14.5.6–9
Metilius Bradua	see Atilius
P. Metilius Nepos	CIL XVI 43
L. Minicius Natalis	had the additional names Quadronius Verus. ILS 1061; CIL II 5410, XI 3002; IGR I 658, improved in the *Jahreshefte* of the Austrian Archaeological Institute 10 (1907), pp. 307ff.

Modius Julius	RIB 980, 1914
P. Mummius Sisenna	CIL XVI 82
P. Mummius Sisenna Rutilianus	ILS 1101; CIL XIV 4244; Lucian, *Alexander* 34.5, etc.
Cn. Munatius Aurelius Bassus	ILS 2740, discussed by H.-G. Pflaum, GP no. 83
Narcissus	Ch. II, n.
Nectaridus	Ammian. 27.8.1
L. Neratius Marcellus	CIL XVI 48; ILS 1032; Vindolanda tablets (information by courtesy of Dr A. K. Bowman)
M. Oclatinius Adventus	RIB 1234, 1462; cf. Dio 78. 14. 1 ff. and see the discussion by H.-G. Pflaum, CP no. 247 + add.
Octavius Sabinus	RIB 605
P. Ostorius Scapula	Tacitus, *agr.* 14; *Ann.* 12.31–39
M. Ostorius Scapula	Tacitus, *Ann.* 12.31.4, 16.15.1
L. Papius Pacatianus	*Cod. Theod.* 11.7.2; PLRE I, p. 656
Cn. Papirius Aelianus	had the additional names Aemil[ius] Tuscillus. CIL XVI 93; II 2075 + add.
Q. Petillius Cerialis	had the additional names Caesius Rufus. Tacitus, *Agr.* 8.2, 17.1–2; *Ann.* 14.32.3; *Hist.* 3.59.2; Josephus, *B.J.* 7.8.2–3. I have discussed this man in Brit. 1973, pp. 179 ff.
P. Petronius Turpilianus	Tacitus, *Agr.* 16, *Ann.* 14.39. For the relationship with A. Plautius, see R: Syme, *Tacitus* (1958), 386, and for Turpilianus' father see esp. Seneca, *Ludus* 14.2; Philo, *Leg.* 243
A. Platorius Nepos	had the additional names Aponius Italicus Manilianus C. Licinius Pollio. RIB 1340, 1427, 1634, 1637–8, 1666, 1935; CIL XVI 69, 70; ILS 1052
A. Plautius	Tacitus, *Agr.* 14; *Ann.* 11.36.5, 13.3; Suetonius, *D. Claud.* 24.2, *D. Vesp.* 4.1; Dio 60.19 ff., 30.2; Eutropius 7.13. On his family the article by L. R. Taylor, *Mem. American Acad. Rome* 24 (1956), pp. 10 ff. is the major study. Note also R. Syme, *Tacitus* (1958), esp. p. 386 and the same author's remarks in *The Roman Revolution* (1939), p. 422.
Polus Terentianus	see Aurelius Polus
Q. Pompeius Falco	By his full names Q. Roscius Sex. F. Quir. Coelius Murena Silius Decianus Vibullius Pius Julius Eurycles Herculanus Pompeius Falco. CIL XVI 69; ILS 1035; AE 1957. 336; 172.577; *Digest* 28.3.6 probably refers to his British governorship
Cn. Pompeius Homullus	had the additional names Aelius Gracilis Cassianus Longinus. ILS 1385, discussed by H.-G. Pflaum, CP no. 89
T. Pomponius Mamilianus	has the additional names Rufus Antistianus Funisulanus Vettonianus on the inscription set up by his household at Chester, RIB 445. Presumably the consul of AD 100, who has the *cognomen* Mamilianus, unlike the consul of 121.
M. Pontius Laelianus	has the additional names Larcius Sabinus on the inscription which gives his career, ILS 1094 + 1100, discussed in my article in R. M. Butler (ed.), *Soldier and Civilian in Roman Yorkshire* (Leicester U.P., 1971), pp. 81 f.
Priscus	Dio 72.9.2a

L. Roscius Aelianus	has the additional names Maecius Celer on ils 1025
M. Roscius Coelius	Tacitus, *Agr.* 7.3 (unnamed); *Hist.* 1.60
C. Sabucius Major Caecilianus	ils 1123
Sallustius Lucullus	Suetonius, *Domitian* 10.2
C. Salvius Liberalis	has the additional names Nonius Bassus on ils 1011
P. Septimius Geta	*Inscriptions of Roman Tripolitania*, ed. J. M. Reynolds and J. B. Ward-Perkins (British School at Rome, 1952), no. 541, discussed in A. Birley, *Septimius Severus* (1971), p. 302 f.
Sosia Juncina	rib 644
M. Statius Priscus	has the additional names Licinius Italicus on his career-inscription, ils 1092. The early part is discussed by H.-G. Pflaum, cp no. 136. See also ae 1910. 86 for the governorship. His tribe, Claudia, first appointment, in Britain, and the existence of a first-century legionary called Statius, whose home was Colchester (Chs. ix, xi, n.), make it just possible that Priscus was a native of this British *colonia*
Stilicho, Flavius	Claudian, *in Eutrop.* 1. 391–3 and *de cons. Stilichonis* 2. 247–55, is the only direct evidence for the great general taking any measures in Britain; if allowance is made for poetic licence, its value is virtually nil
C. Suetonius Paullinus	Tacitus, *Agr.* 5, 14; *Hist.* 2.37; *Ann.* 14.29–39; Dio 62.7–8. Mrs M. T. Griffin has shown, in an important study, *Scripta Classica Israelica* 3 (1976/77), pp. 138 ff., that there are grounds for supposing that Tacitus deliberately omitted to record honours paid to Paullinus by Nero for his achievements in Britain
Theodosius, Fl(avius)	Ammian. 27.8–9; 28.3; *Panegyrici Latini Vet.* 2 (12).5.1–2; ae 1931.53, etc. See the important study of the chronology by R.S.O. Tomlin, Brit. 1974, 303 ff.
M. Trebellius Maximus	Tacitus, *Agr.* 7, 16.3; *Hist.* 1.60.2, 2.65.2.
Ulpius Marcellus (I)	Dio 72.8.2–6
Ulpius Marcellus (II)	rib 976 (?), 1329, 1463–4
Valentinian	see under Theodosius
M. Valerius Maximianus	see Ch. iv, n.
C. Valerius Pansa	cil v 6513
C. Valerius Pudens	jrs 1961, corrected in jrs 1969 by G. Alfoldy
Sex. Varius Marcellus	ils 478, discussed by H.-G. Pflaum, cp no. 237, and – with an alternative chronology – by A. Birley, *Septimius Severus* (1971), pp. 304 ff.
Q. Veranius	ae 1953. 251; Tacitus, *Agr.* 14, *Ann.* 14.29.1. See E. Birley, rbra, pp. 1 ff.
M. Vettius Bolanus	Statius, *Silvae* 5.2.54–6, 140–9; Tacitus, *Agr.* 7.3, 8.1 16.5; *Hist.* 2.97.1, 3.44–45
M. Vettius Valens	cil xi 383
Victorinus	Rutilius Namatianus, *de reditu suo* 491–508
L. Vitellius	See esp. R. Syme, *Tacitus* (1958), p. 386
Vitulasius Laetinianus	rib 334; Schulze, p. 153
unknown under Probus	Zosimus 1.66.2, 68.3; Zonaras 12.29; *Anecdota Graeca* 2.291

unknown *iuridici*	
from Palestrina	AE 1973. 133
from Tivoli	CIL XIV 4248
unknown military tribune	RIB 1132 (Corbridge): the *praenomen* L. and the first letter of the *gentilicium*, C or O, are all that survive of the name

Notes to Chapter IV

I was not able to consult the *Prosopographia Militiarum Equestrium* by H. Devijver (Symbolae Facultatis Litt. et Philos. Lovaniensis, Louvain-Leuven, I, 1976, II, 1977) in time to make use of it in the present work. The major studies of equestrian officers are by E. Birley. See his RBRA, esp. pp. 130 ff.; also the following articles by the same author:

'Alae and Cohortes Milliariae', in *Corolla memoriae Erich Swoboda dedicata (Römische Forschungen in Niederösterreich*, V, Graz-Cologne, 1966), pp. 54 ff.; 'Septimius Severus and the Roman army', *Epigraphische Studien* 8 (1969), pp. 63 ff.

See further the following;

B. Dobson	'Legionary centurion or equestrian officer? A comparison of pay and prospects', *Ancient Society* 3 (1972), pp. 193 ff.

and articles in the *Transactions of the Cumberland and Westmorland Antiquarian and Archaeological Society*, new series, by

L. P. Wenham	'Notes on the garrisoning of Maryport', 39 (1939), pp. 19 ff.
M. G. Jarrett	'Roman officers at Maryport', 65 (1965), pp. 115 ff.
R. W. Davies	'Cohors I Hispanorum and the garrisons of Maryport', 77 (1977), pp. 7 ff.

For possible British equestrian officers, see Aelius Modestus and Aelius Titullus (Ch. XIV, nn.), Q. Florius Maternus, the Macrinii, and M. Statius Priscus (Ch. XI, nn.)

Special abbreviation: PIR² (see p. 170, above)

Notes on units mentioned in this chapter:

ala Tampiana	CIL 48 (AD 103), 69 (AD 122), army of Britain; III 5531, 5632 (Noricum); and see Flavius Crensces
coh. I Aelia Dacorum mill.	CIL XVI 93 (AD146); *Notitia Dig.* XL 44; RIB 1365 (east end of Hadrian's Wall) and large numbers of inscriptions from or near Birdoswald
coh. I fida Vardullorum mill. eq. c.R.	CIL XVI 43, (AD 98), 51 (AD 105), 69 (AD 122), 70 (AD124), 82 (AD 135), 93 (AD 146), 130 (*c.* AD 149–60); RIB 2149 (Castlecary), 2118 (Jedburgh), 1083, etc. (Lanchester), 1083 (? Corbridge), 1265, etc. (High Rochester)
coh. III Bracaraugustanorum	CIL XVI 48, 69, 70, 93, army of Britain; CIL VII 1230, EE IX 1277, tiles from Manchester; cf. CIL XVI 87 (Palestine, AD 139), 55, 17, 121, etc. (Raetia)
coh. I Thracum	see M. G. Jarrett, *Israel Explor. Journ.* 1969, pp. 215 ff.
coh. IV Gallorum	RIB 619 (Templeborough); unpublished tiles (Castleford);

RIB 2195 (Castlehill, Ant. Wall), 1227 (Risingham), 1979–80 (Castlesteads); numerous inscriptions at Vindolanda; and *Not. Dig.* XL 41

Sex. Adgennius Macrinus
CIL XII 3175, Nîmes; Holder I 40, III 505; cf. Evans pp. 128 ff.

P. Aelius Erasinus
RIB 1280, 1286; cf. ILS 8227 for an imperial freedman of this name

P. Aelius Magnus
RIB 894, AD 191

P. Aelius Septimianus Rusticus
RIB 903, AD 185: the editors read Septimenus

Aemilius Crispinus
RIB 897

L. Aemilius Salvianus
RIB 1215, 1234, AD 205/207; cf. CIL VIII 2758; AE 1939. 37, Lambaesis

L. Antonius Proculus
RIB 1544, discussed by E. Birley, RBRA, pp. 174 ff.

A. Atticus
Tacitus, *Agr.* 37.6. R. Syme, *Tacitus* (1958), p. 784 n. 2 suggests that he was a Narbonensian Julius Atticus, the *cognomen* perhaps being native 'adapted to a Latin form'.

Attius Tuticanus
ILS 2755, Langres; Holder I 272, II 2022, III 737

T. Attius Tutor
RIB 830, 837, 842; cf. ILS 2734, Solva; Holder II 2021 ff., III 737

Aur(elius) Verinus
JRS 1961 = AE 1962.263

Aurunc. Felicissimus
RIB 988

Q. Baienus Blassianus
Ch. III, n.

C. Caballius Priscus
RIB 817–820; see E. Birley, RBRA, pp. 90 f.

Caecilius Nepos
RIB 2189

L. Caecilius Optatus
RIB 1265, 1268, 1272; cf. ILS 6957, Barcelona

Caesennius Silvanus
Pliny, *Ep.* 3.8

L. Cammius Maximus
RIB 827–9; cf. CIL V 961, Aquileia

Caristanius Justianus
RIB 2167; cf. Ch. III, n. to Caristanius Fronto

Ti. Claudius Balbillus
AE 1924.78, Ephesus; H.-G. Pflaum, CP no. 15

Ti. Claudius Cogidubnus
Ch. II, n.

Cl(audius) Epaphroditus Claudianus
RIB 1075; cf. CIL IX 3624, Aveia

Ti. Claudius Justinus
RIB 893, AD 188

M. Cl(audius) Menander
RIB 1914

Ti. Claudius Paulinus
Ch. III, n.

A. Cluentius Habitus
RIB 1545; see E. Birley, RBRA, pp. 172 ff.

Cornelius Minicianus
Pliny, *Ep.* 7.22; cf. ILS 2722, Bergomo.
E. Birley, RBRA, p. 141, n. 17, doubted the identity of the man from Bergomo with Pliny's client. But he now tells me that, as the cohort mentioned in ILS 2722, I Damascenorum, was in the army of Palestine in 139 (CIL XVI 87) and probably belonged to the army of Judaea earlier, he accepts it.

C. Cornelius Peregrinus
RIB 812

Desidienus Aemilianus
RIB 1589, AD 258; cf. CIL III 12916, Salona

L. Domitius Proculus
ILS 8866, Prusias ad Ilypium

T. Fabius Liberalis
RIB 2160; cf. CIL XIII 11780, Stockstadt

Fl(avius) Ammausius
RIB 605; Holder I 129

Flavius Cerialis   A. K. Bowman, *Historia* 24 (1975), p. 474 (*Cognomen* only
– I am grateful to Dr Bowman for information about
the *gentilicium*)

Fl(avius) Martinus   RIB 1912
Fl(avius) Maximianus   RIB 1896
Funisulanus Vettonianus   RIB 1879; cf. Ch. III, n. to T. Pomponius Mamilianus
T. Furius Victorinus   ILS 9002, Rome; H.-G. Pflaum, CP no. 139

Q. Gargilius Martialis   ILS 2767, Auzia; cf. CIL VIII 20751, ib. See PIR² G 82.

P. Helvius Pertinax   *HA Pertinax*, 1–2, confirmed and illuminated by the
inscription from Brühl near Cologne: H.-G. Kolbe, *Bonner
Jahrbücher* 162 (1962) 410 ff. (= AE 1963.52); see also
Dio 73.3.1. I discuss the career in my *Septimius Severus*
(1971), pp. 106 ff.

C. Julius Camillus   ILS 2697 + add., Avenches
Julius Candidus   Brit. 1970
C. Julius Marcellinus   RIB 2172
Jul(ius) Melanio   RIB 1273: I hope to discuss this reading in a future article.
Cf. AE 1968. 229–231, Astorga, and H.-G. Pflaum, CP
no. 276

T. Julius Valerianus   CIL XII 2608, Geneva
D. Junius Juvenalis   ILS 2926 + near Aquinum. See R. Syme, *Tacitus* (1958),
pp. 774 ff.

T. Junius Severus   CIL II 3538, Dianium

P. Licinius Agathopus   CIL VIII 4800, Gadiaufala
M. Lucretius Peregrinus   AE 1961. 330 = G. Alföldy, *Die Römischen Inschriften von
Tarraco* (1975), no. 172, Tarragona.

M. Maenius Agrippa *cet.*   Ch. III, n.
Marcius Gallicus   RIB 1883
L. Marcius Optatus   ILS 6948, Iluro
L. Minthonius Tertullus   RIB 2134; see E. Birley, RBRA, p. 166

L. Naevius Verus Roscianus   ILS 2603, near Piacenza
L. Neratius Marcellus   Ch. III, n.

Paternius Maternus   RIB 966, probably from Bewcastle rather than Netherby
Q. Peltrasius Maximus   RIB 989
M. Peregrinius Super   RIB 1231
Q. Petronius Urbicus   RIB 1686; cf. Tacitus, *Hist*. 1.70 and CIL III 11551 for the
homonymous procurator of Noricum
Q. Pisentius Justus   RIB 2195
Pituanius Secundus   RIB 1685; cf. CIL IX 4694, Reate
A. Platorius Nepos   Ch. III, n.
Q. Pompeius Falco   Ch. III, n.
Pomponius Desideratus   RIB 1885
Paulus Postumius Acilianus   RIB 810, 832–3, 847, 850. See H.-G. Pflaum, CP no. 62
for the procurator recorded at Cordova.
Probius Augendus   RIB 1886
Publicius Maternus   Brit. 1970

C. Rufius Moderatus   CIL III 5202, Celeia

C. Sempronius Fidus   CIL II 4245 = G. Alföldy, *Die römischen Inschriften von*

	Tarraco (1975), no. 306, Tarragona.
Sennius Sollemnis	Ch. III, n. to Claudius Paulinus
Septimius Nilus	RIB 1465, 1467
L. Septi[mius?] Petro[nianus?]	AE 1958. 156, Caesarea (Mauretania); H.-G. Pflaum, CP no. 146 *bis*
Q. Servilius Pacuvianus	CIL III 2049, Salona
M. Simplicius Simplex	RIB 1546; discussed by E. Birley, RBRA, pp. 176 ff.
Sittius	CIL VIII 5532, Thibilis. P. Sittius of Nuceria, the Campanian *condottiere* of the Caesarian age, is frequently mentioned by Cicero, Sallust, the author of the *bellum Africum* and the historians of the period; and his influence in this region is recalled by Pliny, *Nat. Hist.* 5.22 and by the numerous Sittii attested epigraphically (see indices to CIL VIII).
Q. Sittius Caecilianus	RIB 278
M. Statius Priscus	Ch. III, n.
C. Stertinius Xenophon	H.-G. Pflaum, CP no. 16.
C. Suetonius Tranquillus	Pliny, *Ep.* 3.8.
Sulpicius Secundianus	RIB 2057–8
L. Tanicius Verus	RIB 2187; cf. ILS 8759b, Thebes (Egypt), discussed by E. Birley, RBRA, p. 91
M. Tituleius Victor	CIL XIII 5382, Besançon
Trebius Verus	RIB 2149; see also Verus, below
Ulpius Titianus	RIB 838, 843
M. Valerius Maximianus	AE 1956. 124, Diana Veteranorum (Numidia), much discussed, notably by H.-G. Pflaum, CP no. 181 *bis*
M. Valerius Speratus	CIL III 12659, Viminacium (Upper Moesia); cf. the *Jahreshefte* of the Austrian Archaeological Institute, Vol. 15 (1912), p. 184, fig. 123.
Verus	CIL XVI 130, Colchester; M. M. Roxan, *Roman Military Diplomas 1954–1977* (London: Inst. of Arch., 1978), p. 26, discusses the date
L. Vinicius Pius	JRS 1961, corrected in JRS 1969 by G. Alföldy, who also reinterprets RIB 722–3
unknown from Ilipa	ILS 2712
unknown from Verona	CIL V 3376–7

Notes to Chapter V

The following are the works which I have found most useful:

E. Birley	RBRA, esp. pp. 87 ff.
id.	'Promotions and transfers in the Roman army. II. The centurionate', *Carnuntum Jahrbuch* 1963/4, pp. 21 ff. (see also refs. on p. 175)
B. Dobson	'The significance of the centurion and "primipilaris" in the Roman army and administration', in H. Temporini (ed.), *Aufsteig und Niedergand der Römischen Welt* II.1

	(Berlin) 1974, pp. 393 ff.
id.	'The centurionate and social mobility during the principate', in *Recherches sur les structures sociales dans l'Antiquite classique* (Colloques, Paris, 1970), pp. 99 ff. (see also his article cited on p. 175, above)
C. E. Stevens	*The Building of Hadrian's Wall* (Kendal, T. Wilson, 1966)
Adauc. Pudens	RIB 1512
Aelius Aelianus	RIB 1498
Ael(ius) Bassus	RIB 754
Ael(ius) Surinus	RIB 754; cf. now AE 1972.445, Mursa, an Ael. Surinus who was a councillor of that town and designated *quinquennalis*
Q. Albius Felix	CIL XI 3108, cf. RIB 1814 for a Felix on the Wall
Alexander	see Fenius
P. Anicius Maximus	CIL III 6809
Anto(nius) Aratus	RIB 2156
Antonius Felix	RIB 1513
Arrius	RIB 1345–6, 1402
C. Arrius Domitianus	RIB 2122–4
Atilius Natalis	JRS 1959
Audac. Romanus	RIB 1779
M. Aufidius Maximus	RIB 143–4
M. Aur(elius) Nepos	RIB 491
Aur(elius) Super	RIB 679
Aurunc.	RIB 1969
Avidius	RIB 1564–5
Avidius Rufus	RIB 1368, 1567
Babudius Severus	RIB 256
Barrius	EE IX 1327b; Schulze, pp. 207, 350, 423
Blandius Latinus	CIL XII 2601
Caledonius Secundus	RIB 1679, 1854; JRS 1960, 1962
Cari. Scipio	RIB 1936; JRS 1959
T. Cassius Firmus	CIL V 906
Cassius Martialis	RIB 254
Cassius Primus	RIB 1415, 1869; JRS 1963
Caecilius Clemens	RIB 1440, 2081
Caecilius Moni . . .	RIB 1057
Caecilius Proculus	RIB 1475–6, 1570
Cl(audius) Augustanus	RIB 1770, 1811, 1855; CIL VII 1268; cf. note to the procurator of this name in Ch. III.
Cl(audius) Cleonicus	RIB 1648
Cl(audius) Priscus	RIB 1972–3, 2021
Ti. Cl(audius) Vitalis	ILS 2656, Rome
Clemens	see Julius, Vibius
M. Cocceius Firmus	RIB 2174–7; and see Ch. XV, n.
Cocceius Regulus	RIB 1652, 1860, 1862
Commidi (?)	RIB 1514
Congaonius Candidus	RIB 1917
Cornelius Severus	RIB 535
C. Curiatius Saturninus	RIB 146
Delluius	RIB 1505
Dossenius Proculus	RIB 258

M. Favon(ius) Facilis	RIB 200
Felix	see Albius
Fenius Alexander	JRS 1958
Fl(avius) As . . .	RIB 1387
Fl(avius) Basus	JRS 1958
Fl(avius) Betto	RIB 2144; Holder III 268 f. (Vetto)
Fl(avius) Civis	RIB 1474: the editors read Civ[i]l[i]s
Flavius Cre(scens)	RIB 1763
Fl(avius) Julianus	RIB 1507
Fl(avius) Latinus	RIB 1409
Fl(avius) Martinus	RIB 1912
Fl(avius) Noricus	RIB 1664, 1812; JRS 1960; cf. CIL III 5548; Kajanto, p. 204
Sex. Flavius Quietus	Ch. III, n,
Fl(avius) Verecu[nd]us	JRS 1964
T. Fl(avius) Virilis	ILS 2653, Lambaesis
T. Floridius Natalis	RIB 587
Gellius Philippus	RIB 1572, 1668
Glicon	RIB 2164
Julius Candidus	RIB 1632, 1646, 1674
Julius Clemens	RIB 476
Julius Commidus	RIB 1514: the reading of the *cognomen* is rather uncertain
Julius Florentinus	RIB 1677, 1762
Jul(ius) Janal(is)	Brit. 1977; for the type of *cognomen*, see Kajanto, p. 54
Julius Juv(enalis?)	RIB 1375
Julius Marcellinus	RIB 1880
C. Julius Maritimus	CIL VIII 2907
Julius Pri[. . .]	RIB 1369
Julius Primus	JRS 1958
Julius Proculus	RIB 1374
M. Julius Quadratus	AE 1957. 249
Julius Rufus	RIB 1356–7, 1386
Julius Secundus	RIB 157
Julius Subsio	RIB 2013; Holder II 1652
Julius Tertullianus	RIB 1970, 2016
Julius Valens	RIB 1774
Julius Vitalis	RIB 2023
Junius Rufus	RIB 1509
Lib. Fro.	RIB 1330
Libo, see Olc.	
M. Liburnius Fronto	RIB 2077
C. Ligustinius Disertus	CIL XI 5960
Lollia Bodicca	ILS 2653
M. Lollius Venator	JRS 1967
Lousius Suavis	RIB 1499, 1506, 1681, 1859, 1861; Holder II 292; according to Evans, p. 457 'the name is entirely without etymology'; but cf. Lovesius, Holder II 293 f.
Marit. (?)	RIB 1656
Marius Dexter	RIB 1760, 1771; JRS 1961. 194
L. Maximius Gaetulicus	RIB 1775, 2120; *Ztschr. f. Pap. u. Epig.* 57, 181ff.
Metius Ferox	RIB 483
Obc. Libo, see Olc.	
C. Octavius Honoratus	ILS 2655

Octavius Sebanus	RIB 2082
Olc(inius?) Libo	RIB 1647 (Olc. Libo), 1849 (Libo), JRS 1964 (Obc. Libo); Schulze, p. 99
Ostorianus	RIB 1676; Kajanto, p. 152
P. Palpellius Clodius Quirinalis	ILS 2702; Tacitus, *Ann.* 13.30
Petronius Fidus	RIB 481
Petronius Fortunatus	ILS 2658 + add.: see E. Birley, *Promotions*, for a discussion of this career, from which I differ slightly, mainly by associating it with the activities of Q. Antistius Adventus, q.v., Ch. III, n.
Pompeius	RIB 1649; JRS 1959, 1961
Cn. Pompeius Homullus	Ch. III, n.
Pontius Proculus	RIB 253
T. Pontius Sabinus	ILS 2726: see E. Birley, RBRA, pp. 29, 38; M. G. Jarrett, Brit. 1976, pp. 145 ff.
Rom. Pro.	RIB 1519
M. Sabidius Maximus	RIB 104: see Ch. XI, n.
Secundinius Verullus	JRS 1958
L. Senecianius Martius	RIB 575; Holder II 1472 f.
C. Severius Emeritus	RIB 152
Sextius Proculus	RIB 1754
Socellius	RIB 1675, 1768; JRS 1964
Sorio	RIB 1821, whose editors detect the figure of a shrew-mouse (Lat. *sorex*) below the name; Holder II 1617 takes it to be Celtic
Statil[ius] Solon	RIB 1439; cf. CIL III 11034, as noted by E. Birley, RBRA, p. 109; see further H.-G. Pflaum, CP no. 124, dealing with another member of Solon's family, which derived from Heraclea ad Salbacum in Caria, and was noted for producing physicians, two of whom treated Trajan and Antoninus Pius respectively
Sta(tilius?) Telesphorus	RIB 2138
Terentius Cantaber	RIB 1568
M. Tillius Rufus	ILS 2667
Turrianius Priscus	RIB 1416
Ulpius Paullus	JRS 1958
Ulpius Volusenus	JRS 1962; Schulze, p. 104
L. Valerius Proculus	ILS 2666
Varius Quintius Gaianus	CIL VI 33033
Verullus	JRS 1958
Vesnius Viator	RIB 2031, discussed by E. Birley, RBRA, pp. 179 f.
Vesuius Rufus	RIB 1858, 2084
Vibius Clemens	RIB 475

Notes to Chapter VI

H. M. D. Parker, *The Roman Legions* (Oxford, 1928 and repr.) is now rather outdated. G. Webster, *The Roman Imperial Army* (Black, 1969) and G. R. Watson, *The Roman Soldier* (Thames & Hudson, 1969), form the best introduction. The origins of legionaries are discussed in detail by G. Forni, *Il reclutamento delle legioni da Augusto a Diocleziano* (Milan, 1953), with addenda in H. Temporini (ed.), *Aufstieg und Niedergang der römischen Welt*, Berlin, II. 1, 1974, pp. 339 ff. See further the valuable discussion by B. Dobson and J. C. Mann, 'The Roman army in Britain and Britons in the Roman army', Brit. 1973, pp. 191 ff. See on II Augusta and XX Valeria Victrix the studies by M. G. Jarrett, in *Archaeologia Cambrensis* 1964, pp. 47 ff., 1968, pp. 77 ff., and on IX Hispana and VI Victrix by E. Birley and A. R. Birley in R. M. Butler (ed.), *Soldier and Civilian in Roman Yorkshire* (Leicester U.P., 1971), pp. 71 ff., 91 ff.

Aelia Augustina	RIB 574
Aelius Claudian(us)	RIB 448 (Chester, XX Val. Vic.)
Aelius Lucanus	RIB 998 (II Augusta)
Aelius Optatus	CIL V 6632 + Dobson-Mann, p. 263, n. 57: 'specialist function may explain recruitment in Italy'.
Agricola	RIB 1008 (II Augusta)
Agrius Cimarus	RIB 372; Holder I 1015
Albia Faustina	RIB 11
Amanda	RIB 360
Anicius Saturn(inus)	RIB 233
[A]nti[o]chus	JRS 1969
[A]ntonius [Lu]cretianus	RIB 88
Aurelius Cervianus	CIL XV 7164; see M. G. Jarrett, *Archaeologia Cambrensis* 1968, pp. 88 f. and fig. 1.
Au[re]lius Diogen[es]	RIB 521 (Chester, presumably XX Val. Vic.)
Aurelius Herculanus	RIB 356 (Caerleon, II Augusta)
Aurelius Lucius	RIB 522 (Chester, presumably XX Val. Vic.)
Aurelius Modestus	RIB 1696
Aur(elius) Timot[heus]	JRS 1960
L. Bebius Crescens	RIB 671 (York, VI Victrix)
Caesoria Corocca	RIB 371; Holder I 679, 1133
C. Calventius Celer	RIB 475 (Chester, II Adiutrix)
L. Celerinius Vitalis	RIB 659 (York, IX Hispana)
Celsus	RIB 19 (London, II Augusta)
Ti. Cl(audius) Quintianus	RIB 1031
Compitalicius	EE IX 1327 (Newstead, presumably XX Val. Vic.); Kajanto, p. 220 knows no other example (derived from *Compitalia*)
Condrausisius	RIB 1005 (Hadrian's Wall, XX Val. Vic.); Holder I 1097
Q. Cornelius Q.f. Cla.	RIB 254; (Lincoln, IX Hispana) cf. 528–530 for three other tombstones of Quinti Cornelii
Cornel(ius) Castus	RIB 318
Ol. Cor[nel(ius)] Vict(or)	Brit. 1977, where the editors restore Cor[dius], implausibly.
C. Cossutius Saturninus	JRS 1962 (Birdoswald, VI Victrix)
Curatia Dinysia	RIB 562

M. Didius Provincialis	RIB 1085
Domitia Saturnina	RIB 564
L. Duccius Rufinus	RIB 673 (York, IX Hispana)
L. Ecimius Bellicianus Vitalis	RIB 495 (Chester, XX Val. Vic.); Holder I 388, 1405
Egn(atius) D(i)onisius	RIB 1175 (Corbridge, VI Victrix)
S. Epidius [Pu]dens	RIB 486, with revised reading of the name by E. Birley (Chester, probably II Adiutrix)
Fesonia Severina	RIB 563; Schulze pp. 190, 355, 554 (Faesonius)
T. Flaminus T.f. Pol.	RIB 292 (Wroxeter, XIV Gemina)
Flavia Saturnina	RIB 565
Fl(avia) Veldicca	RIB 358; Veldicca is not in Holder, cf. III 142
Fl(avius) Agricola	RIB 11 (London, VI Victrix)
Fl(avius) Callimorphus	RIB 558
T. Flavius Candidus	RIB 357 (Caerleon, II Augusta)
Fla(vius) Lucianus	RIB 2181 (Auchendavy, II Augusta)
T. Fl(avius) Natalis	RIB 358 (Caerleon, II Augusta)
Forianus (?)	RIB 139 (Bath, VI Victrix)
M. G(avius?) Secundinus	RIB 1225
Hermogenes	RIB 461; cf. Dio 69. 22, for Hadrian's doctor
C. Jav[olenus? Sa]tur[nal]is (?)	RIB 147 (Bath, II Augusta); cf. Ch. III, n. to Javolenus Priscus
Julia Belismicus	RIB 318; Holder I 386 f.
Julia Nundina	RIB 372
Julia Secundina	RIB 363, 373
Julia Senica	RIB 374; Holder II 1467 ff., 1476
Julia Veneria	RIB 375
J(ulius) Alesander	RIB 375
J(ulius) Belicianus	RIB 375; Holder I 388
C. Julius Calenus	RIB 252 (Lincoln, VI Victrix)
C. Julius Decuminus	RIB 359 (Caerleon, II Augusta)
C. Jul(ius) Fl(avius) Ingen[uus]	RIB 1292, with slight modification (High Rochester, VI Victrix)
Jul(ius) Julianus	RIB 360 (Caerleon, II Augusta)
C. Jul(ius) Marullinus	RIB 532 (Chester, probably XX Val. Vic.)
C. Julius Quartus	RIB 498 (Chester, XX Val. Vic.)
Jul(ius) Quintilianus	RIB 447 (Chester, probably XX Val. Vic.)
Jul(ius) Secundus	RIB 574
C. Jul(ius) Severus	RIB 499 (Chester, XX Val. Vic.)
Q. Julius Severus	RIB 361 (Caerleon, II Augusta)
C. Jul(ius) Sp[e]ratus	RIB 2151 (Castlecary, VI Victrix)
Jul(ius) Valens	RIB 363 (Caerleon, II Augusta)
Jul(ius) Valens	RIB 13 (London, XX Val. Vic.)
Julius Vitalis	RIB 156 (Bath, XX Val. Vic.)
Justus	RIB 322 (Caerleon, II Augusta)
C. Juventius Capito	RIB 476 (Chester, II Adiutrix)
Litorius Pacatianus	RIB 1599
Lucilius Ingenuus	RIB 544
C. Mannius Secundus	RIB 293 (Wroxeter, XX – not yet Val. Vic.)
Martia	RIB 566

M. Minu(cius) Aude(ns)	RIB 653 (York, VI Victrix)
Modius Julius	RIB 980, 1814
C. Murrius Modestus	RIB 157 (Bath, II Adiutrix)
Oppius [F]elix	RIB 2024 (Hadrian's Wall, II Augusta)
M. Petronius L.f. Men.	RIB 294 (Wroxeter, XIV Gemina)
Pomponius Donatus	RIB 1030
C. Pomponius Valens	JRS 1962
Restita	RIB 566
C. Saufeius	RIB 255 (Lincoln, IX Hispana)
L. Sempronius Flavinus	RIB 256 (Lincoln, IX Hispana)
Serapio	RIB 558
Sur(ius) Justus	RIB 1175 (Corbridge, VI Victrix?)
Tadia Vallaunius	RIB 369; Schulze, pp. 89, 425; Holder III 94
Tadius Exuper(a)tus	RIB 369 (Caerleon, II Augusta)
T. Tertinius . . .	RIB 1134 (Corbridge, legion unknown); Holder II 1799
T. Tertinius Virilis	*Nehalennia-Catalogue* (see p. 198) no. 29
Thesaeus	RIB 558
Ulpius Silvanus	RIB 3 (London, II Augusta)
Ursus	RIB 327 (Caerleon, II Augusta)
Valerius	RIB 1577 (Housesteads, VI Victrix)
C. Valerius C.F. C[la]u.	RIB 540 (Chester, XX Val. Vic. or II Adiutrix)
C. Valeri[us . . .]	RIB 539 (Chester, XX Val. Vic. or II Adiutrix)
C. Valerius C.f. Maec.	RIB 257 (Lincoln, IX Hispana)
C. Valerius Crispus	RIB 478 (Chester, II Adiutrix)
Q. Valerius Fronto	RIB 479 (Chester, II Adiutrix)
C. Val(erius) Justus	RIB 507 (Chester, XX Val. Vic.)
L. Val(erius) Justus	RIB 1175 (Corbridge, VI Victrix)
M. Valerius Latinus	RIB 158 (Bath, XX Val. Vic.)
M. Valer(ius) Martialis	RIB 541 (Chester, XX Val. Vic. or II Adiutrix)
L. Valerius Pud[ens]	RIB 542 (Chester, XX Val. Vic. or II Adiutrix)
T. Valerius Pud[ens]	RIB 258 (Lincoln, II Adiutrix)
L. Valerius Seneca	RIB 480 (Chester, II Adiutrix)
C. Valerius Tullus	RIB 1826 (Carvoran, XX Val. Vic.)
C. Valerius Victor	RIB 365 (Caerleon, II Augusta)
M. Vari(us) Severus	RIB 235
Q. Varius Vitalis	RIB 725
Vibenius Lucius	RIB 602; cf. Schulze, pp. 101 f. + add. (Vibennius), 105 (Vibienus)

Notes to Chapter VII

G. L. Cheesman, *The Auxilia of the Roman Imperial Army* (Oxford, 1914), is now badly in need of replacement. See now the works by Watson and Webster and the article by Dobson and Mann cited on p. 182; most of the items in the bibliography on p. 175 are also relevant. The evidence of the diplomas published in CIL. XVI is now greatly enhanced by the publication of M. M. Roxan, *Roman Military Diplomas 1954–1977* (London: Institute of Archaeology, interesting study of the sizes of the various types of unit. See now especially P. A. Holder, *Studies in the auxilia of the Roman army from Augustus to Trajan* (BAR Int. Ser. 70, 1980), and the same scholar's monograph on the army in Britain (cf. p. 10).

Ael(ius) Gemellus	RIB 1480
Albanus	RIB 108
Ammonius	RIB 2213; Schulze, pp. 121 f. shows that this name is probably Egyptian, although Holder I 131 regards it as Celtic
Aurel(ius) Armiger	RIB 1991
Aur(elius) Campester	RIB 1524
Aurelius Crotus	RIB 1525; Holder I 1177
M. Aur[el(ius)] Januarius	RIB 1459 (reading a little uncertain)
Aur(elius) Marcus	RIB 1828
Candidus	RIB 580 (Manchester)
Candidus	RIB 1172 (Hexham)
Caravi(us)	JRS 1960, citing Appian, *Iber.* 43.; Holder I 781
Carinus	JRS 1969
Ceanatis	JRS 1969
Cintusmus	RIB 619; cf. the *aerarius* of this name, Ch. XII, n.; Holder I 1024 f.
Claudius Paulinus	Ch. III, n.
Ti. Claudius Tirintius	RIB 291
Comes	JRS 1969
Comitinus	JRS 1969; cf. Holder I 1074 for Comit- names
Consortius	JRS 1969
Crocus	*Epit. de Caes.* 41.3; Holder I 1173
Crotus	RIB 620; Holder I 1177
Cudre(nus)	RIB 579
Cunittus	JRS 1969; cf. Holder I 1192 (Cunita)
Damio	RIB 2213; listed by Holder I 1218 as Celtic, but see under Ammonius above and the Greek doctor cited by Pliny, *nat. Hist.*, ind. to Bks. 20–27
Dannicus	RIB 108; Holder I 1223
Deciba[lus]	RIB 1920
Elpis	Brit. 1974
Enestinus	JRS 1969
Excingus	RIB 621; Holder I 1488
Fabius Sabinus	CIL XVI 69
Flavia Peregrina	RIB 620
Flavinus	RIB 1172
Fl[av]ius Bitucus	RIB 108; Holder I 431
T. Flavius Crensces	ILS 2515, Carnuntum
Fl(avius) Hilario	RIB 2003
Flavius Silvanus	ILS 2515, Carnuntum
Frumentius	RIB 2109
Fulvius Natalis	RIB 108
Q. Gargilius Martialis	Ch. IV, n.
Gemellus	CIL XVI 69
Genialis	RIB 109

Hnaudifridus	RIB 1576
Hurmio	RIB 1619
M. Ingenuius Asiati[cus]	RIB 586
Julius Augustalis	RIB 918
D. Julius Candidus	RIB 1350
Jul(ius) Carantus	RIB 1266
Jul(ius) Gr[ati]nus	RIB 1101
Jul(ius) Pastor	RIB 1795
Jul(ius) Rufinus	RIB 2042
Jul(ius) Victor	RIB 1247
Longinus Sdapeze	RIB 201: see Dobson-Mann, p. 198 n. 34, taking Sdapeze to be the second name of Longinus rather than the first part of his father's name (Matycus)
Maduhus	RIB 1526; cf. Holder II 370 (Madu, etc.)
Masavo	RIB 577; Holder II 450
Maslorius	JRS 1969; cf. Holder II 453 (Mas(o)lacus)
Maus	RIB 1523: cf. the names of the usurper Carausius in RIB 2291, *M. Aur. Maus. Carausio*, Holder II 487 f.
Melisus	RIB 619; Holder II 537 f.
Motius	JRS 1969; cf. the potter Mottius Bollus, Ch. XIII, n.; Holder II 646
Obsequens	RIB 1828
Quintianus	RIB 578
Rufus Sita	RIB 121
Sattua	Brit. 1974; cf. Holder II 1376 (Sattia)
Senorix	JRS 1969; Holder II 1500
Similis	JRS 1969
Smertrius	RIB 804; cf. Holder II 159 ff.
Tetrecus	Brit. 1974
Tiberinus	JRS 1969
Sex. Valerius Genialis	RIB 109; for 'Frisiaus' = 'Frisiavo', see J. C. Mann, Brit. 1971, p. 224
Val(erius) Vitalis	RIB 279
Ved . . .	RIB 639; cf. Holder III 135 ff.
Verecud. Rufilia	RIB 621
L. Vitellius Tancinus	RIB 159. P. A. Holder points out to me that Tancinus' father had probably become a citizen, obtaining a grant presumably from the censor of this name, q.v. in Ch. II, n. – while the *ala* need not have been given the title *c(ivium) R(omanorum)* until the Flavian period. Holder II 1717 f.; Evans, p. 260

Notes to Chapter VIII

B. Dobson and J. C. Mann, 'The Roman army in Britain and Britons in the Roman army', Brit. 1973, pp. 191 ff. is the main study. See also the items on pp. 178, 182, and on veterans' privileges, P. Garnsey, *Social Status and Legal Privilege in the Roman Empire* (Oxford, 1970), pp. 245 ff.

C. Aeresius Saenus	RIB 685; Schulze, pp. 112, 241; Holder I 52, II 1284
Albanus	CIL XVI 70
[A]mabilis	JRS 1960 = M. M. Roxan, *Roman Military Diplomas 1954–1977* (London: Inst. of Arch., 1978), no. 8. The name recurs on a graffito found at Flint, kindly shown to me by G. D. B. Jones
Antigonus	RIB 160
M. Aur[el(ius)] Januarius	RIB 1459 (the inscription is now lost and the reading of the name is rather uncertain)
T. Aur(elius) Aurelianus	RIB 627
Aur(elius) Mucianus	RIB 729
T. Aur(elius) Quintus	RIB 623
Aureli(us) Romulia[nus]	RIB 748
Aur(elius) Tasulus	RIB 887; Holder II 1751
Crotus	RIB 620
L. Ecimius Bellicianus Vitalis	RIB 495; Holder I 388, 1405 (Ecimius is not in Schulze)
Fl(avia) Augustina	RIB 685
Flavia Peregrina	RIB 620
Fl(avia) Veldicca	RIB 358
Fla(vius) Fuscinus	JRS 1963
T. Fl(avius) Natalis	RIB 358
Genialis	RIB 367
Julia Secundina	RIB 363, 373
C. Julius Calenus	RIB 252, reading Galenus; for Calenus, Kajanto, p. 191
C. Julius Decuminus	RIB 359
Jul(ius) Januarius	RIB 600
C. Jul(ius) Martinus	RIB 363, 373
C. Jul(ius) Sp[e]ratus	RIB 2151
Jul(ius) Valens	RIB 363
Lucius	CIL XVI 82
[Ma]nsuetus	CIL XVI 82
Ramm(i)us	see under [A]mabilis, above
Reburrus	CIL XVI 48; Holder II 1089 ff.
Saenius Augustinus	RIB 685
[Satu]rninus	CIL XVI 130
Se[. . .]ius [Se]necianus	RIB 367
Severus	CIL XVI 48
Sigilius	RIB 892, where *emeritus* is taken as a *cognomen*; cf. Holder II 1544

Ulpius Silvanus	RIB 3
C. Valerius Crispus	RIB 478
Valerius Verecundus	Brit. 1977
Vindex	RIB 620; Holder III 328 ff. lists names in *vind-; vindos =* white, 342

Notes to Chapter IX

B. Dobson and J. C. Mann, Brit. 1973 (see p. 182, above) is the main study. See also E. Birley, RBRA, pp. 76 ff. I cannot follow the arguments of D. Kennedy, 'The *ala I* and *cohors I Britannica*', Brit. 1977, pp. 249 ff. On the *numeri Brittonum* in Upper Germany, see Dobson-Mann, p. 200, and M. P. Speidel, in H. Temporini (ed.), *Aufstieg und Niedergang der römischen Welt* (Berlin) II.3, p. 202 ff. It may be helpful to list the other British units in chronological order. I am grateful to E. Birley and P. A. Holder for advice.

i. formed before AD 69, probably soon after conquest:

ala Britannica	Tacitus, *Hist.* 3.41; CIL XVI 47 (Pannonia, AD 102)
cohors I Britannica equitata (*Britannorum*, XVI 185)	CIL XVI (Pannonia, AD 80); XVI 31 (Pann., AD 85 – *milliaria*); XVI 54 (Moesia sup., *c.* AD 105; *c.R.*); XVI 185, etc. (Dacia, AD 164)
coh. II Britannorum eq. (*milliaria* at least AD 100)	CIL XIII 12425 (Germania inf., Flavian); XVI 46 (Moesia superior, AD 100); XVI 163 (Dacia, AD 110)
coh. III Britannorum eq.	CIL V 7717 (?AD 69/70); XVI 55 (Raetia, AD 107)

ii. formed c. AD 70 and sent to Danube:

coh. I Flavia Brittonum (*eq.*) (*milliaria?*)	CIL III 2024 (Dalmatia); III 5668 (Noricum); III 4811, XI 6337 (third cent. officers, tribunes)
coh. II Flavia Brittonum eq.	CIL XVI 45 (Moesia inf.; AD 99)

iii. formed c. AD 80, sent to Danube c. 85:

ala I Brittonum (*c.R.* in Dacia)	AE 1973. 459 (Pannonian recruit, *c.* AD 98); AE 1973. 459 (Dacia, AD 123); CIL. XVI 175 (Pannonia inf., AD 139)
coh. I Brittonum mill, eq.	CIL XVI 31 (Pannonia, AD 85); XVI 54 (Moesia sup., *c.* AD 105); XVI 163 (Dacia, AD 110, Ulpia mill. torquata *c.R.*)
coh. II Brittonum eq.	CIL XVI 56 (Mauretania Caes., AD 107)
coh. III Brittonum eq.	CIL XVI 46 (Moesia sup., AD 110); XI 393
coh. IV & V Brittonum eq.	are postulated from the above and from:
coh. VI Brittonum eq.	CIL XIII 12423 (?) (tile, Germania inf.); AE 1972 (Danube, *c.* AD 106); cf. II 2424, VIII 5363

iv. formed c. AD 90–98, sent to Danube:

coh. I Augusta Nervia Pacensis Brittonum milliaria	AE 1962. 264 (Dacia, AD 140)
coh. II Aug. Nerv. Pac.	CIL XVI 61 (Pannonia inf., AD 114); XVI 110 (Dacia,

mill. Brittonum   AD 158)

v. formed by Hadrian, sent to Noricum:

coh. I Aelia Brittonum   CIL IX 5357; III 4812 (AD 238)
mill.

Adcoprovatus	CIL XVI 160; Evans, pp. 128 ff. on names in *Ad-*
P. Aelius Urbicinus	CIL VI 3337
Ael(ius) Mercurialis	RIB 1742
[P.A.]elius [. . .]ogont[ius?]	CIL VI 3343, following a suggestion of E. Birley; cf. JRS 1952 for a potter called Moguntius.
Aemilius Saeni (*filius*)	AE 1956. 249, Cologne
L. Aemilius Flaccus	CIL VI 3357
Q. Aemilius Marinus	CIL VI 3339
Albanus	CIL XVI 70
Aur(elius) Macrinus	RIB 714; R. W. Davies, Brit. 1976, 139 f. regards this man as a *singularis* of the governor rather than of the emperor, amending the reading of the now lost inscription from Malton
T. Aurelius Pius	CIL VI 3344
Aurelius Verecundus	CIL VI 3344
Bodiccius	CIL III 3256; Holder I 455 ff.
Calidius Quietus	CIL VI 3346
Canio	RIB 1483
Catavignus	ILS 2560; Holder I 839
L. Ecimius Bellicianus Vitalis	RIB 495; Holder I 388, 1405
Fidelis	CIL III 2024, Salona
T. F(lavius) Verecundus	CIL III 4576
T. Flavius Verecundus	CIL VI 3338
Ingenu(u)us	CIL III 4576
Italicus	CIL III 4576
Ivomagus	ILS 2560; Holder II 112
Ivonercus	CIL XVI 110, with new fragment giving improved reading of the name in M. M. Roxan, *Roman Military Diplomas 1954–1977* (London: Inst. of Arch., 1978), no. 47 with n. 5. cf. Holder II 112
Julia	RIB 1483
Julius Vitalis	RIB 156
M. Junius Capito	CIL VIII 21669, Albula (Mauretania Caesariensis)
Lucca, Lucco	CIL XVI 49; Holder II 296 f.
Lurio	RIB 1483
[Ma]nsuetus	CIL XVI 82
M. Minicius Mar[ce]l[linus]	CIL XIII 6679, Mainz
Mog. Ursus	CIL III 5455; Holder II 607 ff. for names in *Mog-*
Molacus	see under Ivonercus; Holder II 617
Nectovelius	RIB 2142; Holder II 746
Nig. Marinianus	CIL VI 3279

Novantico	CIL XVI 160; cf. Holder II 778 f.
Paternus	ILS 2560
C. Pomponius Valens	JRS 1962
Priscinus	CIL III 4576
Pro . . .	CIL III 4576
[Satur]ninus	CIL XVI 130
D. Senius Vitalis	ILS 2572, Cologne
T. Sempronius Pudens	CIL VI 3357, cf. 3359
Sepenestus	JRS 1961
Similis	CIL XVI 49
T. Statius Vitalis	CIL III 11233, Carnuntum
Tadia Vallaunius	RIB 369; Schulze, pp. 89, 425; Holder III 94
Tadius Exuper(a)tus	RIB 369
M. Ulpius Faustinus	CIL VIII 9764, Portus Magnus (Mauretania)
M. Ulpius Justus	CIL VI 3301
M. Ulpius Longinus	CIL XVI 163
M. Ulpius Novantico	CIL XVI 160
M. Ulpius Quintus	ILS 2365, Rome
M. Ulpius Respectus	CIL VI 3301
Ursa	RIB 1483
Vacia	RIB 1742; Holder III 79; Evans, pp. 475 f.
Val(erius) Paternus	CIL VI 3358
L. Valerius Simplex	ILS 4789
Virssuccius	CIL III 3256; Holder III 397
Vitalis	CIL XVI 163

On the *cohors I Cornoviorum*, see E. Birley, *Archaeologia Cambrensis* 1953, pp. 9 ff. and *Historia-Augusta-Colloquium Bonn 1972/74* (1976), p. 72, CIL VII 1243; EE IX 1285.

inscription from Castlecary	RIB 2147 & 2152, rejecting the reading in CIL VII 1094, which, however, remains a possibility

Notes to Chapter X

See. P. Salway, *The Frontier People of Roman Britain* (Cambridge, 1965); R. Birley, *Civilians on the Roman Frontier* (F. Graham, Newcastle, 1973); D. J. Breeze and B. Dobson, *Hadrian's Wall* (Allen Lane, 1976); R. Birley, *Vindolanda. A Roman Frontier Post on Hadrian's Wall* (Thames & Hudson, 1977); M. G. Jarrett, *Maryport, Cumbria: A Roman Fort and its Garrison* (Kendal, T. Wilson, 1976); C. Daniels, *Handbook to the Roman Wall by J. Collingwood Bruce*, 13th ed. (H. Hill, Newcastle, 1978). I have also benefited from a forthcoming study of 'The deities of Roman Britain' by E. Birley, to be published in the *Aufstieg und Niedergang der römischen Welt* (De Gruyter, Berlin and New York); on the Veteres I have also consulted with profit the article by F. Heichelheim in the *Real-encyclopädie der classischen Altertumswissenschaft* (Pauly-Wissowa: Stuttgart, Druckenmüller), Vol. IX A.I (1961), columns 408–415.

Aelius Mansuetus	JRS 1957; a graffito on a black jar found in turret 34A on Hadrian's Wall has the name Ma(n)suetus: Brit. 1972

Ahtehe	RIB 1180
Alimahus	RIB 1620
Amatius Ingenuus	RIB 906
Annamoris	RIB 784; Holder I 44 (interpreting as Adnamorix)
Apullio	JRS 1963; cf. Holder I 167 (Apullonus)
Arcavius	RIB 926; cf. Holder I 182, on names in *Arc-*
L. Arruntius Salvianus	RIB 1062
Aspuanis	RIB 1603
Audagus	RIB 774; Holder I 283; Evans, pp. 145 ff.
Aur(elia) Aia	RIB 1828
Aur(elia) Aurelia(na)	RIB 959
Aurelia Caula	RIB 1745; cf. Holder I 867 (Caul-)
Aur(elia) C[uno]vinda	JRS 1967; cf. Holder I 1193 ff. (*cuno-*), III 342 (*vindo*)
Aur(elia) Eubia	RIB 612
Aur(elia) Lupula	RIB 1250
Aur(elia) Quartilla	RIB 1251
Aurelia Rom[ana]	RIB 749
Aurelia Sabina	RIB 749
Aur[e]lia S[abin]illa	RIB 1745
Aurelia Victor[i]na	RIB 1435
Aur(elius) Mucianus	RIB 727
Aur(elius) Pr[o]p[inquus]	RIB 612; JRS 1969
Aur(elius) Pus[i]nnus	RIB 612
Aur(elius) Quartinus	RIB 1251
M. Aurelius Vic[t]or	RIB 1481 (Chesters)
[A]ure[l]ius Vict[or]	RIB 1255 (Risingham)
Aure(lius) Vict(or)	RIB 1606 (Housesteads)
Aurel(ius) [Vic]tor	RIB 1435 (Haltonchesters)
Baculo	RIB 773; Holder I 325
Baib(ius) Duvianus	JRS 1965; Holder I 1388 (Duvius)
Barathes	RIB 1065, 1171
Blescius Diovicus	RIB 1254; Holder I 452, 1285
Burcanius	RIB 926
Canio	RIB 1483
Cistumucus	JRS 1968
Clanova	Brit. 1974
Claudia Turi[a]nilla	RIB 1789
M. Cocceius Firmus	RIB 2174–7; see Ch. xv, n.
Crescentinus	RIB 785
Crotilo	RIB 934
Cunovindus	Brit. 1971; see under Aur(elia) C[uno]vinda
Dailus	RIB 1620
Deccius	RIB 1805
Delfinus	RIB 1620
Diodora	RIB 1129
Dionysius Fortunatus	RIB 1250
Duihno	RIB 1046; Holder I 1365
Durio	RIB 2063; Holder I 1380
A. Egnatius Pastor	RIB 808
Enemn[o]genus	RIB 742
Fersio	RIB 1620
Fersomeris	RIB 926: I see no reason why this name and the one

which follows it, Unsenis, should not be those of
dedicators, rather than – as the editors assume – epithets
of *omnibus dibus*; cf. RIB 2109, a dedication to *dib(us)*
deab(us)q. omnib(us), unqualified.

Fla(viu)s Antigonus Papias	RIB 955
Fl(avius) Martius	RIB 933, explained by the milestone published in JRS 1965
Fontia	Brit. 1974
Fortunatus	RIB 969 (where E. Birley reads *d(eo) Hv[e]ter(i)*)
Gratus	RIB 1620
Greca	RIB 934
Hermione, Q(uinti) f(ilia)	RIB 813, 845
Hermes	RIB 758
Hnaudifridus	RIB 1576
Huctia	JRS 1963
Ivixa (?)	RIB 1804; cf. Holder II 111 ff. (*Ivi-*)
Januarius	RIB 780 (Brougham); cf. 744, 1833 for the name
Javo[l]ena Monime	RIB 967: E. Birley's reading; for Javolenus Priscus, see Ch. III, n.
Julia	RIB 1483
Julianus	RIB 775
Jul(ius) Pastor	RIB 1795
Jul(ius) Senecianus	JRS 1967, improved reading by G. Alföldy in JRS 1968. See now M. G. Jarrett, *Maryport, Cumbria: A Roman Fort and its Garrison* (Kendal: T. Wilson, 1976), pp. 42 ff.
Justina	RIB 1743
Longinus	Brit. 1973
Lunaris	RIB 786 (Brougham), 1521 (Carrawburgh); cf. AE 1922. 116
Lurio	RIB 1483
M.	RIB 787
Mamma	JRS 1965; Holder II 400
Maximus	RIB 1103; cf. 1915 for another Maximus
Meni(us) Dada	RIB 1799; Holder I 1214
Mocux[s]oma	JRS 1962; cf. Holder II 604 (*mocu*)
Morirex	RIB 861; Holder II 636 ('sea-king')
Necalames	RIB 1793–4, 1801
Nittiunis	JRS 1968
Nobilis	RIB 1180
Novel(lia) Justina	RIB 1743
L. Novell(ius) Lanuccus	RIB 1743
Pervica	RIB 1747; Holder II 971
Pervinca	RIB 1620
Pluma	RIB 786
Pov . . c . arus	RIB 926
Primulus	RIB 660
Ramio	RIB 2063; Holder II 1072
Rautio	RIB 1620
Regulus	RIB 1602
Ressona	RIB 784; Holder II 1177 f.

Rianorix	RIB 862; Holder II 1181
Romana	RIB 1729
Romulus	RIB 1620
Rufinus	RIB 1271

Sabina	JRS 1963
Salmanes	RIB 2182
Senaculus	RIB 1699
M.Senec[ia]nius V . . .	RIB 2064; Holder II 1472 f.
Senilis	Brit. 1973
Similis	RIB 1620
Sotera	JRS 1968; see also under Jul(ius) Senecianus
Suadnus (?)	RIB 1458; cf. Holder II 1642 (Suadinus); Evans, p. 258
Sucabus	Brit. 1971
Superstes	RIB 1602

Talio	JRS 1968; Holder II 1709; Evans, pp. 259 ff.
Tancorix	RIB 908; Holder II 1718
Tertulus	RIB 1455
Tittus M . . .	RIB 787
Titullinia Pussitta	RIB 984; Holder II 1054
Trupo	RIB 2063

Uccus (?)	RIB 1548
Ulpius Apolinaris	RIB 959
Unsenis	RIB 926: see note under Fersomeris
Unthau[s]	RIB 1088
Ursa	RIB 1483

Vagdavarcustus	RIB 926
Venustin[i]us Lupus	RIB 1986
C. Verecundius Severus	RIB 1984
Vetti[a] Mansueta	RIB 1789
Viasudri(us) (?)	RIB 1048; cf. Holder III 273 f. for Via- names
Victor	RIB 1064
Vidaris	RIB 785; Holder III 288
Vindicianus	RIB 934
Vrocata	JRS 1953; cf. Holder III 454 f.
– orix	JRS 1967

Notes to Chapter XI

There is a useful study of the general background in the article by P. A. Brunt, 'The Romanisation of the local ruling classes in the Roman empire', *Assimilation et résistance a la culture greco-romaine le monde ancien. Travaux du VIe Congres International d'Etudes Classiques (Madrid, Septembre 1974)*, (Paris, Les Belles Lettres, 1976), pp. 161 ff. *The Towns of Roman Britain* (Batsford, 1974), by J. Wacher, provides very full coverage and full documentation.

Special abbreviation:
Kubitschek   J. W. Kubitschek, *Imperium Romanum tributim discriptum* (Vienna, 1889)

Aelia . . . Cauva	RIB 94; Holder I 870
Ael(ia) Severa	RIB 683
P. Ael(ius) Fi[r](mus)(?)	JRS 1955
(A)emilia Theodora	RIB 677
Aesubilinus	RIB 193. I prefer the reading in CIL VII 87; *Aesurilini* in RIB; Holder I 53
Aetern[ius ?]	RIB 648
Agessilus	Brit. 1971: the name, in the genitive, was scratched on a pipe-clay statuette before firing, and need not therefore represent an inhabitant of Canterbury
Q. Agrius Auspex	RIB 650
Agustalis	RIB 154
A. Alfid. Pomp. Olussa	RIB 9. Pomp. might be either a second *gentilicium*, Pomp(eius), Pomp(onius), etc.; or a tribe, Pomp(tina); but it is possible that the man had the *cognomen* Pompolussa, as suggested by Kubitschek, p. 222 n. 314. NA ATHENI is read in line 5, interpreted as *na(tus) Atheni(s)*, 'born at Athens'. The third letter is very uncertain, and could be an I; note that Atina in Italy was enrolled in the Pomptina tribe, Kubitschek, p. 45.
Ammin(i)us	RIB 90, cf. Adminius, Ch. II, n.
Andoc . . .	JRS 1969
Andronica	RIB 691
C. Antistius Frontinus	RIB 247
Anto(nius) Gargilianus	Brit. 1970
Anto(nius) Step(h)anus	RIB 695
Apollonius	RIB 2065
Attic[us]	Brit. 1972
Attius	RIB 192; Holder III 737
Attius Ch . . . uvus	RIB 101
Atto . . .	JRS 1957
Aur[eli . . .	RIB 709
Aur(elia) Eucarpia	RIB 10
M. Aurelius Eucarpus	RIB 10
Aurelius Euticianus	Brit. 1972
Aurelius Igennus	Brit. 1972
Aur(elius) Sat(urninus)	JRS 1944
Aur(elius) Senecio	RIB 250; Holder II 1473 f.
M. Aurinius Simn[us]	RIB 689; cf. Schulze, p. 558 (Aurini, Aurius); Holder II 1566
Austalis	EE VII 1141
Barita, see Candida	
Bitudacus	JRS 1937
Brica, see Julia	
Bruscius	RIB 262
C. Calpurnius Receptus	RIB 155
Candida Barita	RIB 689; cf. Holder I 350 (Baricca)
Carina	RIB 188
Carinus	RIB 188
Carssouna	RIB 262; Holder I 816
Cassavus	RIB 110; Holder I 824
Cast. Castrensis	RIB 112

Catia . . . Cens[o]rin[a?]	RIB 95
Cata	JRS 1956
Catiotuos, see Claudia	
Catus	RIB 154: I prefer to separate this name from Minianus, following G. Alföldy in his review of RIB, citing CIL XIII 5780 (*Bonner Jahrbucher* 1966)
P. Cicereius Felix	RIB 6
Cintusmus	RIB 194; Holder I 1024
Civilis	JRS 1964
Classicianus, see Julius	
Claudia Catiotuos	RIB 250; cf. Evans, pp. 171 ff.
Cla(udius) Florentinus	Brit. 1970
[C]laudius Ligur	RIB 141
Cominius Familiaris	JRS 1944
Comitianus	RIB 154; cf. Holder I 1075
Comitinu[s]	Brit. 1972
Q. Core(llius) Fortis	RIB 684
Cor(nelius) Sim(ilis) (?)	JRS 1955, reading CCRSM; the photograph in K. Branigan and P. J. Fowler (edd.), *The Roman West Country* (1976), p. 74, pl. 8, justifies the reading offered here
Q. Creper(e)ius Marcus	Brit. 1973
Dagobitus	RIB 22; Holder I 1215
Deuccus	RIB 295; Holder I 1272
Diodora	RIB 1129
Eberesto	JRS 1925
Eglecta	RIB 695
T. Egnatius Tyrannus	RIB 6
Exsupereus	RIB 154
Felicula	RIB 710
Fl(avia) Ingenua	RIB 251
Fl(avia) Martiola	RIB 933, interpreted in the light of the milestone of Postumus in JRS 1965
Fl(avia) Victorina	RIB 83
Flavinus	JRS 1958
Fl(avius) Bellator	RIB 674; Holder I 387
P. F(lavius?) Hyginus	CIL VII 1322
Fl(avius) Martius	RIB 933: see under Fl(avia) Martiola
Flor(ius?) Cogitatus	RIB 202
Flor(ius?) Fidelis	RIB 202
Q. Florius Maternus	RIB 1578, 1591
Gaius	JRS 1933
Germanilla	RIB 154
Grata	RIB 22
Hermes	RIB 195
Hyginus, see F(lavius)	
Igennus, see Aurelius	
Julia Brica	RIB 686; Holder I 529
Julia Casta	RIB 113

Julia Velva	RIB 688; cf. Holder III 154 ff.
Jul(ius) Flor(us)	JRS 1955
Julius Primus	JRS 1936
Jovina	RIB 154
Jovinus	Brit. 1971
Justus	Brit. 1971
Karinus	Brit. 1971
T. Licinius Ascanius	RIB 14
Lossio Veda	RIB 191; see K. H. Jackson in F. T. Wainwright (ed.), *The Problem of the Picts* (1955), pp. 137 f.
Lucanus	JRS 1962
Lucianus	RIB 617
Lucius	CIL VII 1335, 4
Lucret[ius]	JRS 1948
Lucullus	RIB 90; cf. Holder II 196, 304
Lupinus	JRS 1958
Macr . . .	RIB 202
M. Macrinius Avitus Catonius Vindex	H.-G. Pflaum, CP no. 188 + add.
M. Macrinius Vindex	H.-G. Pflaum, CP no. 161
Mantinia Maerica	RIB 689; cf. Holder II 392, 411 f.
L. Marcius Memor	JRS 1966
Marcus	JRS 1962
Marinus	Brit. 1977
Martia[lis]	JRS 1952
M. Martiannius Pulcher	Brit. 1976
Martina	JRS 1952
[Mi]nervalis	JRS 1962
Minianus	RIB 154: see comments under Catus
M. Minicius Mar[ce]l[linus]	CIL XIII 6679; cf. CIL VII 1338, 15, for Min . . . on a graffito from Lincoln. For the cavalry officer of this name, see the new diploma of AD 123, and H. Devijver (op. cit. in notes to Chapter IV), M61
Nata[lis?]	JRS 1956
Nemmonius Verecundus	Brit. 1972; Holder II 713
Nican[or]	JRS 1951
M. Nonius Romanus	RIB 309
Novantico, see Ulpius	
Octobrianus	Brit. 1971
Olussa, see Alfid(ius)	
P. Oranius Facilis	Brit. 1977; Schulze, pp. 349, 364
Paratus	JRS 1944
T. Perpet[uius ? . . .]	RIB 648
Petronius	Brit. 1972
Philus	RIB 110
Placida	RIB 295
Pomp(eius?) Nic.	CIL VII 1323
Pompolussa, see Alfid(ius)	
Primus	EE VII 1143
Primu[s]	CIL VII 1257

C. Protaciu[s . . .]	RIB 141
Pulcher	RIB 1124
Quintus	RIB 262
Romana	RIB 188
Rufinus	RIB 188
Rufus	JRS 1954
Rusonia Avent[i]na	RIB 163
M. Rustius Massa	RIB 654
Sabidius Maximus	RIB 104, cf. AE 1937. 101 (Macedonia), a centurion called M. Sabidiu[s] Ma[ximus], who served in several legions, including perhaps I[I Aug.] under Hadrian and Antoninus Pius
Sabina	JRS 1959
M. Sabinius Victor	RIB 68
Sacer	RIB 262
Saen(i)us Tammon(i)us	RIB 67; Holder II 1715
Senicianus	RIB 306; CIL VII 1305; see R. G. Goodchild, *Antiquity* 27 (1953), pp. 100 ff.
Severinus	RIB 154
Silvianus	RIB 306: see under Senicianus
Similis	RIB 192 (Colchester)
Similis	JRS 1936 (Verulamium)
Solinus	RIB 22
M. Statius Priscus Licinius Italicus	Ch. III, n.; cf. Statius Vitalis in Ch. IX. Priscus was in the tribe Claudia (ILS 1092), in which Camulodunum was enrolled
Sulinus	RIB 105, 151; Holder II 1665
Tacita	JRS 1958
T. Tammon(ius) Vitalis	RIB 67
Tretia Maria (? = Maria Tertia)	RIB 7
Ulpius Felix	RIB 691
M. Ulpius Januarius	RIB 707
M. Ulpius Novantico	CIL XVI 160
M. Ulpius Quintus	ILS 2365
L. Ulpius Sestius	RIB 163
Val(eria) Frontina	RIB 202
Valerius	JRS 1952
Valerius Amandinus	RIB 16
Valerius Marcellus	RIB 16
Valerius Superventor	RIB 16; Kajanto, p. 320; Ammian. 18.9.3
[V]al(erius) Theodorianus	RIB 677
Vanus	JRS 1925
Vassedo	JRS 1944
Veda, see Lossio	
Velva, see Julia	
Velvinna	RIB 154
Venusta	JRS 1954
Vepogenus	RIB 191; see under Lossio Veda
Verecunda	CIL VII 1335, 4
P. Vicana	RIB 111; Holder III 276

Victoricus	JRS 1957
Vilbia	RIB 154
P. Vitalis	RIB 111
Vitalis	JRS 1952
Viventia	JRS 1957
Volusia Faustina	RIB 250
Vol(usius? Iren[aeus]	RIB 641
Unknown centurion from Nicaea	RIB 203

Notes to Chapter XII

For general background, see M. I. Finley, *The Ancient Economy* (London, 1973). See now also, on an important aspect, J. du P. Taylor and H. Cleere (eds), *Roman Shipping and Trade: Britain and the Rhine provinces* (C.B.A. Res. Rep. 24, 1978).

Special abbreviation:

Nehalennia-Catalogue	*Deae Nehalenniae*. Gids bij de Tentoonstelling Nehalennia de zeeuwse godin, Zeeland in de romeinse tijd, romeinse momumenten uit de Oosterschelde (Middelburg, Koninklijk Zeeuwsch Genootschap der Wetenschappen, Leiden, 1971)
,Q. Antistius Adventus	Ch. III, n.
,Arisenius Marius	*Nehalennia-Catalogue*, p. 35: the altar was found too late to be illustrated, and is only mentioned briefly
Ascattinius Rascua	CIL XIII 8780; Holder I 245, II 1075
Atticus	RIB 69; cf. 70–1 for resident aliens at Silchester
M. Aur(elius) Lunaris	JRS 1921 = AE 1922. 116
C. Aurelius Verus	ILS 7522
Axius	Galen 12, p. 786K
[Ba]rathes/Barates	RIB 1065, 1171
Caesar	see *B.G.* 20 on merchants trading with Britain
Callisunus	JRS 1954; cf. Holder I 700 ff.
T. Calvisius Secundinus	CIL XIII 8782
Cassavus	RIB 110; Holder I 824
Cillenticus (?)	JRS 1957; cf. Holder I 1014
Crescens	JRS 1931
Epillicus	JRS 1954; cf. Eppillus, Ch. II, n.; Holder I 1445
Fla(viu)s Antigonus Papias	RIB 955
Fl(avius) Helius	RIB 251
Fl(avius) Secundus	CIL VII 1310
Fufidius	CIL XIII 7300
Gimioga	AE 1972. 380; cf. Holder I 2022 (Gimio)
Julia Fortunata	RIB 687
Julius Jucundus	CIL VII 1309

Julius Ju(v)enis	CIL VII 1310
Q. Julius Martinus	Brit. 1976
Q. Julius Murranus	CIL VII 1311
M. Julius Satyrus	CIL VII 1312
Sex. Julius Sedatus	CIL VII 1313
Q. Jul(ius) Senex	CIL VII 1314
L. Jul(ius) Senex	JRS 1929
Lossio Veda	RIB 191; see Ch. XI, n.
Lunaris, see Aur(elius)	
Nat. Sol.	CIL VII 1200
Nepos, A. Platorius	Ch. III, n.
M. Nonius Romanus	RIB 309
Papias, see Fla(viu)s	
Peregrinus	RIB 140
Philus	RIB 110
C. Piscius Fagus	JRS 1934; cf. CIL XIII 33, 323-5
Placidus, Viduci f(ilius)	*Nehalennia-Catalogue* no. 45; see also Viducius, below
Rufus	JRS 1954
Salmanes	RIB 2182
L. Secundinius Moderatus	ILS 4749
M. Secund. Silvanus	ILS 4751; AE 1972. 370
Secundus	RIB 140
C. Silvius Tetricus	JRS 1932
L. Solimarius Secundinus	ILS 7523
Stolus (?), see Axius	
Urbicus, Q. Lollius	Ch. III, n.
L. Val(erius) Latinus	CIL VII 1319
Vepogenus	RIB 191; see Ch. XI, n. to Lossio Veda
M. Verec. Diogenes	RIB 678, 687
L. Viducius Placidus	Brit. 1977; note the potter Viducus, Ch. XIII, n.
T. Vindac(ius) Ariovistus	CIL VII 1320; Holder III 328 f., 686
M. Vitel(lius) Cres(cens)	CIL VII 1321
— onianus	RIB 2059

Notes to Chapter XIII

Most books on Roman Britain have something to say on craftsmen. Apart from those mentioned in the notes to other chapters, see esp. J. Liversidge, *Britain in the Roman Empire* (Routledge, 1968), esp. pp. 169 ff. The makers of mortaria are a special subject, on which the definitive study by Mrs K. F. Hartley is eagerly awaited. In the meantime one must rely on her publications of stamps from particular sites, or studies of particular groups of potters; several of these are listed below as 'Special abbreviations'. On tile-makers, see now A. McWhirr and D. Viner, Brit. 1978, pp. 359 ff.

Special abbreviations:

Bar Hill	A. Robertson *et al.*, *Bar Hill: A Roman Fort and its Finds* (Brit. Arch. Reports 16, 1975)
Corbridge	E. Birley and J. P. Gillam, 'Mortarium stamps from Corbridge, 1906–1938', *Archaeologia Aeliana*[4] 26 (1948), pp. 172 ff.
Fenland	C. W. Phillips (ed.), *The Fenland in Roman Times* (London, Royal Geographical Soc., 1970)
Fish	B. W. Cunliffe, *Excavations at Fishbourne 1961–1969* Leeds, Soc. of Antiquaries, 1971)
GAJ 4	K. F. Hartley, 'Were mortaria made in Roman Scotland?', *Glasgow Archaeological Journal* 4 (1976), pp. 81 ff.
Rich.	B. W. Cunliffe (ed.), *Fifth Report on the Excavations of the Roman Fort at Richborough*, Kent (Oxford, Soc. of Ant., 1968)
RPKC	M. R. Hull, *Roman Potters Kilns at Colchester* (Oxford, Soc. Ant., 1963)
RPS	K. F. Hartley, 'Two major potteries producing mortaria in the first century AD', *Roman Pottery Studies in Britain and Beyond* (Brit. Arch. Reports, Supp. series 30, 1977), pp. 5ff.
SCRY	B. M. Dickinson and K. F. Hartley, 'The evidence of potters' stamps on samian ware and on mortaria for the trading connections of Roman York', in R. M. Butler (ed.) *Soldier and Civilian in Roman Yorkshire* (Leicester U.P., 1971), pp. 127 ff.
VE	S. S. Frere, *Verulamium Excavations* I (Oxford, Soc. Ant., 1972)
Wilders	K. F. Hartley and P. V. Webster, 'Romano-British pottery kilns near Wilderspool', *Arch. Journ.* 130 (1973), pp. 77 ff.
Winterton	I. M. Stead, *Excavations at Winterton Roman Villa* (London, HMSO, 1976)

L. Aeb(utius) Thales T. F.	Brit. 1971
Aesico	SCRY
Aesuminus	Fenland; see Evans, pp. 200 ff. (*esu-*)
Agripp.	SCRY
Alb.	RPS
Albinus	Rich.; SCRY; VE
Amandinus	RPKC
Amandus	RIB 2091
Amminus	RPKC; see Ch. II, n. to Adminius
Anavill.	JRS 1942
Arontuis	see Summacus
Arveri(us)	EE VII 1130, etc.; Holder I 232
Atepaccius	Winterton
C. Attius Marinus	SCRY; VE
Austinus	Wilderspool; GAJ 4
Avienu[s]	JRS 1959
Avitus	JRS 1961

Baro	RPKC; SCRY; Holder I 351; Kajanto, p. 264
Bellicianus	CIL VII 1255; Holder I 388
Bellicus	Corbridge
Bilce	Winterton; Holder I 419 (Bilic-), Evans, pp. 149 ff.
Boduogenus	CIL VII 1292; Holder I 462; Evans, p. 151
Bollus	see Mottius
Bonos(us)	Brit. 1972; Holder I 488
Bonoxus	SCRY; Holder I 489
Brigia.	GAJ 4; Holder I 542
Briginus	JRS 1969; Holder I 543
Bruccius	VE; Holder I 622
Bruccius	RIB 274
Brucetius	RIB 105, 151; Holder I 622
Bruscius	SCRY; VE; Holder I 624
Buc(c)us	Rich.; Fish.; RPS; Holder I 626
Cabriabanus	CIL VII 1238; Brit. 1971; Holder I 666
Cacumattus	Rich.; RPS; Holder I 668 ff. (Cacu-)
Camulacus	Fenland; cf. Holder I 724; Evans, pp. 160 f.
Candidus	Rich.
Can[d]idus	Brit. 1977
Caratius	RIB 274; Holder I 774; Evans, pp. 162 ff.
Castus	Fenland; VE
Catullus	see Vettius
Celatus	RIB 274
Cintugnatus	RPKC; Holder I 1022 f. ('first-born') Evans, pp. 179 f.
Cintusmus	RIB 194; Holder I 1024; Evans, pp. 179 f.
P. Cipius Polybius	CIL VII 1293, etc.; cf. J. C. MacPeake and C. N. Moore, Brit. 1978, pp. 331 ff.
Civilis	RIB 99
Clementinus	EE IX 1292
Cogidubnus	Ch. II, n.
Colasuni	RIB 274; Holder I 1064 f.
Constantius I	the quotation is from *Panegyrici Latini Veteres* 8(5).21.2
Crico	SCRY
Cunoarda	J. P. Wild, *Arch. Journ.* 131 (1974), p. 147; cf. Holder I 1193 (*cuno*), 186 (*ardu*): both elements seem to mean 'high'
Cunobarrus	CIL VII 1267; JRS 1931; Holder I 1193
Cunopectus	RPKC; cf. Holder I 1193 ff. (*cuno-*)
Cupitus	Winterton
Curmissus	Winterton; Holder I 1203
Dares	K. F. Hartley, Brit. 1978, pp. 388 f.; cf. Homer, *Iliad* 5.9 f., Virgil, *Aeneid*, 5.368 ff.
Decmitius	Wilders.; cf. Holder I 1247 ff.
Dignus	Brit. 1971
Doccius	CIL VII 1218; Holder I 1298
Doccius	Rich.; SCRY; GAJ 4
Docilis	Corbridge
Doinus	Rich.; VE
Driccius	VE
Dubitatus	RPKC
Dubnus	JRS 1960; Holder I 1360 f.; Evans, pp. 196 f.

Emi.	GAJ 4; Holder I 1433 f.
Fronto	Fish.; GAJ 4
Galvisius	JRS 1935, 1961
Glaucus	RIB 213
Gracilis	Rich.; RPS
Helenus	CIL VII 1284
Honorinus, Fl(avius)	CIL VII 1196
'Inemituobon'	Corbridge
Ingenuus	JRS 1969
Invomandus	GAJ 4
Juc. Dignus	CIL VII 1241; JRS 1937; Brit. 1970, 1976; see now Brit. 1978, pp. 359 ff.
T. Ju(lius?) Af(er?)	RPS
C. Jul(ius) Pri(mus?)	Rich.; SCRY
P. Jul(ius) Sur(us?)	JRS 1942
Junius I	VE
Junius II	SCRY
Junius Loccius	Corbridge
Q. Justius Cico	Winterton
Q. Jus(tius) Cres(cens)	Winterton
Juventinus	RIB 132
Littera	RPKC; Holder II 246 f.
Litugenus	RPKC; Rich.; Holder II 247 f.; Evans, pp. 217 f.
Loc(cius) Pro(culus?)	Bar Hill; cf. Holder II 278; Schulze, p. 426 (Locceius)
Loccius Vibius	SCRY
Maenalis	JRS 1955
Malliacus	RPKC; Holder II 396
Marinus	see Attius
Martial(is)	JRS 1956
Martialis	Corbridge
Matuacus	RPKC; Holder II 479
Matugenus	Fenland; VE; Holder II 480 f.; Evans, pp. 228 ff. ('son of bear – or 'son of good')
Maturus	JRS 1961
Mercator	SCRY
Messor	RPKC
Messorius Martius	Corbridge; Holder II 576 ff.
Metilius	SCRY
Moricamulus	Rich.; SCRY; cf. Holder I 724 ff. (Camulos), II 628 f. (Mori-); Evans, pp. 160 f., 232 f.
Mossius	VE; Holder II 645
Mottius Bollus	Rich.; RPS; Holder II 646; Evans, pp. 233 f.
Muco	SCRY; Holder II 648
Olondus	CIL VII 1298; Holder II 848
Orbissa	Rich.; RPS; Holder II 865
Orgil(lus)	RPS; Holder II 876 (suggesting possible Greek origin for the name)
T. C. Paca(tus)	JRS 1925
P. Pas(sienus?) Libo	CIL VII 1298
Patendinus	JRS 1951, 1965

Patricius	CIL VII 1297
Paullus	Fish.; RPS
Priscus	RIB 149
[Pud]ens, Pudentinus	RIB 91
Quintus	RIB 1542
Regulus	RPKC
Ruf(us)	RPS
Q. Rutilius Ripanus	VE
Sagus	JRS 1969; Holder II 1349
Sangus	JRS 1959
Sarrius	SCRY; Holder II 1370
Saturninus	VE
Secundus	Rich.; VE
T. Senbon(ius?) Avitus	JRS 1961
Senilis	RPKC
Sennianus	JRS 1940; Holder II 1479
Sennius	VE
Setibogius	JRS 1960, p. 220; Bar Hill; Holder II 1529; Evans, pp. 152 f.
Servandus	see JRS 1969, correcting RIB 608
Silvius	JRS 1926
Simplicia	RIB 213
Sollus	SCRY; VE
Sulinus	RIB 105, 151; Holder II 1665
Sulinus	RIB 150
Sulloniac(us)	GAJ 4
Summacus	Rich.; RPS; Evans, p. 472
Tamesubugus	Brit. 1974; cf. Holder I 629 (-bugios), II 1713 ff. (tames-)
A. Terentius Ripanus	SCRY
Tout(i)us	RIB 149; Holder II 1898; Evans, pp. 266 ff.
Sex. Valerius C(. . .)	RPS
Sex. Valerius Eclectus	information from K. F. Hartley
Q. Valerius Esunertus	RPS; Holder I 1478
Va(lerius) Gemel(lus)	JRS 1935
Sex. Valerius Jus(tus?)	information from K. F. Hartley
Sex. Valerius Saturninus	information from K. F. Hartley
Q. Val(erius) Se . . .	Rich.; SCRY; RPS
Q. Valerius Suriacus	Rich.; RPS
Q. Valerius Veranius	Rich.; RPS
Sex. Valerius Viroma	information from K. F. Hartley; perhaps abbreviated for Viromarus, cf. Holder III 388 ff.; Evans, pp. 286 ff.
Vassinus	RIB 215; cf. the potter Vassonus (Rich.); Holder III 121
Vediacus	Fenland
Veluvi(us)	information from G.D.B. Jones
Verctissa	JRS 1961; Evans, pp. 279 f.
Verus	JRS 1965
Q. Vet[tius] Catullus	JRS 1961
Victor V. F.	JRS 1969
Viducus	RPKC; cf. Ch. XII, Viducus, n.
Viribonis	JRS 1963, but cf. Brit. 1986
Vitalis	RPKC; SCRY: Winterton: there were five separate potters of this name

CCM	Wilders
LVL	Brit. 1977, pp. 275 ff., 1978, pp. 359 ff.
ROA	VE
TMH	VE
TPF	Brit. 1977, pp. 275 ff., 1978, pp. 359 ff.

Notes to Chapter XIV

The literature on the countryside in Roman Britain is large. I have derived particular benefit from C. Thomas (ed.), *Rural Settlement in Roman Britain* (CBA Research Report no. 7, 1966); A. L. F. Rivet (ed.), *The Roman Villa in Britain* (Routledge, 1969); and S. Applebaum, 'Roman Britain', in H. P. R. Finberg (ed.), *The Agrarian History of England and Wales*, vol. I, ii AD 43–1042 (Cambridge, 1972). On the various *civitates* (Dobunni, etc.) see esp. A. L. F. Rivet, *Town and Country in Roman Britain* (Hutchinson, 1958 and repr.); and his forthcoming *Place-Names of Roman Britain* (Batsford, 1979).

Special abbreviations:

Applebaum, CBA RR: see above

Abe . . .	JRS 1969
Adalma	JRS 1966
Aelia Augustina	RIB 574
Aelius Modestus	EE VII 812
P. Aelius Modestus	RIB 1580
A(e)l(ius) Pri(mus?)	Brit. 1971
Ael(lius) Titul(lus)	JRS 1962; Kajanto, p. 171 (only 36 examples)
P. Aelius Titullus	RIB 1395
Albinus	Ch. II, n.
Allectus	Ch. II, n.
Alpinianus	JRS 1952; see Ch. III, n. to Julius Classicianus
Amatius	Brit. 1970
Anicetus	Applebaum, p. 21, discussing RIB 148
Ann.	Brit. 1970
Ant.	JRS 1963
Ariconius (?)	Applebaum, pp. 24 f.; Ch. XV, n. to Aruconius
Attius	RIB 219; Holder III 737
Aurel(ia) Con[ce]ssa	JRS 1965
T. Aur(elius) Aurelianus	RIB 627
[A]ur(elius) Pu . . .	JRS 1969
T. Aur(elius) Quintus	RIB 623
M. Aurelius Riespetecus (?)	JRS 1956
Aur)elius) Senopianus	RIB 628; Holder II 1499
Aur(elius) Serenus	JRS 1957
Ausonius Avitus	JRS 1957
Bassi . . . ti . . .	Brit. 1971
Bel. Januaris	JRS 1965; cf. Holder I 385. 391
Bellicia	Brit. 1973, 1975; Holder I 388 ff.

Bellicus	RIB 304
Beronius	Applebaum, p. 24; cf. Holder I 407 (Berones)
Bodeni(us)	CIL VII 3; Holder I 456
Boudica	Ch. II, n.
Bruccius	RIB 274; Holder I 622
Campana	JRS 1963
Candiedinia Fortuna[ta]	RIB 632; cf. Schulze, p. 142 + add.
Canius Dignus	JRS 1963; Schulze, pp. 142, 144
Caratius	RIB 274; Holder I 774
Carausius	Ch. II, n.
Cartimandua	Ch. II, n.
Censorinus	CIL VII 1288
Cingetissa	RIB 630; Holder I 1018; Evans, pp. 177 ff.
Claud . . .	RIB 275
Ti. Claudius Primus	RIB 219
Cogidubnus	Ch. II, n.
Colasuni	RIB 274; Holder I 1064 f.
Colon . . .	Applebaum, p. 21
Concess . . .	JRS 1939
Corotica	JRS 1962; cf. Coroticus, Ch. XVI, n.
Cosc(onia) Mammiola	JRS 1957 (the *cognomen* is not in Kajanto)
Cupit(us)	JRS 1942; Kajanto, p. 296
Curatio	JRS 1961
Curati(us)	CIL VII 1270
Decimius	JRS 1962
Donatus	JRS 1966
Dum. Censorinus	RIB 218; Holder I 1371 suggests Dum(nonius)
Etterna	Brit. 1973
Fausta	JRS 1969
Faustinus	Victor, *de Caes.* 35.4, with which C. E. Stevens, CBA RR 7, p. 122 n. 118, compares *Itin. Ant.* 474.5
Ferna	JRS 1965
Fidelis	JRS 1962
Firminus	JRS 1968
Flaetio	JRS 1962
Florenti(us)	CIL VII 1270
T. Floridius Natalis	RIB 587
Gemellus	RIB 218
Gulioepius (?)	RIB 132
C. Indutius Felix	RIB 181; cf. Indutiomarus, Caesar, *B.G.* 5.3.2.
Indutius	CIL VII 1232; Holder II 41 ff.
Ing.	Brit. 1971
Ingenti	Brit. 1971
Ing(enuius?) Fabill(us?)	JRS 1962
Isarninus	CIL VII 1270; Holder II 75
Iventius Sabinus	RIB 187; cf. CIL XIII 1190 (Bourges) for the god Rigisamus
Ixarninus	CIL VII 1270
Juc. Dignus	CIL VII 1241; JRS 1937; Brit. 1970, 1976; see now Brit. 1978, pp. 359 ff.

Jul(ia) Ingenuilla	RIB 133
Julius	Brit. 1973
Jul(ius) Secundus	RIB 574
Junia	Brit. 1975
Jun(ius) Ve . . .	JRS 1937
Jut(i)us	JRS 1962
Licinius	CIL VII 1270
Lopiscallus (?)	JRS 1966; cf. Holder II 286 f.
Lovernianus	JRS 1969; cf. Holder II 295
Maecius	Brit. 1971
Martinus	CIL VII 1270
Matugena	Brit. 1975; Holder II 480 f.; cf. Ch. XII, n. to Matugenus
Maxima	JRS 1955
Melluna	JRS 1969; cf. Mellonus, Ch. XVI, n.; Holder II 540
Mettus	RIB 136
Mina	A. C. C. Brodribb *et al.*, *Excavations at Shakenoak* IV (1973), p. 88 no. 10; cf. Holder II 586
Mocux[s]oma	JRS 1962; cf. Ch. X, n.
Naevius	RIB 179
Narina	JRS 1969; cf. Holder II 689 (Naria)
Q. Natalius Natalinus	CIL VII 3
Q. Neratius Proxsimus	JRS 1962; cf. L. Neratius Marcellus, Ch. III, n.
Pacata	JRS 1969
Paet.	JRS 1969
Prasutagus	Ch. II, n.
Q. Pompeius Anicetus	RIB 148, cf. Applebaum, p. 21
Postimia	JRS 1958
Priminus	RIB 631
Quietus	Brit. 1972
Quintus, see Aurelius	
Reburrus	CIL XVI 48; cf. Ch. IX, n.
Remus	Brit. 1972
Riespetecus	see Aurelius
Rubrius Carinus Orientalis	Brit. 1973
Sabi(nus)	JRS 1965
Saini(us?)	Brit. 1970
Sas . . .	JRS 1959
Satavacus	Brit. 1975, correcting 1973; cf. Holder II 1374 ff. for Sat- names
Secunda	Brit. 1973
C. Sentius	RIB 137
Senopianus	see Aurelius
Senuacus	JRS 1961; cf. Holder II 1504 (Senucus)
Serenus	see Aurelius
C. Severius Emeritus	RIB 152
Simplicia	RIB 213
Somia	JRS 1969
Spes	RIB 137
Sulicena	RIB 134
Sulloniacae	Applebaum, p. 20

Tacita	RIB 221
Tamm(onius?)	Brit. 1970; cf. Ch. XI, n.
Tare ...	Brit. 1971
Termo	Brit. 1973
Tertia	Brit. 1976
Tetricus	see note to Faustinus
Timoteus	Brit. 1973
Tit. Pin.	JRS 1965
Titia Pinta	RIB 720; cf. Holder II 1005 f.
Trenico	JRS 1963; cf. Holder II 1911 (*trenos*)
Ulpius	JRS 1969
Vagnius/Vagionius	Applebaum, p. 20, citing *Itin. Ant.* 472.2; see Schulze, 306, for the *gentilicium*
Val(erius) Adjutor	RIB 720
Val(erius) Varialus	RIB 720
Val(erius) Vindicianus	RIB 720
Vassinus	RIB 215
Vatiaucus	Brit. 1973
Veneria	EE IV 712
Venutius	Ch. II, n.
Vernico	JRS 1965; Brit. 1979
Veronius	Applebaum, p. 24
Vital(is)	JRS 1965

Notes to Chapter XV

For useful introductions, see P. A. Brunt, in J. P. V. D. Balsdon (ed.) , *The Romans* (London, 1965), pp. 177 ff.; J. A. Crook, *Law and Life of Rome* (London, 1967); M. I. Finley, *The Ancient Economy* (London, 1973).

Ael(ia) Severa	RIB 683
P. Ael(ius) Bassus	RIB 754
Aesubilinus	RIB 193; (see Ch. XI, n.)
Anencletus	RIB 21
Aquilinus	Brit. 1976
Arrius Paulinus	RIB 1229
L. Aruconius Verecundus	CIL VII 1214; cf. VI 12488 (not in Schulze); Holder I 230 regards Aruconius as Celtic
Atiliana, Atilianus	RIB 560. I differ from the reading in RIB. after prolonged inspection of the stone, prompted by G. Alföldy's suggestion, in his review in the *Bonner Jahrbücher*, 1966
Attius	RIB 219
Audax	Brit. 1976; cf. CIL VII 13383 for this name on a graffito at London
M. Aufidius Maximus	RIB 143–4
M. Aur(elius) Lunaris	AE 1922. 116
M. Aurelius Marcio	ILS 1477.; see P. R. C. Weaver, *Familia Caesaris* (CUP, 1972), 276 ff.

Barates/Barathes · RIB 1065, 1171
Briginus · JRS 1969

Caec(ilius) Musicus · RIB 683
Calpurnia Trifosa · RIB 155; cf. JRS 1957, 231 n. 28, on the name
C. Calpurnius Receptus · RIB 155
P. Campa[nius] Italicus · RIB 2094
Celer · RIB 2094
Cl(audia) Martina · RIB 21
Ti. Claudius Primus · RIB 219
Claudius Severus · RIB 937
Ti. Cl(audius) Trifer(us?) · JRS 1962, where R. P. Wright expands as Trifer(na), without discussion, referring back to JRS 1957, where the most complete reading was *Trif*. But Triferna is very rare (Schulze, p. 107 n. 1), whereas Trypheros of which Triferus would be a simplified form, is common enough, cf. CIL VI 8588, ILS 145, CIL III 2193, 2453.
M. Cocceius Firmus · RIB 2174–7; *Digest* 49.15.6. See the discussion of the case by E. Birley, RBRA, pp. 87 ff.

Epillicus · JRS 1954
Eutuches · RIB 143
Eutyches · RIB 1271

M. Favon(ius) Facilis · RIB 200
Felicissimus · RIB 561
Felicio · RIB 1290

Graec(us) · Brit. 1976
Hardalio · RIB 1436, where the editor interprets Hardalionis as the name of the slave's owner, but I prefer to regard it as a form of *ardelio* = 'busybody' (Martial 2.7; 4.79), hence a typical slave's name
Hermagoras · RIB 561 (Chester)
Hermagoras · RIB 1291 (High Rochester)
(H)imilico (?) · RIB 193. The name might, however, be Voucimilico, and be a Celtic form
Honoratus · RIB 1291
(H)ylas · RIB 937

Imilico (?) · see (H)imilico
Ingenuus · JRS 1969

C. Julius Protus · CIL VII 1216

Lemnus · RIB 144
Lucilla · RIB 1271

Merc. Magnil. · RIB 162; see E. Birley, JRS 1966, 228 f.

Naevius · RIB 179
Nipius Aquila · CIL XVI 30
C. Nipius Ascanius · JRS 1951; G. Webster, *Flintshire Historical Society Publications* 13 (1952–3), 5 ff.
C. Nipius Flavianus · CIL VI 611
Novicius · RIB 200
Numerianus · RIB 1064

Patrick	see Ch. XVI, n.
Pompeius Optatus	RIB 560
T. Pomponius Mamilianus Rufus Antistianus Funisulanus Vettonianus	RIB 445
Regina	RIB 1065
P. Rubrius Abascantus	EE IX 1266
Rufinus	RIB 1271
Rufus	JRS 1954
Tertull(us)	EE IV 717, citing *Arch. J.* 32 (1875), p. 67, a false reference, which should be *Arch. J.* 33 (1876), p. 262
Theodotus	RIB 1229
Sexti Valerii	see Ch. XIII, n,
M. Verec. Diogenes	RIB 678, 687
Verecundus	RIB 200
Victor	RIB 1064
Ylas	RIB 937

the unknown imperial freedman at York is known from RIB 643, where the reading P. NIKOMEDES seems to me too uncertain to accept.

Notes to Chapter XVI

On the various topics discussed in this chapter, see, in addition to the works cited under individual names, below, and J. Morris and A. H. M. Jones (cited, on p. 165, 170, above), M. W. Barley and R. P. C. Hanson (eds), *Christianity in Britain, 300—700* (Leicester U.P.), 1968.

Special abbreviations:

Bartrum:	P. C. Bartrum, *Early Welsh Genealogical Tracts* (Cardiff, Univ. of Wales, 1966)
Haddan and Stubbs	A. W. Haddan and W. Stubbs, *Councils and Ecclesiastical Documents relating to Great Britain and Ireland*, I (Oxford, 1869)
PLRE	see p. 165, above
Aaron	Gildas 10.2
Adelphius	text reproduced by Haddan and Stubbs I, p. 7 and J. C. Mann, *Antiquity* 35 (1961), p. 317
Aeternus	CIL VII 1297 (Colchester)
Aeternus	Bartrum, p. 185 (Edern)
Aëtius	Gildas 20.1
Agricola	Prosper, *Chron. s.a.* 429
Albanus	Gildas 10.2, etc. See J. Morris, *Hertfordshire Archaeology* I (1968), pp. 1 ff., discussing the hagiography in the Turin MS published in Germany in 1904

Allectus   Ch. II, n.

Ambrosius Aurelianus   Gildas 25; Bede, *H.E.* 1.16; Nennius, *H.B.* 31 , 42, 48, 66; Bartrum p. 187 (Emrys Wledig). J. N. L. Myres, JRS 1960, p. 35 draws attention to the similarity of names of the great Bishop of Milan

An(i)cilla   Brit. 1976, cf. 1977 and see Jamcilla

Arminius   see under Adelphius

Artorius (Arthur)   Nennius, *H.B.* 56, 66, 73; Bartrum p. 171 (Arthur ab Uthr Bendragon)

Augulus   various versions, of which the principal is in the *Martyrologium Hieronvmianum*, reproduced in Haddan and Stubbs I, pp. 27 ff. Morris, *Age of Arthur*, pp. 14, 335, calls this person Augurius and assigns his death to AD 359. But I do not think one can accept that any Catholics were martyred by the Arians

Augustinus   J. M. C. Toynbee, *Journ. Brit. Arch. Ass.* 1953, 1 ff.

Aurelius, Marcus   Dio 71.16.2 records his despatch of Sarmatians to Britain

Aurelius Caninus   Gildas 30; Bartrum, p. 180 (Cynan). The name Caninus, Lat. = 'doggy' is regarded as a pun by editors; but it is found as a *cognomen*, see Kajanto, p. 326 (including CIL VI 9920 b10, late C4)

Caelestius   see R. P. C. Hanson, *St Patrick* (1968), pp. 36 ff. for a useful summary of Bury's demonstration that he was neither British nor Irish

Calpurnius   Patrick, *Confessio* 1; status as decurion, id., *Epist.* 10. Muirchu, *v. Patr.* I, says that his wife, Patrick's mother, was Concessa

Carausius   Ch. II, n.

Cartimandua   Ch. II, n.

Censorinus   CIL VII 1288

Ceredig   Bartrum, p. 177; see P. H. Blair, *Arch. Ael.*[4] 25 (1947), pp. 25, 29 and under Coroticus, below

Cinhil   Bartrum, p. 177; see Quintilius, below

Clemens, Cluim   Bartrum, p. 177; P. H. Blair, *Arch. Ael.*[4] 25 (1947), p. 27

Cogidubnus   Ch. II, n.

Coel Hen   Bartrum, p. 178; P. H. Blair, *Arch. Ael.*[4] 25 (1947), pp. 25, 46 ff.

Constans   Orosius 7.40.7, etc.

Constantine I   Ch. II, n.

Constantine III   Ch. II, n.

Constantine of Dumnonia   Gildas 28–9; Bartrum, p. 179 (Custennin ap Cadwr)

Coroticus   Patrick, *Epistula* 2, 6, 12, 19, 21; Muirchu, *v. Patr.* pr., 29; see also Ceredig, above

Crocus   *Epit. de Caes.* 41.3

Cunedda   Bartrum, p. 179 (Cunedda Wledig ab Edern); Nennius, *H.B.* 62

Cuneglasus   Gildas 32; Bartrum p. 182 (Cynlas Goch ab Owein Danwyn)

Cunobelinus   Ch. II, n.; cf. the various persons called by this name in the genealogies, Bartrum p. 181 (Cynfelyn)

Cynloyp   see Ceredig

Desiderius	*cod. Theod.* 9.36.1; cf. CIL VII 1287
Eborius	see under Adelphius
Eutherius	PLRE I, pp. 314 f.; Applebaum, p. 25
Fastidius	Gennadius, *de viris illustribus* 56. See the discussion by R. P. C. Hanson, *St. Patrick* (1968), esp. pp. 40 ff.
T. Fl(avius) Senilis	R. G. Collingwood in R. E. M. and T. V. Wheeler, *Report on . . . Lydney Park, Glos.* (1932), pp. 102 f.
Fraomarius	Ammian. 29.4.7
Frontinus	Ammian. 28.1.21
Fullofaudes	Ammian. 27.8.1
Germanus	Constantius, v. Germani 1. 19, 23; 2.1–4; Bede; *H.E.* 1.17–21; Nennius, *H.B.* 32 ff.
Gerontius	Ch. II, n. J. N. L. Myres, JRS 1960, p. 34 draws attention to a Pelagian tract addressed to two women disinherited by their father of this name (*de contemnenda hereditate*, PL 30.45–50). For the name in the Genealogies, see Bartrum, p. 190 (Geraint)
Gildas	H. Williams (ed.), *Gildae de excidio Britanniae* (London: Hon. Soc. of Cymmrodorion, 1899) and M. Winterbottom (ed.), *Gildas, The Ruin of British and other works* (London and Chichester: Phillimore, 1978), both furnish text, translation and introduction
Hnaudifridus	RIB 1576
Igillus	Zosimus 1.68.3
Innocentia	Brit. 1976
Instantius	Sulpicius Severus, *Chron.* 2.51.4
Jamcilla	Brit. 1977
Julian	see Ammian. 21.10.8 for his criticism of Constantine
Julianus	Olympiodorus, frags. 12, 16
Julius	Gildas 10.2
Justinianus	RIB 721; perhaps the general of Constantine III of this name, Zosimus 6.2.2
Lupus	see under Germanus
Maglocunus	Gildas 33–36; Bartrum, p. 202 (Maelgwyn Gwynedd ap Cadwallon Lawhir)
Magnentius	PLRE I, p. 532
Marcus	Ch. II, n.
Melania	*vita Melaniae* 10 (Latin), 11 (Greek) refers to her property in Britain among other places
Mellonus	*Acta Sanctorum*, October, vol. 9 (1858), pp. 570 ff.: *vita S. Melloni archiepiscopi Rothomagensis*; cf. Melluna, Ch. XIV, n.
Q. Natalius Natalinus	CIL VII 3: Brit. 1979
Ninianus	Bede, *H.E.* 3.4
Palladius	Ammian. 22.3.3, etc.; PLRE I, pp. 658 f.
Papittedo	J. M. C. Toynbee, *Journ. Brit. Arch. Ass.* 1953, pp. 1 ff. see Holder I 1407 for the Celtic suffix -*edo*

Paternus	Bartrum, p. 218 (Padarn Beisrudd = Pesrut)
Patrick	see above all his own *Confessio* and *Epistola*, now edited with introduction, translation into French and full commentary by R. P. C. Hanson, *Saint Patrick, Confession et Lettre à Coroticus* (Paris: Sources Chretiennes no. 249, 1978) and by A. B. E. Hood, *St Patrick. His Writings and Muirchu's Life* (London and Chichester: Phillimore, 1978). See also esp. Hanson's *St Patrick. His Origins and Career* (Oxford, 1968). The quotation on p. 157 is from C. E. Stevens, *Ant. Journ.* 50 (1970), p. 136
Paulus	Ammian. 14.5.6 ff.; PLRE I, pp. 683 f.
Pelagius	R. P. C. Hanson, *St Patrick* (1968), pp. 35 ff. gives a useful introduction. J. N. L. Myres, JRS 1960, pp. 21 ff. and J. Morris, *J. Theol. Stud.* 16 (1965), pp. 26 ff. are stimulating but controversial. See further P. Brown, *Augustine of Hippo* (London: Faber, 1968), esp. pp. 340 ff., and id., *Religion and Society in the Age of St Augustine* (1972), pp. 183 ff.; R. F. Evans, *Pelagius: Inquiries and Reappraisals* (London: Black, 1968); J. N. D. Kelly, *Jerome: His Life; Writings, and Controversies* (London: Duckworth, 1975), esp. pp. 187 f., 307 ff.
Potitus	Patrick, *Confessio* 1
Prasutagus	Ch. II, n.
Publianus	Brit. 1976
Quintilius	Bartrum, p. 177 (Cinhil); P. H. Blair, *Arch. Ael.*[4] 25 (1947), pp. 27 ff., suggesting Quintilius – Quintillus is also possible
Restitutus	see under Adelphius
Sacerdos	see under Adelphius
Salmanes	RIB 2182
Saturnia and Senacus	Brit. 1979
Senicianus	RIB 306, CIL VII 1305
Severianus	see under Agricola
L. Septimius . . .	RIB 103
Silvianus	RIB 306
Silvius Bonus	Ausonius, *Epigr.* 107–112
Stilicho	Ch. II, n.
Tacitus	Bartrum, p. 214 (Tegid . . . ap Cein); cf. EE VII 1151: *Taciti* on a piece of lead at Risingham
Tiberianus	Sulpicius Severus, *Chron.* 2.51.4; Jerome, *de viris illustribus* 123
Tullia Tacita	CIL VII 1324
Valentinus	Ammian. 283.4–6, etc.; PLRE I, p. 935
Victoricus	JRS 1957
Victricius	The bishop's letter is in PL 20. 443 ff.
Victricius	EE IX 1300; Applebaum, p. 23
Vindicianus	RIB 721
Vindomorucius	RIB 2053
Vitalinus	Uley curse-tablet: information from M. W. C. Hassall
Viventia	JRS 1957
Viventia	Brit. 1976

Vortigern   Gildas 23 (unnamed: 'superbus tyrannus'); Bede, *H.E.* 1.14; Nennius, *H.B.* 31 ff.; Bartrum, p. 194 (Gwrtheyrn). The Pillar of Eliseg (Bartrum, pp. 2 f.) makes him son-in-law of Magnus Maximus.

Vortipor   Gildas 31; perhaps the Voteporix *protector* of *EE* IX 1030, Carmarthen; and presumably Guortepir map Aircol ('son of Agricola) of the Harleian Genealogy (Bartrum, p. 10 no. 2)

Zosimus   6.5.2–3 describes the expulsion of Roman officials and self-defence against Germanic invaders by the Britons, in AD 409; see E. A. Thompson, Brit. 1977, pp. 306 ff. who rightly stresses that the date was 409, not 410; I cannot follow him in his other arguments

Platorius Nepos inscription—see plates section

'To Aulus Platorius, son of Aulus, Sergia [voting-tribe], Nepos Aponius Italicus Manilianus Gaius Licinius Pollio, consul, augur, imperial pro-praetorian legate of the province of Britain, pro-praetorian legate of the province of Lower Germany, pro-praetorian legate of the province of Thrace, legate of the legion I Adiutrix, quaestor of the province of Macedonia, curator of the Cassia, Clodia, Ciminia and Nova Traiana roads, recommended for election by the Deified Trajan, military tribune of the legion XXII Primigenia, Loyal and Faithful, praetor, tribune of the plebs, one of the three superintendents of public prisons, their patron, by decree of the decurions [town-councillors of Aquileia]'.

Note: as customary, the most honorific posts, consul and augur, are placed first, out of order; the consulship would actually have been held between the governorships of Thrace and Lower Germany. The career is listed otherwise in 'descending' order, with the latest post, the governorship of Britain coming first, and the first appointment, as a superintendent of prisons (at Rome) coming last. But several items towards the end are misplaced: 'quaestor of the province of Macedonia' should probably go before 'recommended for election by the Deified Trajan', while 'praetor, tribune of the plebs' should be placed immediately before 'quaestor'.

Index

3 Writers

(a) Ancient